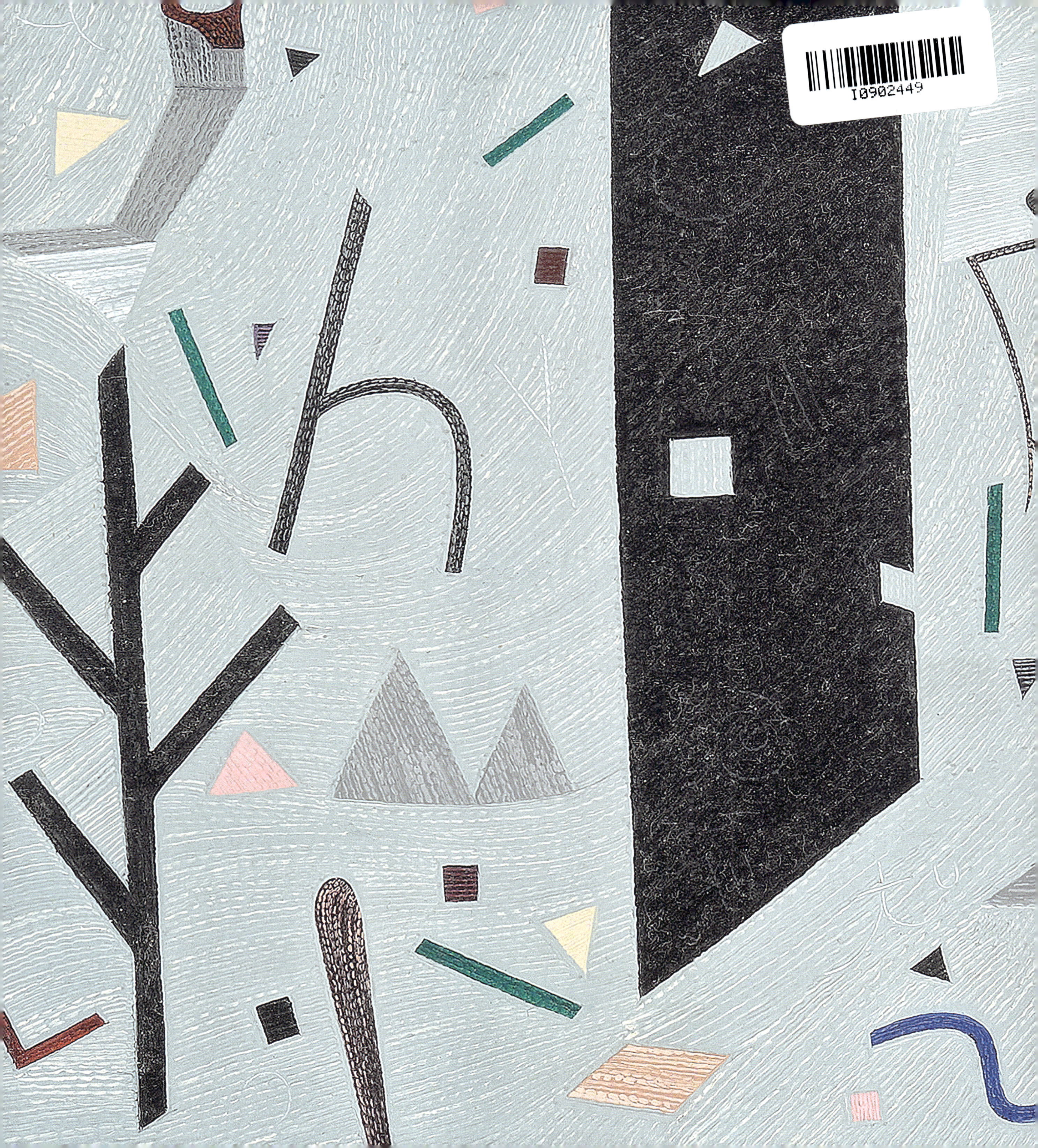

SUZANNE ADAN
I'M NO SPRING CHICKEN

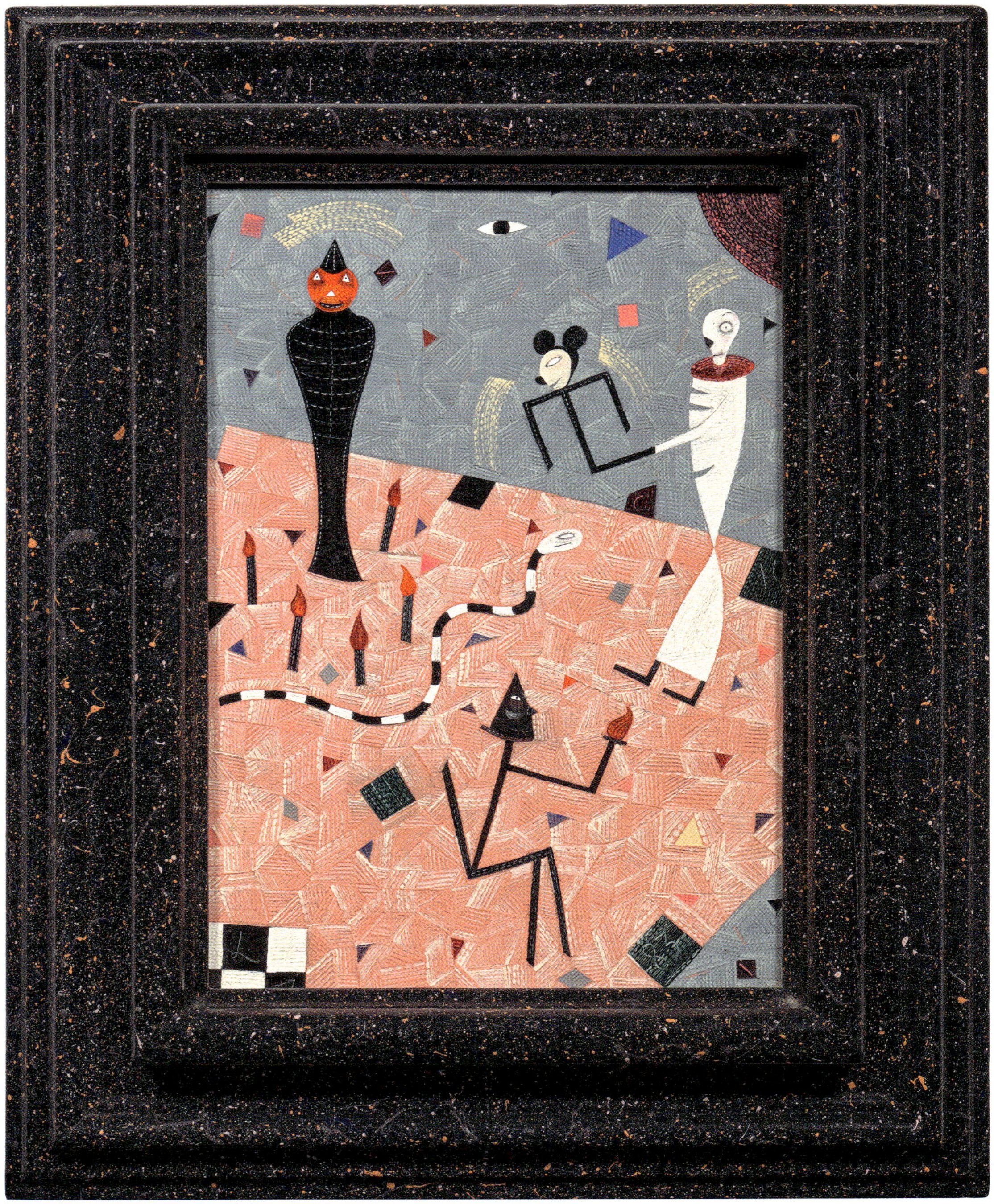

SUZANNE ADAN
I'M NO SPRING CHICKEN

Scott A. Shields

with additional essays by
Diana L. Daniels and Elaine O'Brien

and a foreword by Gladys Nilsson

CROCKER
art museum

HIRMER

Dedicated to Myrtle and Raymond Adan, James Adan, and Michael Stevens. Their love and support gave me the courage to be a creative person throughout my life.

Suzanne Adan

Contents

[p. 2] *Trick or Treat*, 1983.
Oil on canvas, 9 ⅞ × 7 ⅞ in. Collection of Elizabeth Adan.

Unless otherwise noted, all artworks are by Suzanne Adan (American, born 1946).

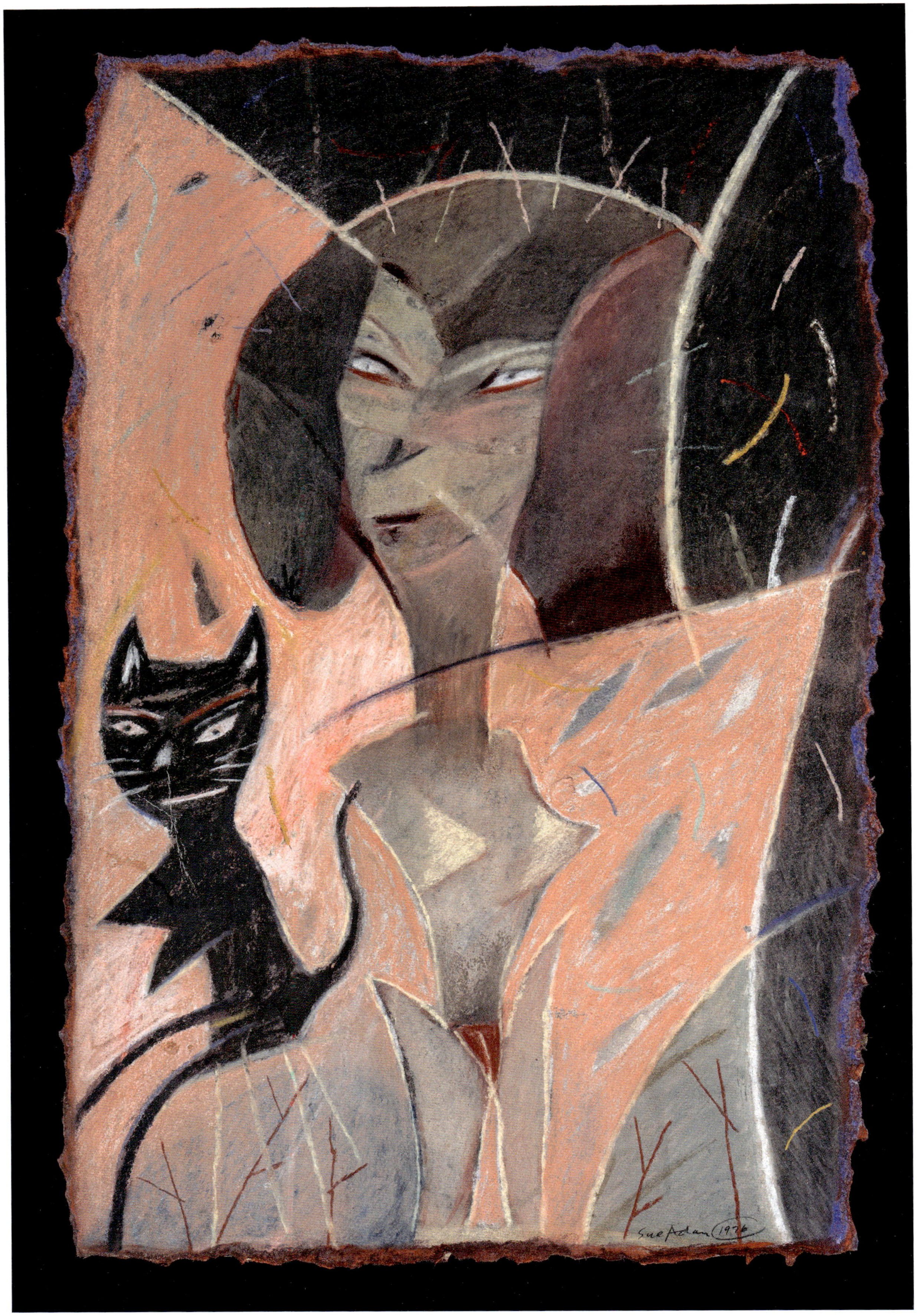

Victoria's Homecoming with Adolph, 1976.
Chalk on paper, 28 × 23 in. Collection of Vicky Wallace and Ron Peetz.

Acknowledgments

Suzanne Adan (born 1946) creates personal universes that combine fantasy, popular culture, and autobiography. This catalogue, *Suzanne Adan: I'm No Spring Chicken,* assembles more than 120 of her paintings, works on paper, and ceramics, along with archival photographs and images. Like the exhibition it was created to accompany, it celebrates her eightieth year and documents more than fifty-five years of her artistic production.

A native Californian, Adan was born in Woodland and raised in nearby Yolo. She earned her BA and MA from Sacramento State College in 1969 and 1971, respectively. It was during this time that she met her husband, sculptor Michael Stevens, and began to encounter artists from Sacramento, Davis, the San Francisco Bay Area, and Chicago who appreciated the place that humor, satire, and irreverence could have in art. At the trail-blazing Candy Store Gallery in Folsom and elsewhere, Adan's pieces stood or hung alongside California Funk and Nut art, as well as work by Chicago's Hairy Who. Over time, the vintage toy collections that she and Stevens assembled proved inspirational as well. Today, she continues to create surreal images of whimsical characters, toys, and animals that simultaneously disturb, charm, and disrupt, all through a beautifully fastidious approach and a signature application of paint.

The Crocker Art Museum thanks Adan for her enthusiasm in presenting her art to the public in such a significant way. We also thank those from the Sacramento region and beyond who have contributed to this project through their expertise, shared stories, loans of artwork, and financial contributions. This project is, to be sure, more than a celebration of a single artist, it honors a community and an aesthetic approach that has helped define the Sacramento region. It also manifests a widespread affection for Adan herself.

The Crocker is grateful to those who have provided exhibition and catalogue support. For their lead co-sponsorship, we thank Marcy Friedman and Paul Kaufmann, as well as Mark and Marjorie Friedman, who have supported not only this project but many others at the Crocker. We are also indebted to presenting sponsors William Ishmael and David Gibson, Susan Willoughby, and an anonymous couple, as well as to supporting

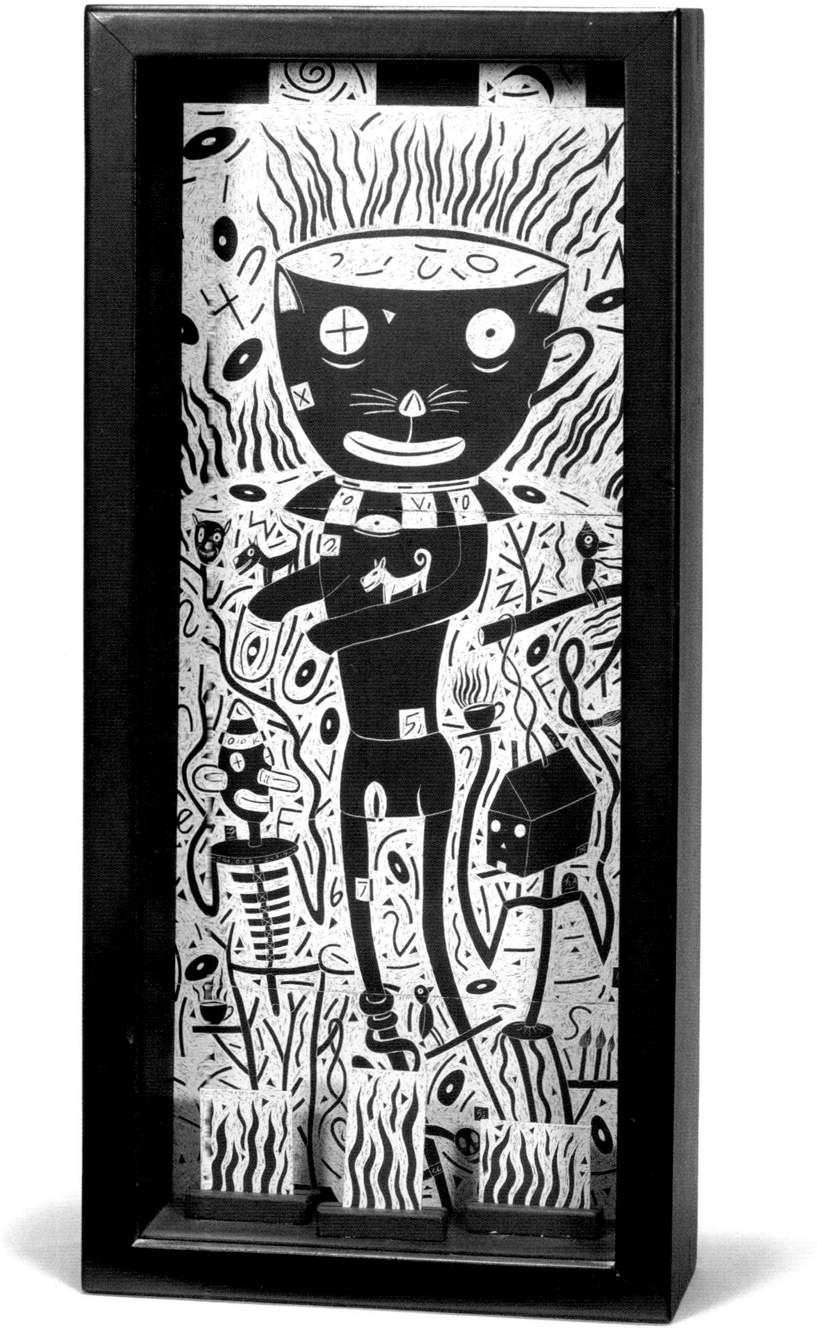

Kit'n Ca'boo'dle (For Vicky), 1996.
Scratchboard, 15 × 7 × 3 in. Collection of Vicky Wallace and Ron Peetz.

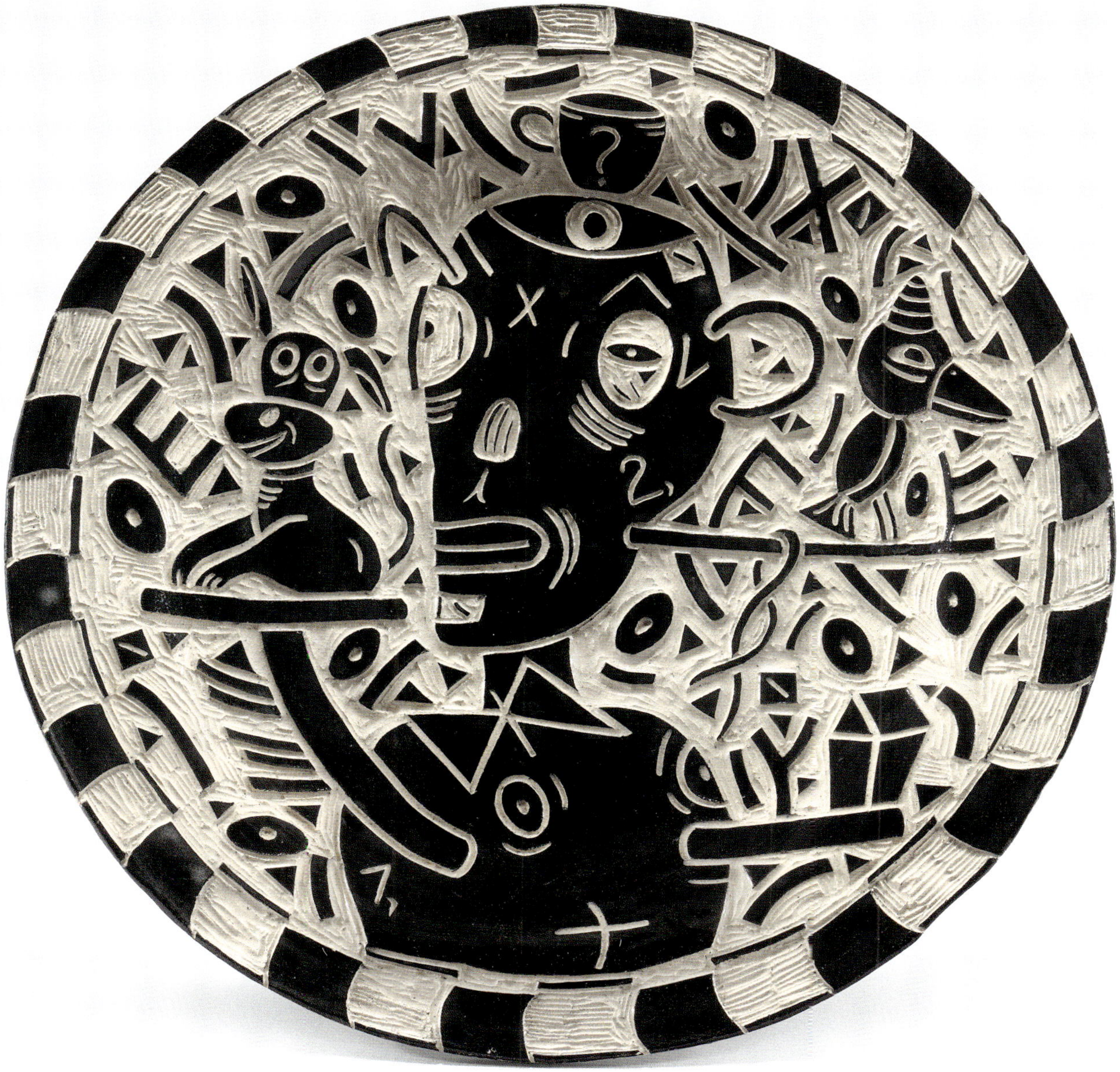

E-Eye-E-Eye-Oh!, 2015.
Clay and black underglaze, 18 in. (diam.). Collection of Rita Gibson.

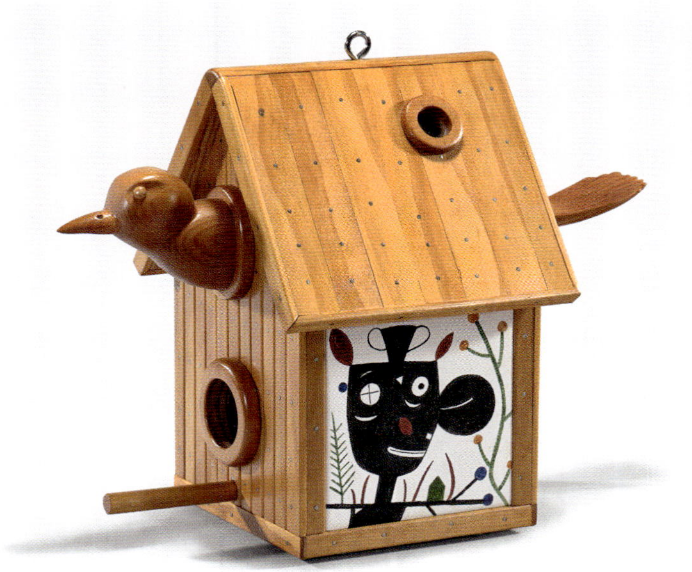

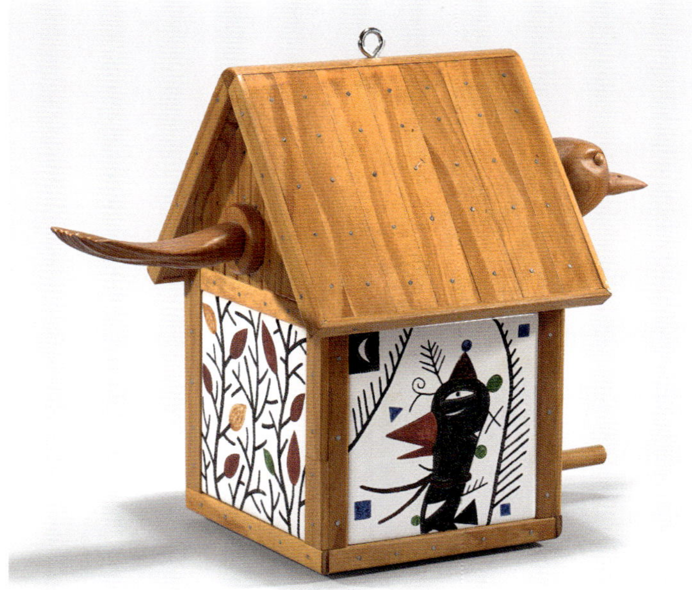

sponsors Marilyn Isenberg and Kay Lehr. There were also a host of contributing sponsors. We thank them all, since it is because of their largesse this beautiful, internationally published catalogue was made possible.

Numerous others were gracious in lending artwork. Their support in acquiring the artwork in the first place and subsequent willingness to share it with the public are enormously appreciated. Lenders include Alexander Adan, Elizabeth Adan, Jane K. Adan, Mima and Numan Begovic, Susan Bitar, Ellie and John Cary, William Chambers, Caleb Counts, Julia Couzens and Jay-Allen Eisen, Phil and Ginny Cunningham, Michael and Lindy Dunlavey, David and Karen Ewing, Marcy Friedman, Mark and Marjorie Friedman, Rita Gibson, Jeff Goodrich and Mary Jameson, Carla Hills and Frank LaPena, Julia Himovitz, Lucas Himovitz, Catherine Hopper, Pamela Hopper, Susan Hopper, Scott and Ruixia Howe, Susan Howe and Rebecca Goodchild, Marilyn Isenberg, Lynda Jolley, Steve and Beth Jones, Vince and Sage LaPena, Kay Lehr, Carol Livingston, Pat Mahony and Randy Getz, Mark Marvelli, Donna and Tony Natsoulas, D. Oldham Neath, Gladys Nilsson and Jim Nutt, Elaine O'Brien, Ron Peetz, Libby and Kevin Sanchez, the Jan Shrem and Maria Manetti Shrem Museum of Art, Jerald Silva, Jennifer Kim Sohn, Julie Spezia, Beau Stevens, Keri Stevens, Jon Stevenson, James Sundquist, Angela Tahti, Thane Tahti and Janet Crecelius, Marny and Rick Wasserman, Sheri Watson, Tom Weborg and Sandra Singer, Phil and Patricia Weidman, Patrick Whitnell, and Paul Wortman. Emily Leff not only agreed to lend the piece she owned but then decided to donate it. Marilyn Isenberg and Michael and Lindy Dunlavey have long planned to leave their wonderful paintings to the Crocker as bequests. Numerous other art colleagues, friends, and family members graciously put up with exhibition openings, lectures, and workshops, when most probably had better things to do. We thank them all.

Producing a catalogue of this scale requires the help of many. Adan's friend and fellow artist Gladys Nilsson contributed the publication's foreword, Nilsson's own Crocker exhibition (curated by Francesca Wilmott, PhD) overlapping with Adan's. Diana L. Daniels and Elaine O'Brien, PhD, contributed essays elucidating Adan's enigmatic iconography and her time

Michael Stevens (American, born 1945) and Suzanne Adan (American, born 1946), *Bird House (House Warming Gift)*, 2010. Wood, ceramic tile, glaze, and scratchboard, 14 × 18 ½ × 10 in. Collection of Phillip and Marilyn Araki Isenberg.

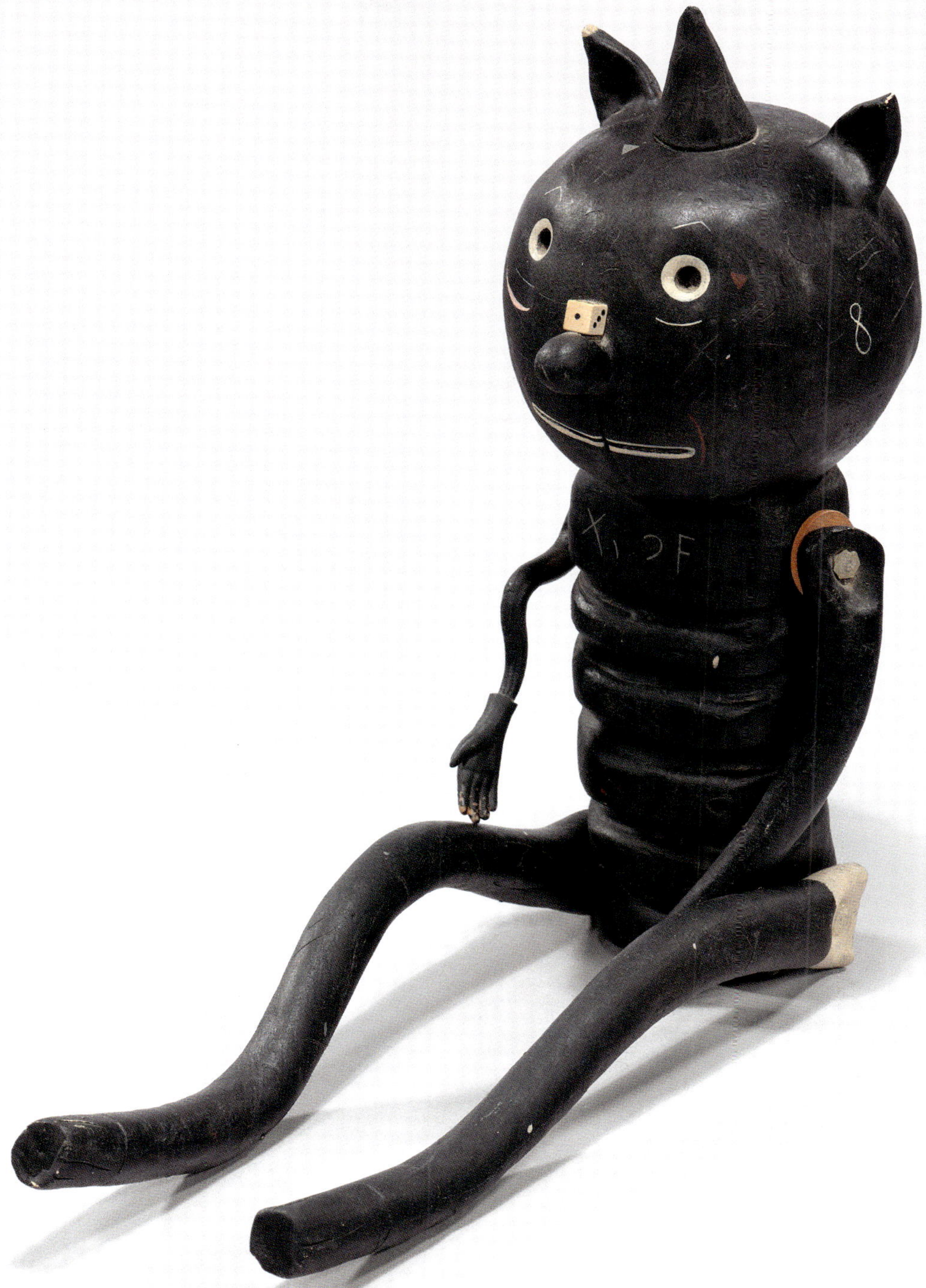

Pussy, 1996.
Clay, acrylic paint, plastic, and wood, 22 × 5 × 5 ½ in. Collection of the Artist.

at Sacramento State respectively. Susan Willoughby offered edits and contributed a firsthand historical perspective. Adan and Stevens patiently answered questions, attended meetings, and read texts. They also spent hours digging through archival material, finding old photographs, catalogues, newspaper clippings, and historic works of art buried deep in their Tuff Shed. A special acknowledgment also goes to four of Adan's primary painting instructors: Jack Ogden, Jim Nutt, Jerald Silva, and the late Irving Marcus, as well as her ceramics teacher, the late Ruth Rippon. All made a profound impact on her artistic development and helped foster a narrative direction in her work.

At the Crocker, Caitlin Schwarz and Mariah Briel coordinated checklists and worked with lenders in multiple photography sessions both at the Crocker and off-site; photographer Gerard Vuilleumier expertly captured most of the pieces reproduced herein, and David M. Roth, Rob Stone and Muzi Li Rowe also contributed images. Jessica Barclay coordinated loans and paperwork; Matthew Isble, Tyler Turner, and Brian Suhr (who also took some photographs) made the exhibition itself—and its accompanying collateral—both whimsical and beautiful. Former Mort and Marcy Friedman Director & CEO, Lial A. Jones, championed the project from its inception, while the Crocker's current director, Agustín Arteaga, supported it to completion. The Crocker staff broadly, along with the ever-supportive Co-Trustees, contributed in myriad other ways.

Beth Jones and Lynda Jolley, who exhibited Adan's work for many years at JAYJAY, provided space and assistance with photography sessions. Elizabeth Adan helped secure loans and images from the Adan Family. Sheri Watson at Raven's Corner assisted with framing. Hirmer Publishers captured Adan's mischievous spirit in the catalogue, their team including Elisabeth Rochau-Shalem, senior editor; Rainer Arnold, editor; David Sánchez Cano, copyeditor; and Lukas Winkler, graphic designer. Finally, Michael Stevens, who since 1967 has been Adan's best friend and collaborator, contributed to the process throughout, participating in every step from beginning to end.

At the Crocker, we especially acknowledge Suzanne Adan, whose provocative, whimsical body of work and presence in the community has added immeasurably to the Sacramento art scene and helped give it national importance. Using her formidable technical skills and razor-sharp wit, she has created artworks that are exquisite, playful, clever, and unafraid to bare their teeth.

Agustín Arteaga, PhD
Mort and Marcy Friedman Director & CEO
Crocker Art Museum

Scott A. Shields, PhD
Ted and Melza Barr Chief Curator and Associate Director
Crocker Art Museum

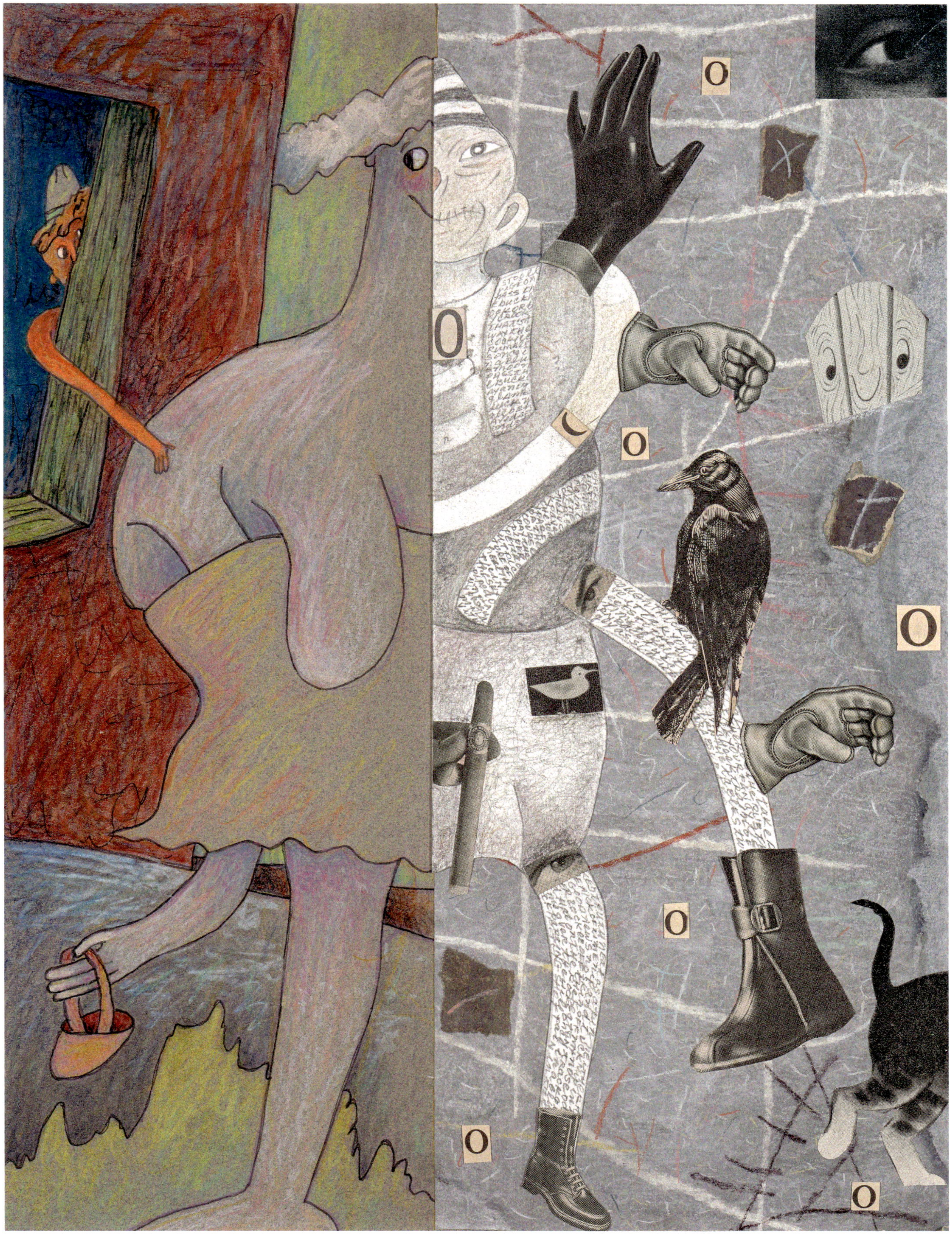

Gladys Nilsson (American, born 1940) and Suzanne Adan (American, born 1946) *Untitled II*, 2025.
Mixed media, 12 × 9 in. Courtesy of Gladys Nilsson and Suzanne Adan.

Foreword

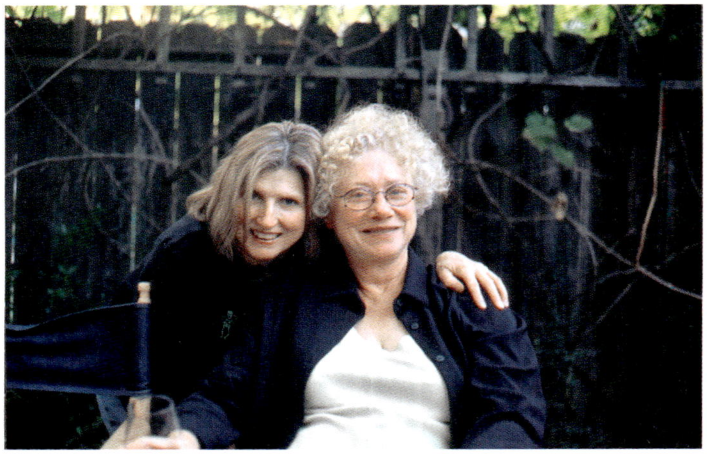

Suzanne Adan and Gladys Nilsson, 2003.
Courtesy of Suzanne Adan.

Dear Suzanne,

Thank you for asking me to write the foreword to your catalogue. I am honored to do so! Having accepted, I found myself writing and rewriting in my head, to try and get a handle on the how and what I'd say. This of course doesn't help the nod-off factor in bed. We all know I write about as well as I cook (not much and never correctly spelled). So, I decided to simply write you a letter.

We've known each other for years, since I and mine moved to Sac in late '68. If you figure it out, that's more than half a century—yikes—we are two old broads—as you have titled your show—No Spring Chicken! Oh boy, a lot of wrinkling and sagging going on—you went the slim route while I embraced a more rounded one—oh tee hee!!

At any rate, I'll just say that I've always liked your straight forwardness, never afraid to state your opinion. A fearless trait that your work also states. It's strong and good and wry and fun. Your explorations have continued in a variety of ways and materials. I laud your ability to do so, your invention on many levels.

One of the first pieces of yours I remember seeing was *Panty Hose.* **[p. 107]** It stopped me in my tracks, so funny, what word play! I broke out laughing. Ah ha, says I to myself, a kindred spirit! Being able to laugh and share that laugh, one of the most important things ever!

And we have shared many giggles. So much fun—I can't pass a goofy dress without thinking back to our shopping excursions, loading our arms with what might pass as really terrible prom dresses. We'd scurry to the changing rooms, get cubbies across from one another, then wait for the other's "ready" signal and burst into the open, collapsing with glee at how outlandish we looked. Oh what naughty women! We were so bad! We'd never skip over the old-fashioned hat bar either. Alas, they seem to have gone the way of missing socks in the dryer—non-existent.

All this has absolutely nothing to do with art, except it does. I think it's fed a necessary part in both our quests to create.

Your work is terrific, and you are so deserved of every accolade!

With much love and admiration,

Fondly,
Gladys

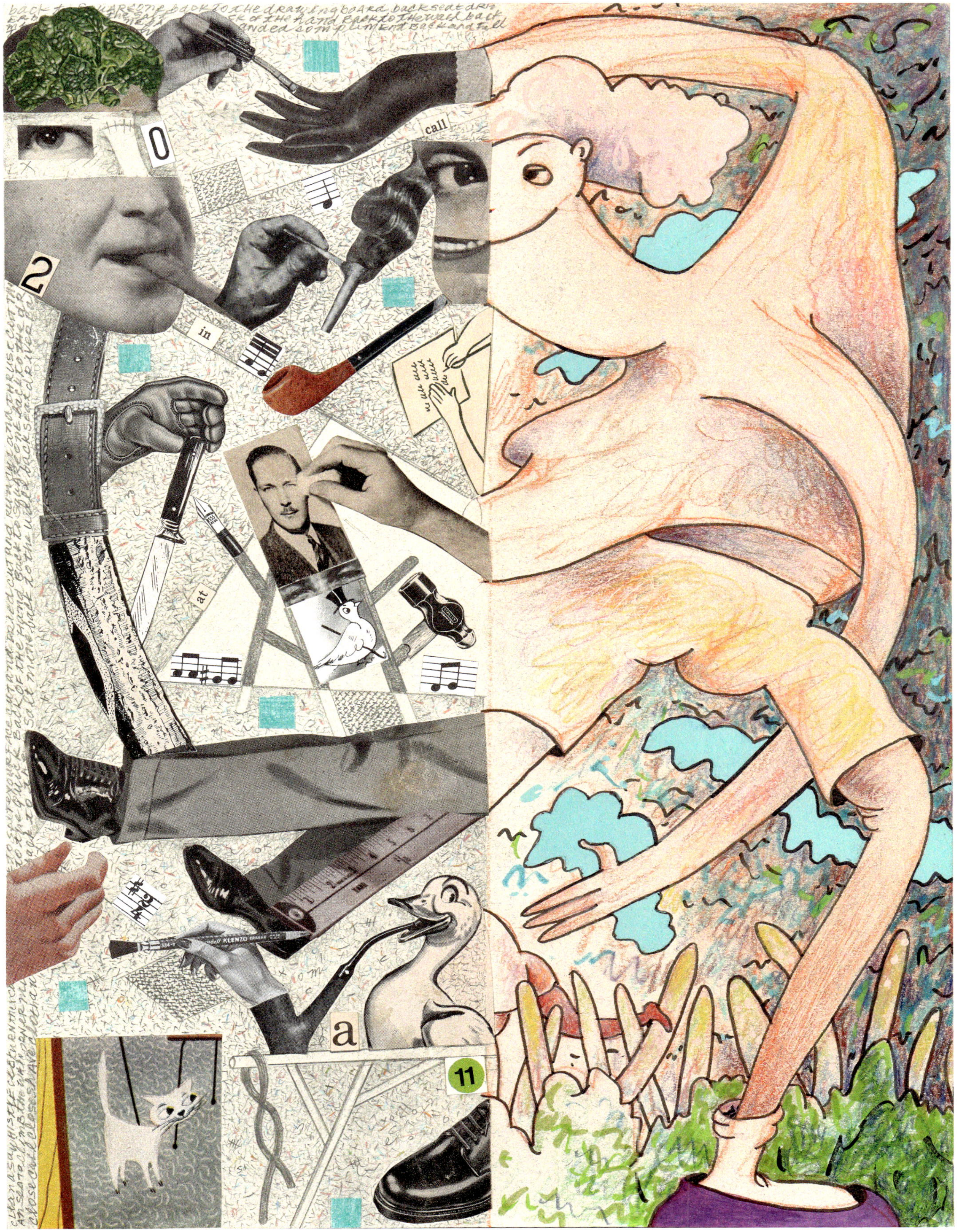

Suzanne Adan (American, born 1946) and Gladys Nilsson (American, born 1940), *Untitled I,* 2025.
Mixed media, 12 × 9 in. Courtesy of Suzanne Adan and Gladys Nilsson.

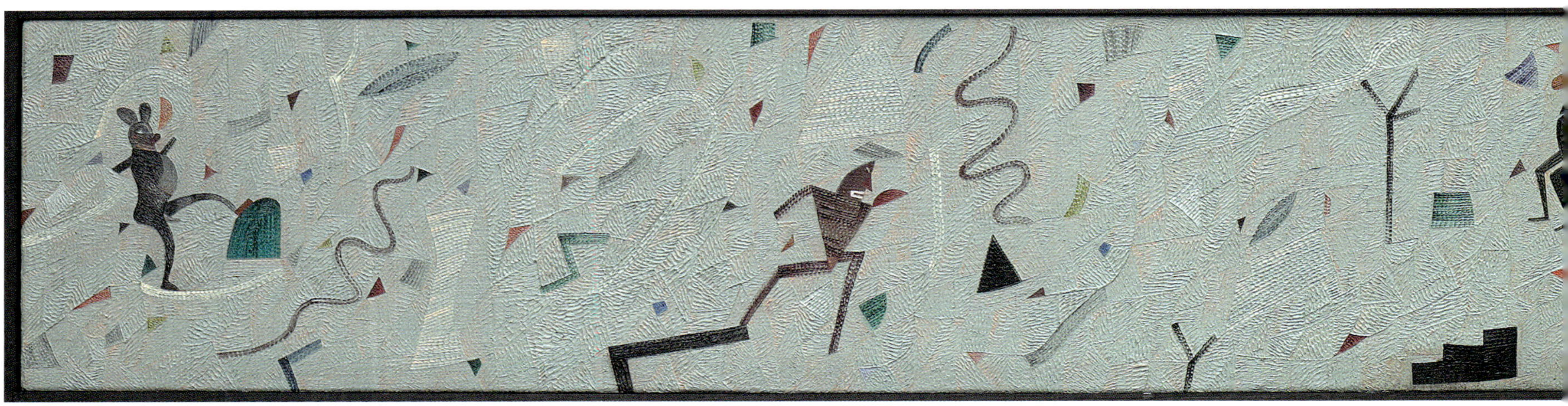

Full Moon, 1980–1981.
Oil on canvas, 8 ½ × 92 in. Collection of Gladys Nilsson and Jim Nutt.

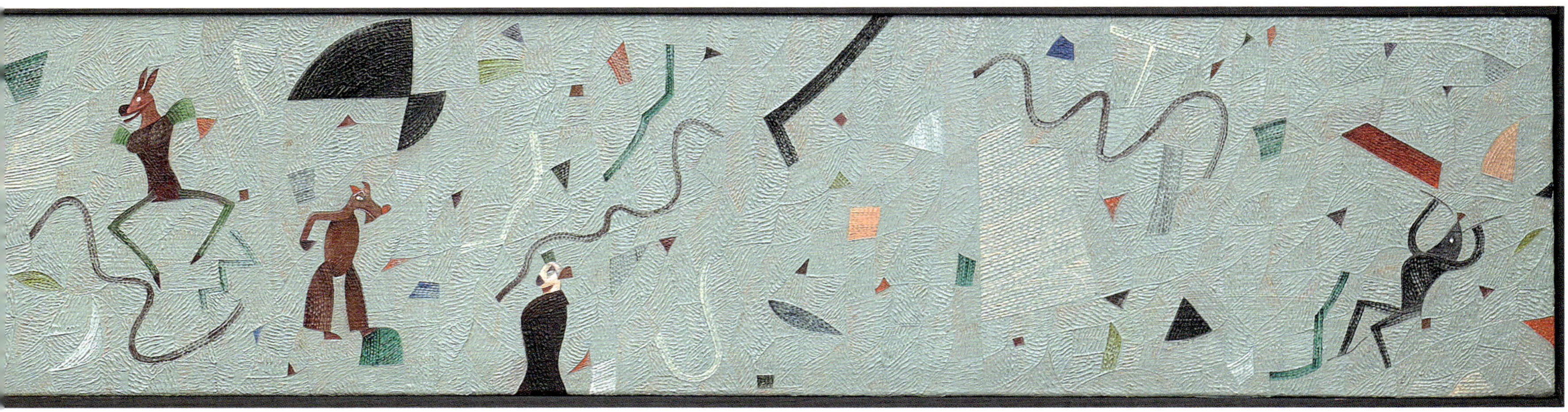

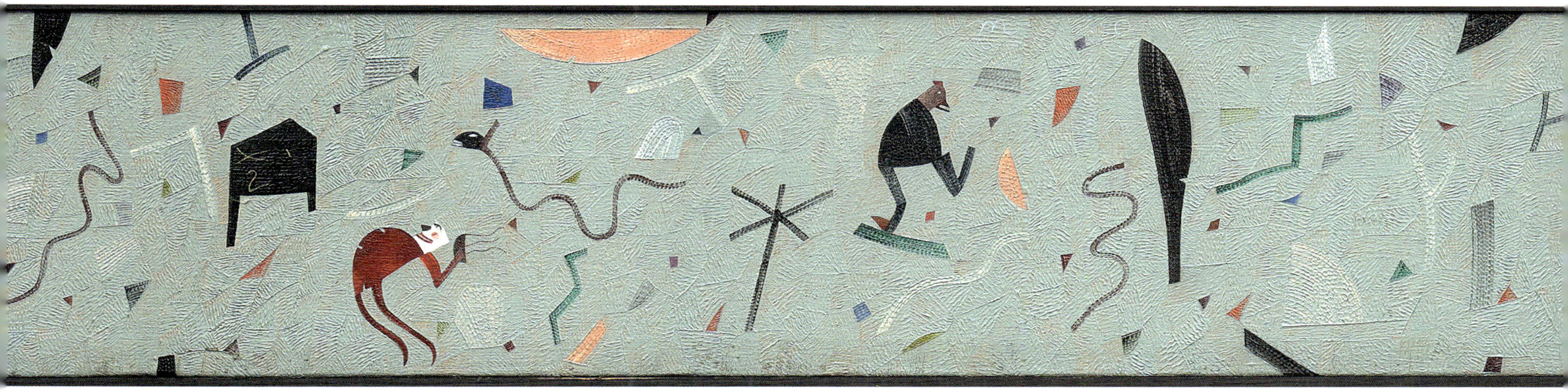

Suzanne Adan: I'm No Spring Chicken

Scott A. Shields

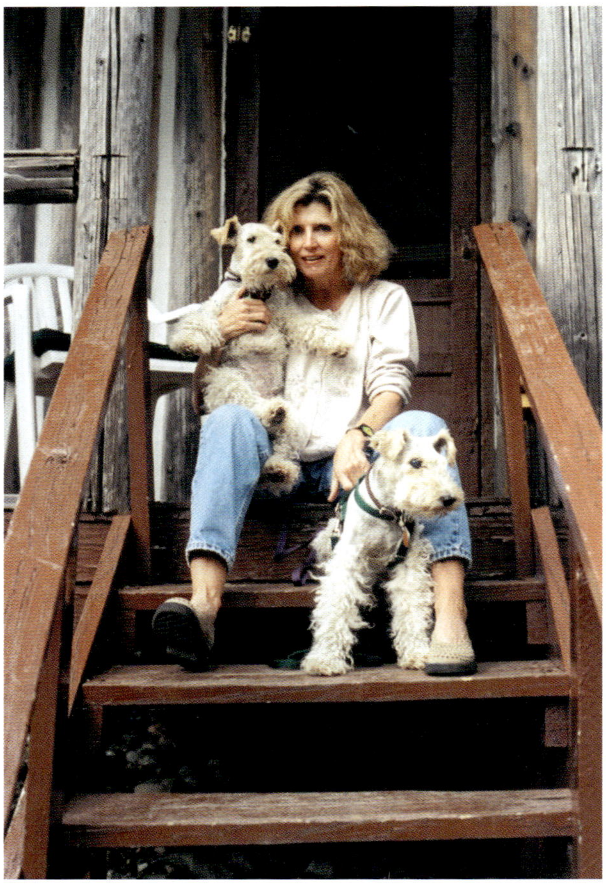

Suzanne Adan with dogs Reilly and Murphy in front of Cabin Number 7, Sardine Lake Resort, 2001. Courtesy of Suzanne Adan.

Much like her art, Suzanne Adan is animated, funny, and a little dark. She has always included figurative and narrative elements in her paintings and works on paper, creating a personal and visual vocabulary that is most certainly American but informed by sources internationally. Adan developed her practice within a rich context of eclectically irreverent Northern California artists, whose everyday subject matter, tongue-in-cheek humor, and penchant for the subversive or naughty led to her own absurd and satirical edge. Folk and outsider art also informs her practice, as do craft traditions. The latter is especially evident in her signature brushstrokes, which are laid down in small swatches and suggest sewing stitches (she became an expert on the sewing machine while growing up). Comic books and childhood toys also bring much to her aesthetic, these low-brow elements sharing equal space with more elevated art historical traditions such as German Expressionism and, especially, Surrealism, both of which foster her visionary spirit and penchant for narration. Curator Renny Pritikin describes just some of the myriad influences that make up her highly individual work:

> Tony Millionaire, whose character Drinky Crow . . . is a personal favorite and distant relative of Adan's black birds. The Chicago painter Tony Fitzpatrick's world of boxers and pinups is a soulmate, as are most of the mannered and hilarious Hairy Who artists, also in Chicago. The former UC Davis art professors William T. Wiley and Roy De Forest are also presences haunting these works for the recurring use of personal symbols and the way each page is saturated with imagery.

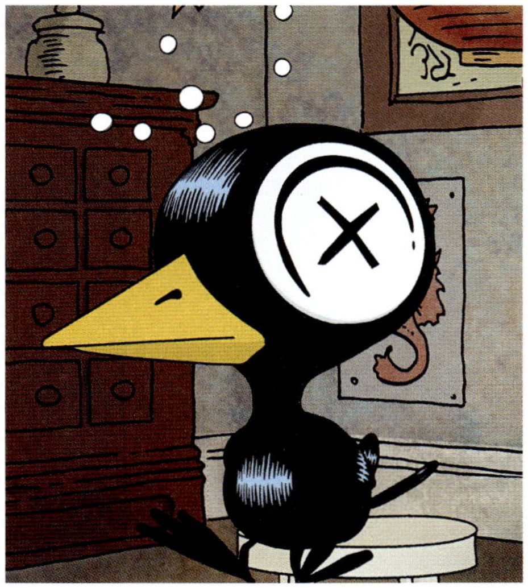

Suzie

One of the greatest influences on Adan also continues to be her sheltered, small-town upbringing, her childhood memories later combining with adult themes and accompanying implications of innocence lost. She was born Suzanne Rae Adan on February 12, 1946, in Woodland Memorial Hospital in Woodland, California. Her parents, Myrtle Irene Adan and Raymond Adan, had a home in the nearby village of Yolo, an unincorporated community twenty-four miles northwest of Sacramento. She had one brother, James (Jim), who was born two years earlier and also became an artist.

Adan's paternal grandparents were from Jaén in southern Spain but moved to Hawai'i in 1912 or 1913 to work in the pineapple fields. Her father was born there on October 1, 1913, his birth certificate listing his name as Ramon and his birthplace as Wailuku, Maui, though he grew up believing he was Raymond and born on the island of O'ahu. The family left Hawai'i when he was five and moved to California, settling in Esparto in Yolo County. Raymond finished eighth grade but progressed no further, as his family needed him to work. Because of this, he was adamant that his own children would receive a college education, whether they wanted one or not.

Adan's mother was eight years younger and born on November 21, 1921, in the small Canadian village of Kelfield in central Saskatchewan. Her maiden name was Cook, her father's family from Norway. Myrtle's mother, an Armstrong, was from Falkirk, Scotland. The Cooks left Saskatchewan for Oregon around 1923 and settled in unincorporated Marcola, near Eugene, where Myrtle graduated from high school. She and Raymond both ended up in Napa County, California, and met at a baseball game in 1941. They married the following year and subsequently moved to Woodland. Just months before Suzanne was born, they settled in Yolo.

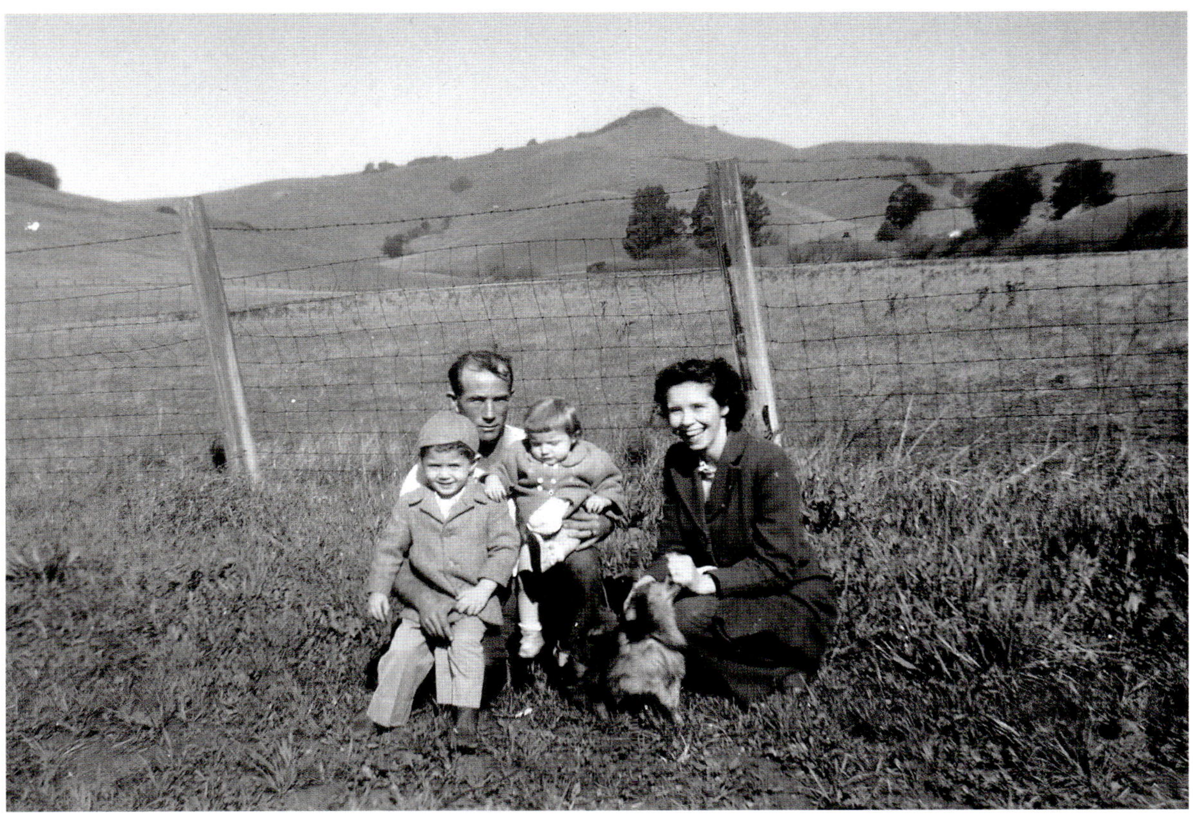

↑ Tony Millionaire (American, born 1956), *Drinky Crow*, from the comic strip *Maakies*, 2008. © Tony Millionaire and Fantagraphics Books.

→ Suzanne Adan with her mother, father, and brother, Jim, Sonoma, 1947. Courtesy of Suzanne Adan.

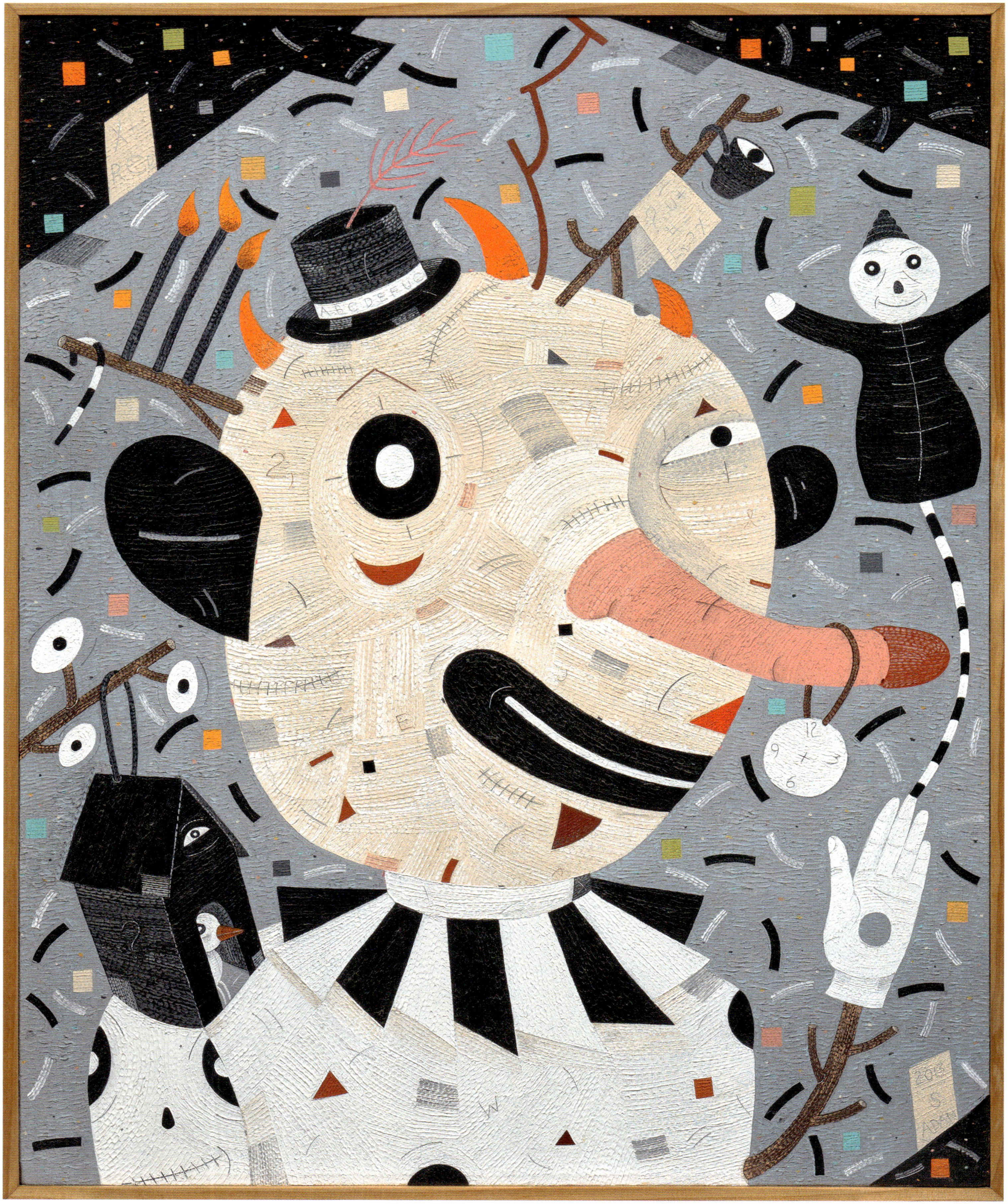

Sugar Daddy, 2013.
Oil on canvas, 29 ¾ × 24 in. Collection of Sandra Singer and Tom Weborg.

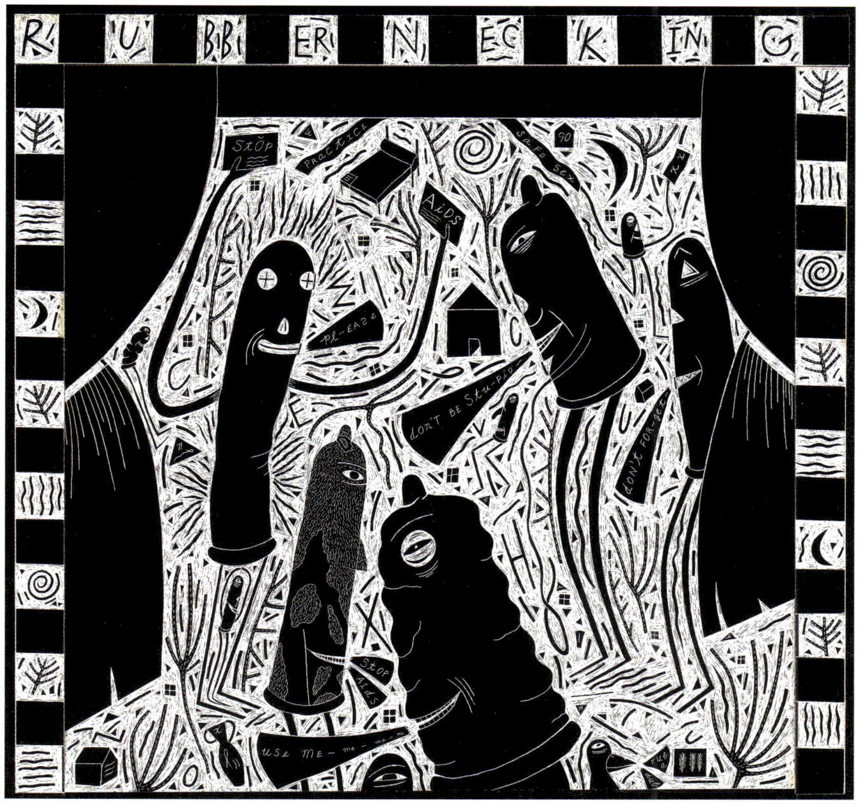

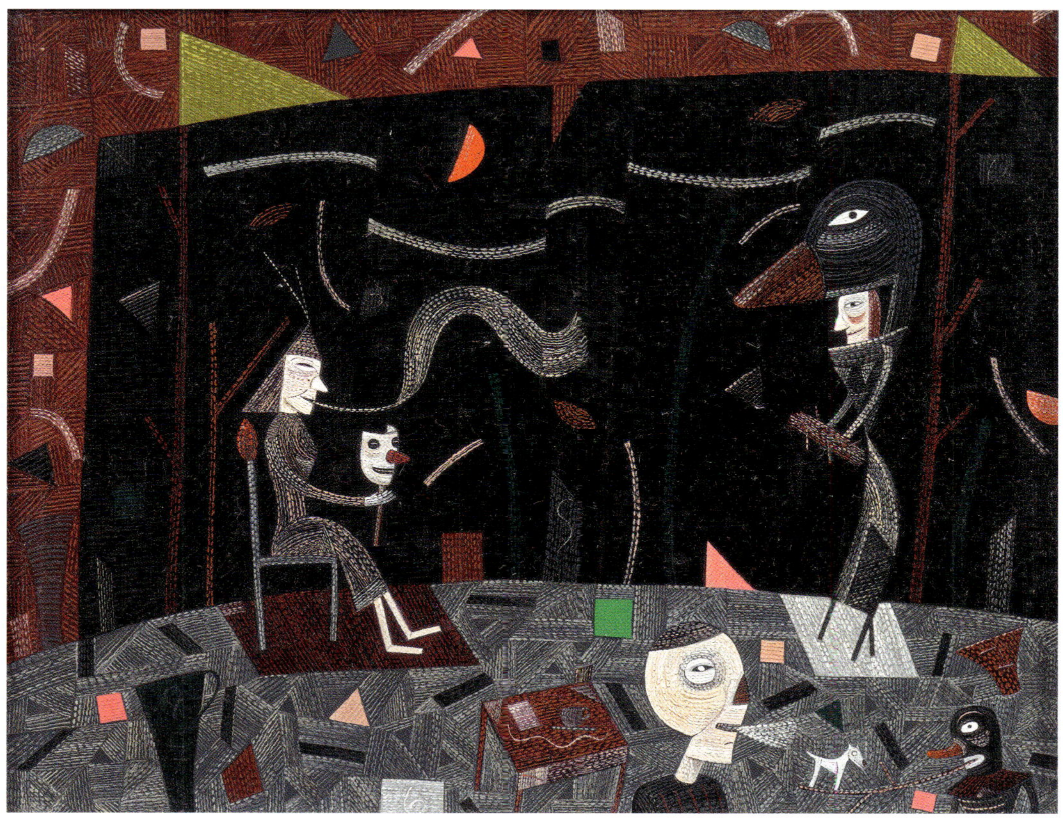

↑ *Rubber Necking,* 1990.
Scratchboard, 8 ½ × 8 ⅝ in. Collection of James A. Sundquist.

→ *Chain Smoke,* 1987.
Oil on canvas, 11 ¾ × 13 ¾ in. Collection of Caleb Counts.

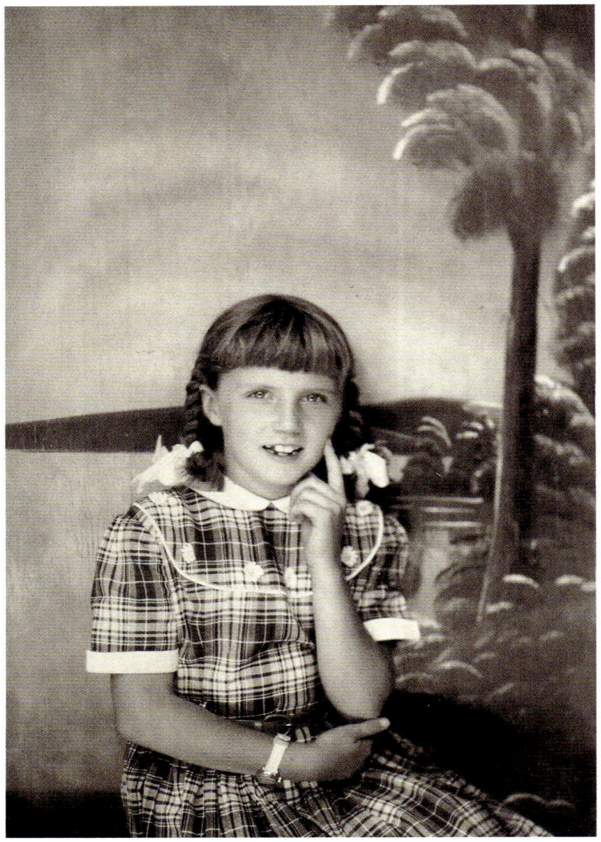

Suzanne Adan, Yolo County Fair, 1952.
Courtesy of Suzanne Adan.

At the time, Yolo had about 300 residents and was much like any small agricultural community in Middle America despite being in California's heartland, the great Central Valley. Adan's kind but pragmatic father worked as a truck driver with the Roy E. Lay trucking firm in Woodland. Raised Catholic, he did not attend church except for special services. Adan's mother was a homemaker and churchgoer, and she made sure her children were baptized and attended Sunday school and weekly services at Yolo Methodist Church.[2] Later, after her children made it through school, Myrtle went to work for the Yolo Post Office. For a short period, Suzanne worked there as well; Yolo's post mistress, Mrs. Eva Hadley, was the Adans' next-door neighbor and a kindly influence on Adan growing up.

Adan attended Cacheville Elementary School (first through eighth grade) in Yolo. She conformed to things expected of girls at the time. She dressed like a proper young lady, wore her hair in braids and pigtails (often with bows at the ends), and joined the Brownie's and Girl Scouts, earning seventeen badges and a first-class rank. A photo of Adan and other girls in Hawaiian grass skirts appeared in Yolo County's *Daily Democrat* under the headline "Cacheville School Plans Fun Festival." Entertainments included a fishpond, balloon darts, bean-bag toss, cakewalk, and bingo. That evening, the students put on a show, which included a barbershop quartet with Jimmie Adan, and a hula performance with Suzanne and other aspiring dancers.[3] Adan also participated in the annual Halloween dance sponsored by her Girl Scout troop (igniting her passion for all things Halloween), as well as other holiday festivities at the Yolo Town Hall.

Despite being relatively shy and quiet, Adan was liked and respected by her small group of classmates, who appreciated her sense of humor and unassuming leadership skills; she was elected to the Cacheville student council more than once. A bit of a goody two-shoes, she tried hard to please her parents and her teachers, behaving well, doing her homework, and making the honor roll. In whatever she tried, her competitive nature caused her to excel.

She was also inherently musical and played the accordion, clarinet, flute, and piano by ear. She credits her love of music both to an excellent first grade teacher, Frances Kergel, who played the piano and conducted sing-alongs in class, as well as to her family's own musical get-togethers. The accordion was something of a family instrument, and in the fourth grade Adan acquired hers from Sears, Roebuck & Co. She took lessons from a music teacher, Jennie Woolworth, who came twice a week to Cacheville Elementary to offer instruction and lead the school's small band.

Adan's brother opted for the clarinet but rarely played or practiced, prompting Suzanne to take it up. She did so in part to prepare for the high school marching band, as she wanted to wear the uniform and perceptively noticed that marching bands did not have accordionists. To the astonishment of her teacher, she also learned to play the flute on her own. A music lover, she never had to be told to practice, even during the summer. Today, she equates her intuitive approach to art-making—trusting her instincts as she is creating rather than starting with a strongly preconceived idea—to the way she once improvised in music. She was also skilled at cooking and sewing, honing her skills through years of participation in her local 4-H club, which also taught her much about how to organize projects and work toward a goal.

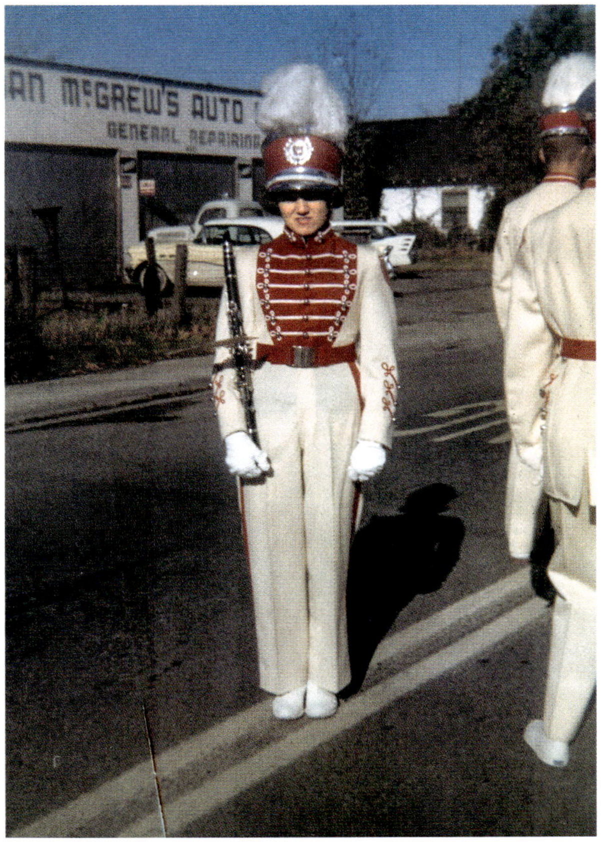

Suzanne Adan in Woodland High School Band uniform, 1959. Courtesy of Suzanne Adan.

Other than these activities and her music, however, there was little else for Adan to do in Yolo, and so she rode her bike often, coming to know every house and building in her town, along with most of the inhabitants. She also spent a good deal of time at the Yolo Branch Library, where kindly librarian Clara Voissard made sure that she and her brother received the books they needed and, at the end of the year, gave her old issues of *LIFE* and *Time* magazines that provided her with glimpses into a world far beyond her own.[4] Adan also remembers when National Rifle Association members came to town to conduct gun safety courses for young 4-H'ers, a thinly disguised recruitment effort in which participants were given junior NRA memberships. Adan still has her membership card.

Head, Heart, Hands, and Health

Most exciting for Adan and her brother was when in June 1957 the Adan family bought their first television, a massive piece of furniture with a tiny black-and-white screen. For Adan, the summer preceding seventh grade was "the best on record," as she and her brother sat in front of the TV for hours and could finally participate in discussions with friends about shows they had seen.[5]

Adan graduated from the eighth grade on June 3, 1959. At the ceremony, she performed with the school band and delivered a rousing clarinet solo, *Sail Along, Silvery Moon*. She attended high school in nearby Woodland, Yolo not large enough to merit a secondary school. Woodland had a population of around 12,000 and was the seat of one of the leading agricultural counties in the United States. In the early 1960s it was home to many wealthy citizens, most of their money made through agriculture, the town boasting rice mills, a sugar beet refinery, and a tomato cannery. Not surprisingly, it also hosted the highly popular—and free—Yolo County Fair, which Adan both attended and contributed to in various divisions relating to food, craft, and sewing through 4-H, and, later on, in art. For a time, she also continued her involvement in band but dropped out in her sophomore year because of the early morning rehearsals. Even today, she is not a morning person.

A photo of Adan in the *Daily Democrat* from 1963 is headlined "A 4-H'er Reports." She was then seventeen and had participated in the Yolo 4-H club for the past seven years. The "report" provided a rundown of her recent activities. "I undertook four projects and completed them: clothing, food preparation, food preservation, and junior leader," she recounted.

> I made a cotton corduroy suit with a print blouse and matching lining for my clothing project this year. I entered them at the Spring Show [the annual display of the 4-H'er's yearly projects or animals] and received three blue ribbons. In food preparation I entered a chocolate cream roll, Starlight Mint Surprises, German Sweet Chocolate cake and Brownie Kisses. . . . I received three blues, one honorable mention, one red and a gold seal certificate. I decided to take food preservation for the first time this year. . . . At our project meetings we canned tomatoes, peaches, bread and butter pickles, sweet pickles, zucchini relish, and apple-grape jelly.[6]

Her contributions to 4-H "Demonstrations and Talent" contests also evidenced her budding sense of humor, such as "How to Make a Purple Cow for Two" (made with ice cream and grape soda) in 1958; "How to Cut a Grapefruit in Sections" in 1963; and back-to-back "Hootenannies" in 1964 and 1965.[7]

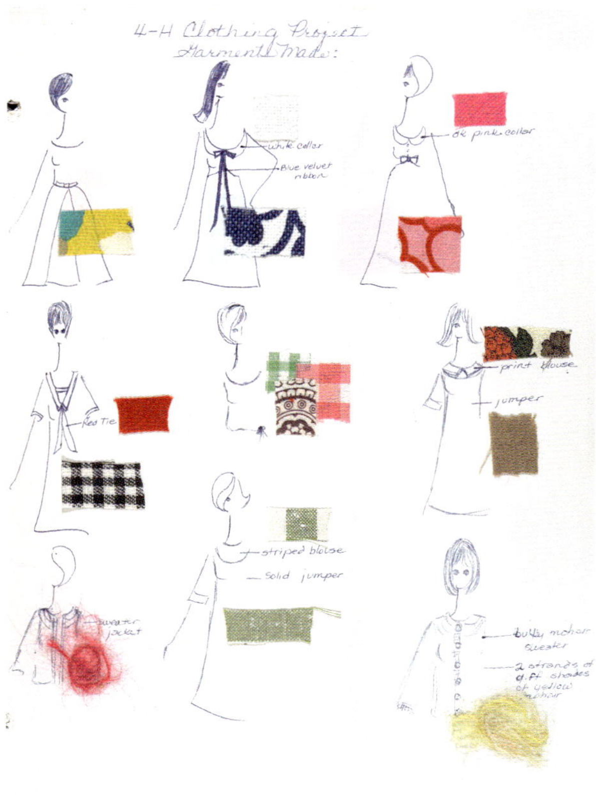

Suzanne Adan's 4-H Clothing Project, 1965. Courtesy of the Artist.

Changing Courses

Adan also pursued projects beyond 4-H, though art was generally not one of them. It was only in her final semester of high school that she took her first formal art class, an entry course called Arts and Crafts. Though it did not cover painting or drawing—those were offered in classes she didn't take—it sparked her interest in ceramics. The piece she made that pleased her most was a ceramic container for her mother's bobby pins. To make it, she used bobby pins to carve the clay, which she thought conceptually very clever. The piece did, in fact, anticipate her love of punning; the process foretold of the sgraffito technique she would one day use to make scratch-boards and hand-carved tiles. Though Adan called the bobby-pin vessel "the only good thing to come out of the Arts and Crafts class," the idea of working in clay stuck in her mind as something fun to do.[8] Her mother cherished the bobby pin vessel until she died.

Adan was relieved to graduate from Woodland High School in June 1963. She had grown restless in Yolo, and it was becoming increasingly difficult for her to remain within the cloistered, small-town environment of her youth. In college, her world view changed dramatically, almost from the outset. She began her freshman year at Sacramento State College (today California State University, Sacramento) when she was 17 years old. Less than three months later, President Kennedy was assassinated. It happened on a Friday, and she was going to her afternoon art history class, but the campus was practically empty. She will forever remember the moment when she heard the news that Kennedy had been killed: "It changed everything, and we kind of knew that life was never going to be the same."[9] She even organized a 4-H cake sale, from which she donated the proceeds to the forthcoming John F. Kennedy Memorial Library and Museum. Jacqueline Kennedy sent her a note of thanks stating, "Of all the many tributes to the memory of President Kennedy, I am sure that none would have pleased him more than the touching response of you young people."[10]

In fall 1964, Adan enrolled in a Costume Design and Selection class in the Sacramento State home economics department, which she found disappointing. The same had been true of her child development and family development classes, especially because she was unsure whether she even wanted to have children. She did, however, enjoy the art department's Introduction to Design, which she took in that same fall semester as a requirement. She asked her brother to suggest other art classes she might take. Jim recommended Introduction to Oil Painting with Irving Marcus.

Marcus's class proved a defining moment in Adan's college education, as it was because of that class that she decided to pursue a career in art. With such little affinity for home economics, she decided to change course, though for a brief time she thought she might be able to combine her skills in this arena with art, either by teaching at the high school level or by pursuing a career in clothing design. Convincing her parents to accept her aspirations would, however, be another matter, and she continued to leave her major undeclared until 1966, when she once again turned to her brother for help, asking him to convince their parents to officially let her declare art as her major and anthropology as her minor. Not immediately supportive, her parents thought being a nurse, secretary, or elementary school teacher made better sense for a young woman. But, after several "heated discussions," they relented, accepting the fact that both of their children were now on the path to becoming artists.[11]

All Star

On July 13th, 1965, Adan and a young man named Ron Timothy appeared on the front page of the *Daily Democrat* as Yolo County 4-H All-Stars, the reporter calling Adan a "pert brown haired lass" and "expert seamstress and talented dress designer." [12] She had continued her 4-H involvement into college but would soon be terming out.

To win an All-Star award was the highest possible achievement in the 4-H program, and Adan was certainly deserving. Chosen by a county-wide committee of 4-H leaders, it was based on the total cumulative record of the contenders and given to top club members from each county: one female and one male. During her nine years in 4-H, Adan pursued a year of farming (swine), three years of food preservation and home furnishing, five years of garment-making, and six years of junior leadership. She also tallied eight years of food preparation, meaning she made most of her family's meals throughout high school and into college, sometimes with her brother's help, as he was also enrolled in food preparation. In 1965 alone, she prepared 604 dishes for her family and served 484 meals. She also won purple ribbons at the annual countywide 4-H Spring Show in home furnishings and food preservation, making 15 decorative items and refinishing furniture, and canning and cold-packing 322 containers of fruits, vegetables, and jellies. She made 17 pieces of clothing as well. The experiences were more relevant to her future than one might think, as she explained in her home furnishings design portfolio: "I arranged it considering such problems as color, scale, balance, texture, center-of-interest, etc. I also learned how to mat and frame a picture which will be useful to me at school since I'm an art major."[13]

Adan additionally prepared her 4-H club's Yolo County Fair booth that year, made food for needy families, led a workshop to make holiday favors for hospital patients at Thanksgiving and Christmas, and taught Sunday school at her church. Over time she served as her 4-H club's historian, sergeant at arms, secretary, and vice president. It was a lot, especially for a busy college student. Years later, she made a painting titled *Four H,* a loose self-portrait that depicts her in a beret and green 4-H tie, wearing a dress that she made herself. [p. 26] Her head, hands, and shoulders balance multiple objects and four to-do lists. A squiggly clarinet issues from her mouth. She also has the nose of a pig, a reference to the one-and-only year she took a pig to the fair. Though she won a blue ribbon, the project ended in personal devastation when she sent her friend "Scotty" to market.[14]

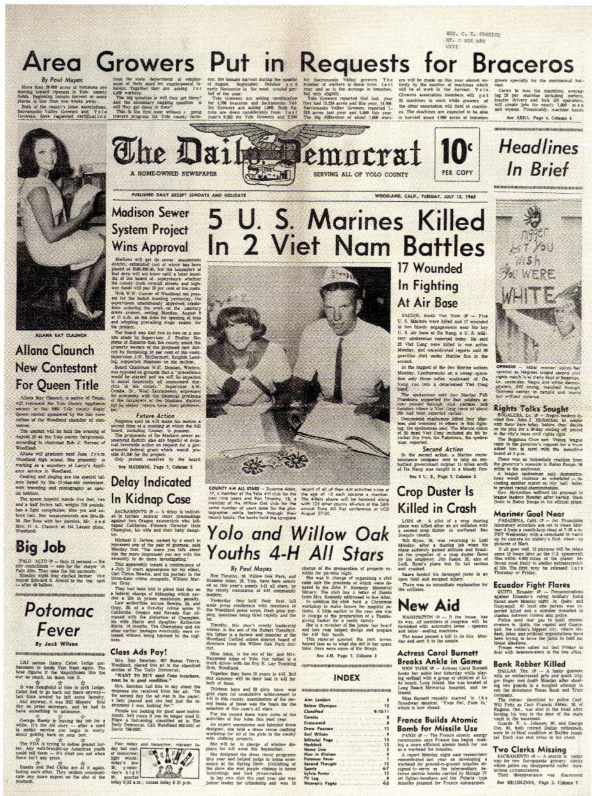

Area Growers Put in Requests for Braceros

The Daily Democrat

A HOME-OWNED NEWSPAPER — SERVING ALL OF YOLO COUNTY

10¢ PER COPY

Headlines In Brief

Madison Sewer System Project Wins Approval

5 U. S. Marines Killed In 2 Viet Nam Battles

17 Wounded In Fighting At Air Base

Allana Claunch New Contestant For Queen Title

Delay Indicated In Kidnap Case

Big Job

Potomac Fever

Class Ads Pay!

Yolo and Willow Oak Youths 4-H All Stars

Crop Duster Is Killed in Crash

New Aid

Actress Carol Burnett Breaks Ankle in Game

France Builds Atomic Bomb for Missile Use

INDEX

Rights Talks Sought

Mariner Goal Near

Ecuador Fight Flares

Bank Robber Killed

Two Clerks Missing

The Daily Democrat front page, July 13, 1965. Courtesy of Suzanne Adan.

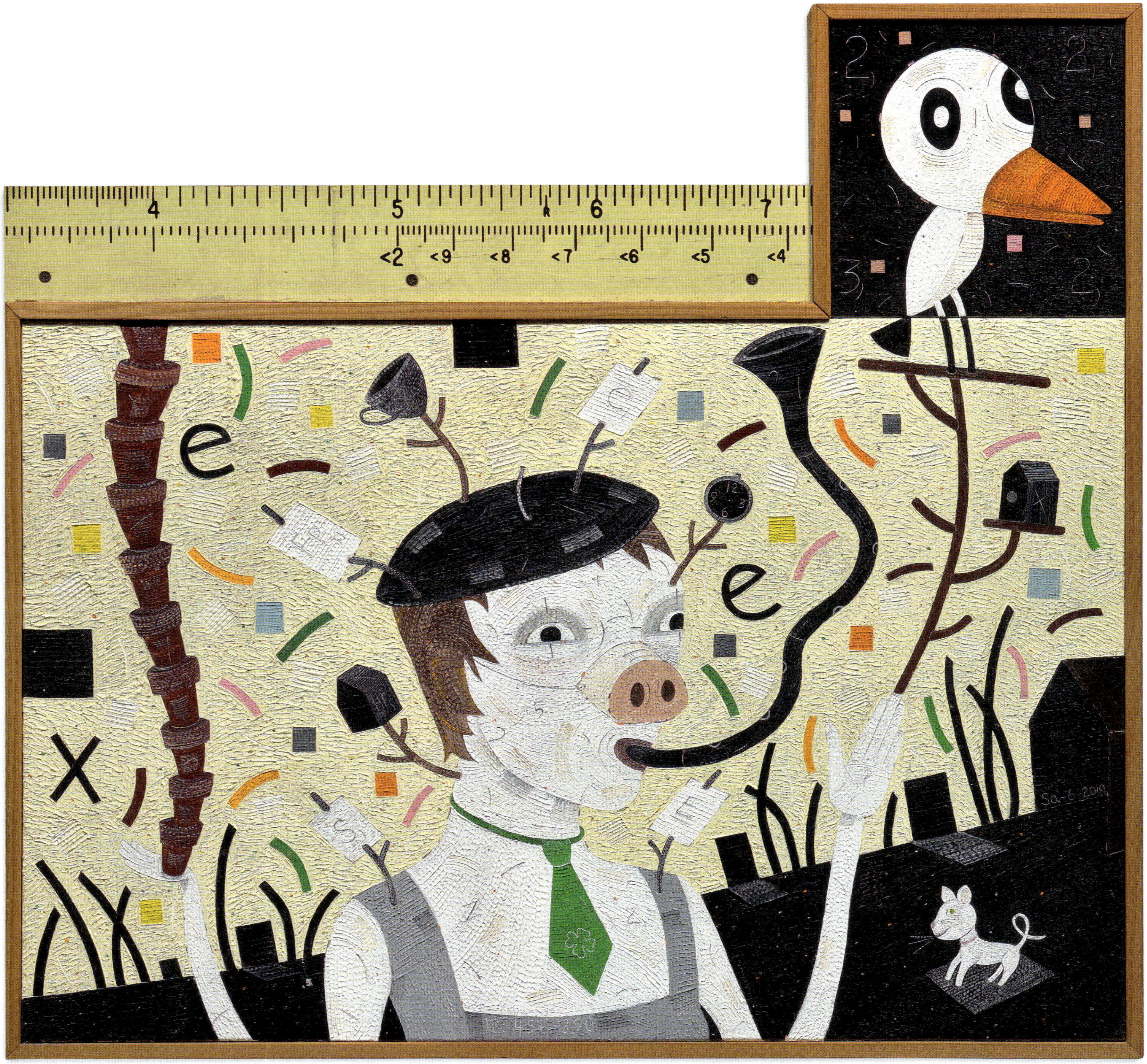

Four H, 2010.
Oil on canvas, 29 ½ × 31 ¼ in. Collection of Caleb Counts.

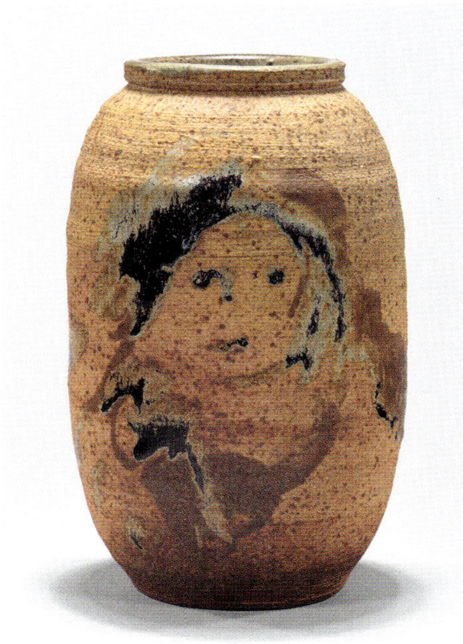

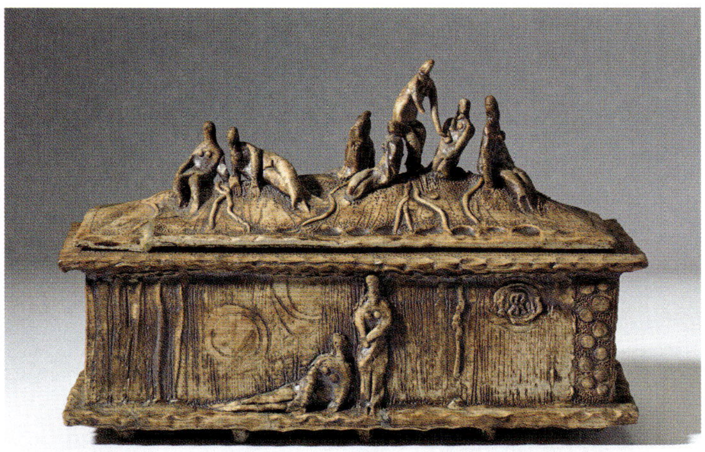

Two-Faced, 1966.
Clay and glaze, 8 × 4 ½ in. Collection of the Artist.

Ruth Rippon (American, 1927–2022), *Fates Box,* 1964–1966. Gray stoneware with iron oxide wash; matte turquoise glaze interior, 8 ½ × 12 ⅜ × 5 in. Crocker Art Museum, gift of Ruth M. Rippon, 2018.130.15.a-b.

Though filled with personal accomplishments, Adan's upbringing was insulated, and she remained largely innocent of the world at large. This dichotomy is evidenced by other stories sharing space with her front-page article in the *Daily Democrat.* Immediately above Adan's photo, the headline reads, "5 U.S. Marines Killed in 2 Vietnam Battles: 17 Wounded in Fighting at Air Base." [p. 25] Immediately to the right, a photograph depicted a woman holding a sign of African American hate, the image accompanying an article about a Civil Rights march.[15] These and other realities of the 1960s were starting to collide with the sheltered, small-town life that she had led.

Steady Progress

Adan attended the 4-H State All-Star conference at the University of California, Davis, in August 1965, an event that gathered 125 honorees from fifty-six California counties. She also submitted an artwork to the Northern California Arts, Inc.'s 12th Annual Open Art Exhibition at what was then called the E. B. Crocker Art Gallery (now Crocker Art Museum) in Sacramento. To her surprise, her work was accepted and put on display in October. Given she was still an undergraduate, the recognition meant a lot.

That same fall, Adan took Beginning Ceramics with Ruth Rippon. She was "fascinated with clay," not just because of her high school art class but because it reminded her of making mud pies as a child. She soon learned, however, that getting clay to conform to expectations on a potter's wheel was not so simple.[16] Rippon, an expert at throwing pots, made the process look easy, but this was not so for Adan, who equated the kick-wheel process with driving a car with a stick shift, neither of which she ever quite mastered.[17] Rippon, however, was equally skilled at hand-building, which Adan realized after seeing her work exhibited at the Artists Contemporary Gallery, an important venue for Sacramento artists at the time. "She [Rippon] created these beautiful hand-built ceramic boxes, and a light bulb went off," Adan remembers. "I came back to class and started doing hand-built pieces."[18] For a while, clay became one of Adan's primary mediums. She would also continue to make small, multi-part ceramic sculptures with landscape elements and animals—and later doll-like figures styled after her painted characters—far beyond Rippon's tutelage, despite harboring an insecurity that her ceramic skills were "technically lousy."[19] She would also use clay to make handmade tiles for public art projects.

A semester after Rippon's class, Adan encountered another impactful instructor, Jerald Silva, who taught watercolor while Professor Robert Else was on sabbatical. Silva earned his own BA and MA from Sacramento State and was an accomplished watercolor practitioner with a unique approach that utilized a selectively opaque application of paint and Elmer's glue. Adan remembers, "When he demonstrated his method of watercolor painting, it was absolutely mind-boggling to watch him elegantly put paint on paper. I took notes and worked diligently to paint like Jerald with little success. But, his techniques did creep into my art in a more crude and primitive form."[20]

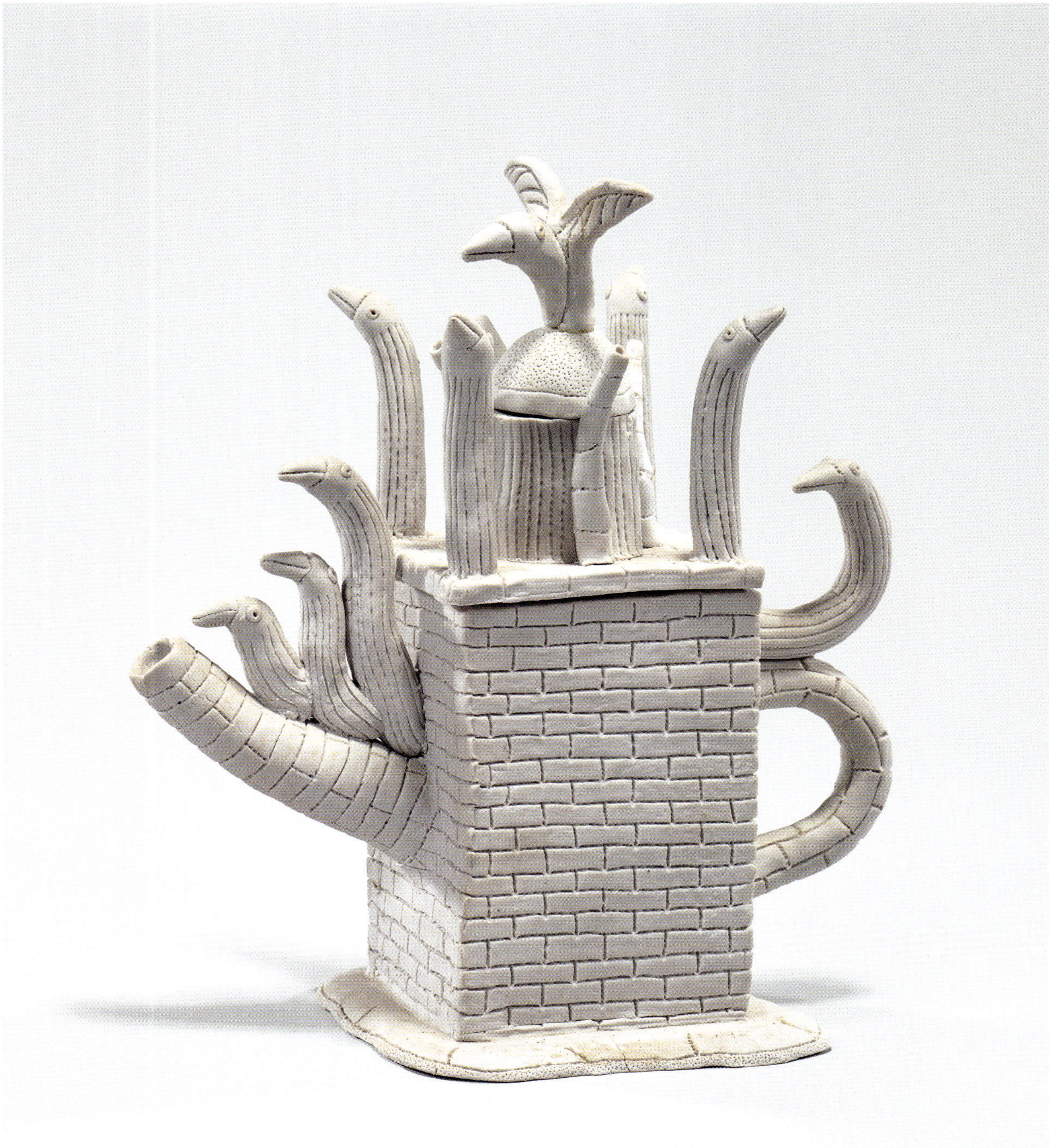

Brick a Bird Teapot, 1976.
Porcelain, 9 ½ × 4 ½ × 8 in. Collection of Susan Howe and Rebecca Goodchild.

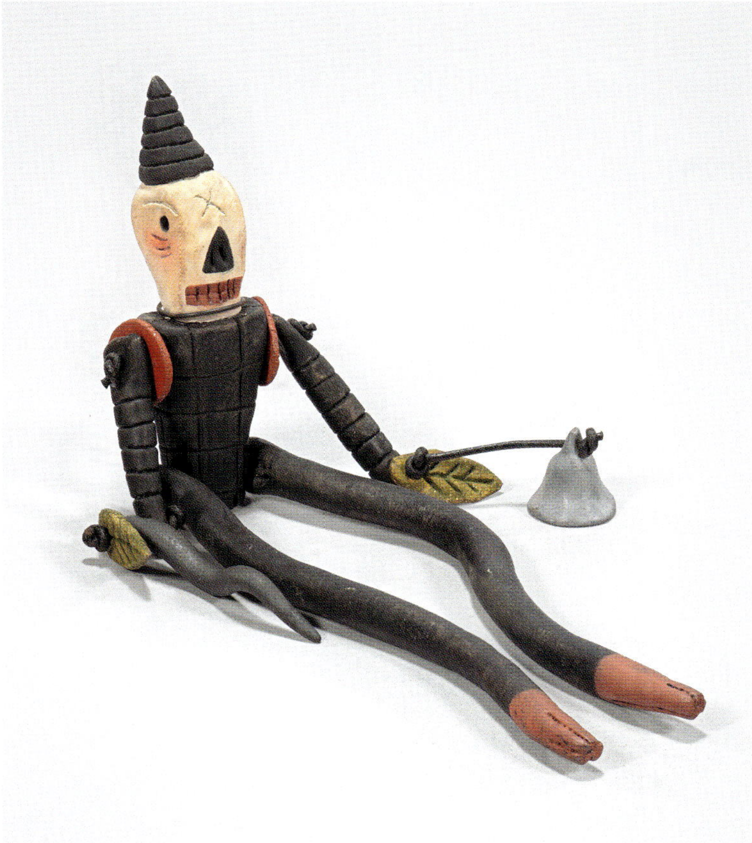

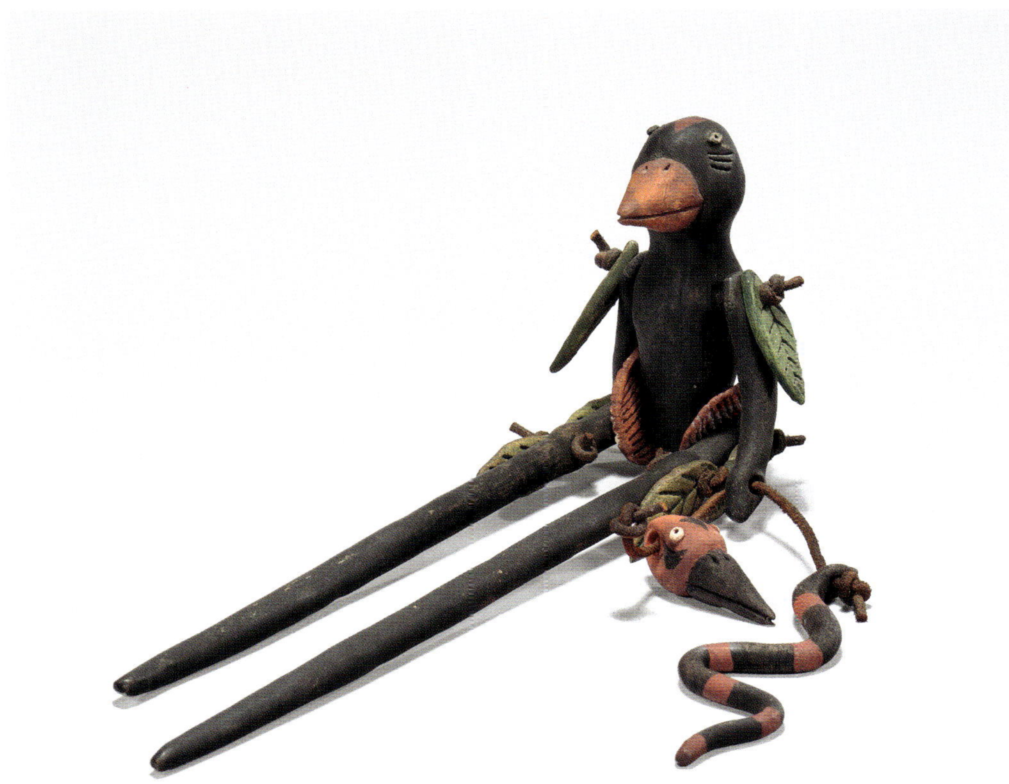

↑ *Clown Doll*, n.d.
Ceramic and leather. Collection of D. Oldham Neath.

→ *Bird Doll*, 1989.
Clay and paint, 11 × 3 ½ × 1 ½ in. Collection of Sheri Watson.

Making steady progress, Adan was starting to find her voice. Her works in clay and efforts in two-dimensional media had begun to evidence her upbringing, sense of humor, and thoughts about the world, hinting at the influence of master artists she had come to admire, especially the German Expressionists and Surrealists, with George Grosz, Otto Dix, Max Ernst, Paul Klee, Jean Dubuffet, and René Magritte all counting among her favorites. She was garnering recognition as well. In the spring of 1966, for instance, she held her first one-person show, an exhibition of drawings, paintings, and ceramics, at Sierra College in Rocklin. Later that year, she took home multiple awards from the Yolo County Fair, winning second prize in the abstract or non-objective graphics category (her brother won first prize in this category), and three first prizes in representational graphics, painting, and pottery. Her submissions to the latter two categories (*Self Portrait in a 1920s Setting* [p. 104] and a ceramic jewelry box) were accorded best-of-show, beating out her brother's work for top honors, this achievement meaning more than the prizes.

Adan also exhibited that year in a group show at Sacramento's Kaleidoscope Gallery and won first and second place prizes in the drawings and collage category at the Sacramento County Fair: *Green Onion at 5th and Broadway* ($50 first place prize) and *Mephistopheles Running Loose* ($20 second place prize). She contributed to the California State Fair that year as well. Just four of the artworks selected were by Yolo County artists, and two of them were by Adan. One was uncharacteristically titled just *Drawing* and displayed in the prints, drawings, and pastels division. The other received a third place prize in the college junior and senior oil painting category. Now lost, it combined her love of food, art, and humor, as evidenced by the title: *The Leopard Skin Snake Takes the Cake (Frosting)!*. It was, by Adan's description, a "goofy" scene of a black-and-white snake devouring a colorfully messy dessert.[21] She made it in part to try to distance herself from Marcus's influence and to create something more uniquely her own. She contributed to Northern California Arts, Inc.'s 13th Annual Open Exhibition at the E. B. Crocker Art Gallery in late 1966 as well, winning third prize in the watercolor division for *Self Portrait in a 1920s Setting*.

Size Matters

Adan now had a steady boyfriend in fellow art student Michael Stevens, whose views on politics and art expanded her own. She met Stevens at Sacramento State in the spring of 1966 in Jack Ogden's drawing class. Ogden told students to choose a classmate to share a locker with, and Stevens asked Adan. They became good friends the following fall in Susan Willoughby's art history class and started dating in the spring. They began going steady that June.

Stevens was born in Gilroy, California, in 1945, and came to Sacramento with his family at age ten. He began to seriously pursue art at La Sierra High School in Carmichael, taking classes with a well-known artist who taught there, Ralph Goings. Adan also came to know Goings, who captured her and Stevens in an informal photograph that he later turned into a painting. [p. 33] After graduation, Stevens enrolled at American

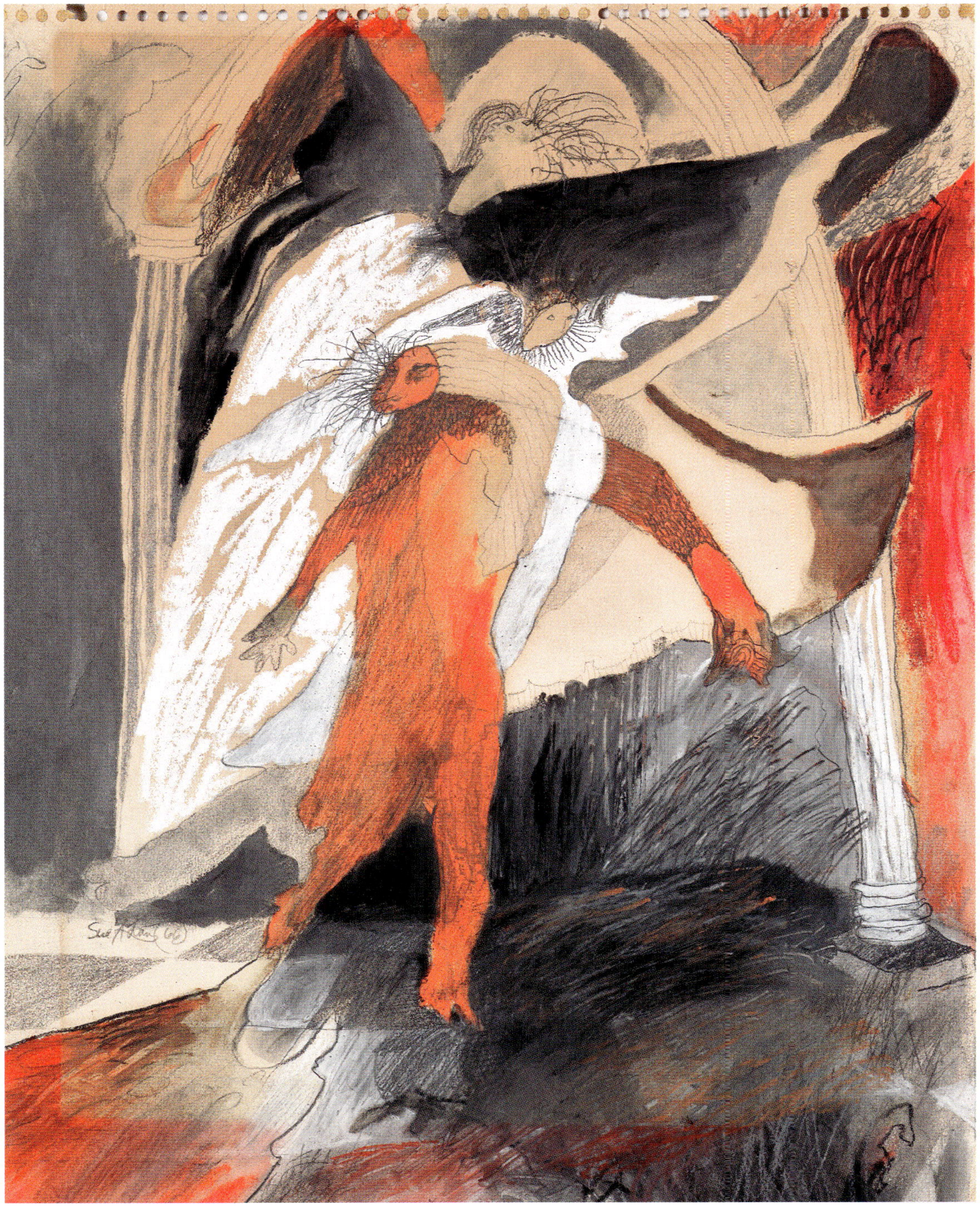

"Mephistopheles" Escape from the Gorgons, 1966.
Oil pastel and pencil on paper, 16 × 12 in. Collection of the Artist.

River College in Sacramento, studying painting with Tony Berlant. He then transferred to Sacramento State, where he continued to focus primarily on two-dimensional work, taking classes with Else, Marcus, Ogden, and others. He also attended a sculpture class with the new instructor Richard Randall and two courses with Rippon: one in sculpture, the other in ceramics.

It was in the spring of 1967 that Adan took her own first oil painting class with Ogden, a course in which she dipped her toe into the international stream of Pop art by making a large painting of Superman. Adan asked Stevens to help her stretch the large canvas for the painting, wanting to compete with the men in the department who liked to make things big. As she recollects, "Size mattered!"[22] Adan's depiction of a comic book figure was indirectly sanctioned by Sacramento artist Mel Ramos, whose paintings of superheroes and pin-ups she knew, his national notoriety—and that of Wayne Thiebaud's—of much interest to her and others in the art department, given that both artists had attended Sacramento State. More important for her own portrayal, however, was the 1950s television show *Adventures of Superman* with George Reeves, which she and her brother watched religiously, as well as her brother's extensive comic book collection. It was also around this time that Adan acquired a Superman lunchbox, which she used for the next several years.

The bold, painterly influence of both Marcus and Ogden was evident in Adan's Superman as well, though her preliminary drawing for the large work—which included multiple Supermen—had more to do with Ogden, as it incorporated rubber stamps. Adan had used her childhood rubber stamps in her work before, which Ogden saw and appreciated, even trying to buy them from her. When Adan refused to sell them, he bought his own set and used them in new ways, in turn influencing Adan.

Members of the Kingsley Art Club came to see Adan's Superman, which she titled *The Face of Fear Showing Sunshine Superman, M & D, or Have You Lost Your Zoo Keys?,* as well as other examples of her work, when she applied to the club for a scholarship. [p. 114] Then, as now, the Kingsley sponsored lectures and exhibitions at the Crocker Art Gallery/Museum and provided merit awards and scholarships to young artists. Adan competed for the funding against Stevens, their friend Ron Peetz, and other Sacramento State artists. Neither Stevens nor Peetz ever let her live it down that she took home the $150 scholarship.

Stevens received his BA from Sacramento State in June 1967, just as he started dating Adan exclusively. Adan, meanwhile, was just finishing her junior year and now regularly putting her work before the public and winning prizes. Her 1967 exhibitions included a juried student show at the Sacramento State College Art Gallery, in which she had three works accepted. She also won a first place prize for a drawing at the Sacramento County Fair, and contributed to a *Sacramento Valley Artists Association Show.* At that year's Yolo County Fair, she won more prizes, receiving first place for her monumental Superman and second place for her whimsical *Star et Smarz, Fuzz and Candy Bars.* Her *Spacey Fur-Lined Airplane Box*, which she had shown in a *California Crafts* exhibition at the Crocker Art Gallery that spring, also won first place in the ceramic division. [p. 34] She exhibited it again with three other ceramics at the California State Fair. Though it did not win any prizes, two other clay pieces

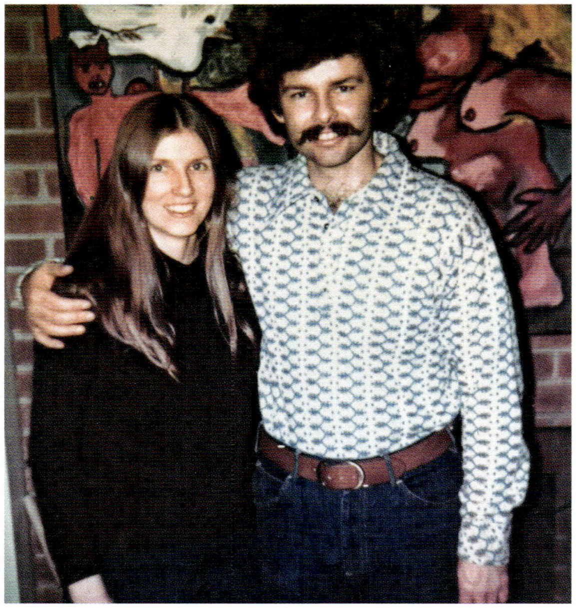

Suzanne Adan and Michael Stevens, Donovan Drive, Carmichael, Christmas 1972. Courtesy of Suzanne Adan.

did: *Giant Size Jewelry Box*, which won a Purchase Award, and *Stoneware Jewelry Box,* which received a non-purchase award.

Adan was well on her way to becoming a practicing artist. In the spring of 1968, she exhibited at the Crocker Art Gallery again, this time winning the Ayling Water Color Award of $75 at the 43rd Annual Crocker-Kingsley exhibition, her submission an *Untitled* rendering of a rainbow. Other rainbow-themed works followed, though these were more conceptual, untidy, and included written narratives and collage elements foreshadowing her punning watercolors soon to come. They also led Adan's friends to bestow her with a new nickname: Rainbow Sue.

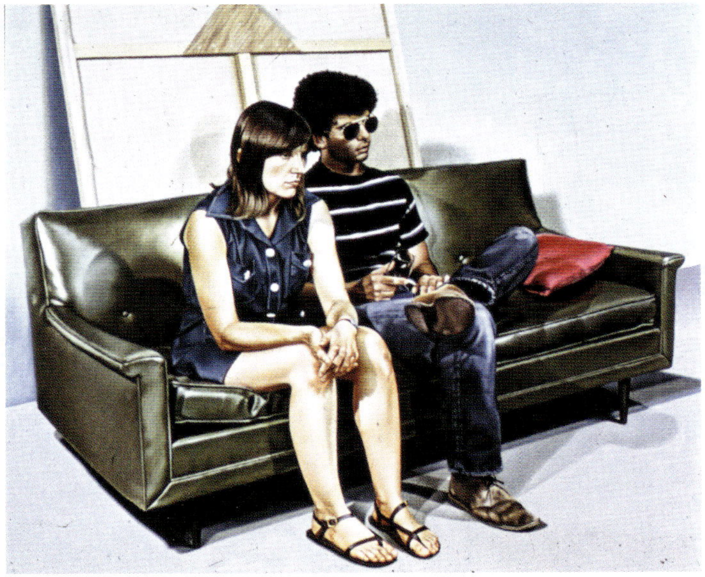

Ralph Goings (American, 1928–2016), *Suzanne Adan and Mike Stevens,* 1969. Oil on canvas. The Goings Family Estate.

Supporting Each Other

Adan's Sacramento State program took a longer-than-normal six years because of her duties as a work-study student in the art department, which did not allow her to assume a full course load. She made photocopies, helped administer tests, pulled slides and loaded slide carousels for the faculty, and performed myriad other tasks. The job paid only minimum wage, which barely got her through the month, but it did allow her to get to know her professors—and fellow students—well.

After receiving her BA in January 1969, Adan immediately entered Sacramento State's MA program. It was a tumultuous time in American history, and a period when Adan would truly begin to question the norms of her cosseted upbringing. In her words:

> 1969 was an astonishing year. Richard Nixon was inaugurated 37th president of the United States on January 20th, and the Vietnam War continued with a vengeance. Women were burning their bras and men were burning their draft cards. Protests continued at People's Park in Berkeley. My brother was in the California National Guard. He and members of his troop were sent to Berkeley, armed with loaded rifles, to fight the protesters.[23]

It was also in that year that Stevens boarded a bus for Oakland to officially refuse military service before federal marshals. For him, getting through college was made difficult, but not by his instructors or the curriculum, but because the Sacramento draft board denied his extensions to finish his education. Adan took matters into her own hands and wrote dozens of letters to local and state politicians on his behalf, asking for their help in keeping him out of the army and Vietnam. The letters were unsuccessful, and so he and Adan hired American Civil Liberties Union lawyers Lawrence Karlton and Coleman Blease to represent his case in federal court. It was not until the fall of 1971 that the case was finally heard. Because the draft board had inappropriately failed to grant his deferment to finish his education, the matter was dropped, with Stevens just weeks away from being sent to federal prison.

Despite the stress and uncertainty of dealing with the draft and the possibility of losing friends and loved ones in Vietnam, Adan, Stevens, and their fellow Sacramento State colleagues found a sense of normalcy in the day-to-day activities of the art department. Though they each made individual work, they also collaborated. In addition to their more

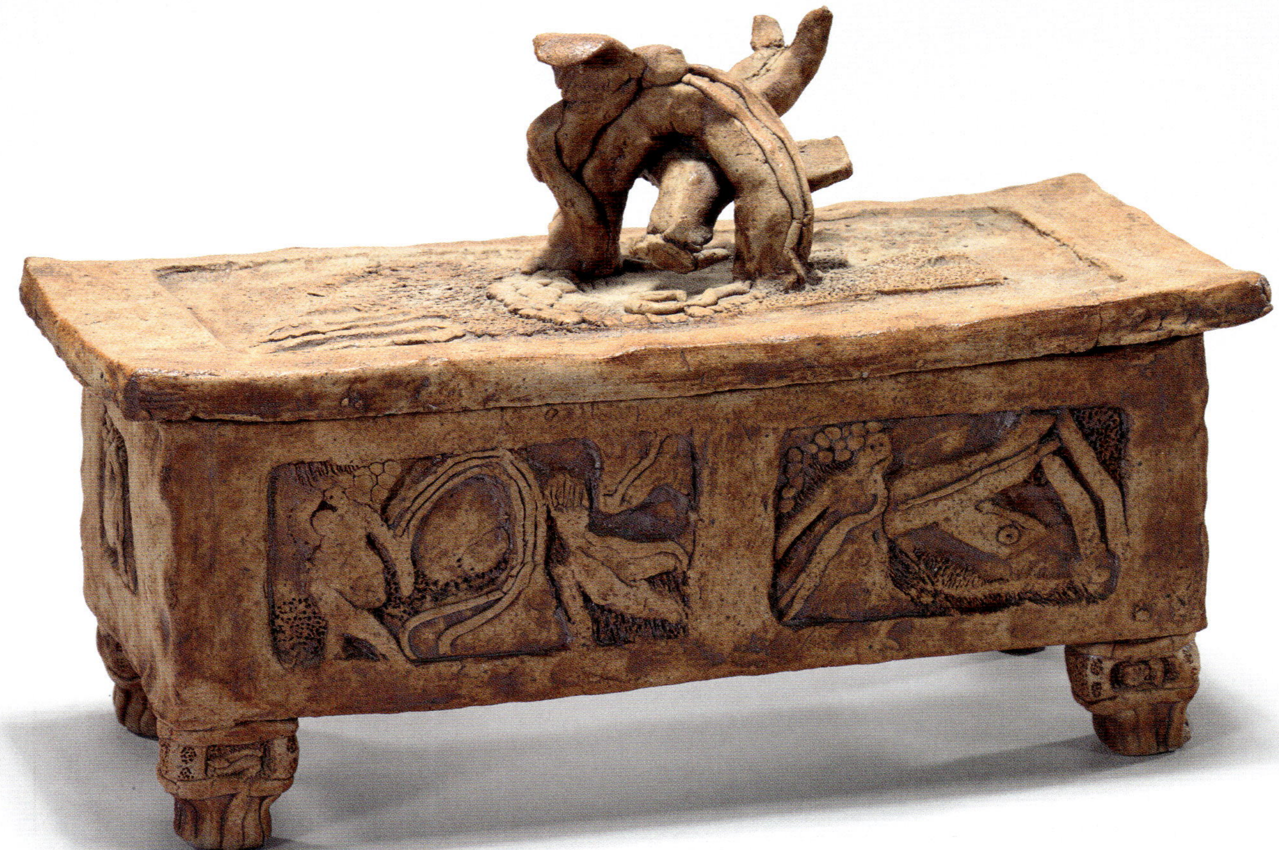

Spacey Fur-Lined Airplane Box, 1966.
Clay, oxide, fur, 6 ½ × 4 ⅛ × 9 ½ in.
Collection of the Artist.

serious solo efforts, Adan, Stevens, and Peetz (respectively Rainbow Sue, Bush Head, and Pink Meat), and sometimes others, used Kodak's new motion picture film to make Super 8 movies, receiving guidance and equipment from artist and poet Phil Weidman.[24] Adan, Stevens, and Peetz even produced a gory little art film called "Brain Wash," which involved a spoof on a cranial surgery at a car wash, Adan being the nurse. The trio also photocopied their faces and other body parts for use in collage drawings and crowded multiple times into the photobooth at Woolworth's five-and-dime to procure smaller images for the same purpose. With the encouragement of Weidman and artist Frank Owen, Adan and Stevens even participated in Ray Johnson's New York Correspondence (later Correspondance) School, a mail-based, performance art project in which participants received a letter or object by post and then added to or subtracted from that item before mailing it on to another participant or back to Johnson. As Adan remembered, "It was a department filled with lots of energy, enthusiasm, humor, and satire; and it definitely fueled how we did our artwork. We were also good friends who socialized and supported each other."[25]

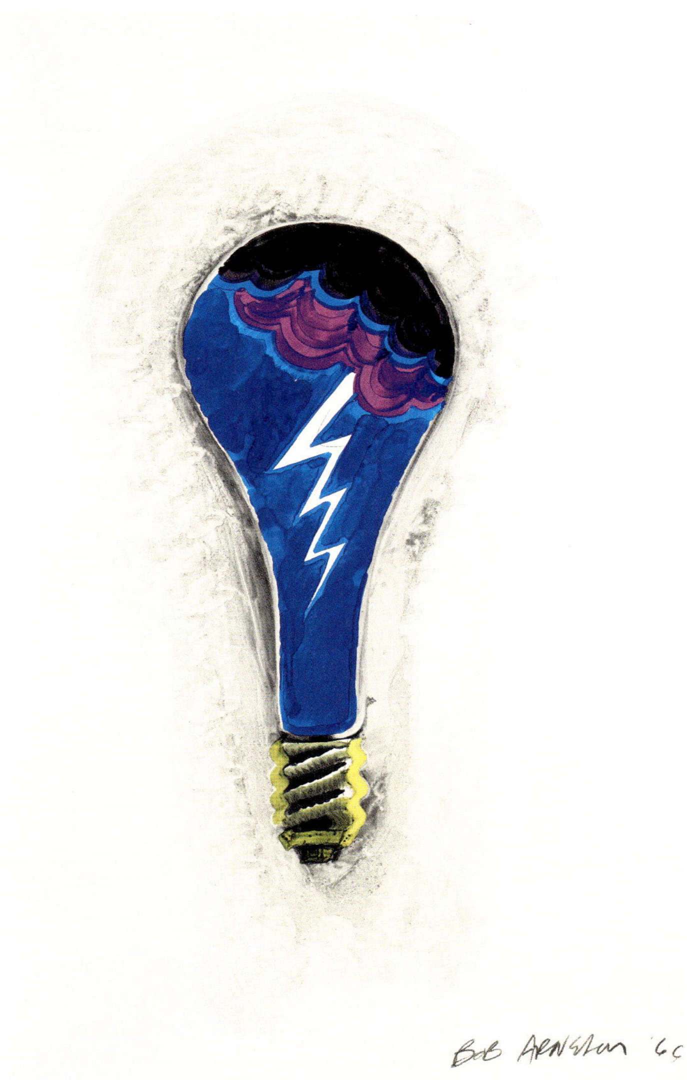

Robert Arneson (American, 1930–1992), *Light Bulb,* 1966. Colored ink on paper, 24 × 16 in. Crocker Art Museum, gift of Robert E. Aichele, 2007.62.1. © 2026 Estate of Robert Arneson / Licensed by VAGA at Artists Rights Society (ARS), NY.

Unorthodox Sources

In June 1969, Stevens managed to graduate with his MA, having shifted his focus from painting to sculpture in graduate school. It was also at this time that he started working as an assistant to Hairy Who artist Jim Nutt of Chicago, who had joined Sacramento State's faculty in the fall of the previous year.[26] Adan's own work progressed through a series of drawings/watercolors that she began to make for her graduate thesis exhibition. One of the artists she personally fancied at this moment—and had for some time—was the New York sculptor Claes Oldenburg, whose drawings and soft, messy, and frequently larger-than-life renditions of everyday objects Adan found appealing. Closer to home, she admired University of California, Davis, ceramics instructor Robert Arneson's work—both in two and three dimensions. As with Oldenburg, she appreciated Arneson's satire and humor. She also enjoyed his sarcasm and use of puns.

Arneson was just one of many artists in the Sacramento region to incorporate humor and a sense of irony into his aesthetic. At UC Davis alone, the terms Funk, Pop, Dude Ranch Dada, Nut, and other labels were variously applied to describe the irreverent wit and California attitude manifested by the school's artists. Roy De Forest and William T. Wiley, with whom Adan's work is often compared, became especially recognized for the subversive comedy of their art. Visiting instructors, including Clayton Bailey, David Gilhooly, and Peter Saul, did too. Wayne Thiebaud, who started teaching at Davis in 1960, also infused his deadpan depictions of confections and people with a wry and subtle humor. Numerous witty and talented students made such work as well, especially in the ceramics realm, thanks to Arneson. The latter included not only Gilhooly, who started out as a student, but Richard Notkin, Richard Shaw, Peter VandenBerge, the painter/ceramist Maija Gegeris Zack (now Maija Peeples-Bright), and others, all of whom Adan would come to know and, in some instances, look to for inspiration. Like Adan, many of these artists also applied funny or punning titles to their work.

Sacramento State certainly had its own share of artist-humorists. Not only had Thiebaud and Ramos been students there, but Ruth Rippon also made sculptures that sometimes manifest a sense of whimsy or irony filtered through a female gaze. When Jim Nutt came to Sacramento State to teach in 1968, he brought his own outrageous aesthetic to town, along with his equally fearless, zany, and talented wife, Gladys Nilsson, both of whom would become Adan's friends and, in Nutt's case especially, mentors.

Nutt and Nilsson met at the School of the Art Institute of Chicago and married in 1961. Nilsson completed her training there in 1962, and Nutt graduated three years later. They became part of the Hairy Who in 1966, when they, along with fellow artist James Falconer, asked the exhibition director at Hyde Park Art Center, where they taught children's classes, to display their work, as well as that of Art Green and Suellen Rocca. The director, Don Baum, agreed, and suggested that Karl Wirsum be included as well. Like the Pop artists in New York, the Chicago artists used American vernacular culture as the basis for their art, though in a less detached, highly idiosyncratic, and more subversive way, drawing inspiration from diverse and unorthodox sources such as advertising, burlesque and pin-up

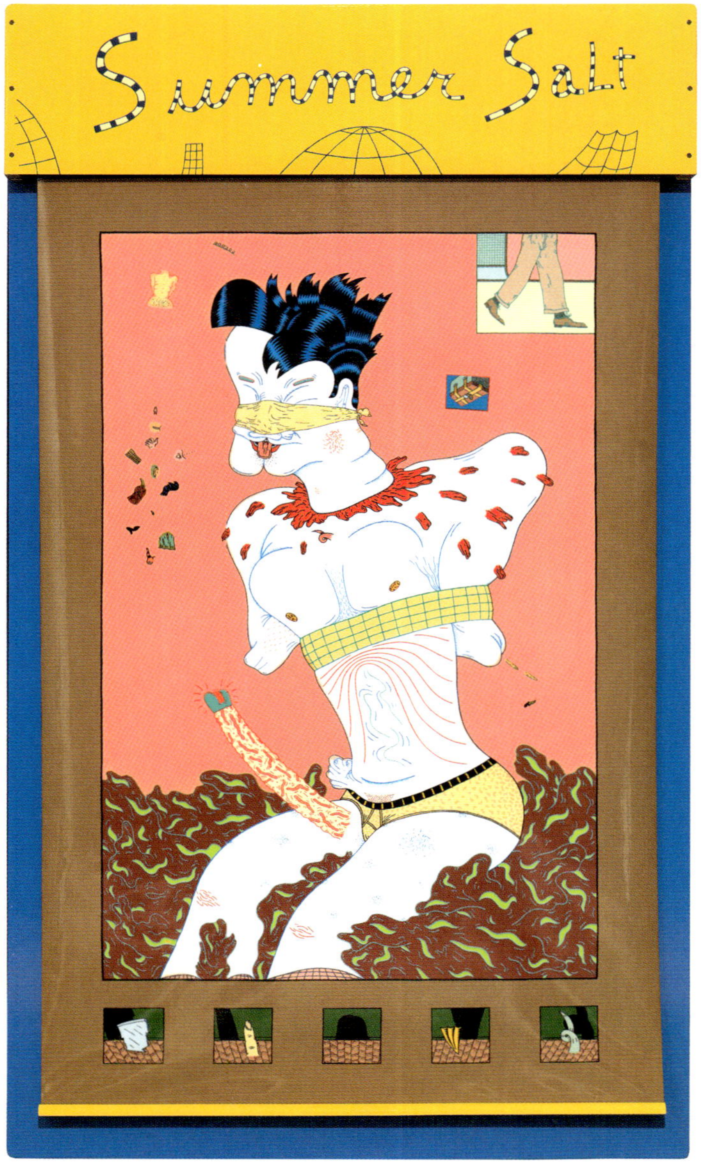

Jim Nutt (American, born 1938), *Summer Salt,* 1970. Acrylic on vinyl and enamel on wood, 61 ¼ × 36 × 3 ½ in. MCA Chicago, Gift of Dennis Adrian in honor of Claire B. Zeisler. Photo by Nathan Keay. Photo courtesy of Museum of Contemporary Art Chicago / Art Resource, NY.

imagery, tattoos, children's toys, tools, fashion magazines, underground comics, arcade imagery, and television, as well as other artists and art history.

All of this appealed to Adan, and she took two special-problems classes with Nutt at Sacramento State. One was research-based (she wrote a paper on Oldenburg); the other was to make watercolors for her thesis project. Nutt's work reinforced her ideas—and Stevens's as well—about humor's place in art and that worthwhile subject matter could be found in places that most artists had never thought to look.

Panty Hose

Betty Friedan's 1963 book *The Feminine Mystique* was inspirational for Adan as well, as it acknowledged the dissatisfaction that she and millions of other women felt about being relegated to narrowly defined roles as homemakers and mothers. To be sure, Adan had been well-trained in cooking, sewing, and how to effectively manage a household, but she now questioned the legitimacy of these responsibilities and wanted something more. She was, in fact, becoming a feminist.

When Adan began her series of watercolors for her thesis project, she hoped to use imagery that would be both familiar to women and have sexual and social connotations in a male-dominated society. Taking cues from her mentors, she invested her work with satire, not-so-subtle witticisms, and puns, using the artworks' titles to create double entendres or complete the joke. Works generally consisted of loosely painted depictions of one or two objects in watercolor mixed with glue, the technique learned from Silva and made on the floor to better create puddles and drips that contributed a shambolic spontaneity and fluidity to the results. That Adan worked on butcher paper was a matter of practicality, as she could source it from the art department for free. Most of the objects portrayed were associated with women and given additional meaning through handwritten explanatory text, use of rubber stamps, and, sometimes, magazine cut-outs or other collage elements.

Adan completed her first piece in the new series in February 1969 and titled it *Panty Hose.* [p. 107] To make it, she cut out a photo from a magazine depicting a woman wearing pantyhose and holding a hose, pairing this image with her own painting of panties, a hose, and rubber stamp letters spelling out PANTY and HOSE, along with written inscriptions. "It was a spoof on pantyhose . . . a fairly new invention for women," she explained. "The miracle of all miracles was the development of 'the pill,' giving women the freedom to have control of our own bodies. Another miracle was the invention of 'pantyhose.' Women could finally ditch the uncomfortable and insufferable girdle, which we had worn for years."[27]

A month later, Adan completed a second work in the sequence, *Fragment of a Formal Idea.* [p. 109] This time, she bought shoes, handbags, and clothing from a thrift store to use as still life props. For this work, she cut an old ballgown in half, rendering the top as the "formal" idea, a satirical reference to art history and critical theory. Because Adan had never owned a formal dress nor been to a prom, she found it amusing and cathartic to cut up a gown and use it in this way. She completed the third and fourth works in the series that April—*Debutante Ball Slippers* and *Pussyfoot Slippers*—this time spray-painting thrift-store shoes silver and pink, covering them with melted wax, and then drawing and painting them and providing narratives. In 1970, she made a second version of *Debutante Ball Slippers*. [p. 38]

Adan's art was getting noticed, and not just in Sacramento. In 1970, curator Philip Linhares included four of her recent pieces in his 1970 *Drawing Invitational Exhibition* held at the San Francisco Art Institute. The exhibition was one of many that Linhares curated at the school highlighting innovative and experimental work by emerging and established artists. Thomas Albright, art critic for the *San Francisco Chronicle,* called out Adan's work for mention, as did Brenda Richardson, who reviewed the exhibition for *Arts Magazine*.

News of the recognition made its way back to Sacramento and, in the fall of 1970, Adan was granted a two-semester graduate teaching assistantship in Irving Marcus's oil painting class. At the same time, Stevens had also started a new job, teaching high school art at his alma mater, La Sierra High School. Once Stevens started his job, but before Adan returned to school, the couple married. Their parents supported the union but were chagrined that the September 5 ceremony took place under a justice of the peace in Placerville, California, rather than as a formal ceremony at a church. Adan's brother and sister-in-law served as the only witnesses.

Candy Store

Adan's teaching assistantship with Marcus was a sought-after assignment, and the experience of working with him and gaining firsthand access to his practice offered Adan new aesthetic alternatives to consider. Originally from Minnesota, Marcus had come to Sacramento State to teach in 1959 and was the chair of the art department for three years starting in 1966, during which time he doubled the size of the faculty. At the time Adan first studied with Marcus, his darkly abstract figurative paintings appealed to her. His work subsequently became more colorful and sometimes even humorous, but by the time Adan went to work for him his art, though still colorful, had started to depict more solemn themes based on newspapers and magazine photographs, which set it apart from the more overtly jocular production of Adan's other mentors.

It was Marcus who introduced Adan to the Candy Store Gallery, as he was the first artist to exhibit there, and he remained a leading member of the gallery's stable until 1976. Adan remembers her first trip to the Candy Store in the fall of 1965 to see a show of Marcus's work. Though disappointed there was no actual candy (she has always had a sweet tooth), she was thrilled with Marcus's paintings and other artists' works on display. In early 1971, she began exhibiting there herself, the exposure helping propel her career.

Owned and operated by Adeliza McHugh, the Candy Store Gallery occupied just two rooms of a small house—once a library—in historic Folsom, about twenty-four miles east of Sacramento. McHugh did, in fact, purchase the house with the idea of selling candy, though health

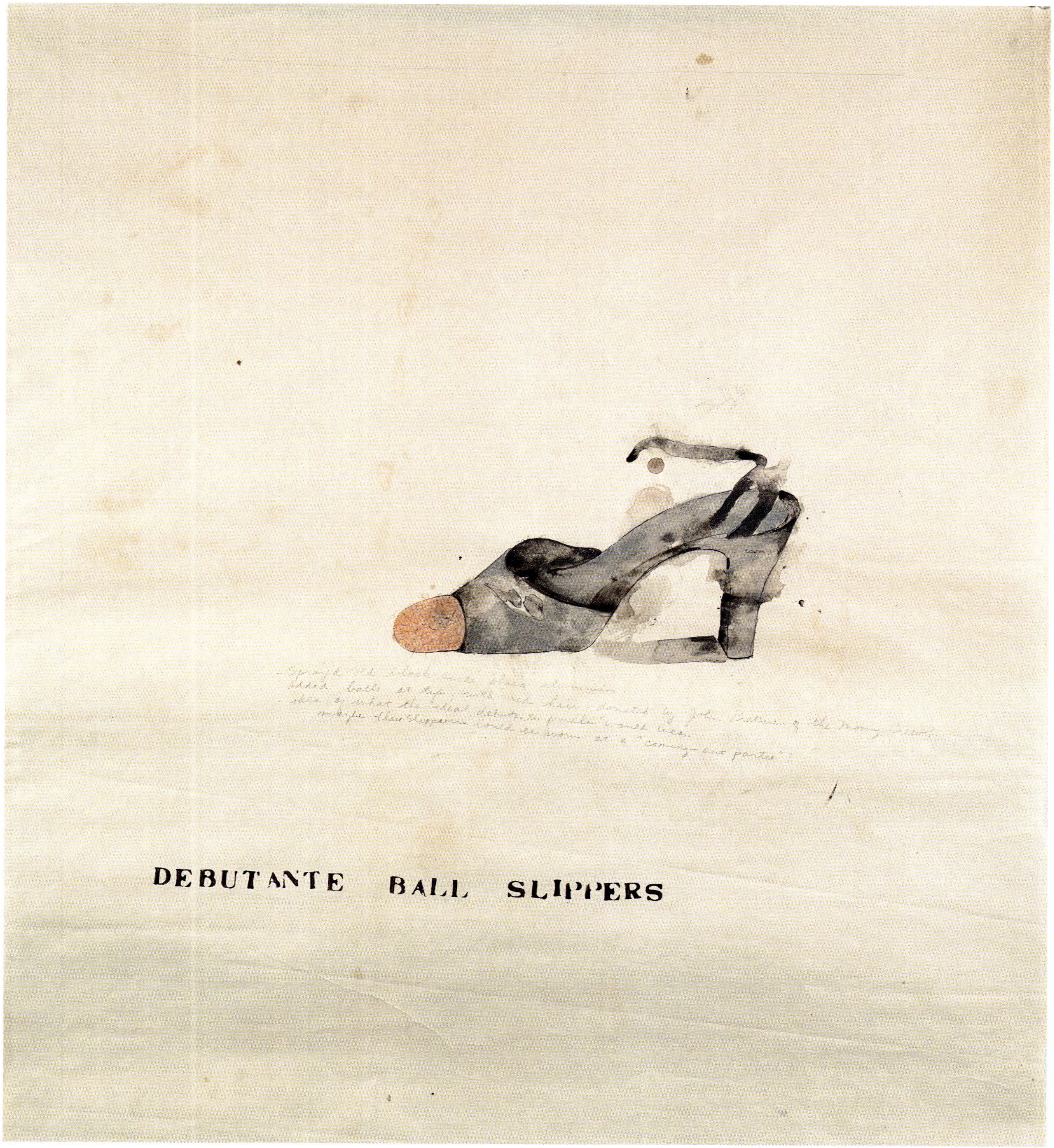

Debutante Ball Slippers, 1970.
Watercolor, pencil, and Elmer's glue on butcher paper, 33 × 27 in. Collection of the Artist.

authorities shut that down. Undeterred, she converted the space into an art gallery, which delighted (and sometimes disturbed) visitors for thirty years and helped put the whimsical and subversive spirit of artists in the Sacramento region on the art historical map.

McHugh invited Marcus to show at her yet-unnamed venue after seeing his art in a 1962 exhibition at the Crocker Art Gallery. He, in turn, introduced her to Jack Ogden and, later, to Nutt and Nilsson. All four artists became part of the ultimate "Candy Store Bunch." Ogden, in turn, introduced McHugh to Arneson and, through him, to other faculty and students at UC Davis. Regular Davis contributors came to include not only Arneson but Roy De Forest, David Gilhooly, Sandra Shannonhouse, Peter VandenBerge, and Maija Gegeris Zack. Don Reich would also join McHugh's primary roster, and other frequent exhibitors in the gallery's early days included Robert Else, Ralph Goings, and Jerald Silva. Members of what might be called the gallery's secondary stable included Luis Cruz Azaceta, Clayton Bailey, Paul Harris, Luis Jiménez, Ben Kypridakis, Tom Rippon, Harold Schlotzhauer, Chris Unterseher, and Joseph Yoakum, as well as Adan and Stevens.

Nutt and Nilsson started showing at the Candy Store Gallery in September 1968. McHugh initially paired the Chicago artists' two-dimensional works with ceramics by Gilhooly and Arneson. That October, she featured Nilsson's art again, this time in a two-person show with Reich. The Hairy Who artists brought greater two-dimensionality to the Candy Store's three-dimensional focus, their penchant for dark absurdity playing nicely with the sculptural work of Arneson and his circle.

Nutt and Nilsson, in turn, helped bring Stevens and Adan deeper into the Candy Store fold, with Adan initially displaying her pun paintings and, subsequently, her ceramic sculptures. In January 1971, Nutt and Nilsson curated a show that included their own work, as well as that of Adan, Stevens, Victor Faccinto, Joan Moment, and Peter Stegall. Adan and Stevens also exhibited with Nutt and Nilsson as a foursome in October–November 1975, a show that took place shortly before the senior couple returned to Chicago. Despite the distance, in late 1976 Nilsson and Adan opened a two-person show at the gallery, and the group of four came together again in October 1977 and, with other artists, in April 1978.[28]

An Attitude of Irrationality

Adan had nearly completed the requirements for her graduate degree in May 1971, but when it came time to go before the faculty review committee and defend her work, she sent her husband instead. In her mind, Stevens owed her a favor for helping him deal with the draft board, and he had little choice but to comply. Sending her husband, who the faculty knew well, was on one level a performance piece. It was also a test meant to convey a message to her professors that her art was good enough to stand on its own. She had long been a model student; she was even a member of the national honor society Phi Kappa Phi. Plus, her art was garnering significant recognition. Earlier that year, her watercolor *Panty Hose* [p. 107] was selected for the *San Francisco Art Institute Centennial Exhibition,* a four-venue juried show of painting, photography, prints,

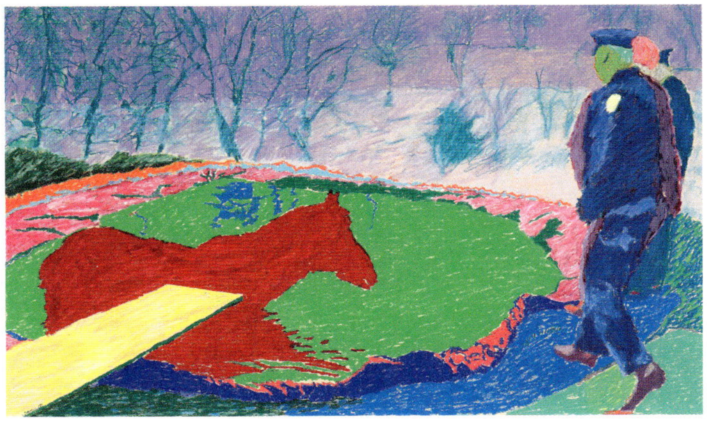

Irving Marcus (American, 1929–2021), *Doesn't Every Horse Have a Pool?,* 1971. Pastel, 25 ⅞ × 40 in. Crocker Art Museum, gift of Anne and Malcolm McHenry, 1991.23.8.

and sculpture that included many important artists and was written about in *Artforum.* The venue for her piece was the San Francisco Museum of Art (today San Francisco Museum of Modern Art), an accomplishment that few of her peers could claim.

Not showing up for her orals was not without risk, however. "I figured that they would deny my degree because I didn't appear before them," Adan remembered. "To be honest, I didn't give a rat's ass what the faculty thought about my work. By this time, I was tired of school and counting the days for my college career to come to an end."[29] Somewhat surprisingly, Adan's thesis committee did approve, and she was awarded her Master of Arts in June. Her brother finished his MA from Sacramento State that same semester. Like Adan, he would go on to become a practicing artist and active member of the Sacramento arts community, though he worked mostly in sculpture, using wood and other materials to create assemblages that dealt with human behavior, the natural world, and people that he loved or admired.

In the month she graduated, Adan exhibited her thesis works at the Kaleidoscope Gallery in a three-person show titled *Shazam: Monumental Arte,* the other exhibitors being her brother, Jim "Alfonso Ambrosio" Adan, and Phil Ito. She subsequently received an invitation from Philip Linhares to contribute to an upcoming *Sacramento Valley Show,* which would open at the San Francisco Art Institute in March 1972. The exhibition was to feature many top Central Valley talents, two of them Adan's former professors (Ogden and Marcus), and other artists who were influences (Arneson, Nilsson, Wirsum). Adan contributed three watercolors; Stevens's work was included as well. That June, she also submitted *Loafer,* one of her punning watercolors, to the 47th Annual Crocker-Kingsley exhibition held at the Crocker Art Gallery.

Recognition continued to come in 1973, as Adan exhibited in multiple juried shows and won prizes. These included the Auburn Arts Festival; the Lodi Art Annual, where she was accorded an honorable mention; the San Mateo County Fair, in which she won second place; and another Crocker-Kingsley exhibition. She won a Patrons' Purchase Award at the latter for her 1971 watercolor *Gumshoe,* a messy, yet elegant depiction of a woman's high-heeled shoe rendered in watercolor, Elmer's glue, and gum—all chewed herself. [p. 42] The purchase, for which she received $100, meant that the piece would become part of the Crocker's permanent collection, both a surprise and a thrill as it was her first museum acquisition. To this day, the painting remains part of the museum's holdings, and despite the paper wrinkling, it has survived quite well given its unusual media.

Farther afield, Adan's work was selected for the *7th National Drawing and Small Sculpture Show* held at the Art Gallery of Del Mar College in Corpus Christi, Texas. Even more exciting was the Whitney Museum of American Art's 1973 acceptance of her 1970 watercolor *Happy Trails to You . . . Until We Meet Again* [p. 121] for its traveling *Extraordinary Realities* exhibition, which would subsequently be shown at the Everson Museum of Art in Syracuse, New York, and the Contemporary Arts Center in Cincinnati. Curated by Robert Doty, it traced an "attitude of irrationality" and "defiance of logic and high art" that could be found in nineteenth-century American painting, traced through Dada and Surrealism, and into recently made work

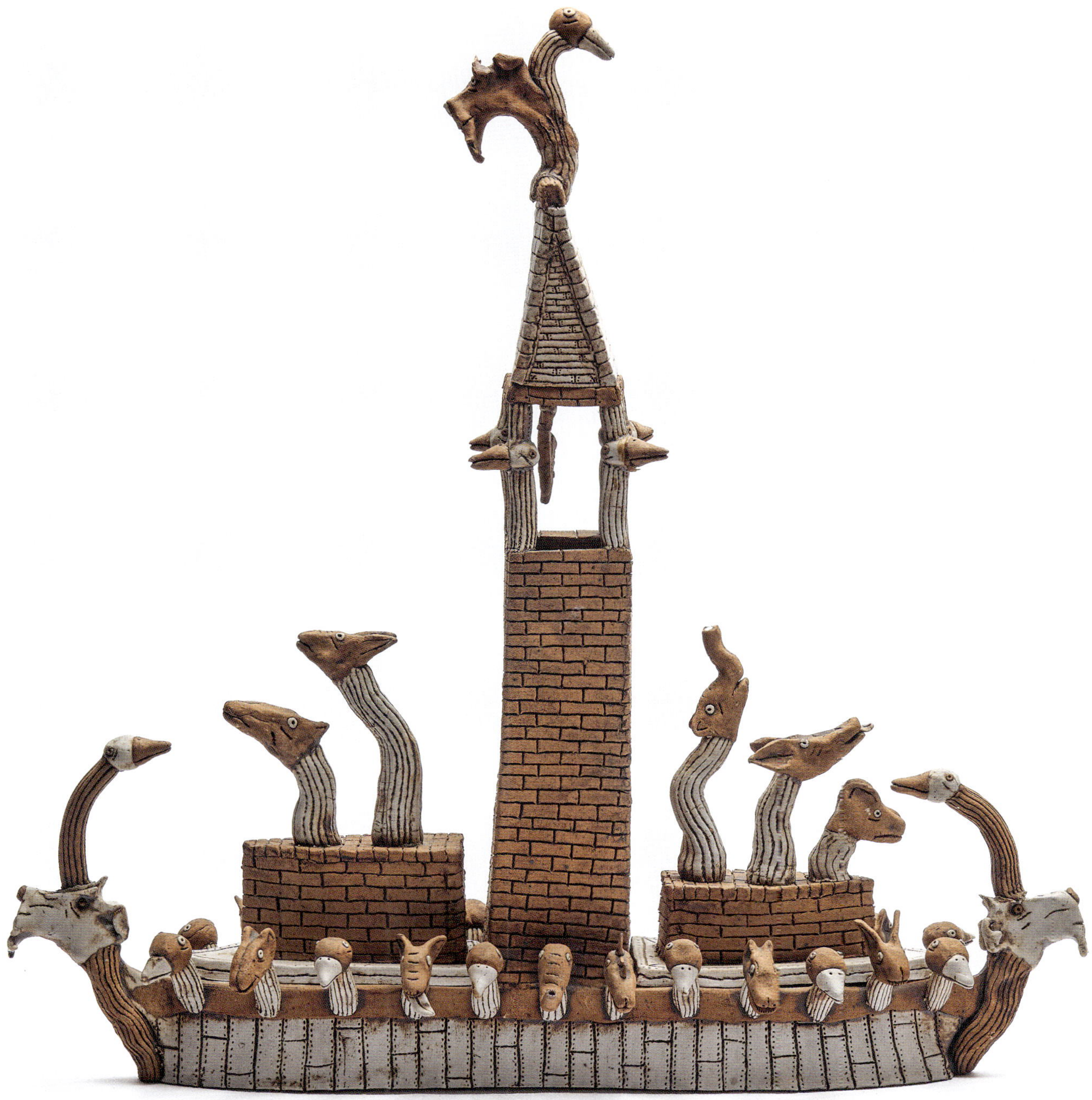

Animal Ark, 1972.
Porcelain and clay, 19 ¼ × 19 × 5 ½ in. The Fine Arts Collection, Jan Shrem and Maria Manetti Shrem Museum of Art, University of California, Davis. Gift of Rita Gibson. Photo by Muzi Li Rowe.

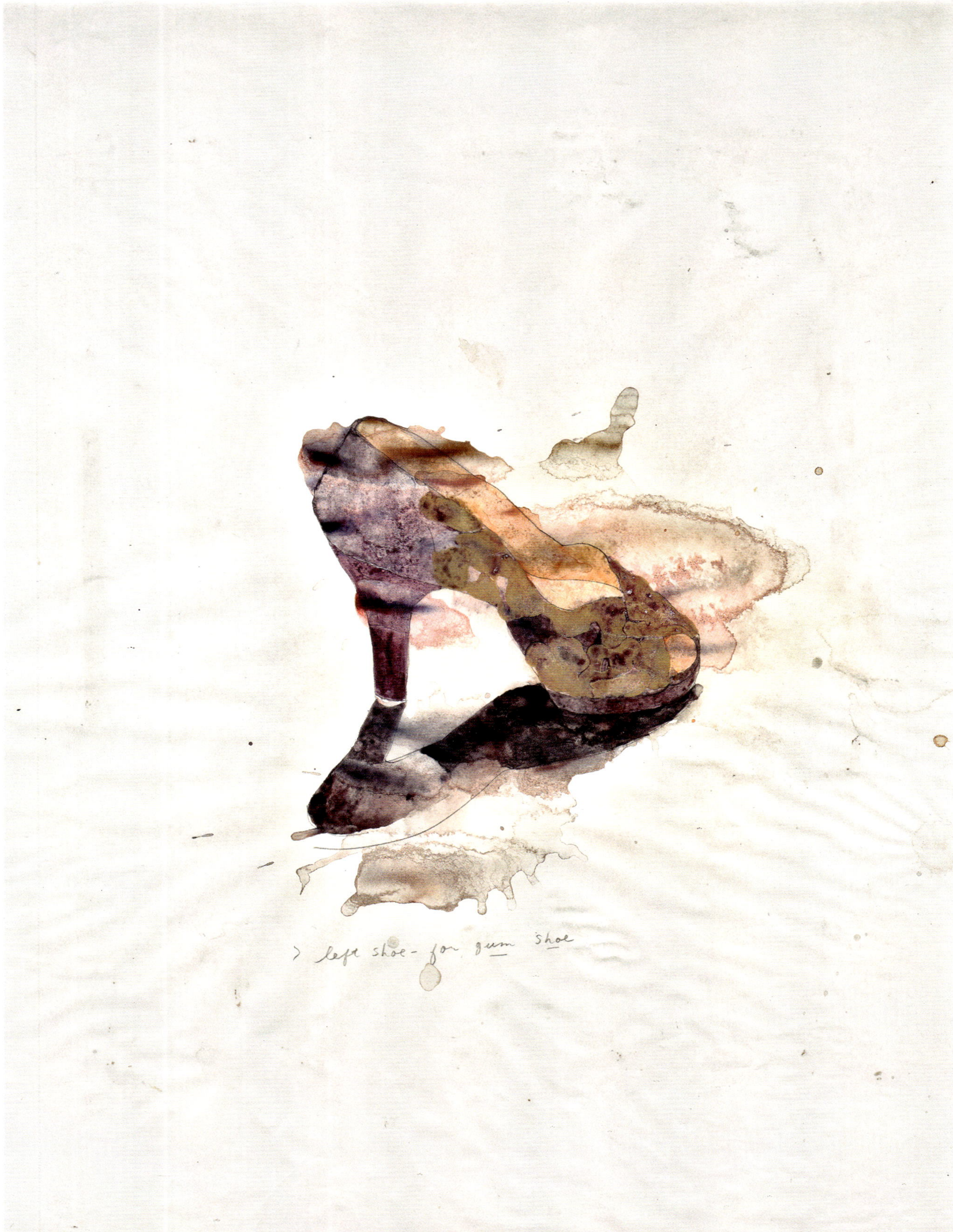

Gumshoe, 1971.
Watercolor, Elmer's glue, and chewing gum on butcher paper, 30 × 23 ¼ in.
Crocker Art Museum, gift of the Kingsley Art Club, 1973.16.

by Chicago's Hairy Who and California Funk artists.[30] The catalogue appropriately included a preface by writer, artist, and illustrator Edward Gorey, but the primary text was by Doty, who wrote that much of the art in the exhibition set out to explore the relationship between "dreams and objective experience, reality and imagination, surface and substance." Doty also noted the pervasive tendency among artists to incorporate "ubiquitous elements which refer to the banal and sometimes ludicrous aspects of the American scene," a state of mind that for him seemed to appeal most to those artists living outside the centers of "mainstream art."[31] Roberta Smith of *Artforum* reviewed the show, and though not enamored of the many works she described as "mean-spirited," took note of the prevalence of "cartoonlike figuration or writing; [and] verbal and visual punning."[32] Her assessment, and Doty's, certainly applied to Adan, whose pieces were made outside the mainstream and were very much thematically and stylistically in sync with what was going on in the outer fringes of the art world. Adan's piece sold while at the Whitney, which was not really a surprise, as she priced it at $29.95, a nod to the exhibition's Dada-like attitude of irrationality. For Adan, it was gratifying that a fellow artist, Sarah Whitworth, purchased it.

Metamorphosis

In May and June 1974, Adan had a one-person show at the highly regarded Womanspace gallery in Los Angeles, an artists' cooperative dedicated to showing and promoting the work of female artists. Adan appreciated the gallery's mission and decided to apply for a show. Notes from gallery records indicate that her "Pun-Drawings" were well received by a four-member selection committee, who ranked her submissions as number one among potential candidates for exhibition. The show, *Suzanne Adan: Drawings—Watercolors,* included sixteen pieces, which Adan described in her artist's statement as dealing with "personal experiences and interests, the combinations and metamorphosis of images and puns, and the dictionary's formal arrangement of words, definitions, and illustration."[33] Artworks were humorous and often accompanied by provocative titles such as *Corn Belt, Pipe Organ, The Restless Balls, Home Cooking, My Cup of Tea, Something Up My Sleeve, Senior Ball Corsage, Pin-Up, Pocket Pool,* and others. **[p. 108, p. 121, p. 44]**

Adan exhibited *Home Cooking* again that November at the 20th Annual Open Art Exhibition held by Northern California Arts, Inc., setting its price at $500. Compared to other watercolors in the show, it was an ambitious amount, yet indicative of her burgeoning confidence and reputation. That fall, Adan started teaching, accepting a job as an adjunct art professor at American River College, a public community college in Sacramento, a position that lasted three semesters. Though her art was finding an audience, neither she nor Stevens were selling enough work to abandon more regular sources of income. In 1976, Adan became a community services art instructor for the San Juan Unified School District in Carmichael. She also continued to sell an occasional piece through the Candy Store Gallery, though most of the group shows featuring her art took place at nonprofit venues. In 1978, she had work included in *Private Vision,* an exhibition

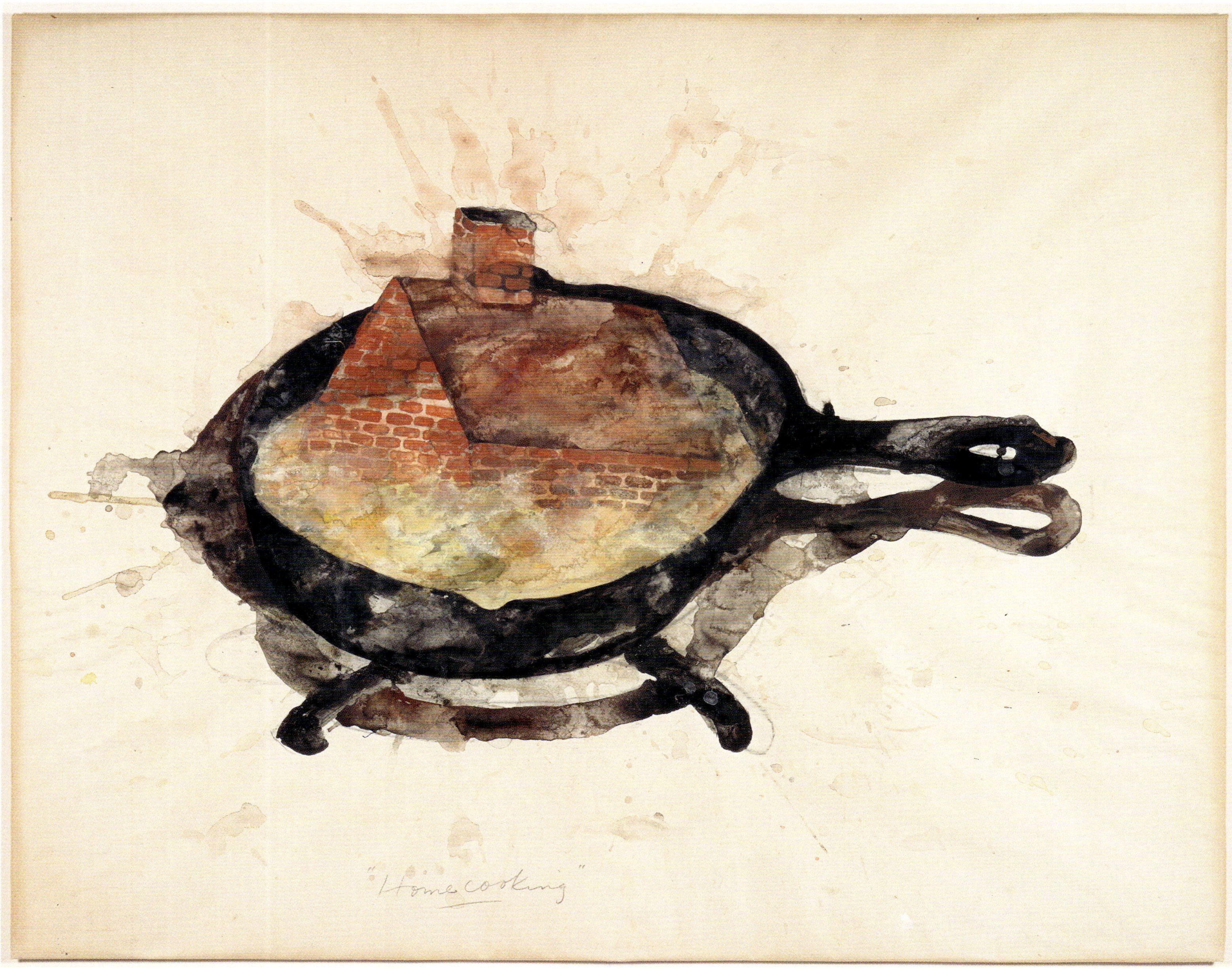

Home Cooking, 1973.
Watercolor and Elmer's glue on butcher paper, 20 × 25 in. Adan Family Collection.

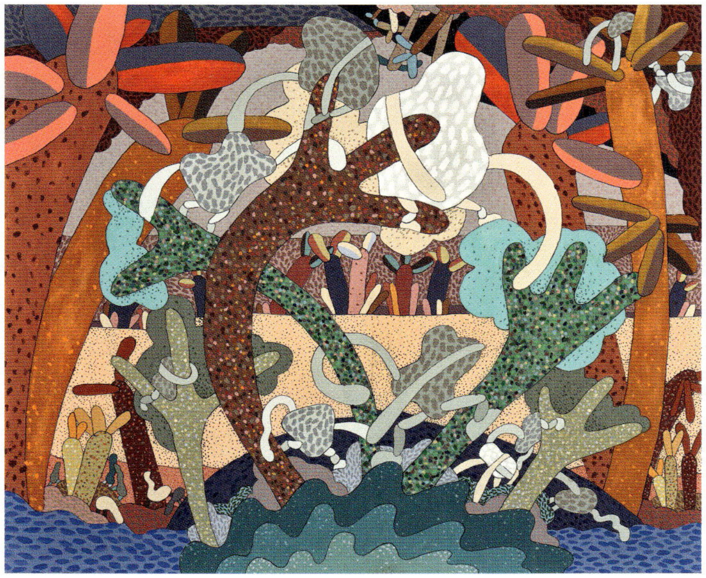

Gladys Nilsson (American, born 1940), *Ape Island*, 1972. Acrylic on canvas, 30 × 36 in. Crocker Art Museum, gift of Anne and Malcolm McHenry, 1973.53.

at Ohlone College in Fremont, and *Your Show*, an all-female display at Cal Expo in Sacramento. She also won a third place prize at the California State Fair for a small painting titled *Carved Images*. A year later, she was in a three-person exhibition with Judith Linhares and Don Meyer at the Richard L. Nelson Gallery at the University of California, Davis.

By this time, Adan was moving beyond the single-object pun paintings into more complex and visionary narratives populated with figures, animals, and enigmatic symbols. Her tastes in the art she admired had also broadened, her own work now informed by international artists with a strong Surrealist bent, including Victor Brauner, Philip Guston, Morris Hirshfield, and Frida Kahlo. Idiosyncratic California-based practitioners such as Jess (Collins) and H. C. Westermann, along with her former teacher Jim Nutt, were important as well.

Brauner, Guston, and Kahlo provided fodder for Adan's own narrative Surrealism, in which she meant to convey disjunctive autobiographical and psychological states. In the case of Westermann, Hirschfield, and Nutt, it was tongue-in-cheek humor and a folksy approach that Adan enjoyed and exploited. Jess's intricate, puzzle-based collages showed her the impact achievable in the use of layered and fragmented images. Adan's friendship with Gladys Nilsson also had an effect, the eccentricity and freedom of Nilsson's jam-packed compositions and spaghetti-limbed figures motivating. "I derived distinct elements from these artists," Adan explains, "which further enabled me to develop my personal and visual vocabulary."[34]

Through all these mentors, along with her own history and biography, Adan arrived at a means of communication that was layered and edgy, yet absurdly satirical. Her personal experiences, objects that she owned or found interesting, and even her pets conveyed "tidbits" of information and "twists of fate" that she infused with irony, satire, and, sometimes, a bit of the macabre. "Humor and satire have always been important elements in my art," she explains. "I work intuitively—weaving fragments together like a puzzle, allowing me to add or subtract pieces to create the composition. I continue revisiting similar themes and symbols, which serve as storytelling devices."[35]

Mr. & Mrs.

Adan has storytelling in common with her husband, whose art is conceptually akin to hers, each spouse influencing the other. Both juxtapose the comedic and sinister, the crude and refined, making art that can be cloyingly cute while simultaneously bleak and dreadful. Childhood plays an outsized role in both artists' work. Because they are so philosophically in sync, they often collaborate. Their art, like their partnership, blends seamlessly, though each brings individual strengths. Adan's drawings and paintings routinely reference her early years, her titles often borrowed from children's games and phrases, some of her iconography evidencing her wholly American upbringing. What gives her art—and Stevens's—its edge, is that it upends the idyllic myth of youth with adult realizations and an occasionally cynical understanding that comes with age. As one writer described, "The couple's work has much in common, yet remains independent.

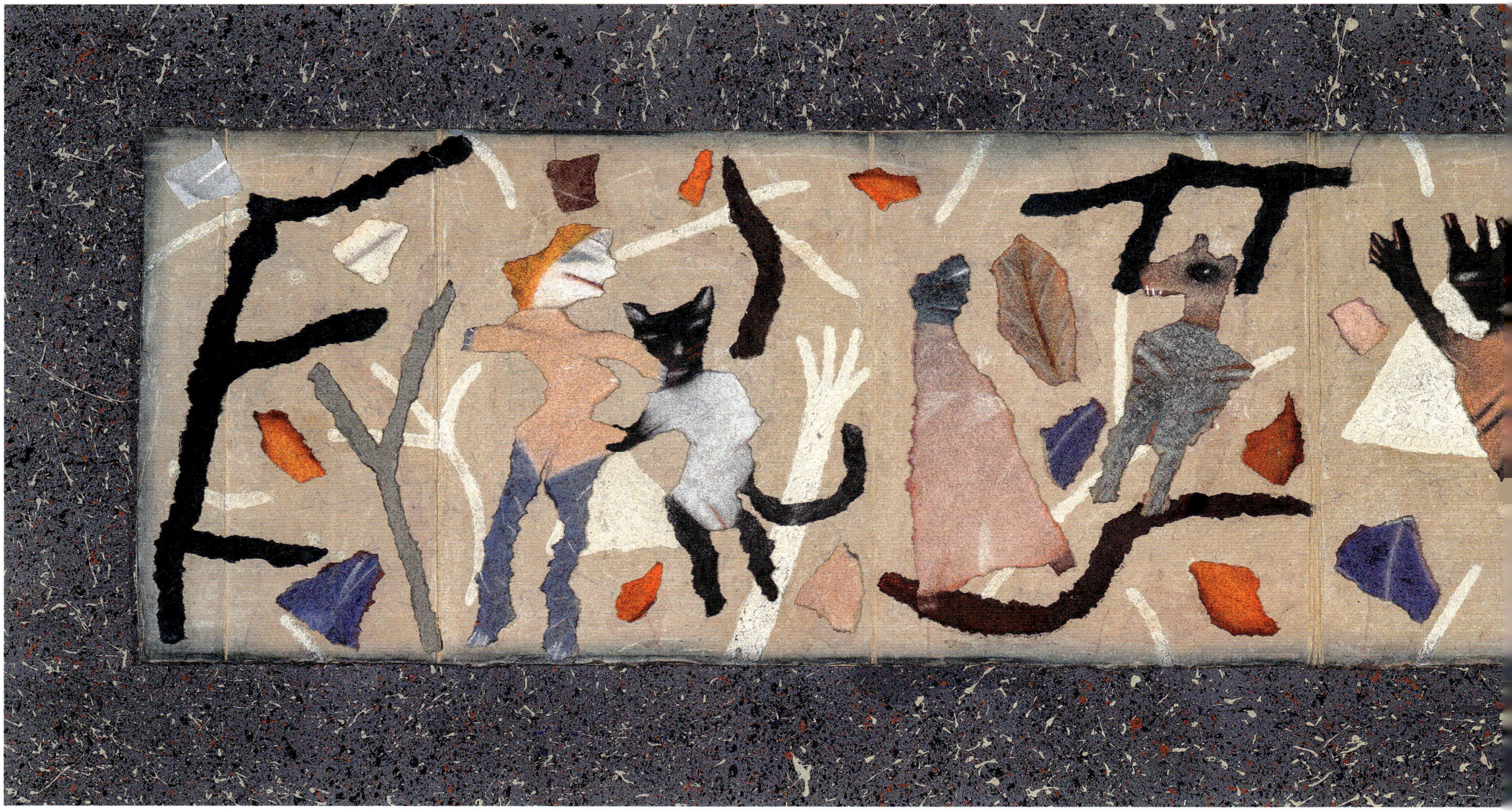

Antler Danse, circa 1976.
Chalk, paper, cardboard, and enamel paint on Masonite, 17 ½ × 62 ½ in. Collection of Jane K. Adan.

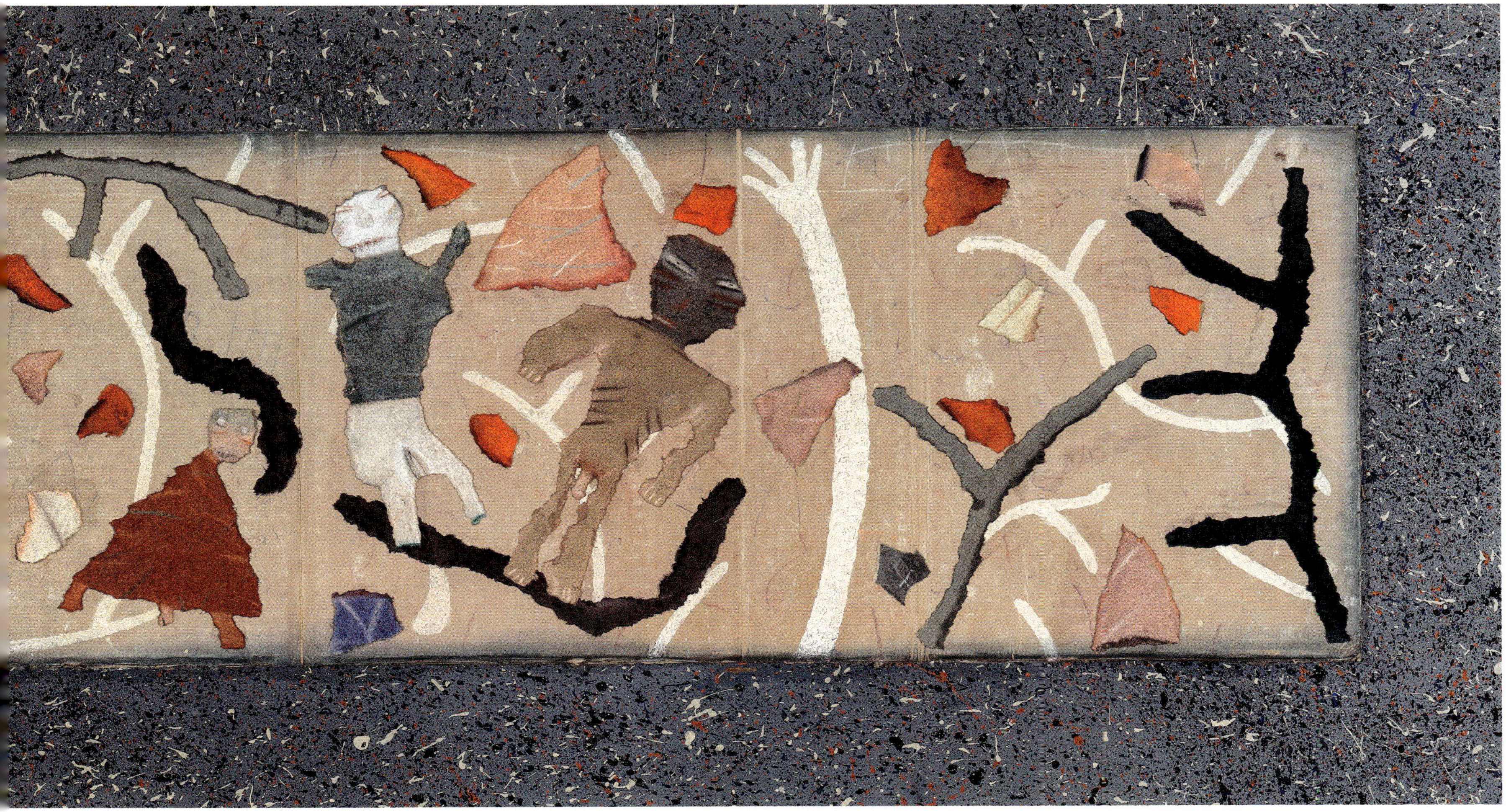

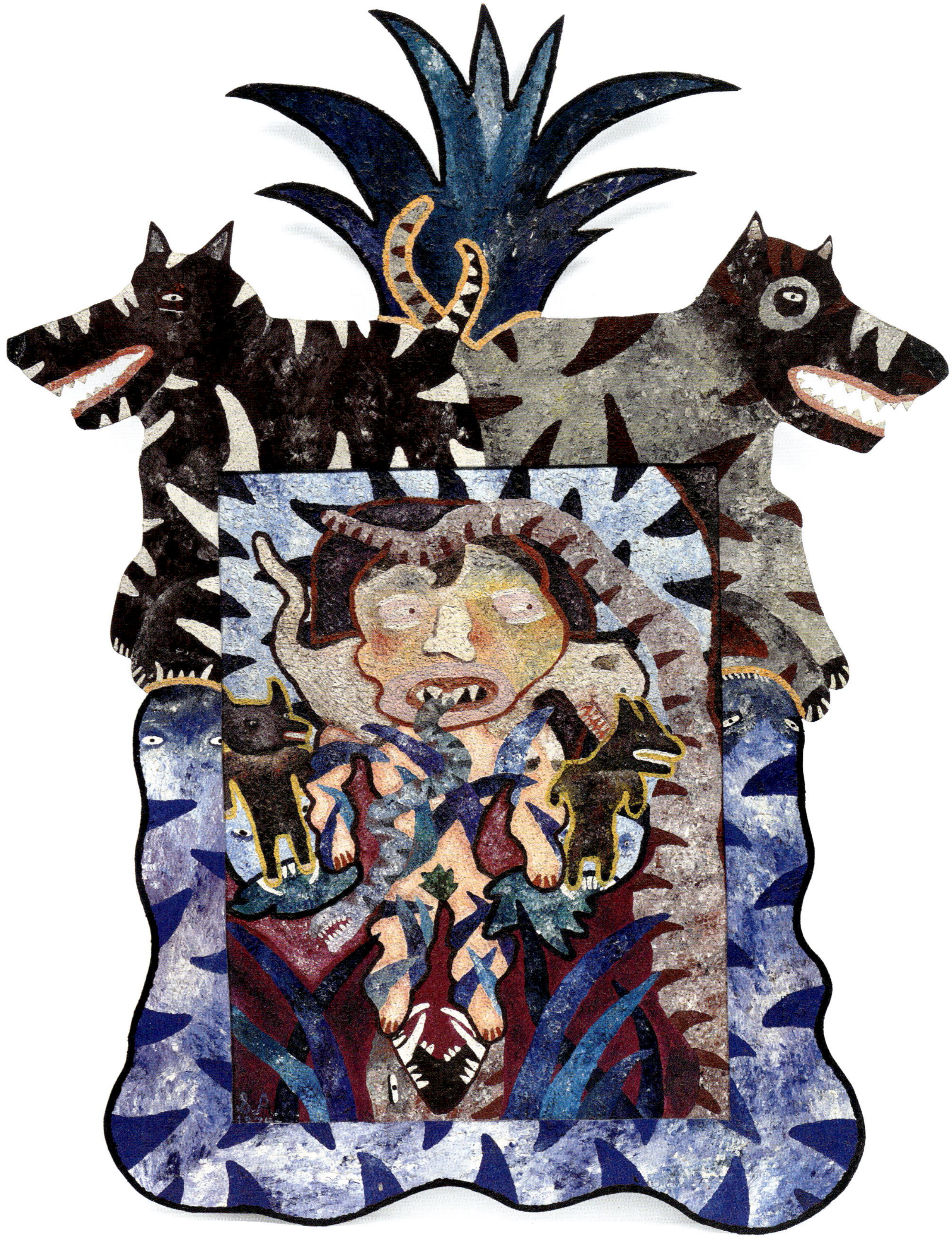

Alexander—The Snake Wrestler, circa 1974.
Oil and acrylic on canvas with carved and painted wood frame, 23 ¾ × 17 ⅝ in. Collection of Alexander D. Adan.

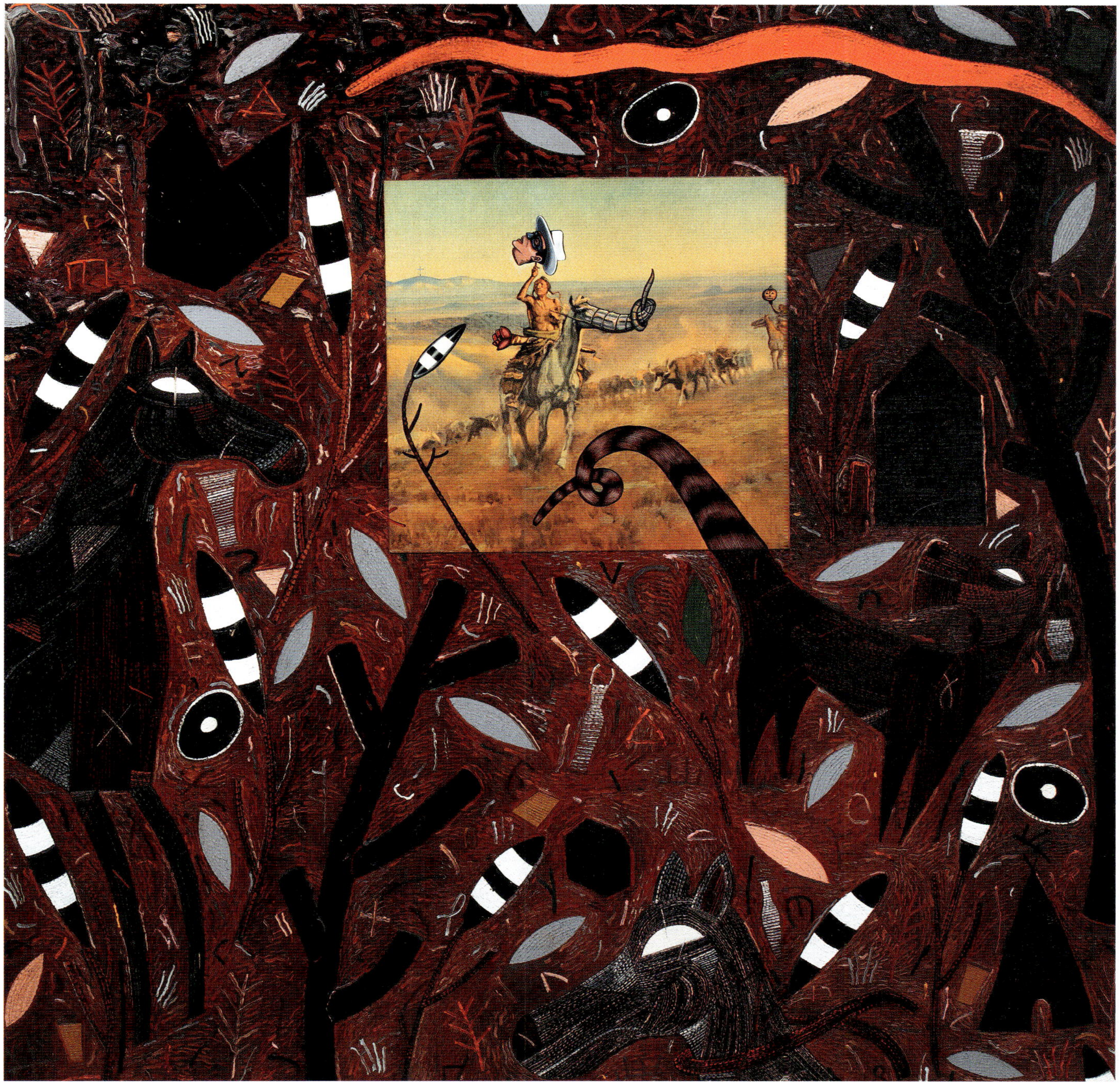

Suzanne Adan (American, born 1946) and Michael Stevens (American, born 1945), *This Title Needs to be Changed,* 1989.
Acrylic on Masonite with dry mount print and enamel paint, 48 × 48 in. Collection of Paul Wortman and the late Brent Smith.

Most obvious in their work is an affectionate, sassy little-kid humor that conceals and then reveals dark, grownup meanings."[36]

Television, especially the golden age of programming in the 1950s and 60s, also informs what Adan and Stevens do. Stevens, by his own admission, practically grew up in front of the television and was captivated by telecasts of silly, slapstick cartoons, local children's programming, and somber stories on the evening news.[37] TV is referenced less overtly in Adan's work, but she nevertheless has fond memories of going to watch it at her aunt and uncle's house before her family owned a set. Not to be missed were the *Honeymooners* on Saturday night, *I Love Lucy* on Sunday, and *Walt Disney's Disneyland* on Wednesdays. She also enjoyed *The Many Loves of Dobie Gillis* and, thanks to Stevens, watched hundreds of episodes of *The Andy Griffith Show,* though the latter was always more Stevens's favorite than hers. Still, it was Andy's Aunt Bee who quipped, "I'm no spring chicken!," inspiring the title for Adan's retrospective and this publication. These shows and others continue to inform her art with a sense of longing for kinder, gentler times.

Playful and Sinister

Humanoid characters that often resemble toys, along with animals, geometric shapes, and ovate polka dots, run amuck throughout Adan's mature work. Letters and numbers, which also factor into many of her pieces, sometimes function as decorative elements but also create cryptic word puzzles that may offer clues about the subject matter or the person a work might honor or memorialize. Dogs and cats, inspired by Adan and Stevens's dearly beloved pets, enliven the rostrum, especially the couple's wire-haired terriers, which appeared while alive and then posthumously. Round-headed black birds, simultaneously playful and sinister, appear frequently, though they seldom fly, preferring a perch or tree branch instead.

One does not need to totally understand Adan's characters or the meaning behind her enigmatic narratives to appreciate them, though familiarity with her source material does add to her art's richness. Those who know Adan have a special inside track, as elements from her life and home are almost always apparent. The collection of vintage items and toys that she and her husband have amassed play directly into their respective approaches in terms of graphic stylization, exaggeration, humor, charm, and sometimes naiveté, all of which help impart a nostalgic feel to the work they make and blur distinctions between lowbrow and highbrow culture. It is a vast collection of Americana that includes metal lunch-boxes, robots, Disney characters (especially Pluto), and tin wind-up toys from the 1930s, 40s, and 50s. There are also depictions of early children's television and storybook icons such as Popeye, Charlie McCarthy, Howdy Doody, and Uncle Wiggily in all shapes and sizes; commercial advertising figures from the 1950s; vintage board games; puppets; Halloween masks; papier mâché snowmen and jack-o-lanterns; Christmas tree ornaments; and miscellaneous "kitschy" items, including an assortment of rubber noses and dog poop. The couple's unofficial motto has long been that if having one item is good, having many is better. Tucked in among these carefully curated displays are examples of the couple's own work, along with that by artist friends and those they admire.

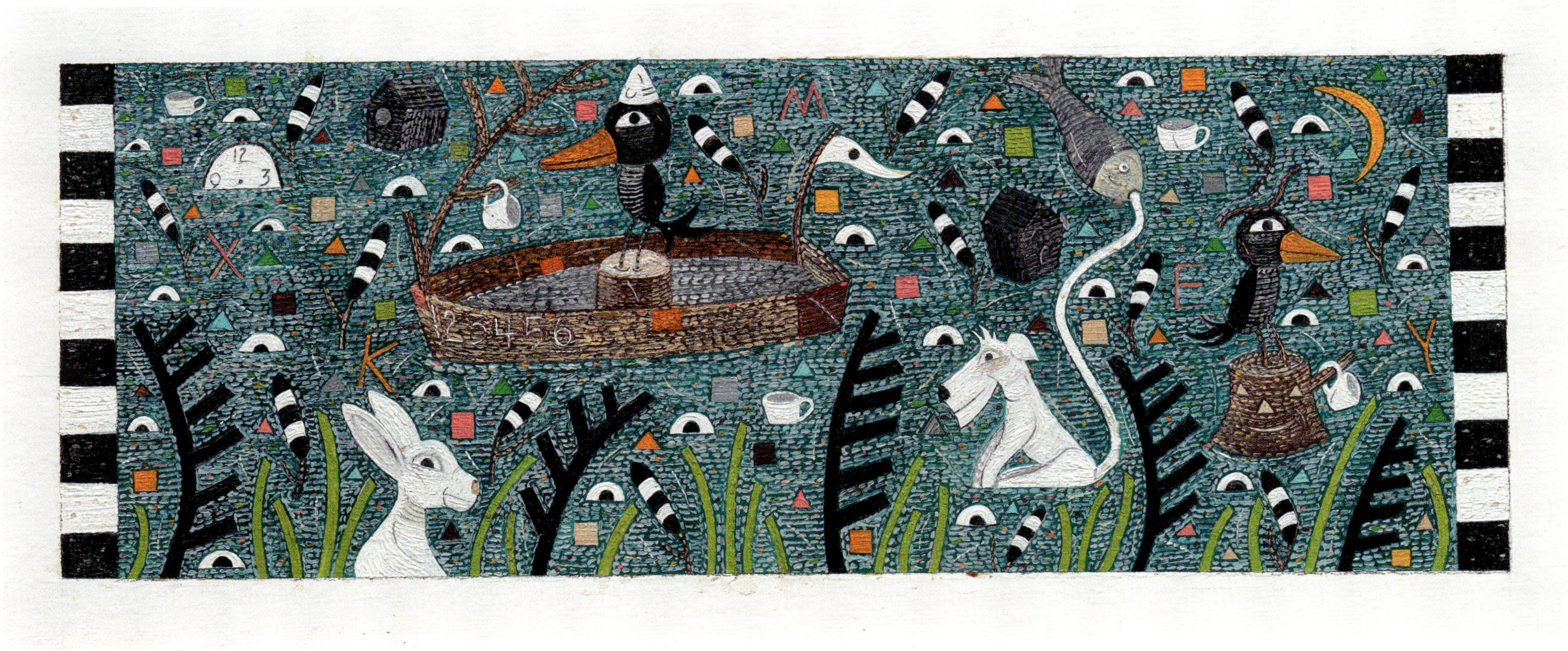

Pieces from Adan and Stevens's collection are sometimes incorporated directly into their work as well, these vintage items sacrificed in the name of art. Adan's *Salty and Peppy (Slant Step),* for instance, combines a pencil drawing beneath a group of vintage salt-and-pepper shakers. [p. 53] The slant-step shape worked into the drawing references an ongoing local fascination with an oddly slanted "stepstool," which became a source of inspiration and amusement for Bay Area artists, the homages first appearing in a 1966 exhibition called *The Slant Step Show* and then in multiple subsequent others. *Wake Up Little Suzie* is a collage drawing mounted atop a child's baby grand piano, the title referencing the artist's name and the music it makes. *Pigtails: Go to the Head of the Class* is both a painting and an assemblage rendered on a child's chalkboard set into an easel, with found object game pieces from a 1960s version of "Go to the Head of the Class." [p. 55] Encapsulating Adan's days in braids and bows, it is a self-portrait of sorts, but in a way that evidences her emergence into the dark comedy of adulthood. The girl's braids are more tree roots than hair, with one emerging from her face where her nose should be. Her schoolgirl uniform and jack-o-lantern hat (inspired by a collection item), along with other attributes of innocence such as a dog (one of Adan's), bird, and tiny teacups, conflict with the painting's general feeling of disarray and the girl's sullied face and ample bosom. It is a vintage world colliding with modern life gone awry.

Tiny Swatches

Stevens incorporates found objects to an even greater degree than his wife and routinely sources "ready-made" reproductions of still lifes, rural scenes, old-master portraits, and religious tableaux from thrift stores. In many of his pieces, he uses these reproductions as theatrical backdrops that provide a place for his subversive, sculpted and painted additions

Dipsy Doodle (Rejected Piece Golden 1 Center), 2016. Oil on paper, 12 ⅛ × 19 ¼ in. Collection of Ellie and John Cary.

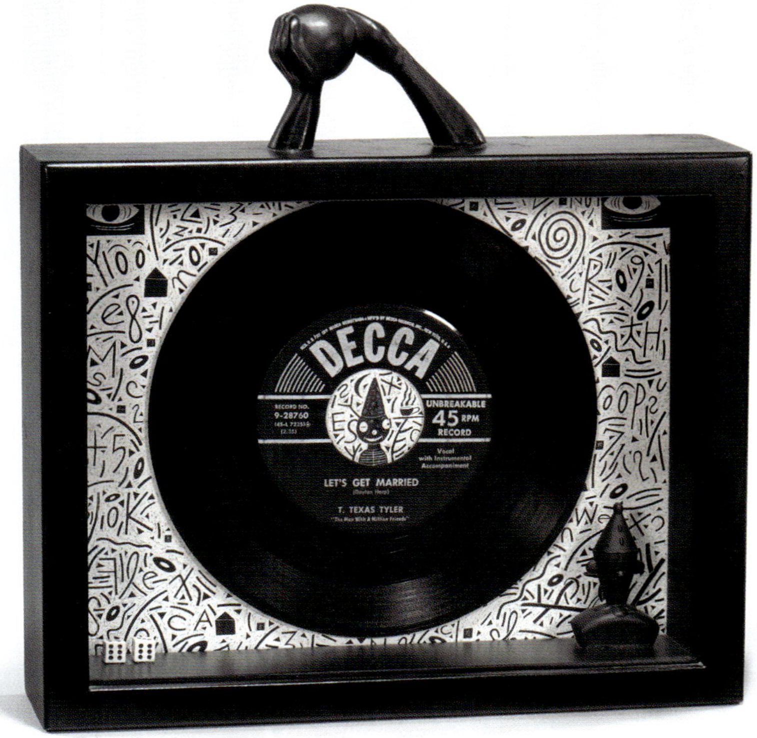

← *Circle Jerk,* 1997.
Scratchboard, record, wood, and rubber, 10 ½ × 10 ½ × 2 ½ in. Collection of the Artist.

↓ *Wake Up Little Suzie,* circa 2016.
Graphite, paper, Plexiglas, and child's baby grand piano, 15 × 13 × 4 in. Collection of Susan Bitar.

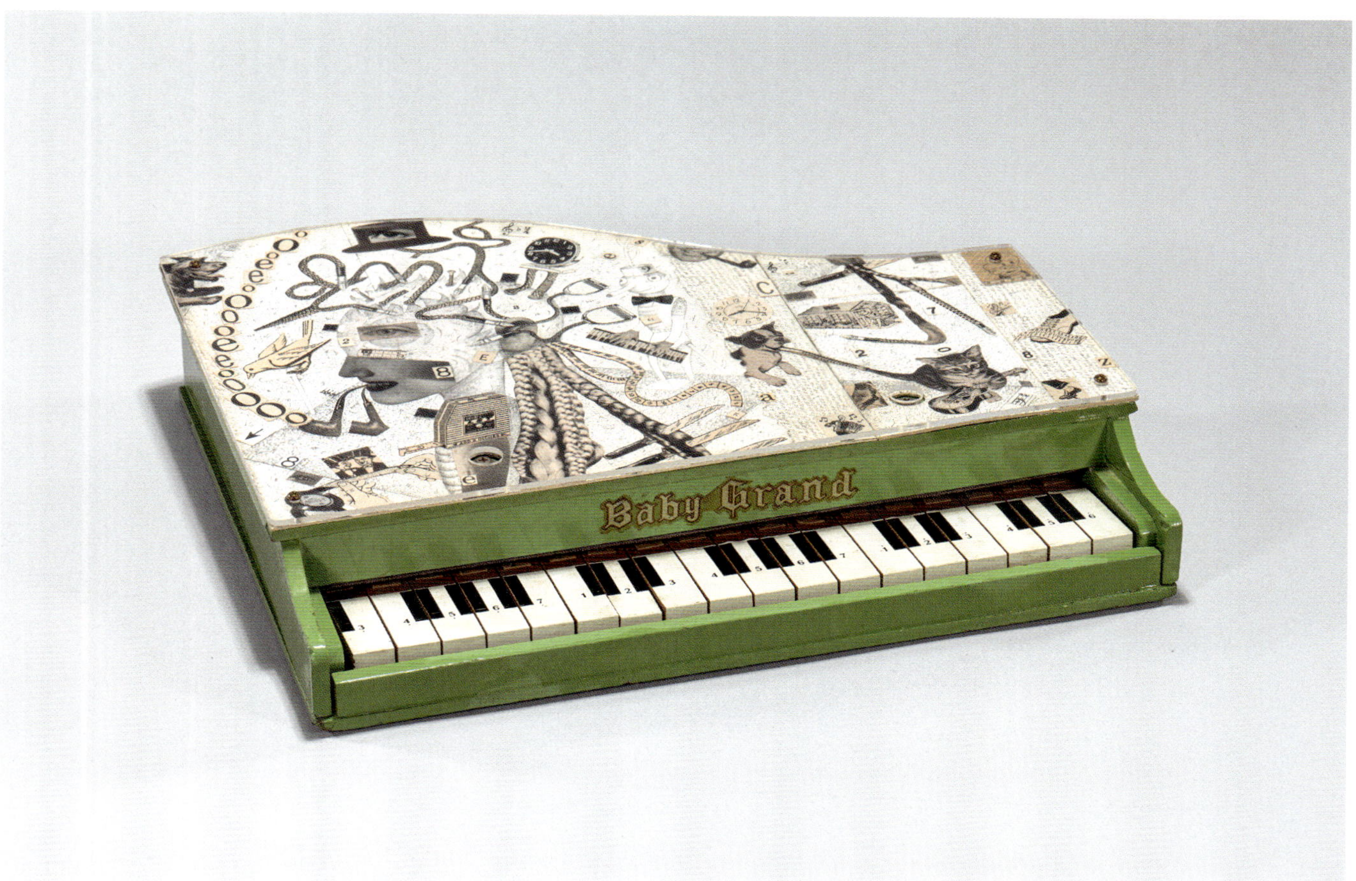

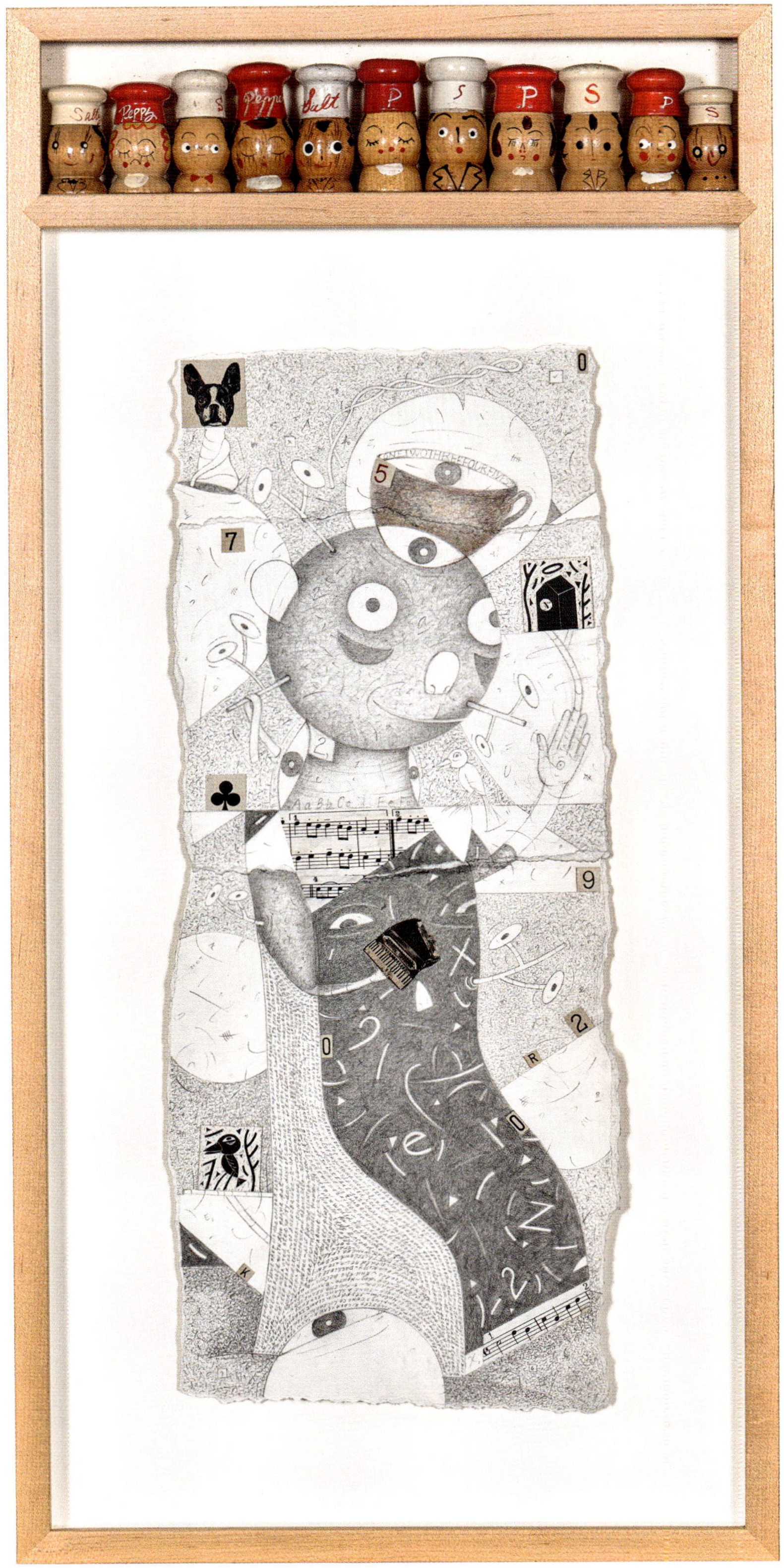

Salty and Peppy (Slant Step), 2012.
Paper, graphite, prismacolor, scratchboard, and wood, 29 1/16 × 13 7/8 × 1 3/8 in. Collection of Carla Hills and Frank LaPena.

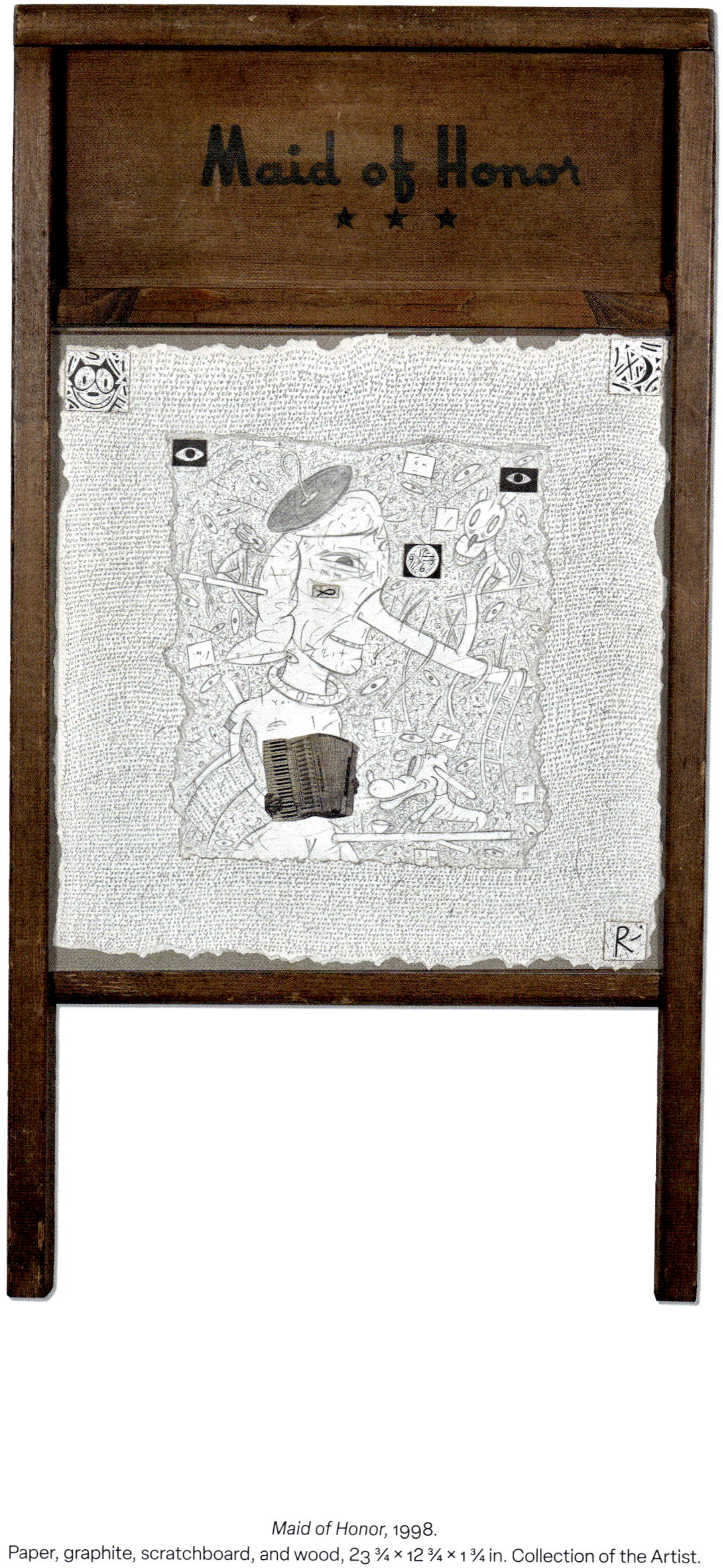

Maid of Honor, 1998.
Paper, graphite, scratchboard, and wood, 23 ¾ × 12 ¾ × 1 ¾ in. Collection of the Artist.

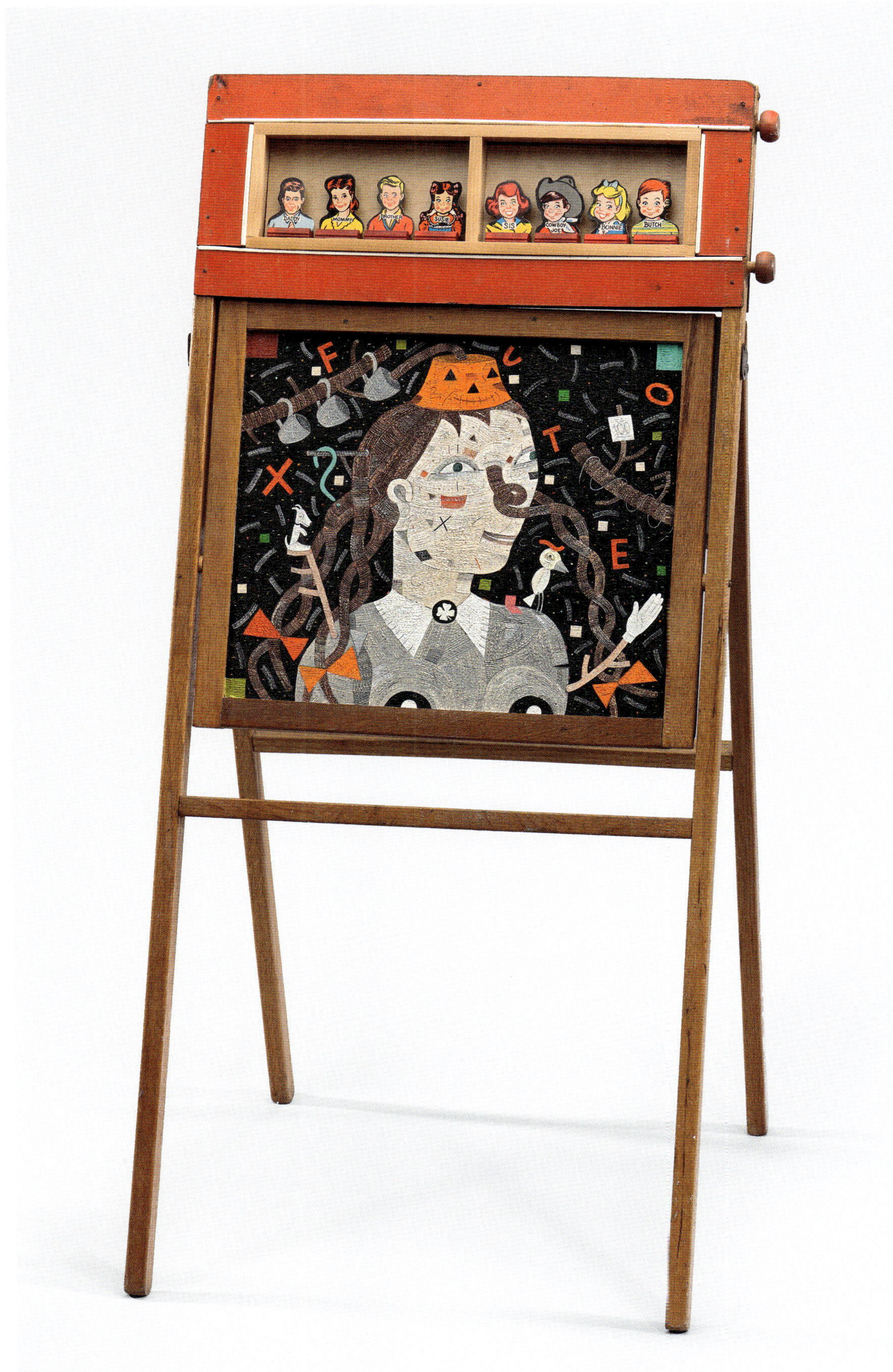

Pigtails: Go to the Head of the Class, 2013–2015.
Oil on slate (chalkboard), cardboard, and paper on wooden easel, 24 ½ × 24 ½ in. Crocker Art Museum, gift of Emily Leff, 2025.92.1.

to inhabit. Adan often paints her subjects into multi-layered, stage-like settings as well, the shifting planes of walls and floors resembling old-fashioned tiles or mosaics that flicker with brushwork and color. Both Adan and Stevens also investigate the intersections between art and craft. Stevens's carved and cut-out wood aligns his art with folk artists and craftspeople, while the textile-like nature of Adan's technique lends her paintings a "homemade" quality.

Adan began to apply her pigment in tiny, obsessive swatches in 1977, having developed the approach after visiting the Art Institute of Chicago. She and Stevens started their three week road trip to Chicago in June, their primary goal being to reconnect with Nutt and Nilsson, who had since returned to the city. They also aimed to do some preliminary planning for their upcoming, four-person Candy Store show. While visiting the Art Institute, Adan encountered Vincent van Gogh's 1887 *Self-Portrait,* a work rendered with flickering dots and dashes of complementary colors laid down, side by side. Though the painting was small, its impact on Adan was profound, and she rushed to the museum store to buy a postcard of it. Back in Sacramento, she utilized van Gogh's approach to make a painting of her father, *Ramón Adan de Yolo,* the work being the first to suggest her new technique. [p. 59] Pleased with the results, she gave it to her father for his birthday, and while her mother liked it, he said little. Shortly thereafter, Adan's mother called to ask if Adan might consent to give her father more hair. Adan acquiesced, but it was the last portrait she made of a family member.

Adan completed two more paintings, *Rock Garden* [p. 60] and *Dance of the Mummers,* in her new style. Shortly thereafter, she refined her approach, making brushstrokes that were more regular and stitch-like, the paint applied like a Pointillist but with tiny rectangles rather than dots. Her 1979 painting *Crosses to Bear* is the earliest example evidencing this more polished technique. [pp. 128–129] The painting was also the first in a series of very long, horizontal works.

Adan's distinctive brushwork would thereafter become an important part of her style. The approach translated equally well to her staccato-like drawings and scratchboards, the removal of the black layer in the scratchboards creating a stitch-like pattern underneath. It is a tidy, yet animated aesthetic that to her felt authentic and appropriate given her early efforts as a seamstress. Her uniformly textured surfaces also helped "weave" disparate elements of her narratives together, bringing an overall unity to compositions that might otherwise feel disjointed. There was just one drawback. Applying paint or making scratchboards in this manner was both laborious and time-consuming, meaning small works would take weeks to complete, and a large one might take several months.

Horse Sense

In 1980, Adan contributed to *Peaceable Kingdom,* a group show dedicated to animals, at San Francisco's Fuller Goldeen Gallery. Also that year, she held one of her most important exhibitions to date, a two-person exhibition with Stevens at what was now the Crocker Art Museum. Both artists were also featured a year later in the Crocker's *Welcome to the Candy Store* exhibition. The recognition helped Adan secure representation at

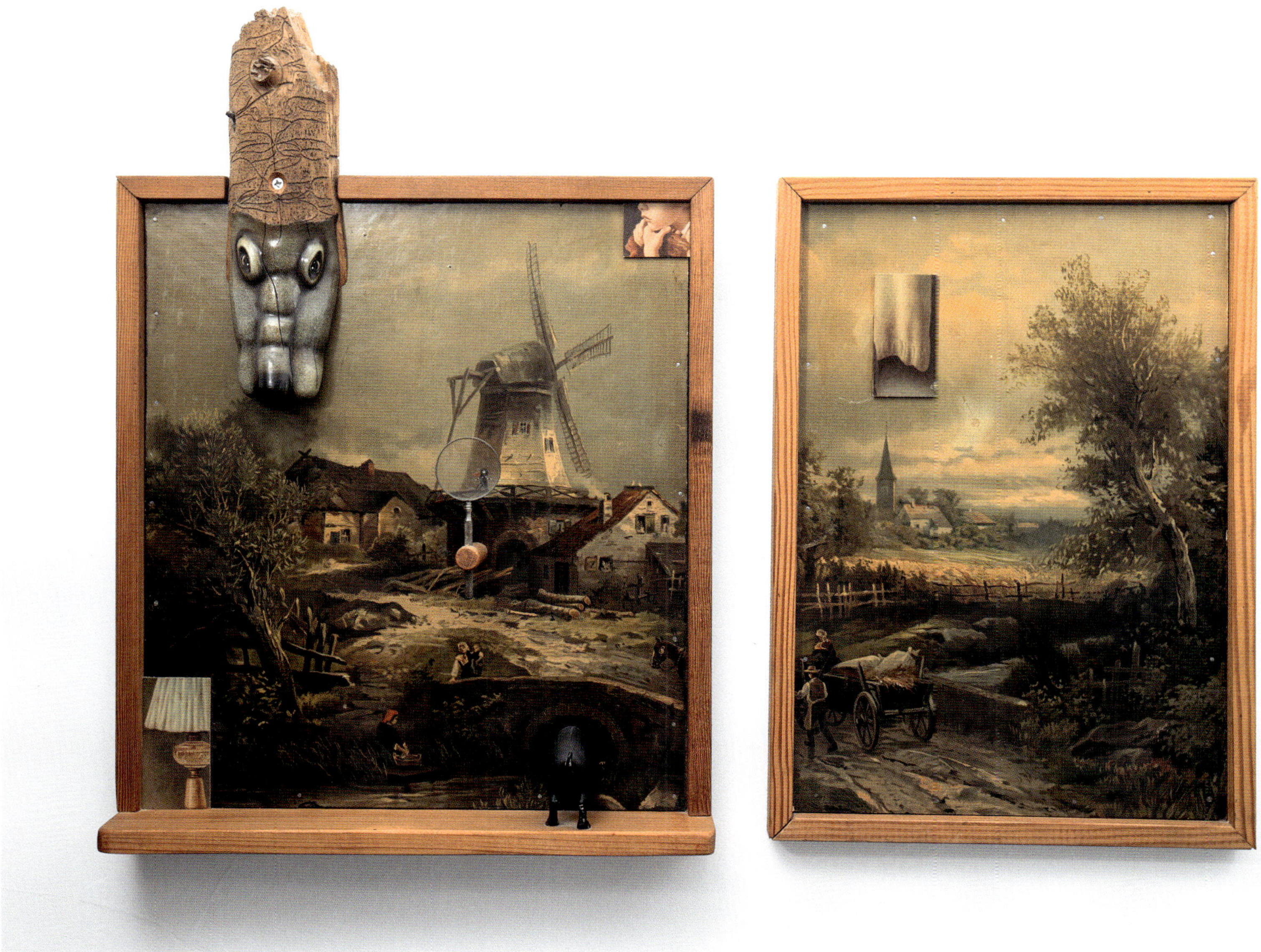

Michael Stevens (American, born 1945) and Suzanne Adan (American, born 1946), *In a Pig's Eye,* 1993.
Wood, enamel paint, plastic, magnifying glass, acrylic, and drymount print, 19 × 42 in.
Collection of Paul Wortman and the late Brent Smith.

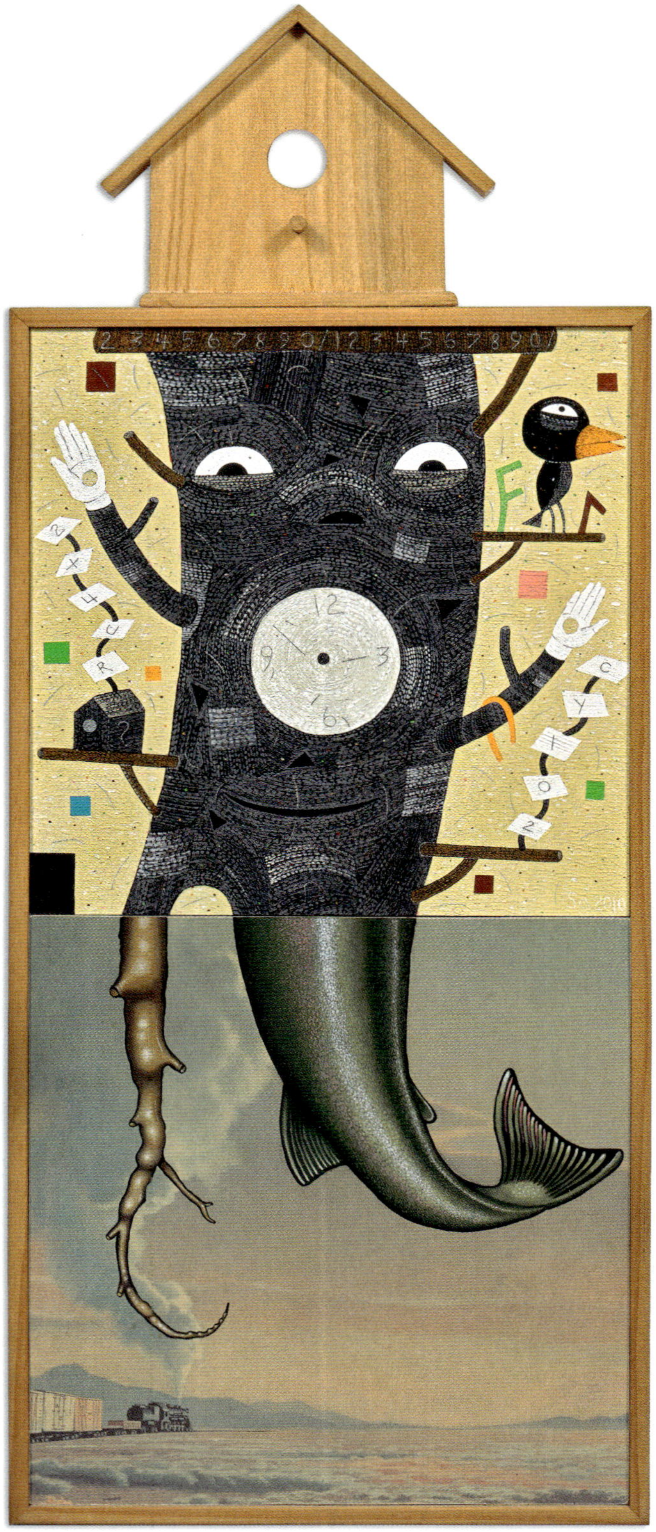

← Suzanne Adan (American, born 1946) and Michael Stevens (American, born 1945), *Ex-quisite Corpse (Bringing Up the Rear),* 2010. Acrylic paint on canvas, drymount print, enamel paint, and wood, 31 × 12 ¼ × 2 ½ in. Collection of Rita Gibson.

↓ *Up Shit (Cache) Creek without a Paddle (For Jim),* 1996. Scratchboard and wood, 15 ½ × 7 × 2 ½ in. Collection of the Artist.

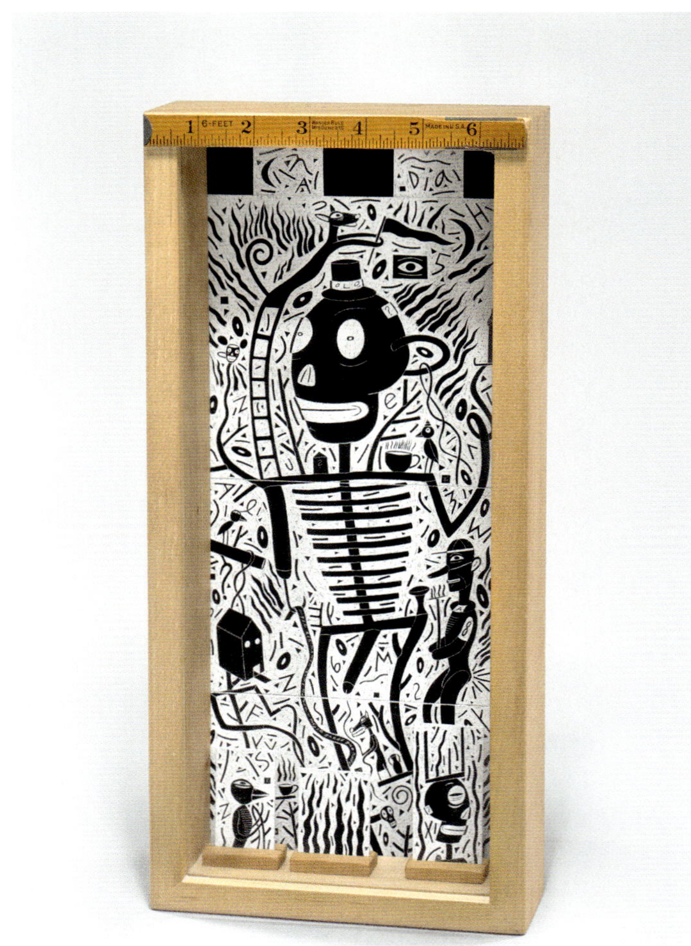

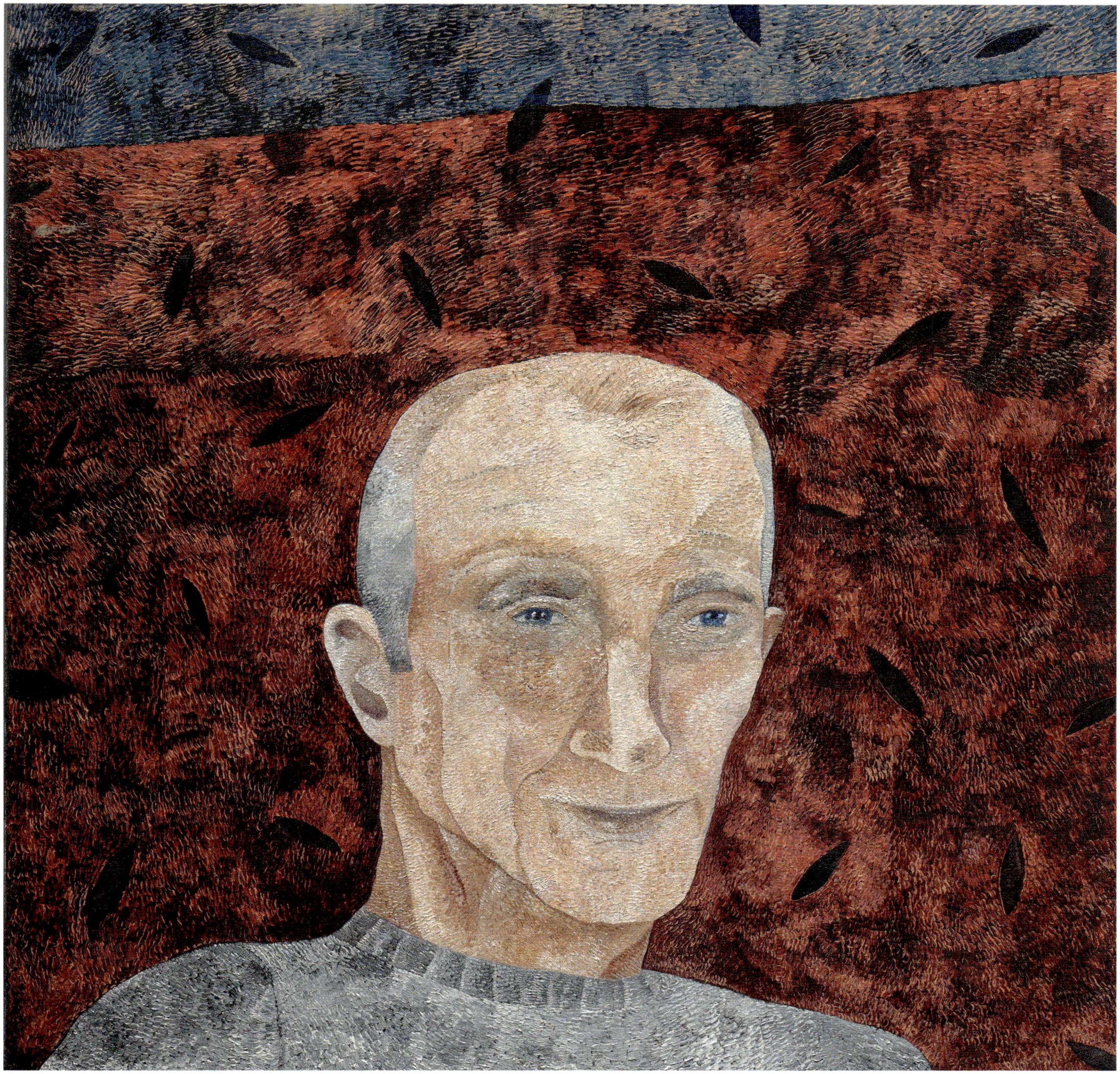

Ramón Adan de Yolo, 1977.
Oil on canvas, 24 × 23 ¾ in. Collection of the Artist.

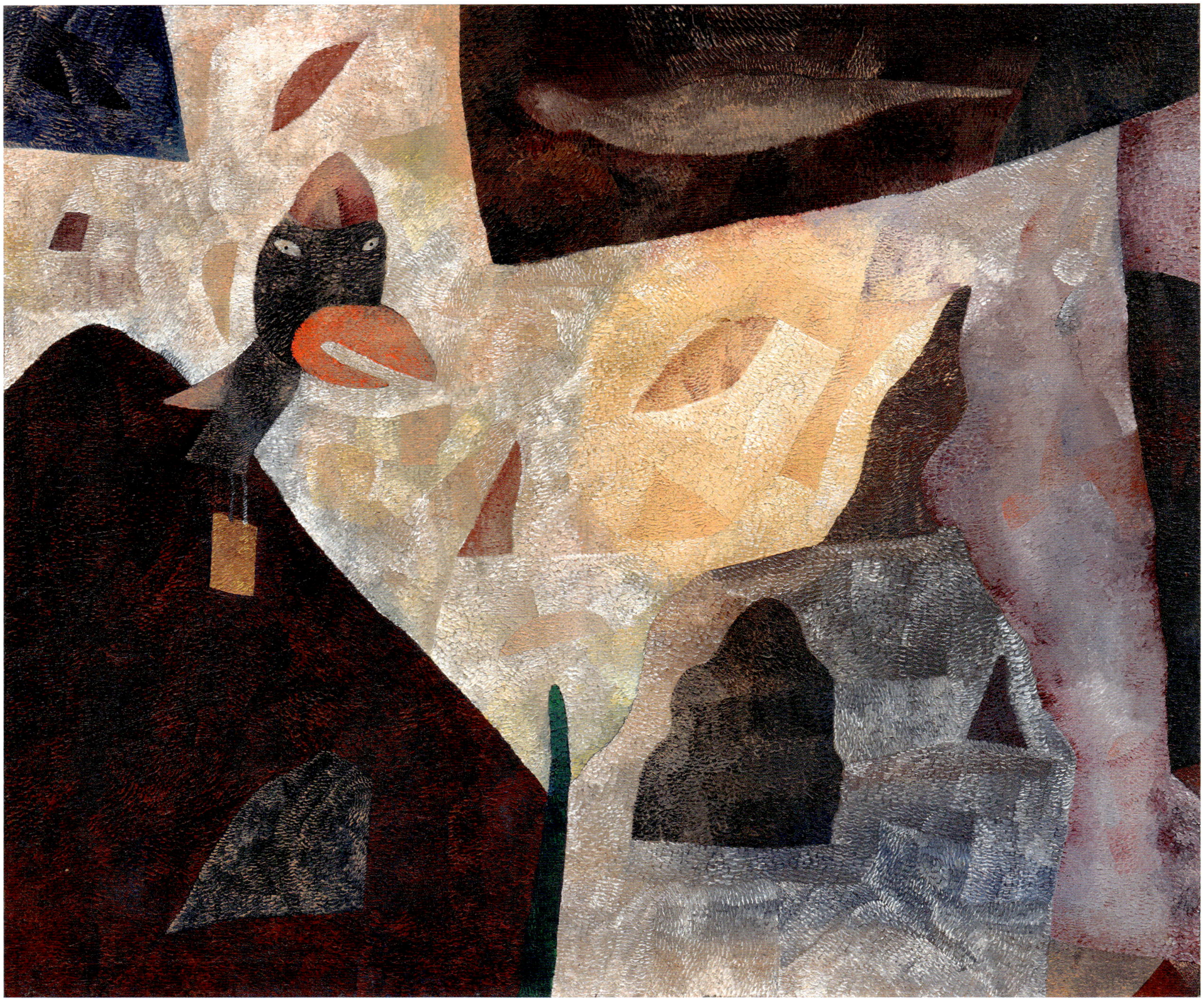

Rock Garden, 1978.
Oil on canvas, 16 × 20 in. Collection of Jennifer Kim Sohn.

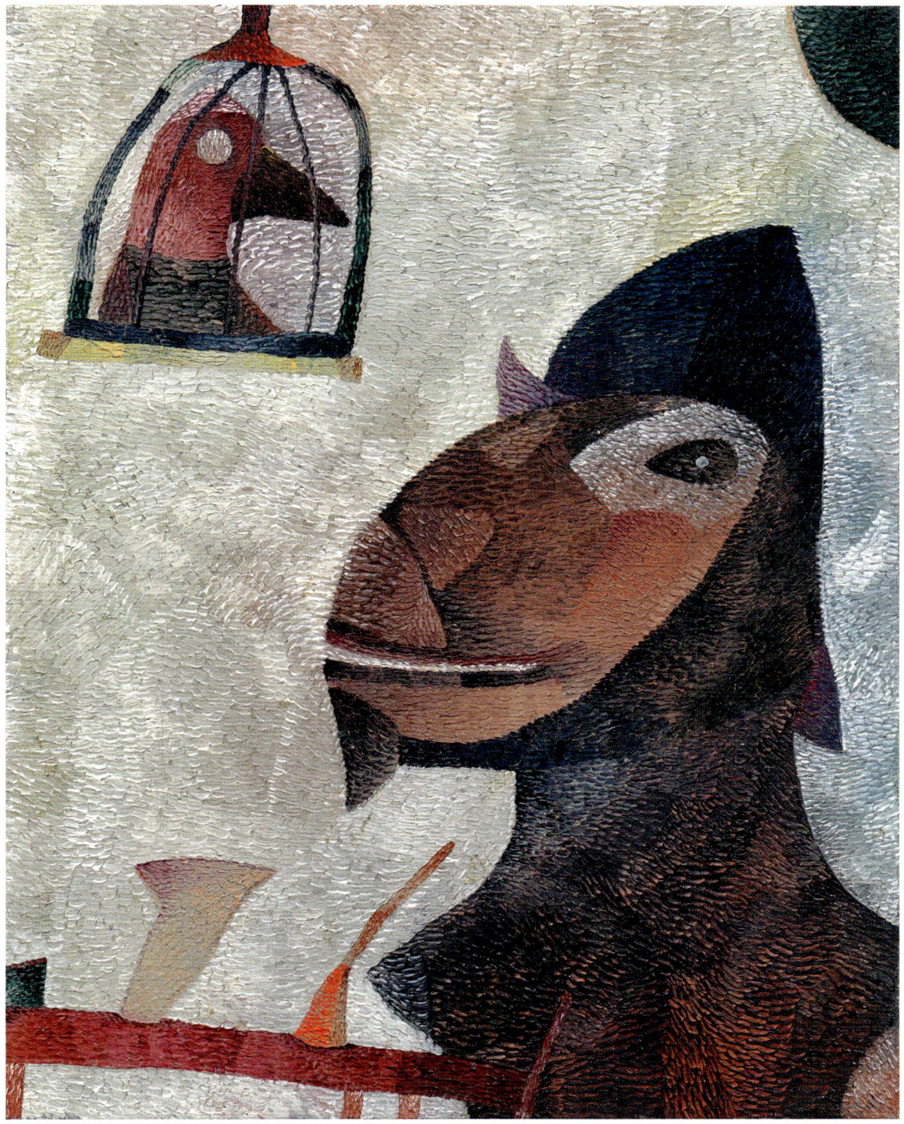

Hocus-Pocus, 1978.
Oil on canvas, 10 × 8 in. Collection of Jerald Silva.

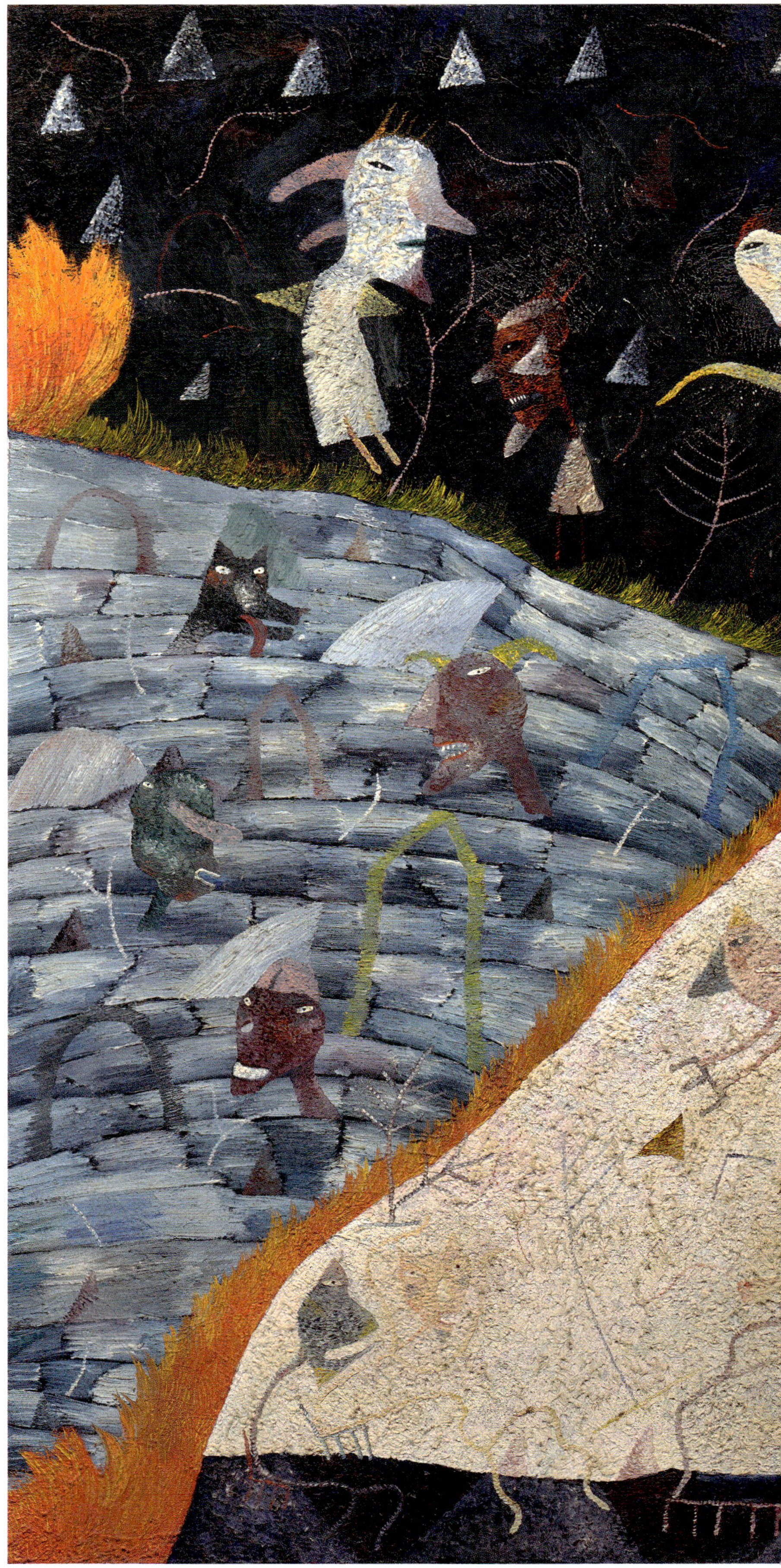

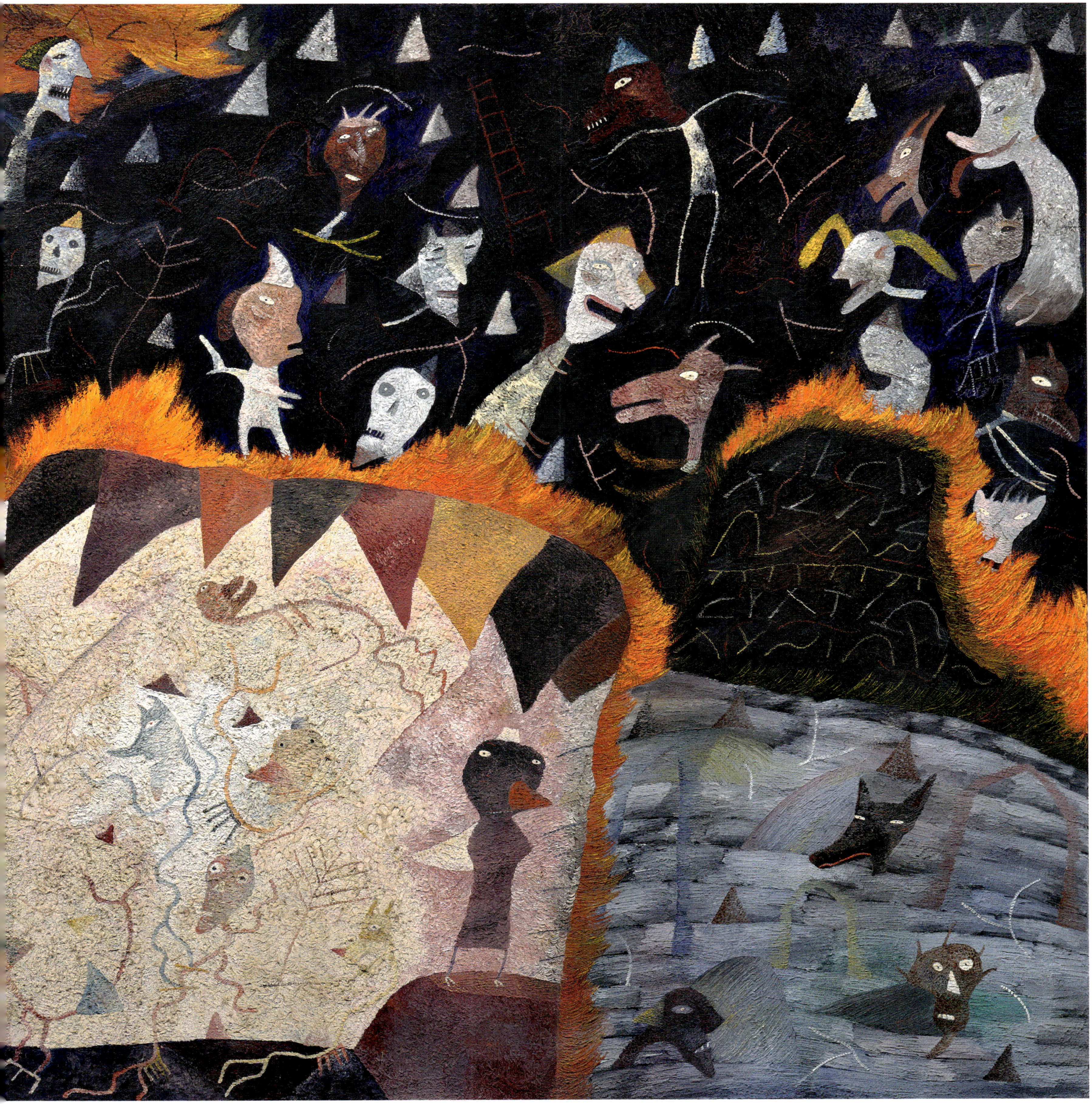

Styx and Stones, 1977.
Oil on canvas, 48 ¼ × 72 ½ in. Collection of Jane K. and the late James R. Adan.

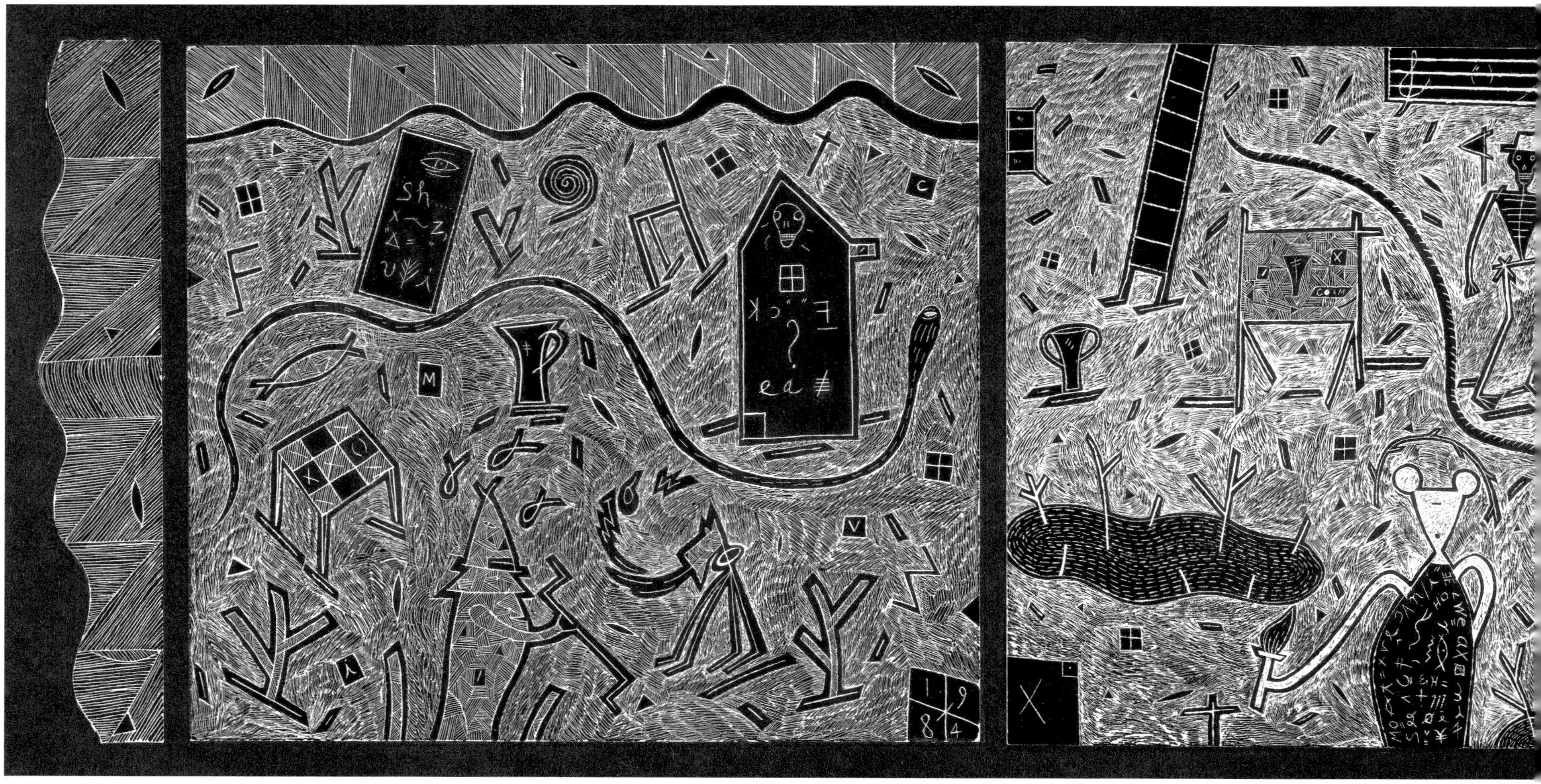

Broken Promises, 1984.
Scratchboard, 10 ¼ × 31 in. Collection of Julia Couzens and Jay-Allen Eisen.

the prestigious Betsy Rosenfield Gallery in Chicago, her first committed gallery outside California. She opened her first one-person exhibition with Rosenfield in 1982, and it was a sellout. Two more solo presentations followed in 1983 and 1985. Stevens also held two sold out shows with Rosenfield, though the frequency of these solo exhibitions slowed after Rosenfield decided to focus more attention on her family. Adan stopped showing with her in 1990, though Stevens continued to send work until 1993. The gallery closed two years later.

In 1984 and 1986, Adan also had one-person exhibitions at the Himovitz/Salomon Gallery in Sacramento. In between, she partnered with Stevens on a show at New Mexico State University in Las Cruces. Also in the late spring of 1987, she held a one-person exhibition at the John Berggruen Gallery in San Francisco. Berggruen met Adan after purchasing one of her scratchboards at the Jan Baum Gallery in Los Angeles; he then asked if he could exhibit her work. Adan agreed, and the show did well financially, but she did not become part of his stable.

To help her bottom line, Adan pursued public art projects. Though she had never taken on a large, outdoor piece, she completed two in 1990: one in the courtyard of the UC Davis Medical Center; the other at Natoma Station, a neighborhood in Folsom. Because these installations needed to withstand the elements, she returned to clay, producing numerous handmade ceramic tiles that together created a mural. Both projects were public-friendly and featured animals and an abundance of other imagery. She titled the Medical Center project *Animal Quilt.*

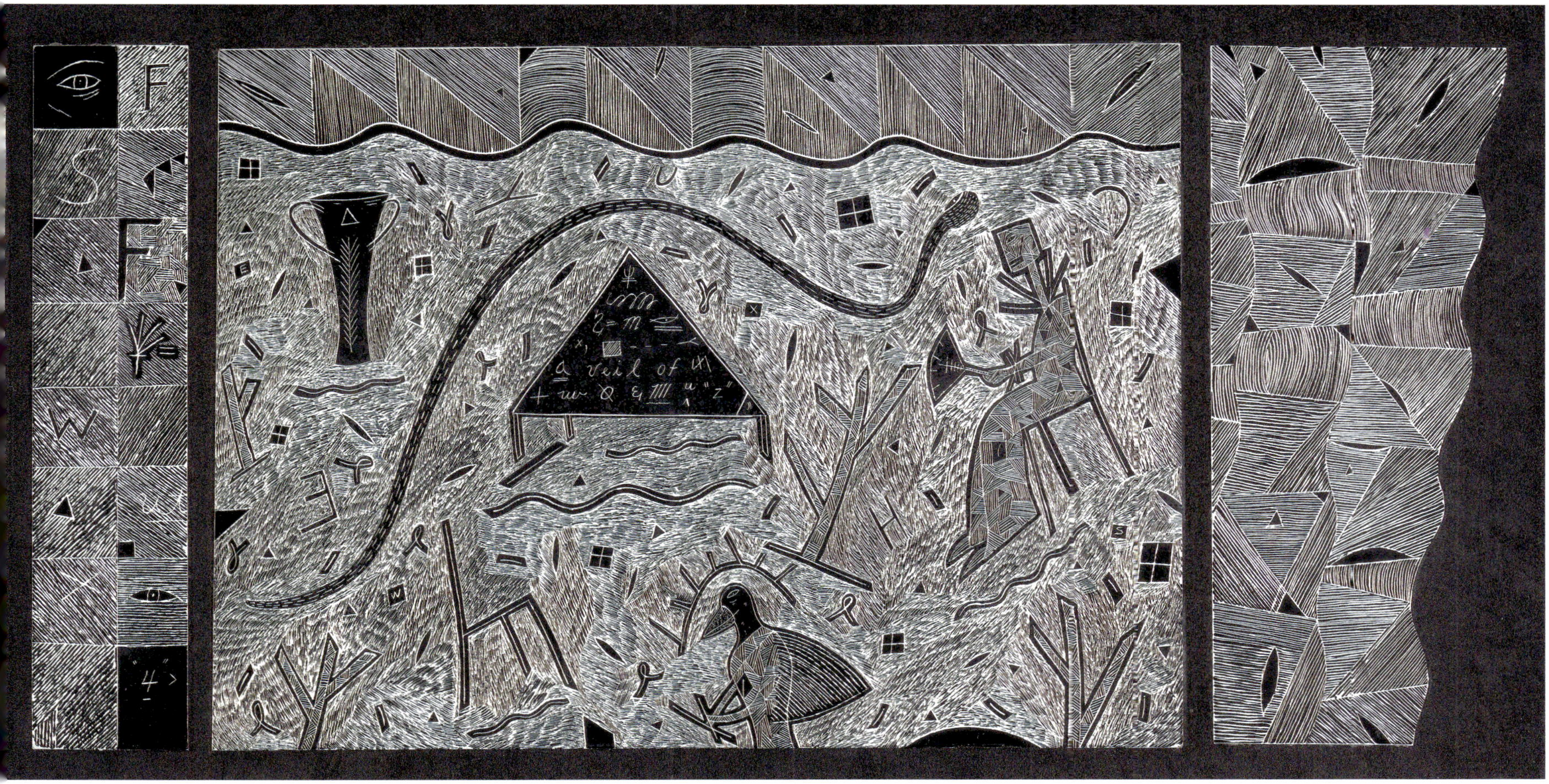

The Natoma Station commission consisted of two separate but related murals in median strips a block apart called *Catawampus* and *Horse Sense.*

Also at this time, Adan pursued another new venture, printmaking, which she had not really attempted since college while studying under Marcus. She did this as part of a Sacramento Metropolitan Arts Commission grant that funded collaborations between artists and commercial businesses. Adan worked with Brent Smith, a Sacramento-based residential designer. She opted for a simple, basic technique, the linocut, using it to create a large and ambitious series of prints featuring the Seven Deadly Sins, which she exhibited at Smith's office, minus one, *Lust* having not yet been printed. [pp. 72–75] She subsequently exhibited the entire group with gallerist Michael Himovitz, and then at the Kala Art Institute in Berkeley. The prints were successful enough that The San Francisco Foundation accorded her the 1991 James D. Phelan Art Award in Printmaking. At the same time, she continued to make scratchboards, the subtractive technique akin to making linoleum cut prints. She contributed a recent scratchboard, *Full Moon,* to a 1991 centennial show at the Crocker of past Crocker-Kingsley exhibitors. [pp. 68–69]

Flying Saucers

By this time, Adan had become a close friend of Himovitz, who continued to display her art in multiple group exhibitions upon forming the Himovitz/Jensen Gallery and then after opening his own eponymous space.

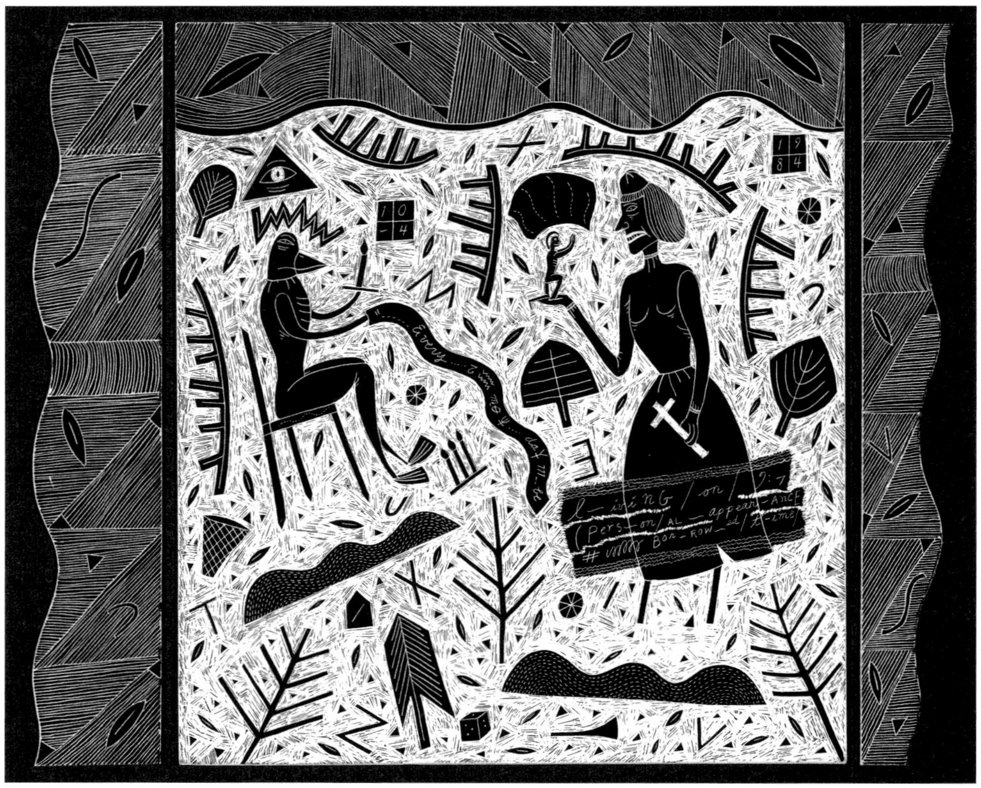

Wishful Thinking, 1984.
Scratchboard, 6 ½ × 8 in. Collection of Karen and David Ewing.

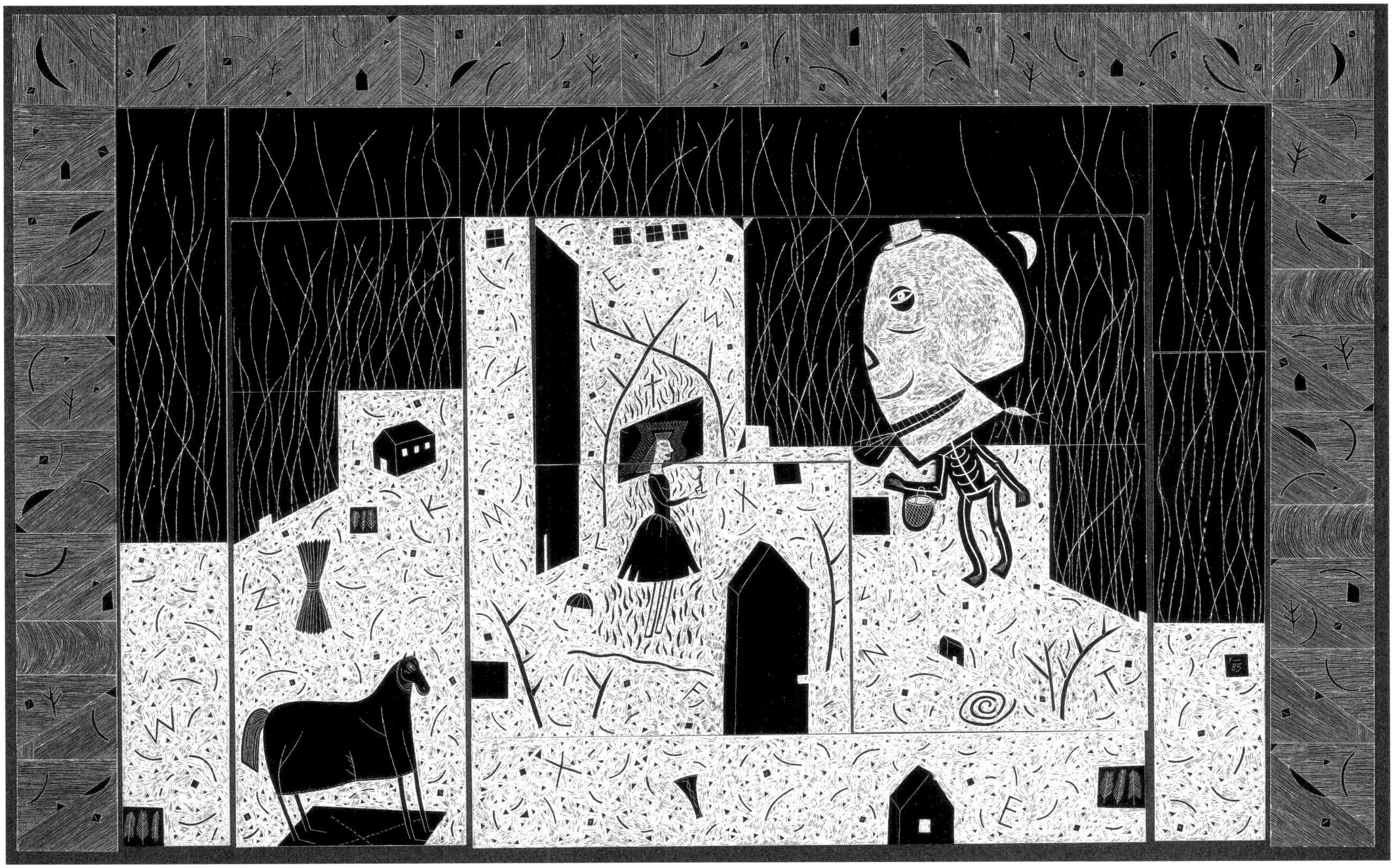

Basket Case, 1985.
Scratchboard and wood, 19 ¼ × 28 ½ in. Collection of Mima and Numan Begovic.

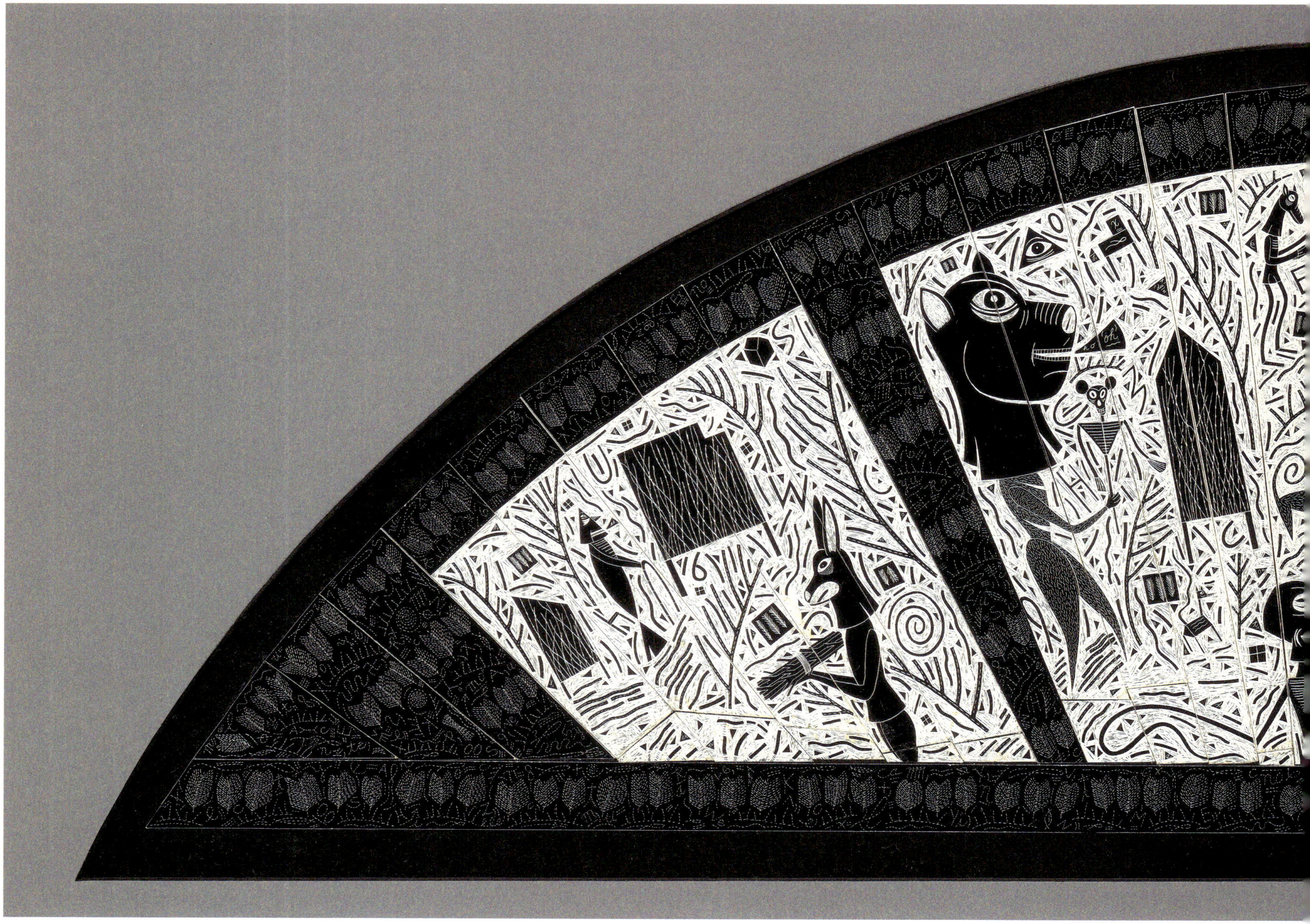

Full Moon, 1989.
Scratchboard, 17 ¼ × 37 ½ in. Crocker Art Museum, gift of the law office of Attia, Bartel, Eng & Torngren, 1989.14.

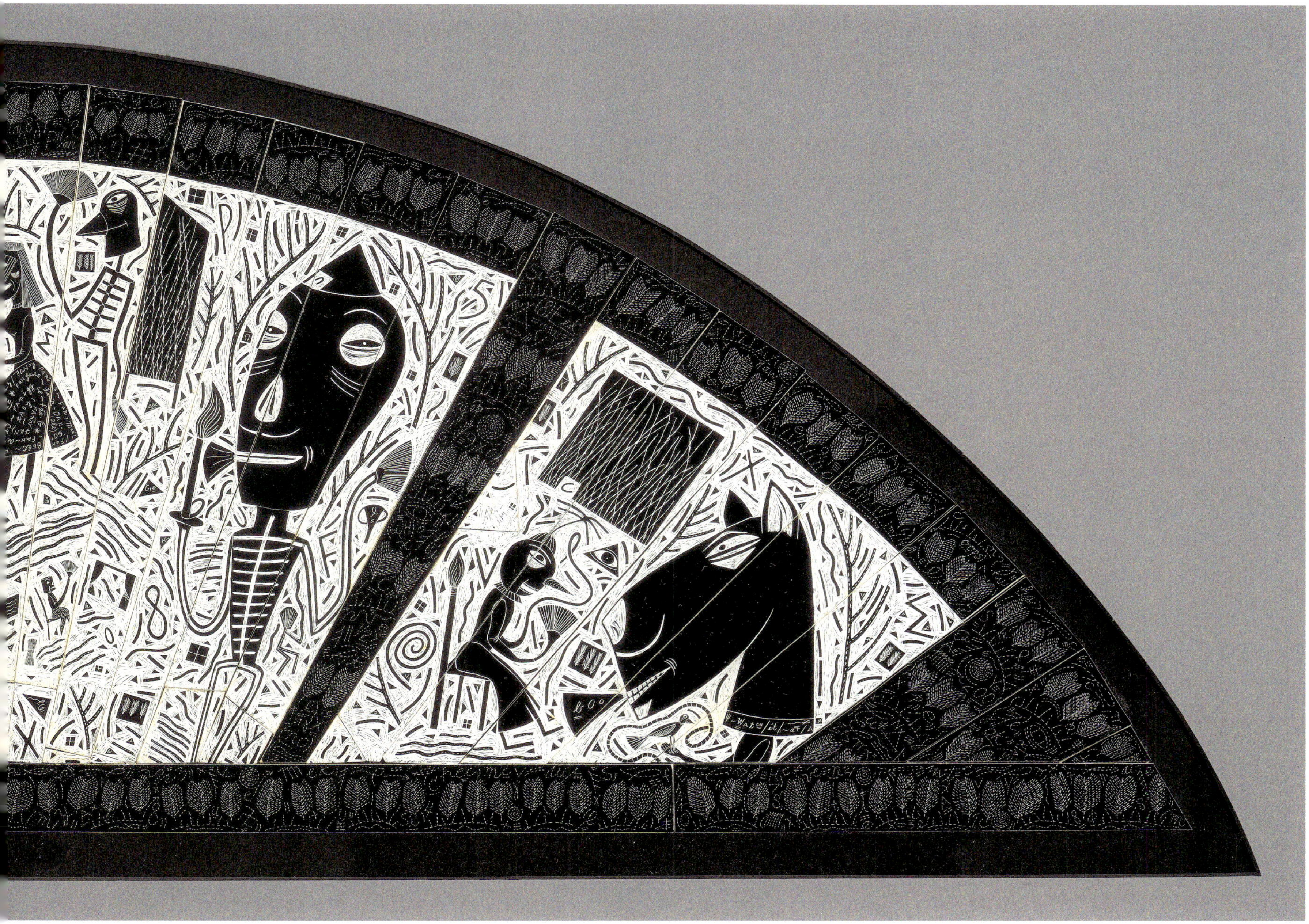

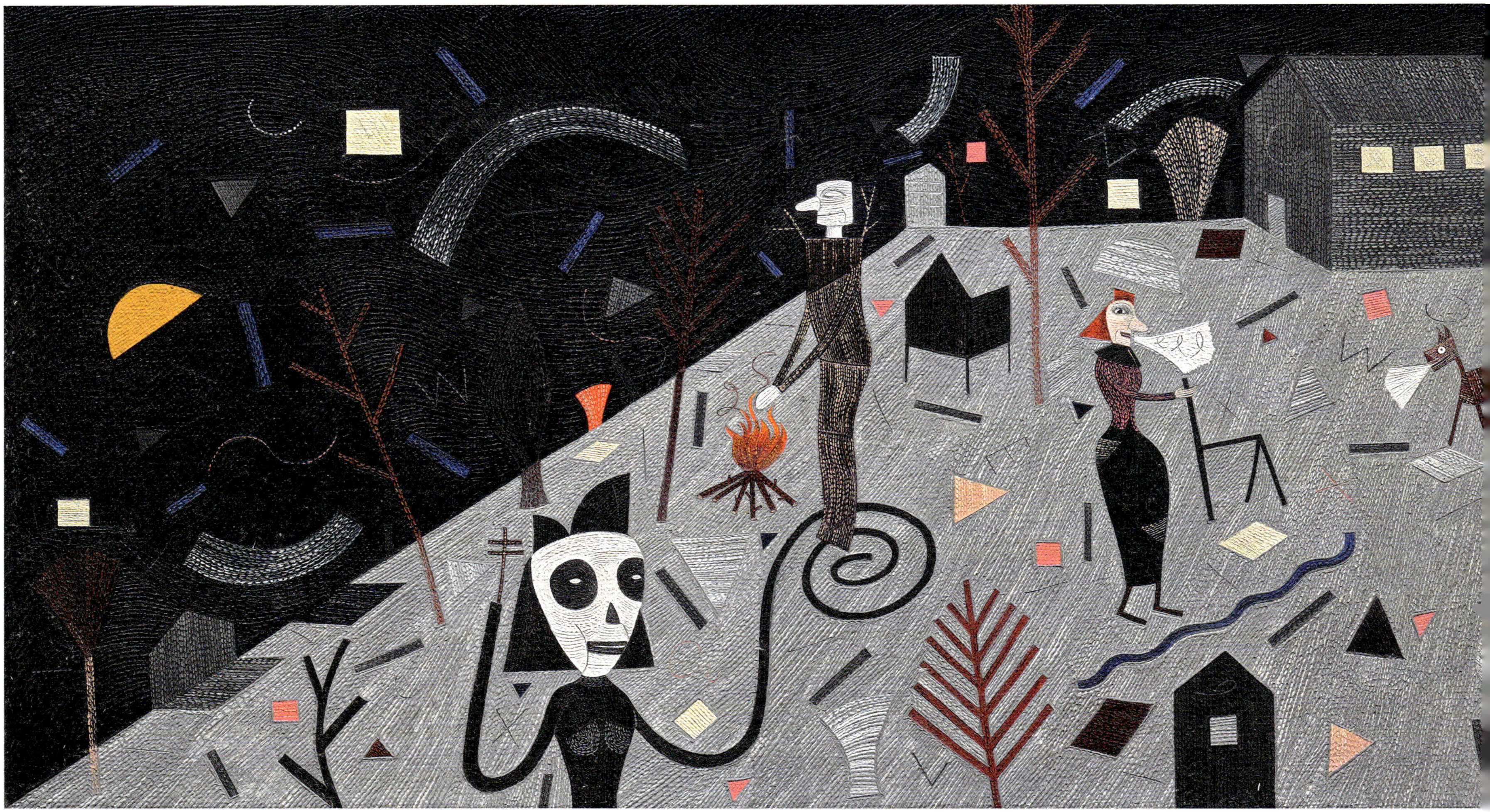

Skin and Bones, 1987.
Oil on canvas, 9 ¾ × 34 in. Collection of Michael Stevens.

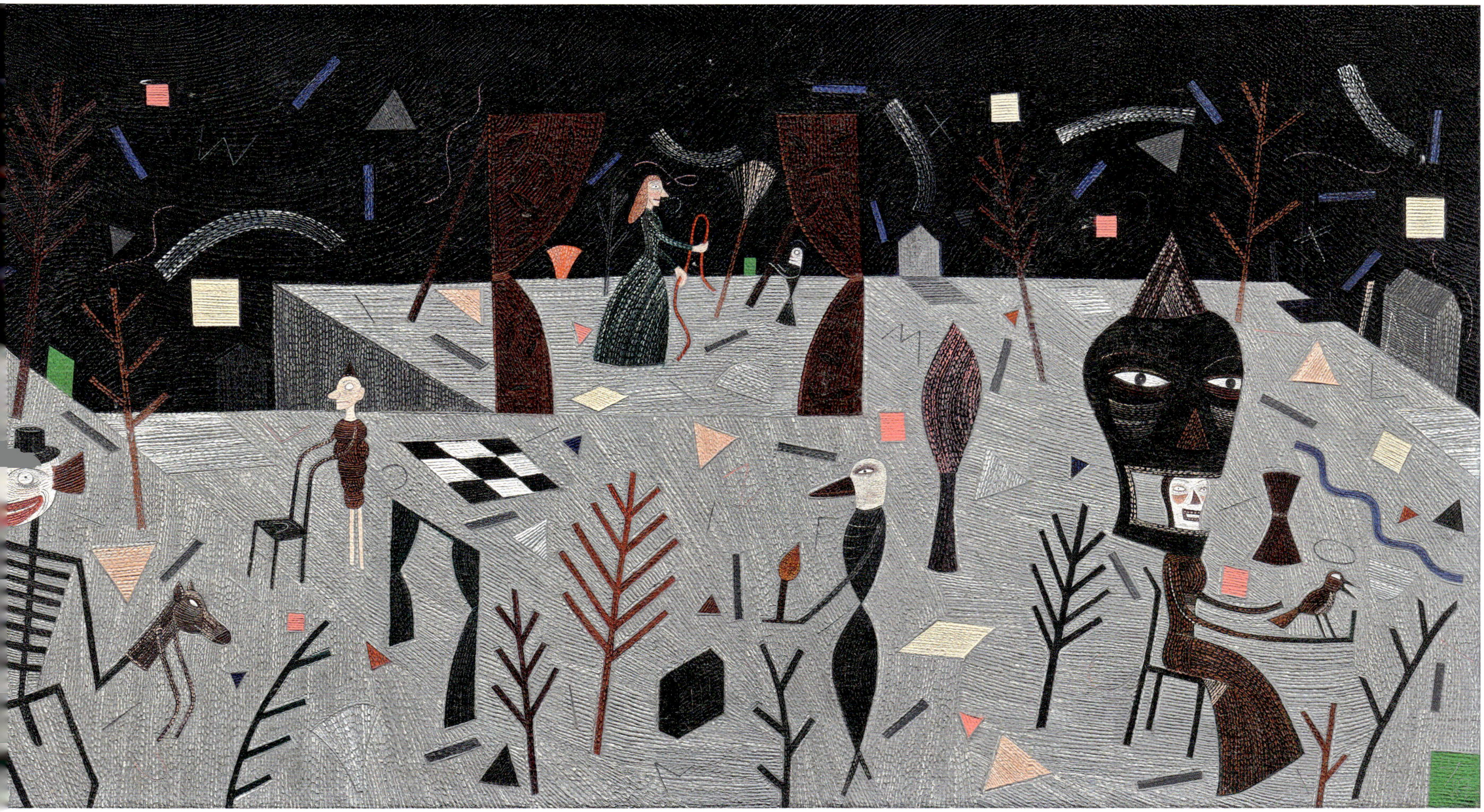

Stevens exhibited with Himovitz as well. In 1993, both artists collaborated on a *Mr. & Mrs.* exhibition, a version of which was reprised in 1996 at American River College Art Gallery and then, two years later, at San Joaquin Delta College in Stockton.

The Crocker Art Museum acquired one of the paintings featured in the 1993 show, *Flying Saucers.* [p. 76] An early work in what is today recognized as Adan's signature style, the painting consists of tens of thousands of tiny brushstrokes and expressive shapes scattered throughout the canvas. This flurry of chaotic activity provides a background for a deeply personal narrative grappling with the fact that Himovitz was dying of AIDS. White and black skeletons, one with a limp body, represent death, while a cat head vase provides a place to hold ashes. A white dog symbolizes the ghost of spirits passed, while a house dangles by a thread and suggests the end is just around the corner. Eyes—the flying saucers of the title—float through the night air like spirits; a crescent moon denotes that darkness has fallen.

Himovitz's 1994 death was a blow to the Sacramento community and, especially, to Adan and Stevens. He was a good friend and, by all accounts, had a keen eye for talent, doing much to nurture the careers of his artists. In the year of his passing, the Crocker Art Museum honored him and his artists with an exhibition, to which Adan and Stevens contributed. Still today, Adan and Stevens remain close to Himovitz's children, his ex-wife and her husband.

For a time, Himovitz's partner, Charles Miller, continued to run the gallery. Adan and Stevens participated in a show he curated called *Gun,* which showcased art by regional artists who sometimes incorporated gun imagery into their work. It was their last exhibition at the gallery, as their relationship with Miller had never quite been what it was with Himovitz. For Adan especially, the loss of gallery representation was a career blow. Stevens showed at Braunstein/Quay Gallery in San Francisco, which occasionally also featured an Adan piece but never represented her like it did him. Plus, the Candy Store Gallery had closed three years earlier. With no formal gallery affiliation, Adan found herself adrift. She turned to Susan Cummins, whose Mill Valley, California, gallery had featured her work in group shows. In 1997, she held a solo exhibition there.

Head of the Class

Adan had no more solo shows for the next several years, though she was now making some of the strongest and largest art of her career, having truly found her signature style by the early 1990s. She did, however, continue to exhibit in thematic group shows at commercial galleries, including the Solomon Dubnick Gallery in Sacramento, the John Natsoulas Gallery in Davis, and the Jean Albano Gallery in Chicago. She also contributed an occasional piece to the Encina Art Gallery at Encina High School in Sacramento. Stevens had been teaching art at Encina since 1990, having served thirteen years as an instructor at La Sierra High School and an additional seven at Rio Americano High School. The Encina Art Gallery, a white box space located within the art classroom, opened in the spring of 1994 at the suggestion of the school's principal,

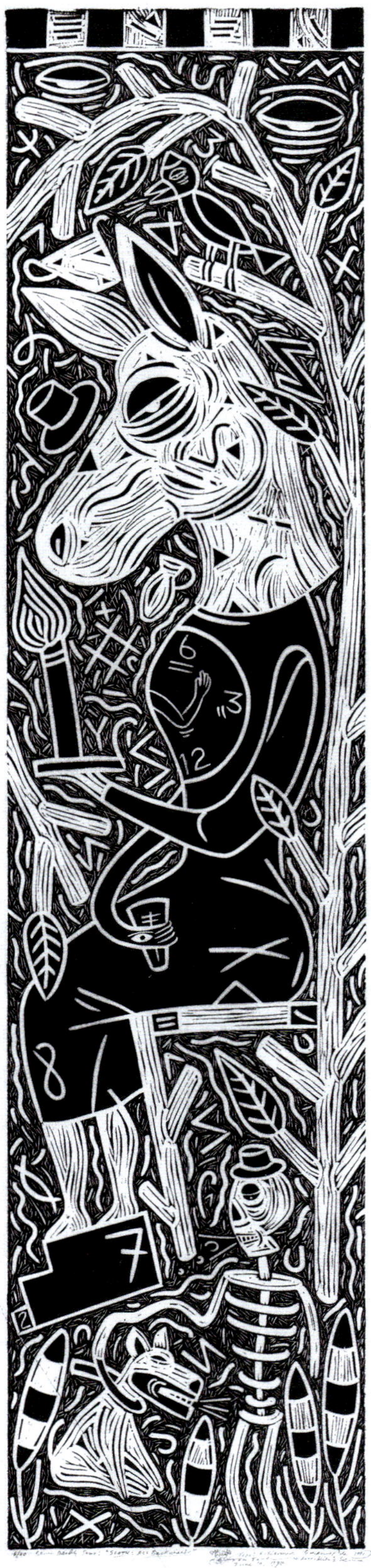

Sloth: Ass Backwards, from the *Seven Deadly Sins* series, 1991. Linocut on rice paper, 57 × 19 × 2 in. Collection of Thane Tahti and Janet Crecelius.

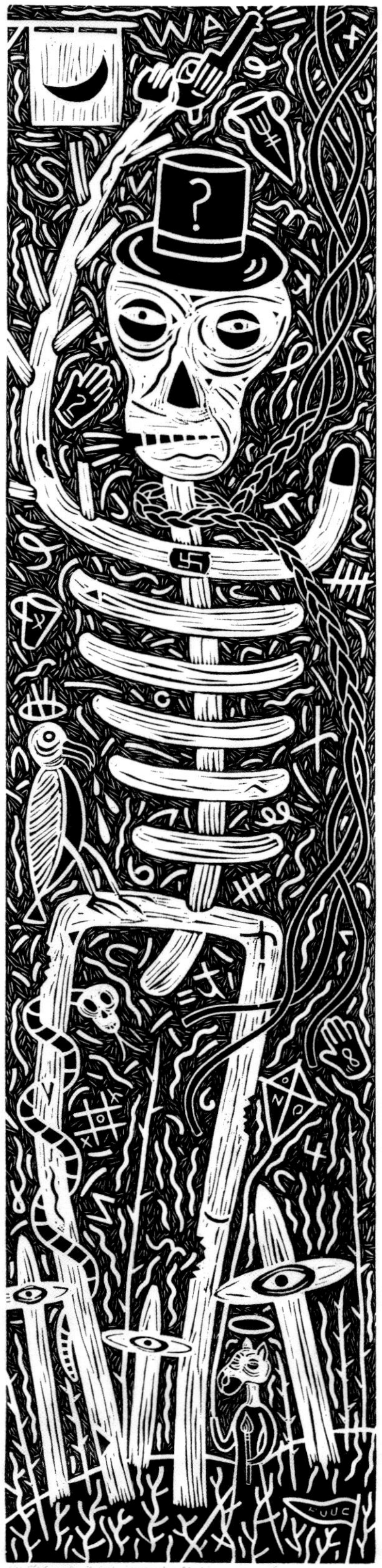

Anger: Bad Blood, from the *Seven Deadly Sins* series, 1991. Linocut on rice paper, 57 ¼ × 19 × 2 in. Crocker Art Museum, gift of Phil and Patricia Weidman, 2024.19.1.

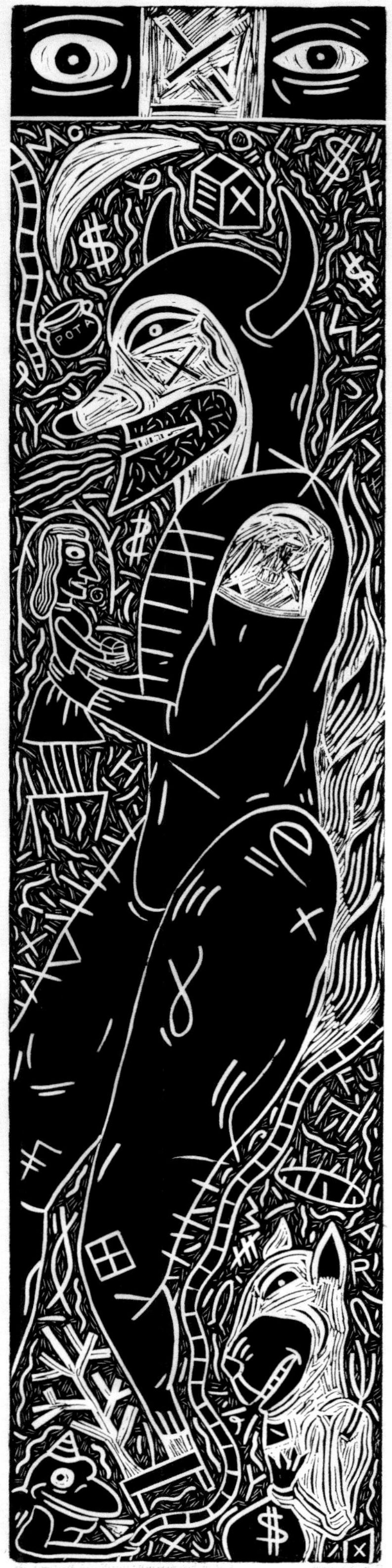

Avarice: Shake Hands with the Devil, from the *Seven Deadly Sins* series, 1991. Linocut on rice paper, 57 ¼ × 19 ½ in. Collection of Donna and Tony Natsoulas.

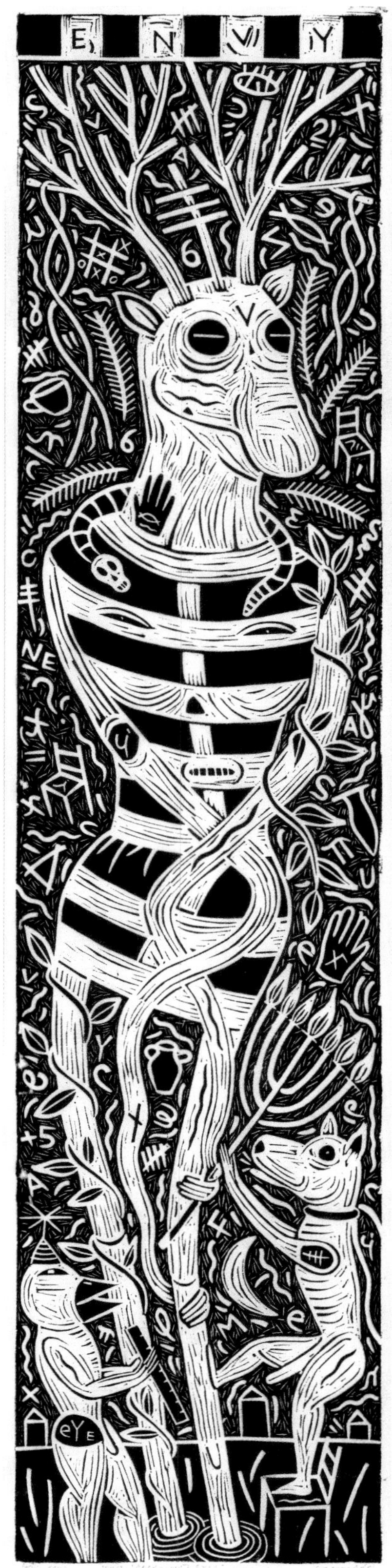

Envy: Green with Envy, from the *Seven Deadly Sins* series, 1991. Linocut on rice paper, 57 ¼ × 19 ½ in. Collection of Vicky Wallace and Ron Peetz.

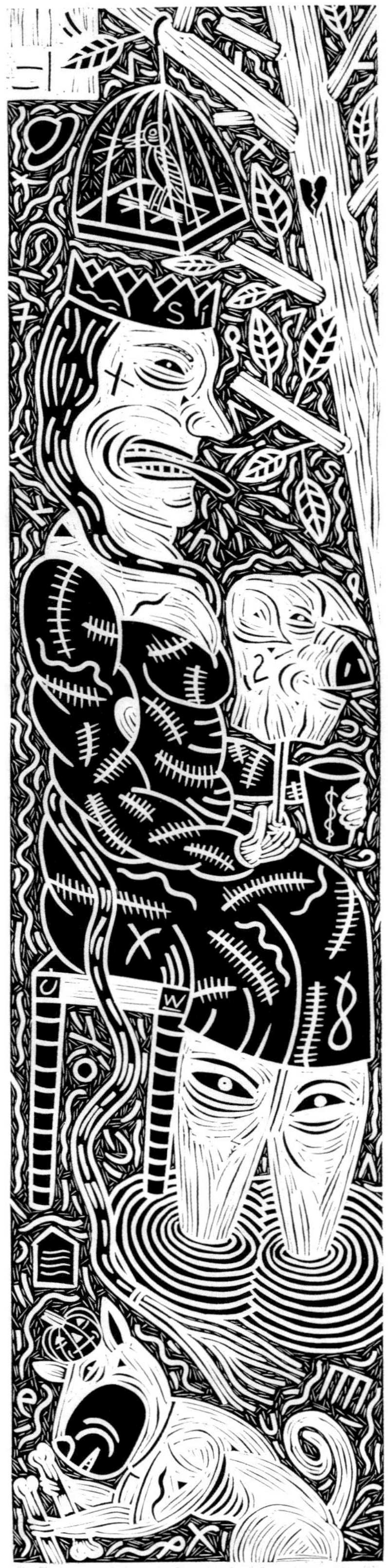

Gluttony: Chew the Fat, from the *Seven Deadly Sins* series, 1991. Linocut on rice paper, 57 × 19 × 2 in. Collection of Karen and David Ewing.

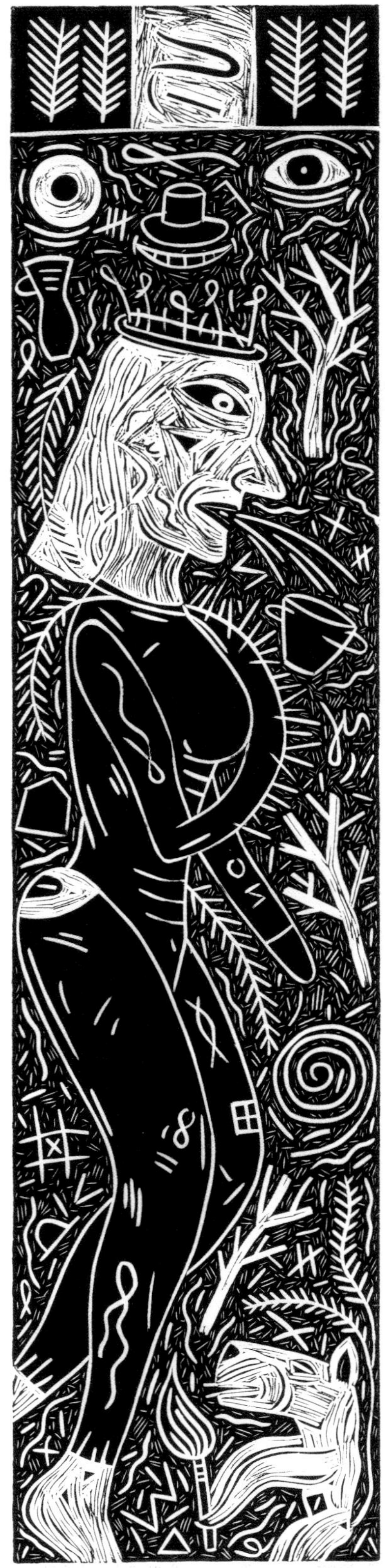

Pride: Crow's Feet, from the *Seven Deadly Sins* series, 1991. Linocut on rice paper, 57 × 19 × 2 in. Collection of Mark Marvelli.

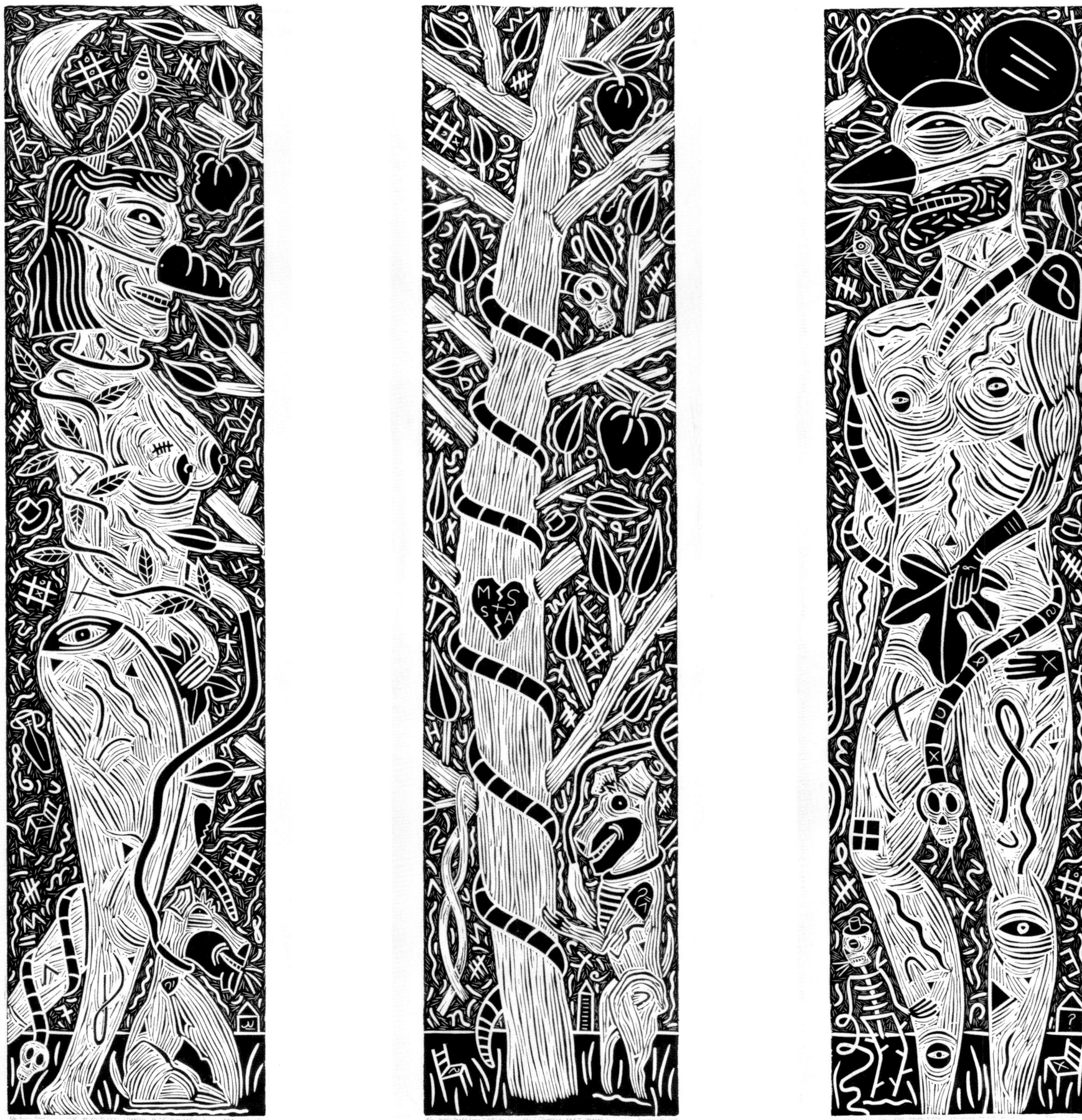

Lust: Garden of Adan (Triptych), from the *Seven Deadly Sins* series, 1991.
Linocut on rice paper, 57 ¼ × 19 ½ in. (each). Collection of Donna and Tony Natsoulas.

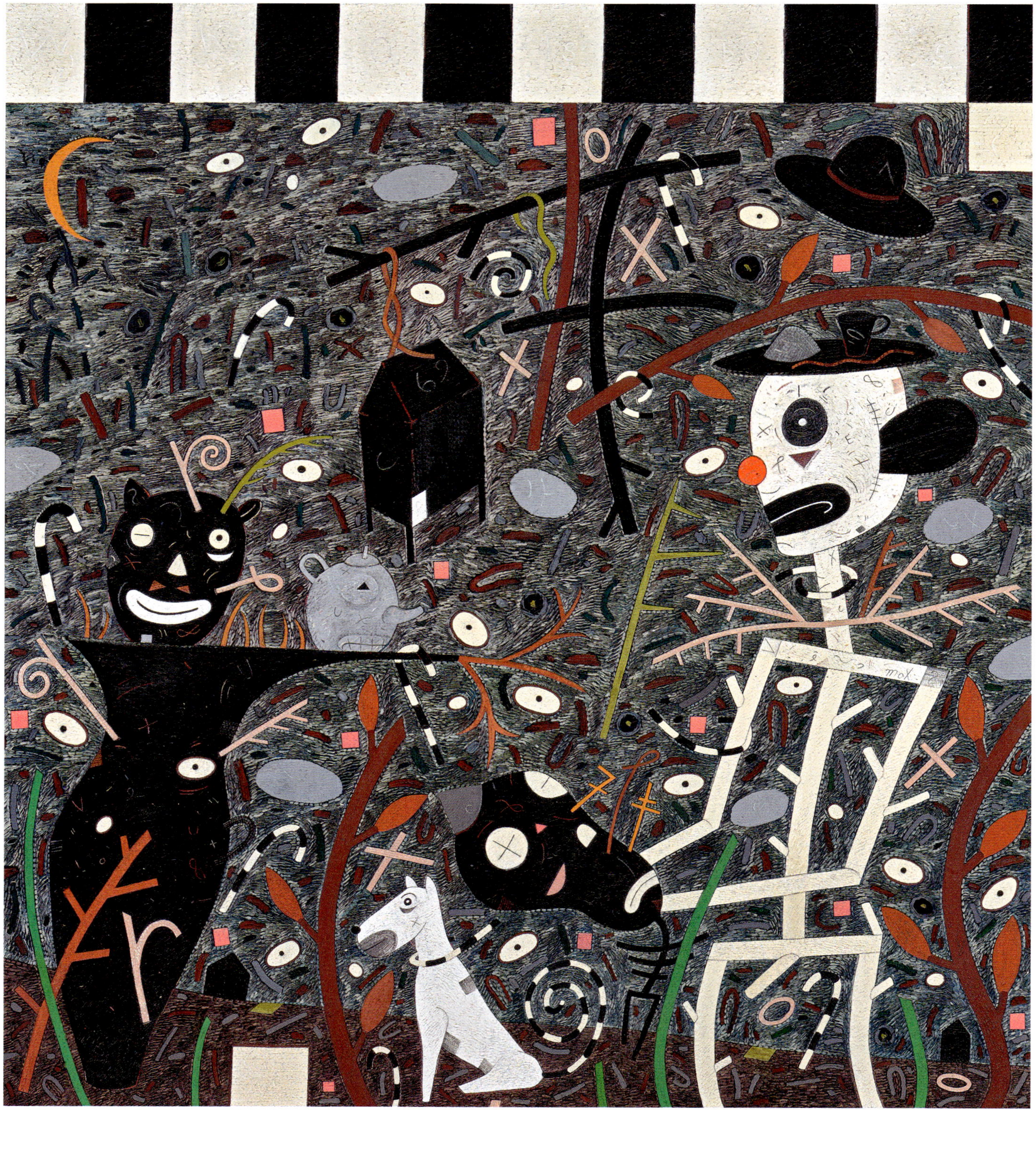

Flying Saucers, 1993.
Oil on canvas, 66 × 60 in. Crocker Art Museum Purchase with funds from the 1993 Paint-A-Plate Fundraiser, 1994.5.

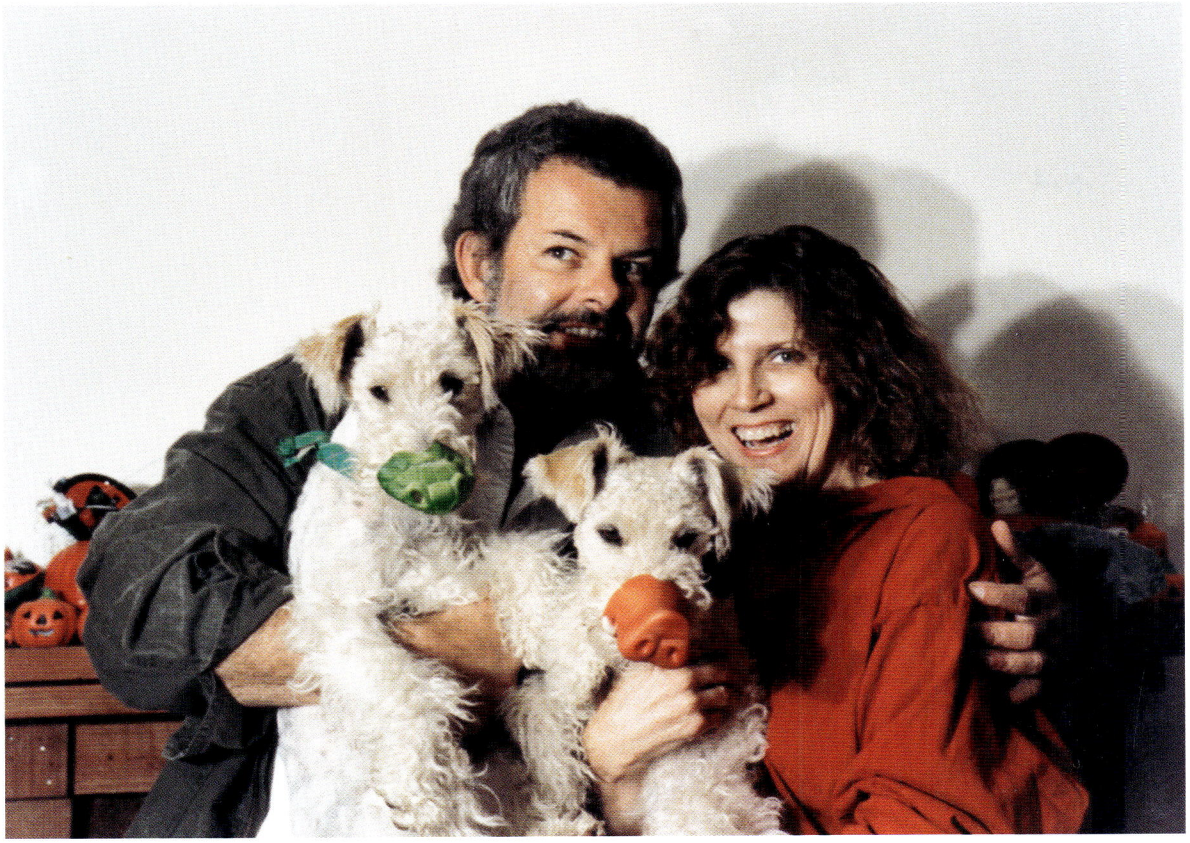

Michael Stevens and Suzanne Adan with their dogs Reilly and Murphy, 1997. Courtesy of Suzanne Adan.

Tom Gemma.[38] It would become a campus attraction, the exhibitions sometimes critically reviewed.

Stevens did the teaching and Adan served as the gallery's curator. She did so from 1994 to 2004, when Stevens retired from high school teaching. As Stevens described it, "We have always been a team, sharing two careers, as artists and teachers."[39] Gemma called both artists "outstanding teachers," noting their passion, their artistic skills, their relationship with students, and their ability to provide excellence in arts education. "The gallery is the pinnacle of their work," he praised, "and I think what they've done surpasses any arts program that I have ever seen."[40] The gallery was, in fact, an excellent teaching tool and an idea that many other schools sought to emulate. "Exposure is the final phase of the creative process," Stevens explained. "We can take the whole class on a field trip in five minutes. The kids can see successful work. They learn from it. They are amazed by it. It became a source of inspiration."[41]

Exhibitions by Encina students took place in the space, as did an annual themed show that attracted entries from top high school students around the region. The gallery also hosted work by professional artists, including not only those who lived in the community but were sometimes from out of state. Sacramento-area community members, including artists, educators, collectors, and designers guest-curated exhibitions providing different points of view, and well-known artists from farther afield came to the school to interact with students. Sacramento arts patrons Mort and Marcy Friedman funded the gallery's first year of operation, and the Sacramento Metropolitan Arts Commission underwrote years two and three.[42] Thereafter, it was important enough to find ongoing support. Because of Adan and Stevens's work at Encina,

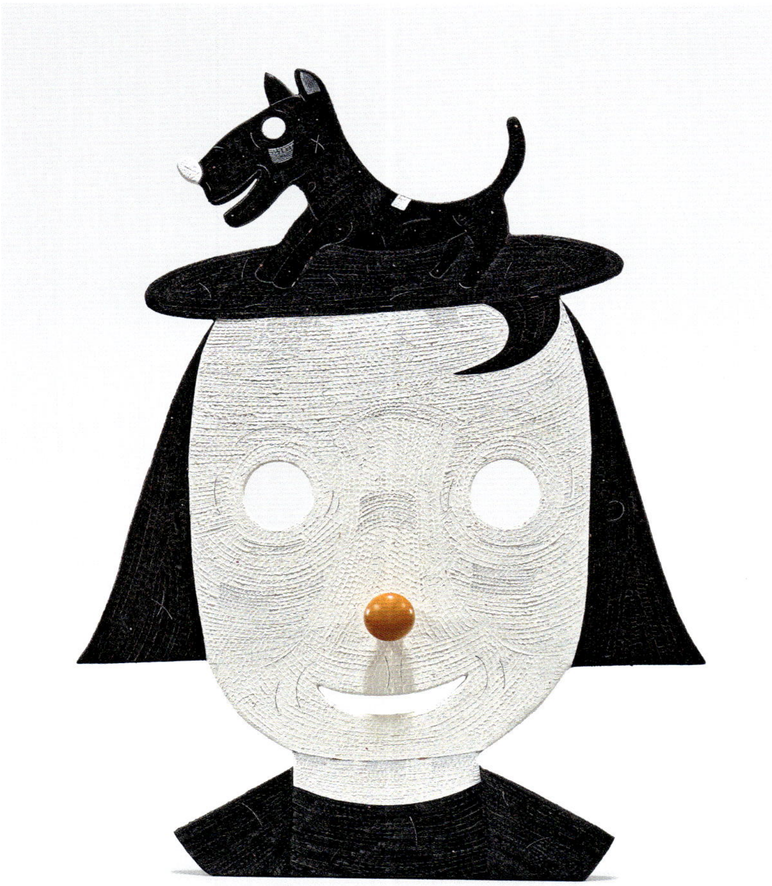

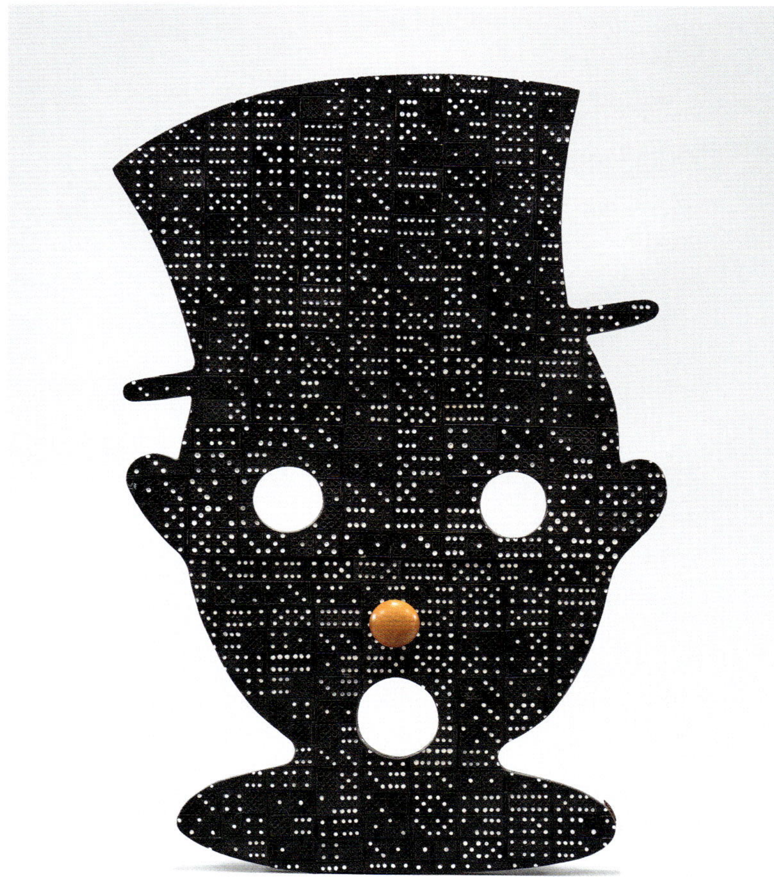

Michael Stevens (American, born 1945) and Suzanne Adan (American, born 1946), *His & Hers,* 2006.
Acrylic paint on plywood, wood, and plastic, 25 ⅜ × 16 ½ × 3 ½ in.; 25 ¾ × 19 × 3 ½ in. Collection of Susan Bitar.

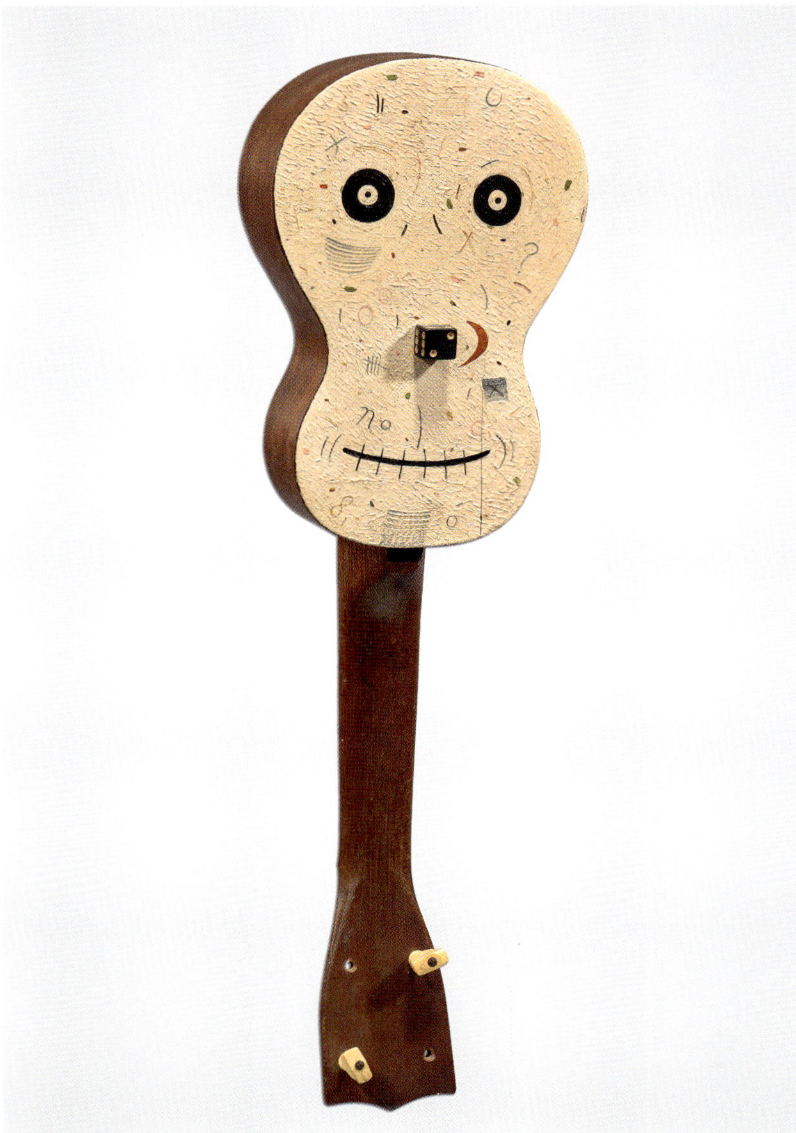

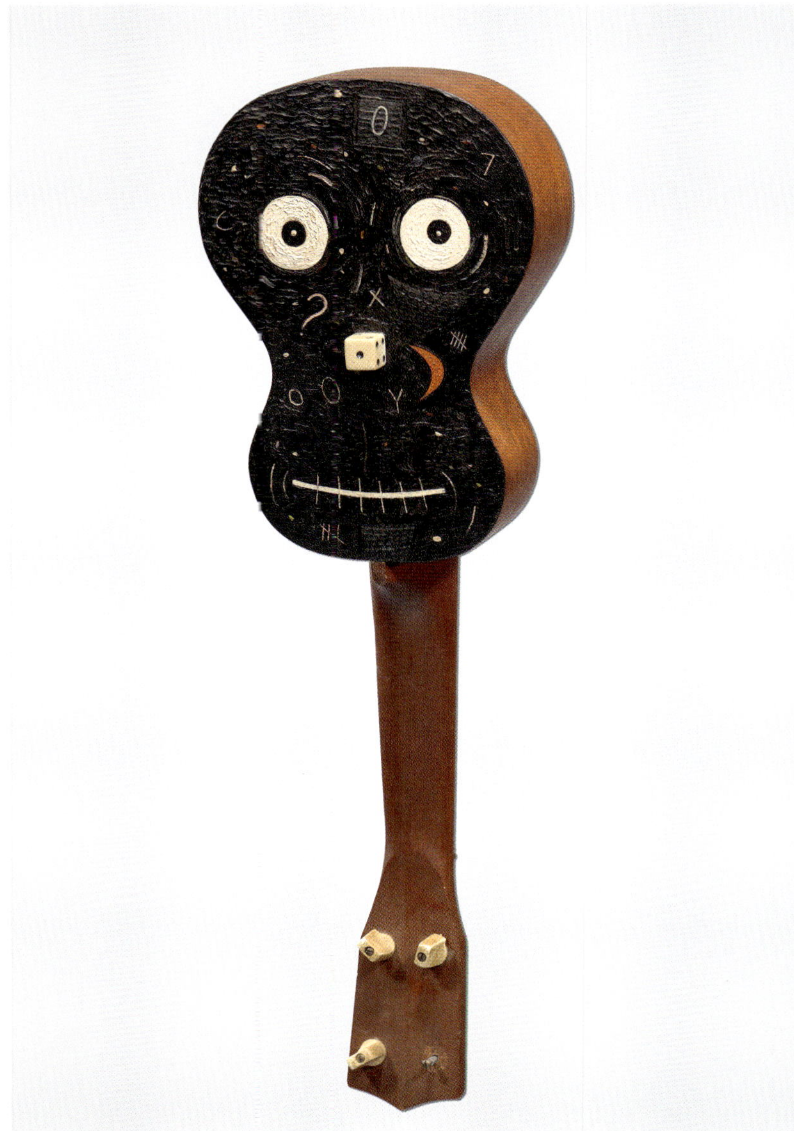

Mrs. Y'Keki, 2001.
Wood ukelele, acrylic, and dice, 21 × 6 ¼ × 3 ½ in.
Collection of the Artist.

Mr. Roy Smeck, 1997.
Wood ukelele, acrylic, and dice, 23 ¾ × 6 × 4 in.
Collection of Michael Stevens.

they received a Distinguished Service Award from California State University, Sacramento, in 2000.

In 2001, Adan and Stevens also held a show at Sacramento State in the Robert Else Gallery, this exhibition also titled *Mr. & Mrs.* and curated by Elaine O'Brien. It not only included art but lunchboxes, wind-up tin toys, and Adan's notorious rubber nose collection. A year later, Adan completed a new public art project: seven site-specific, ceramic-tile murals for the childcare facility in the Capitol Area East End Complex in Sacramento. Titled *Knick, Knack, Paddywhack,* the scenes were destined for the building's exterior and were, as in her previous public art projects, composed of white stoneware clay with black imagery. Adan carved and etched the imagery into the greenware surface of each tile after it was glazed but not yet fired, using a technique akin to that of her scratchboards. Working with ceramic artist Tony Natsoulas, she then bisque-fired the tiles, gave each one a clear glaze to provide a subtle sheen, and fired them a second time. Meant for children, the imagery was nevertheless in Adan's signature style, including letters, numbers, plants, birds, animals, and whimsical abstract shapes. Some images were too large for a single tile and therefore extended onto adjacent ones. Collectively, the seven murals created a running narrative, installed at child height to encourage interaction.

Black-Eyed Susan

In 2004, when Stevens retired from high school teaching, Adan gave up running the Encina Art Gallery. They did not remain idle for long, however, and that fall began team-teaching one day a week as adjunct professors at Sacramento City College. For one semester, they added a night class to their course load but found the students too tired to concentrate and so did not offer it again. For the next fifteen years, Stevens and Adan provided instruction in oil painting, acrylic painting, beginning drawing, two-dimensional design, three-dimensional design, collage and assemblage, and pen-and-ink. In 2010, on top of their teaching duties, they became the directors/curators of the newly remodeled Kondos Gallery on campus, both due to their Encina Art Gallery experience and because of their long and deep relationship with the local arts community. They retired from teaching and curating in 2019.

Another opportunity also presented itself in JAYJAY, a Sacramento gallery owned and operated by Beth Jones and Lynda Jolley, which had been in business for five years by the time Adan and Stevens began showing there in 2005. One of the most respected art venues in the city, it displayed work by the region's top painters, sculptors, and photographers—about twenty in all—Jones and Jolley seeking aesthetic diversity and, at the same time, consistency in the strong reputations of their artists, which for most extended well beyond Sacramento. Adan and Stevens made their 2005 debut in a *New from the Stable Show.* A year later, they partnered on a two-person exhibition, *His & Hers.*

Adan's contributions to JAYJAY shows included oils on canvas, scratchboards, and works on paper. There were also collaborations with Stevens. The *His & Hers* exhibition was named after the show's signature

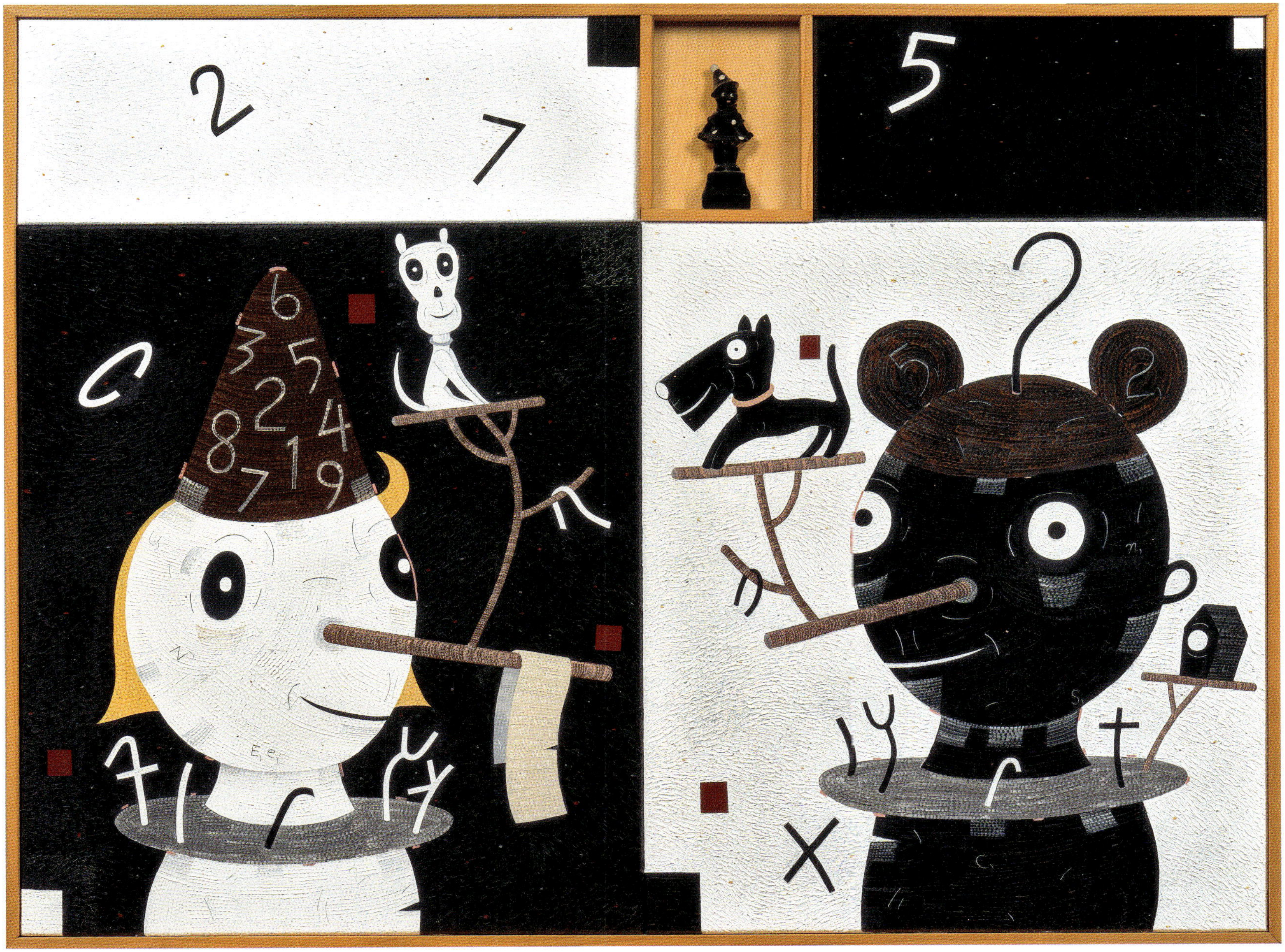

Black-Eyed Susan (In Memory of Reilly and Murphy), 2006.
Oil, ceramic, and acrylic on canvas, 36 × 48 ½ in. Collection of Rita Gibson.

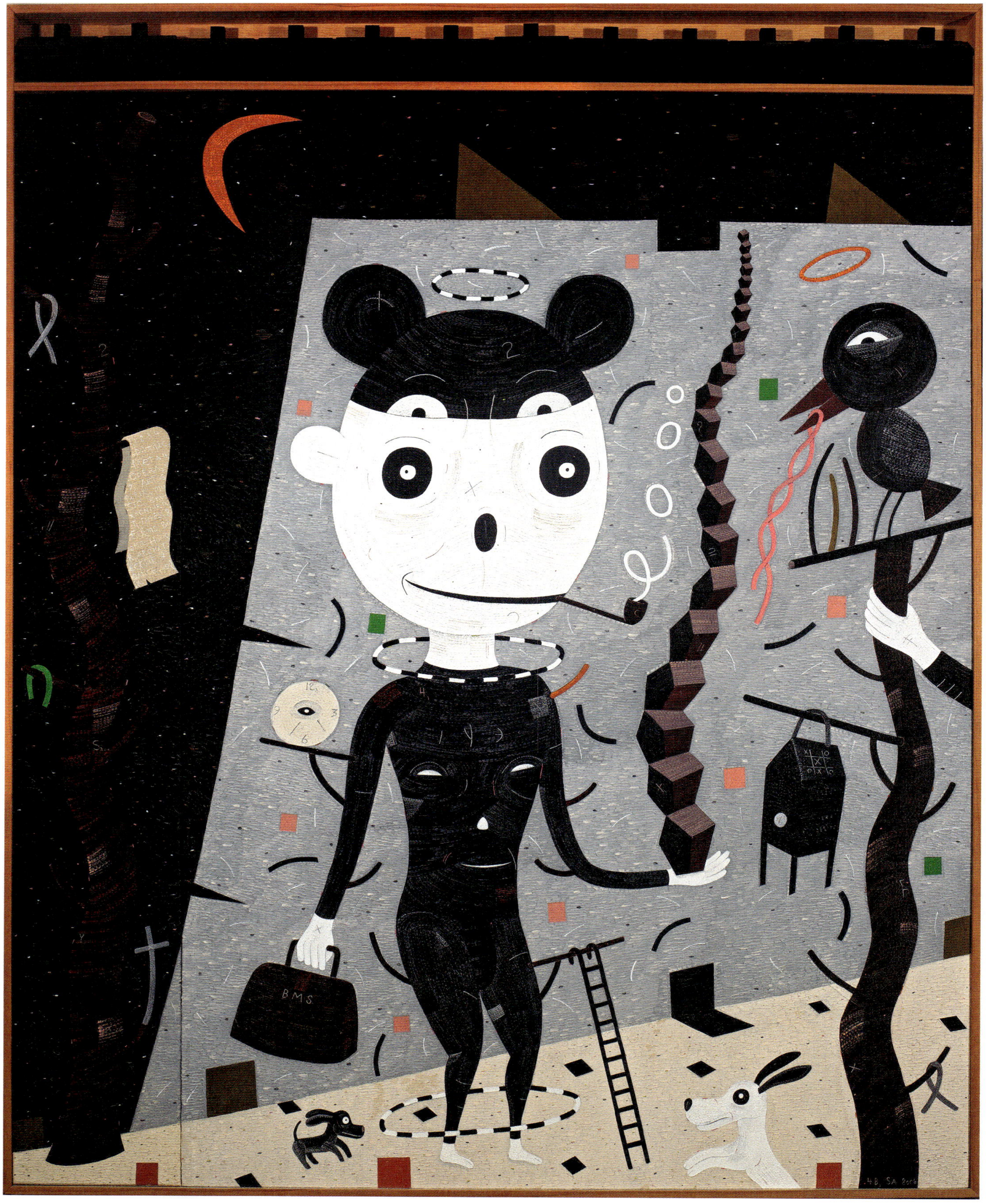

Smoke Signals: Home-Age to Brent Smith (1941–2002), 2006.
Oil on canvas and wood, 65 ½ × 52 ¼ in. Collection of James A. Sundquist.

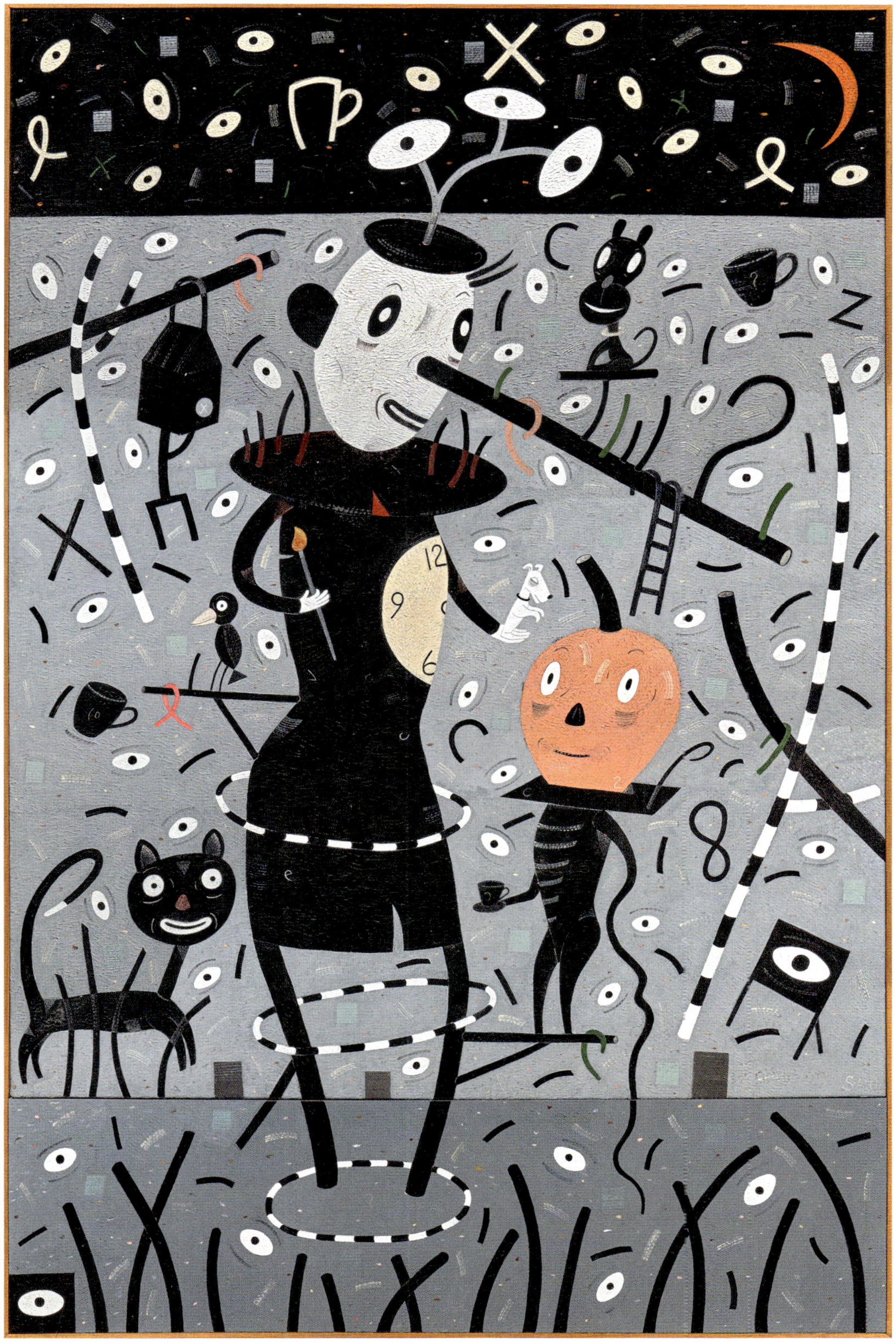

Polka Dots, 2001.
Oil and acrylic on canvas, 58 × 38 in. Collection of Marcy Friedman.

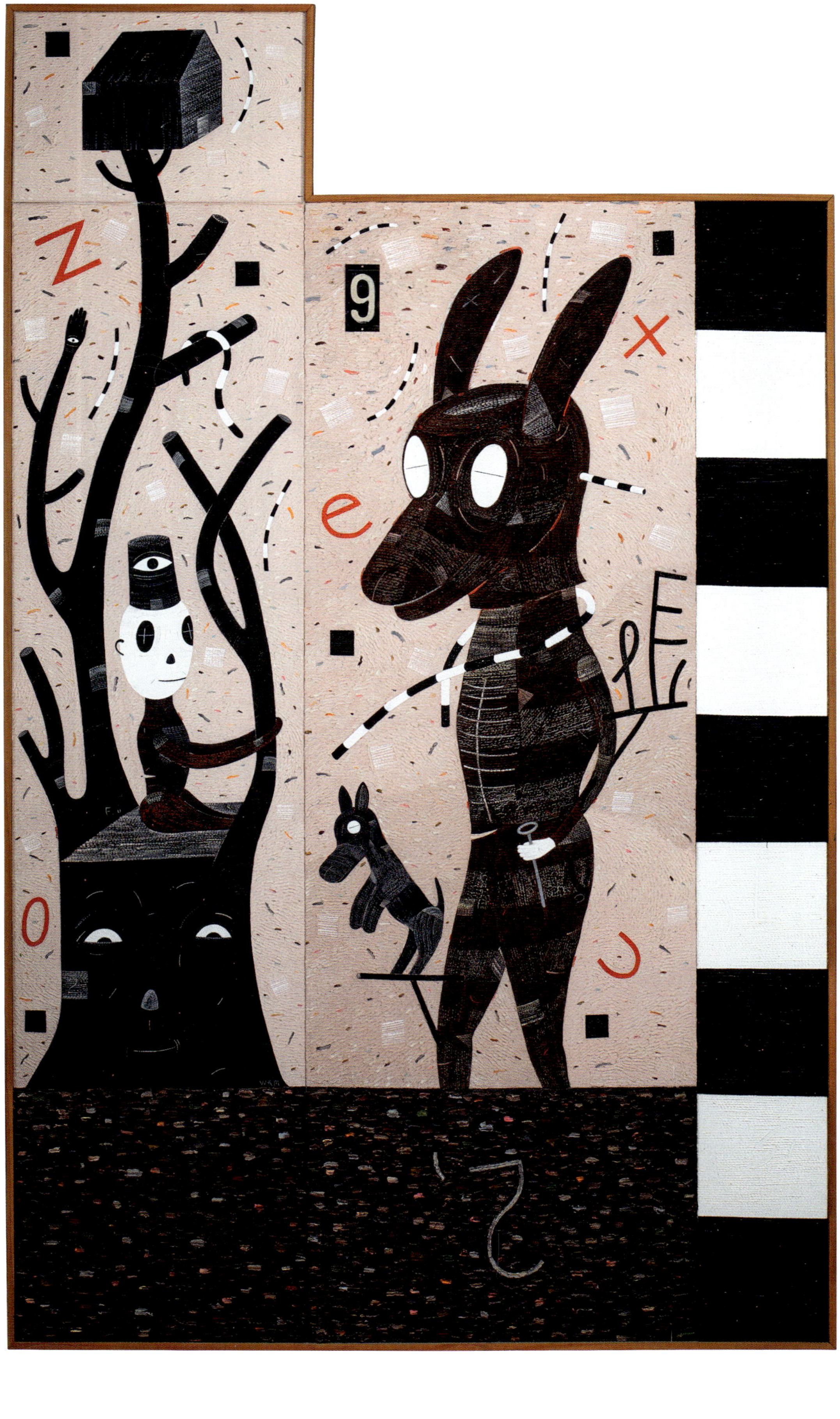

Tough Titty: In Memory of Wulf Meyer, 2006.
Oil, metal, and acrylic on canvas, 85 × 52 in. Collection of Phil and Ginny Cunningham.

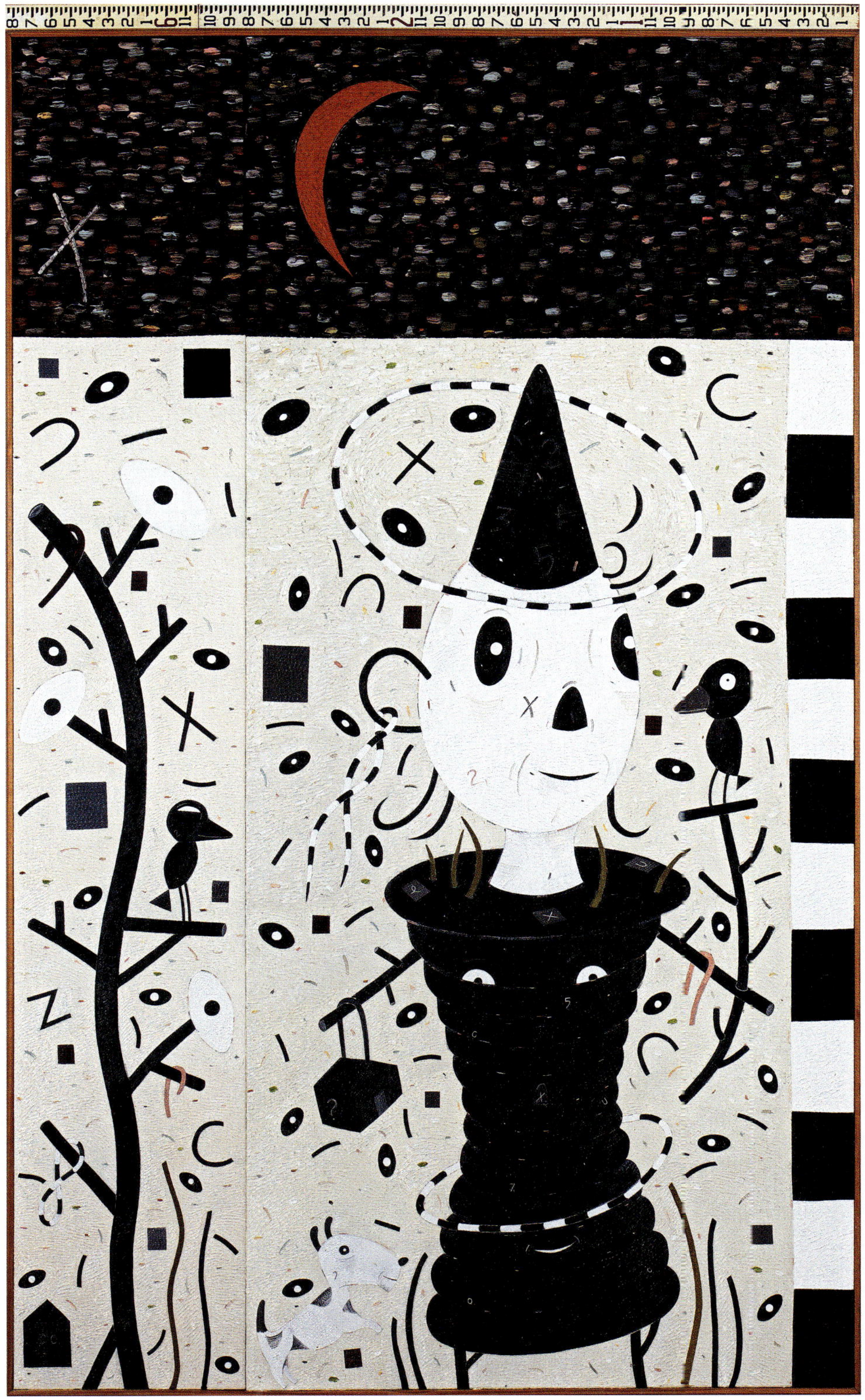

Five O'Clock Shadow, 2002.
Oil on canvas, 74 ½ × 45 in. Collection of Phillip and Marilyn Araki Isenberg.

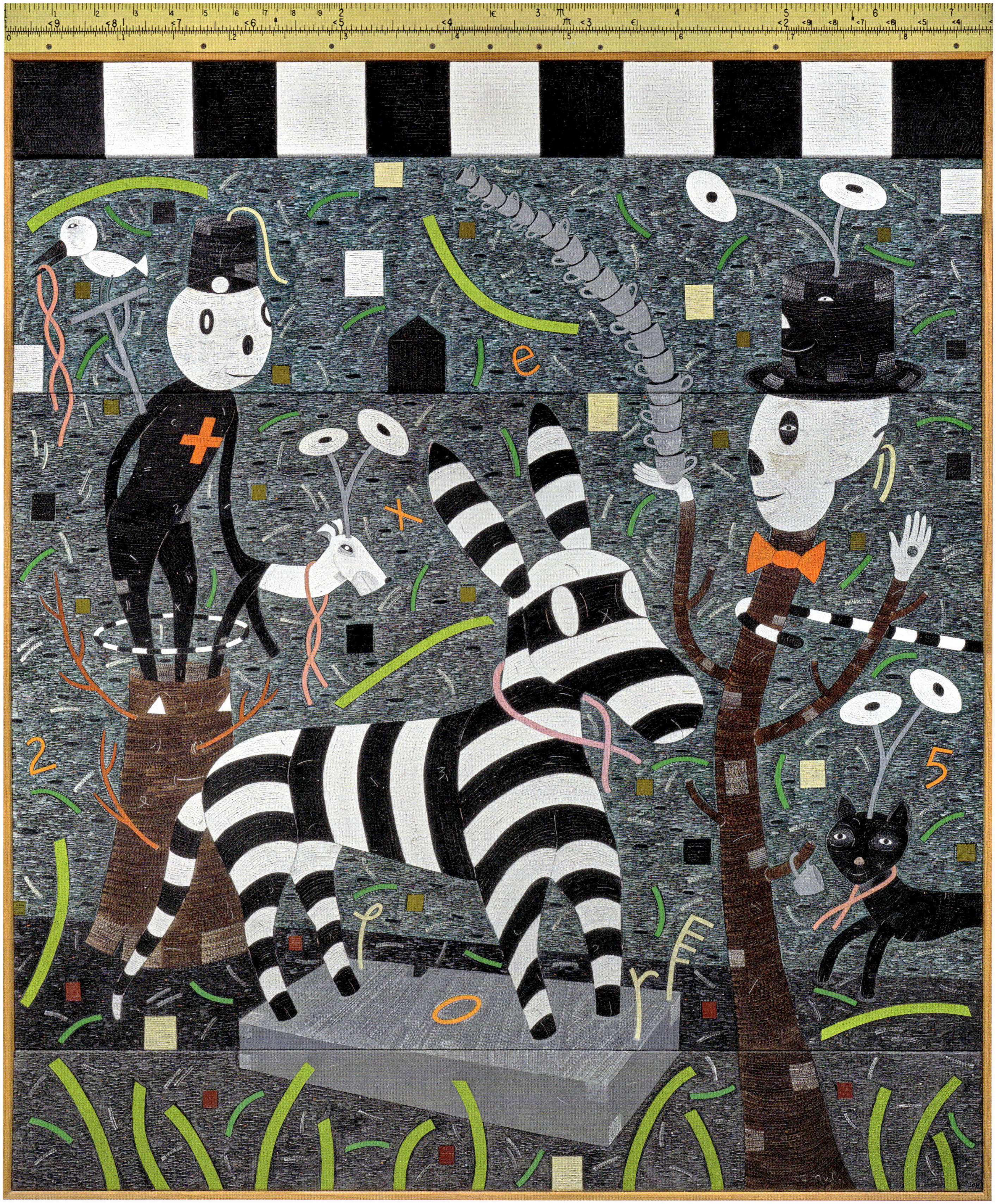

Giddyup: In Memory of Nils Tahti, 2006.
Oil on canvas and wood, 77 × 66 ⅛ in. Collection of Mark and Marjorie Friedman.

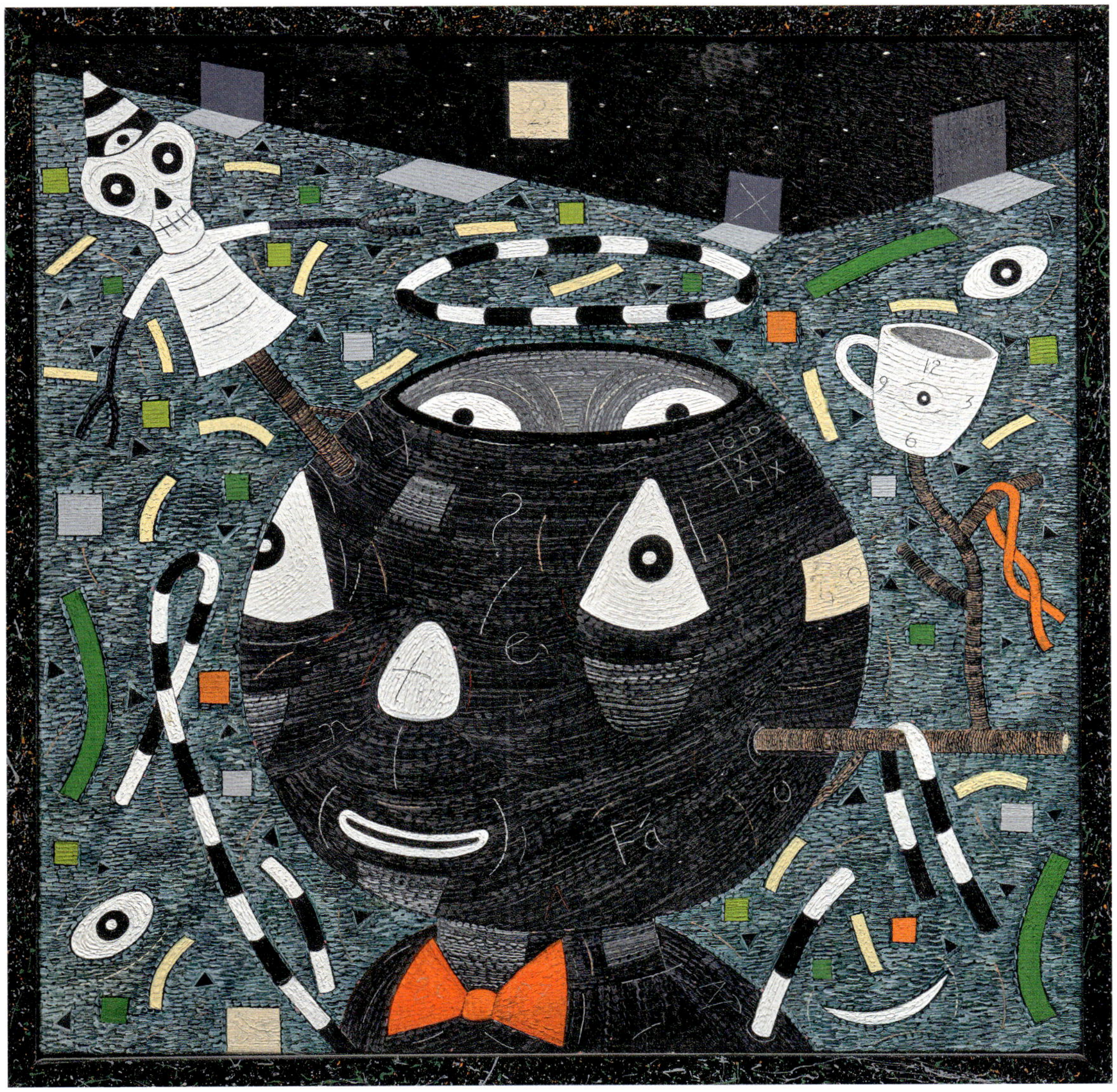

Bug A Boo, 2007.
Oil on canvas, 16 × 16 in. Collection of Donna and Tony Natsoulas.

collaboration, two low-relief heads of a boy and girl. [p. 78] Stevens crafted both heads and created the boy's visage out of dominoes. Adan added her signature brushwork to the girl. While the boy wears a top hat, the girl has a wire-haired terrier on her head, Adan's dog Reilly, who died in 2004, and whose companion, Murphy, would pass away that fall. Between these two sweet faces, a case with small and decidedly less angelic figures inside gave the work what both artists felt was a necessary, darker edge.

Another work in the show, this one entirely by Adan, also memorialized the couple's cherished pets. *Black-Eyed Susan (In Memory of Reilly & Murphy)* included not only the two playfully happy canines but Adan and Stevens as well, both rendered as toys. [p. 81] Indeed, much of the exhibition was about loss, as Adan also included memorials to friends, the works counting among the largest and most complex of her career. Included were *Smoke Signals: Home-Age to Brent Smith,* her friend who died tragically in 2002 [p. 82]; *Tough Titty: In Memory of Wulf Meyer,* an art teacher, graphic designer, and fellow Himovitz artist who died prematurely in 2005 [p. 84, p. 86]; and *Giddyup: In Memory of Nils Tahti,* a painting honoring Tahti, who had died at fifty and was the son of friends Jane and Alvar Tahti, Alvar being a fellow artist.

All these paintings were deeply personal and rendered with a level of detail and brushwork that required many months to complete, a process that was tedious but mentally restorative. Smith, a leader in the "Small is Beautiful"/ Energy Efficiency Movement in housing design, is abstractly depicted with Mickey Mouse ears, a teetering stack of houses in his hand and a row of found-object, wooden cabins above his head. *Tough Titty: In Memory of Wulf Meyer* includes a fez-wearing figure seated on a tree bench and facing off with a large, anthropomorphized rabbit and small dog. *Giddyup: In Memory of Nils Tahti* is a tour-de-force of horror vacui, without an inch of canvas left bare. Two figures—one with a tree-trunk body and holding a stack of teetering teacups surely about to fall and shatter—share space with a bird, puppet-dog, cat, and centrally placed striped toy horse. Running across the top of the multi-sectioned canvas are numbers and a yardstick, the latter, perhaps, a measure of life.

Ruffled Feathers

In addition to easel painting, Adan also pursued new public art projects. In 2008, she applied for and received Sacramento Metropolitan Arts Commission funding to produce a large black-and-white ceramic tile mural for Jacinto Creek Park in Sacramento, which took more than a year to complete. Once again, Adan created it like a scratchboard, carving away the negative space to reveal imagery glazed in black, and leaving the carved layer rough, so it would more closely resemble her other artwork. The scene features trees with cropped limbs; a bevy of animals including cats, dogs, snakes, fish, black birds, and a rabbit; as well as buildings and birdhouses. Other tiles included plant forms, letters and numbers, and abstract shapes. A few mostly black tiles included only letters and numbers, suggesting scientific formulas or the periodic table of the elements. She titled the mural *Ruffled Feathers* due to the preponderance of birds.

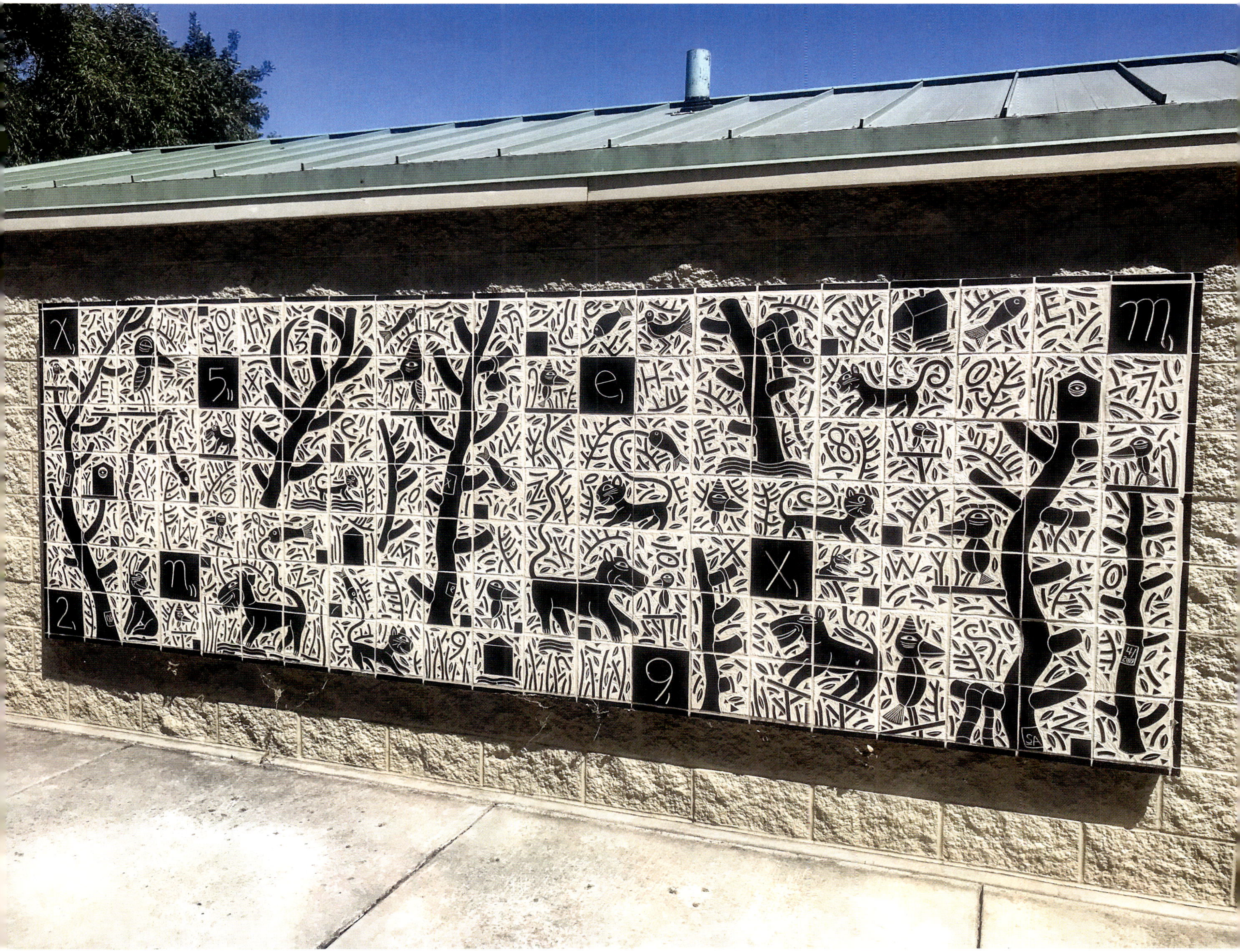

Ruffled Feathers, 2010.
Handmade black and white tile piece for Jacinto Creek Park, Sacramento.
Courtesy of the Sacramento Office of Arts + Culture.

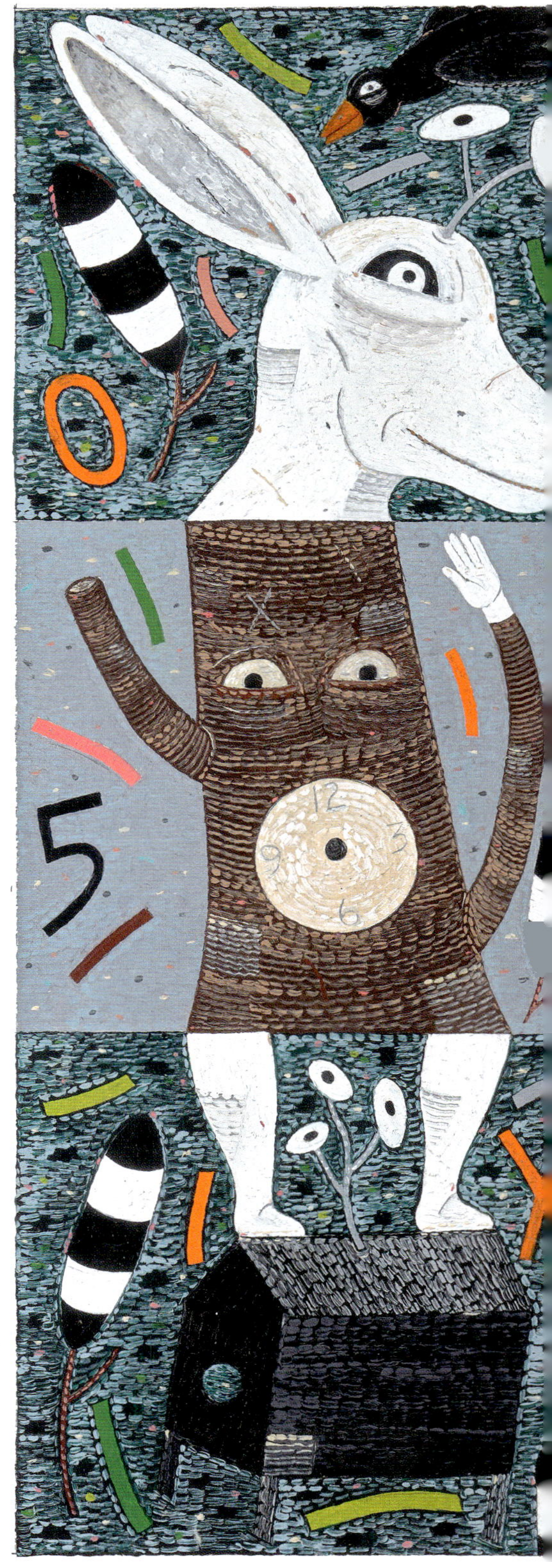

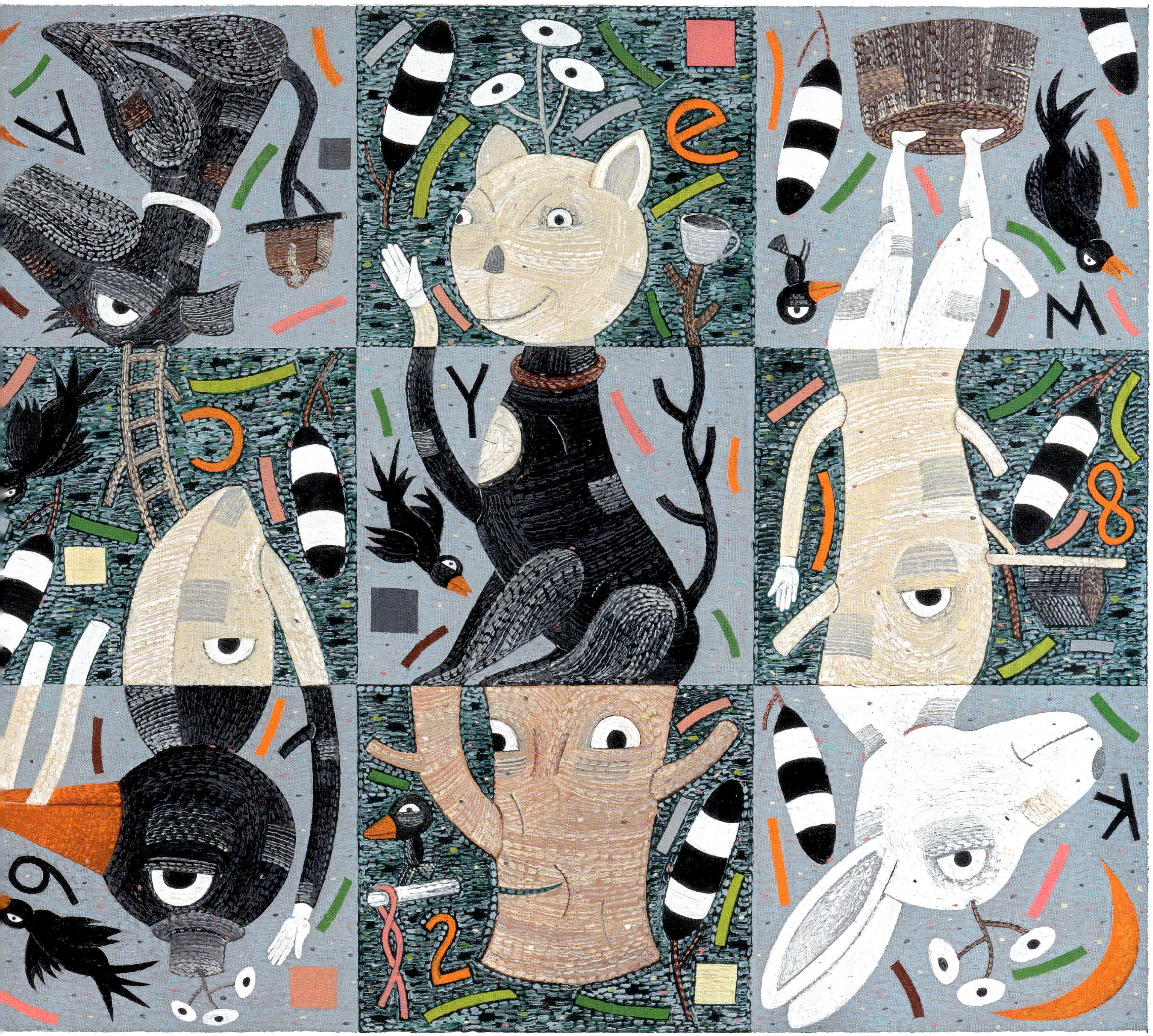

Flying Colors I (Rejected Piece, Terminal B, Sacramento International Airport), 2009.
Oil on gessoed paper, 22 ⅝ × 28 ⅜ in. Collection of Mark and Marjorie Friedman.

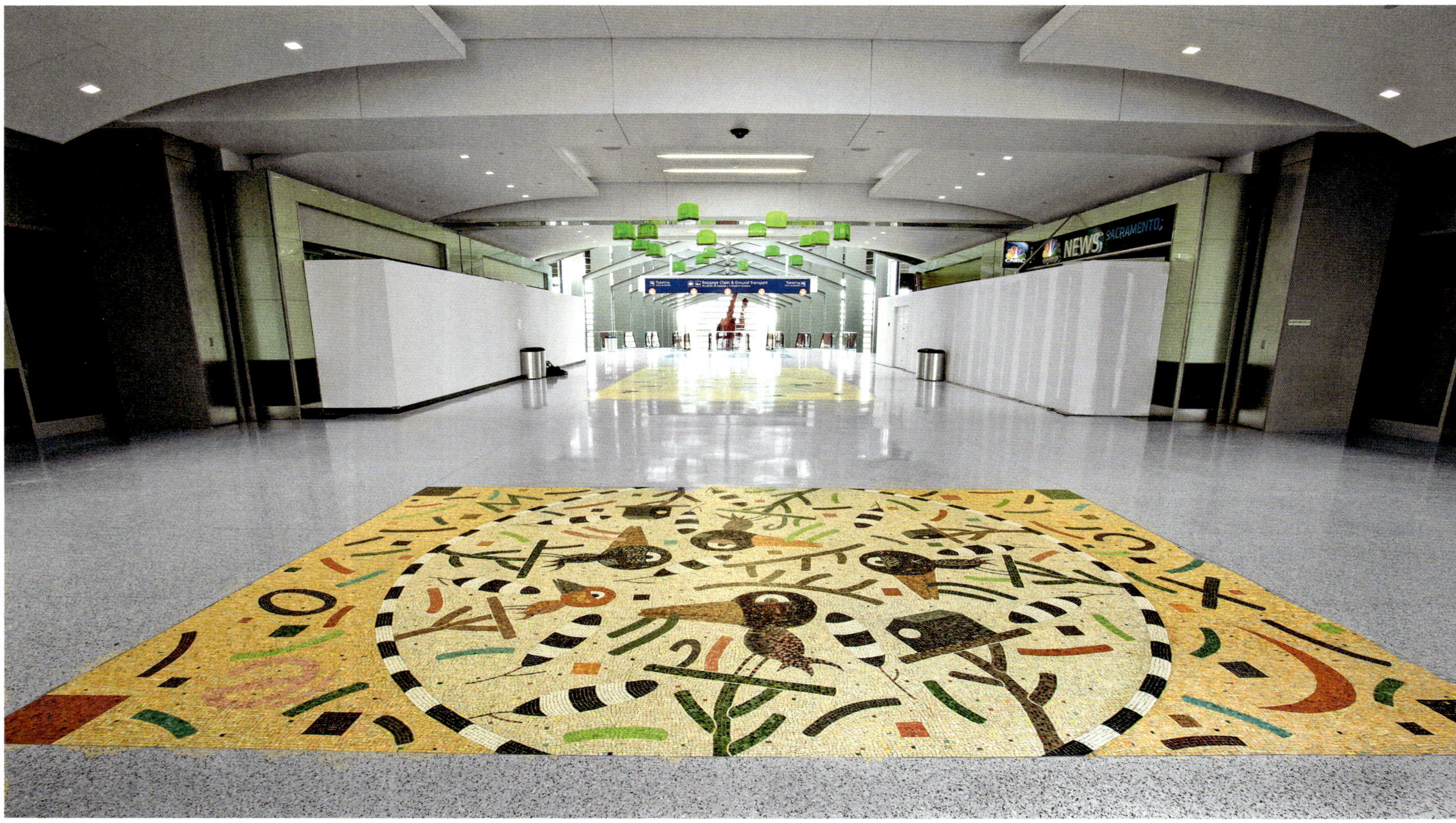

Flying Colors, 2011.
Glass mosaic, 18 × 24 ft. Sacramento International Airport, Sacramento Metropolitan Art Commission.
Photo courtesy of David M. Roth.

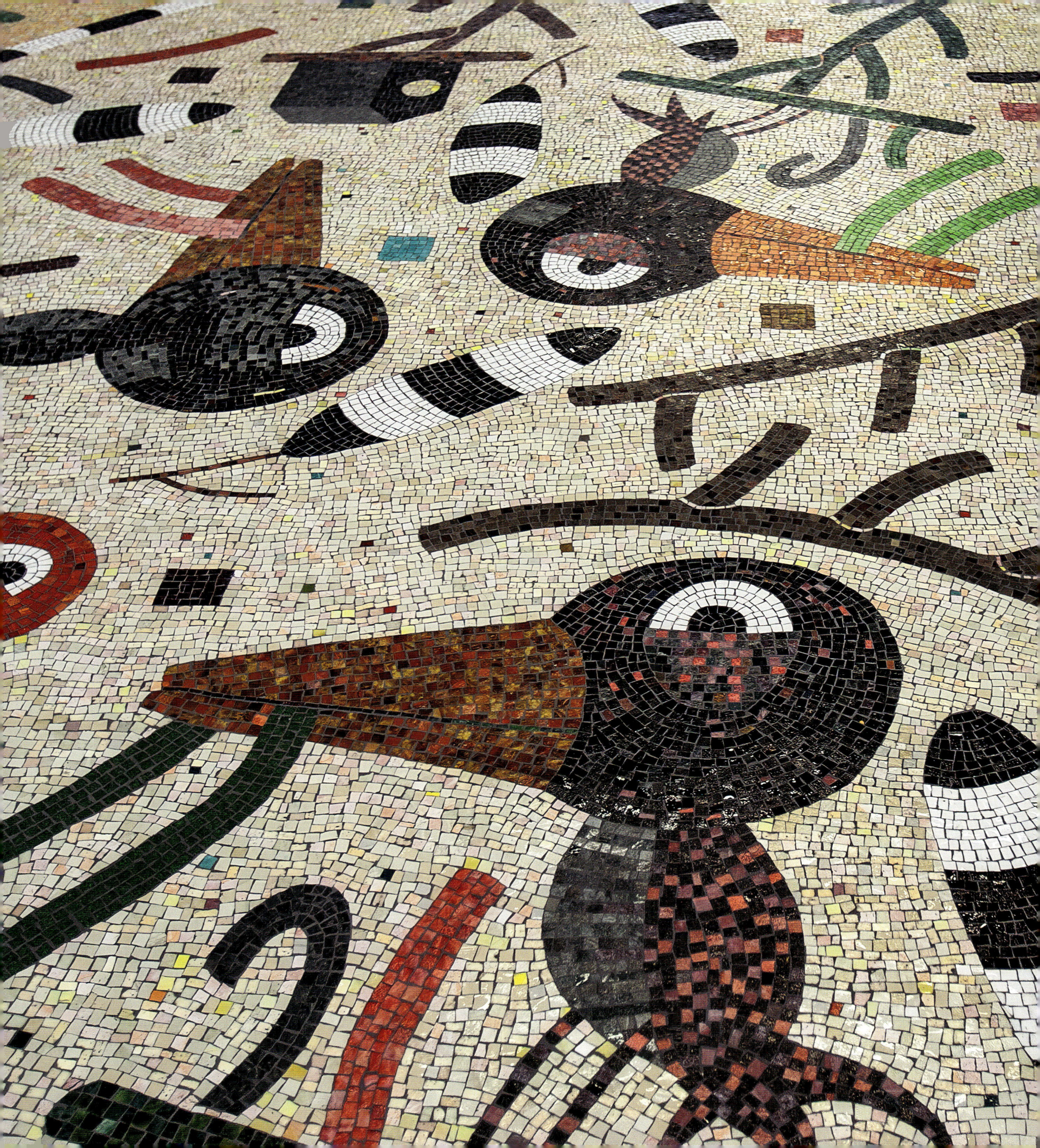

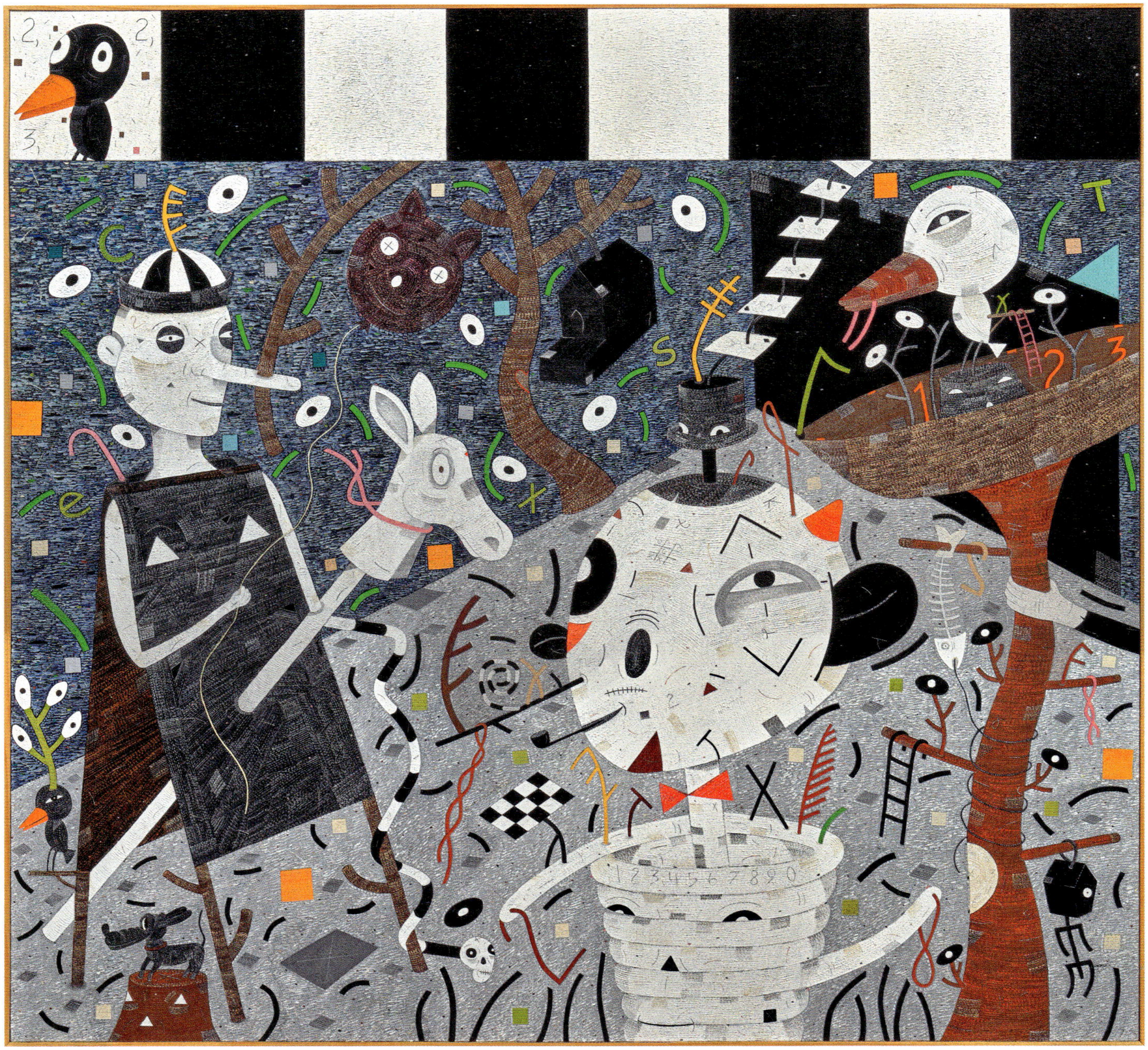

Cabin Number Seven, 2013.
Oil on canvas, 56 × 60 in. Collection of Marcy Friedman.

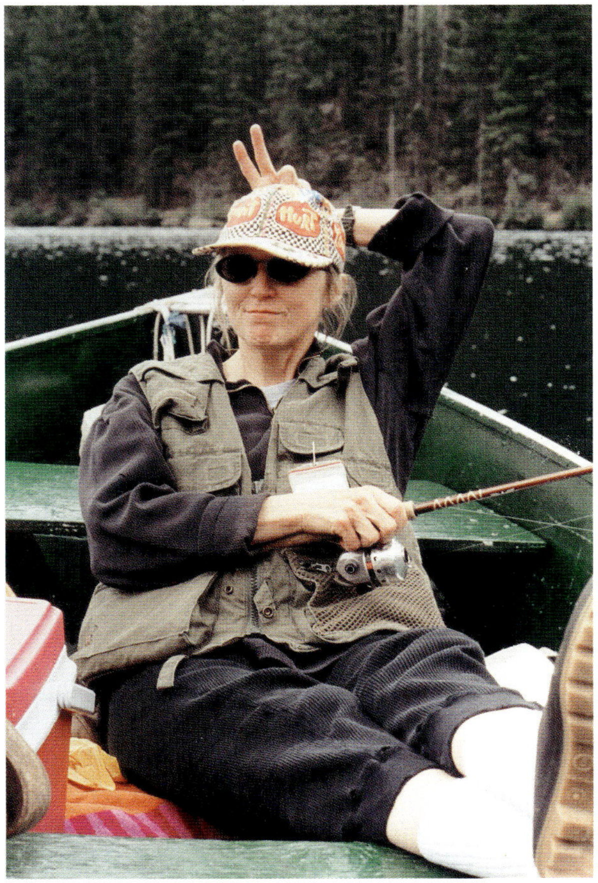

Suzanne Adan in fishing gear at Sardine Lake Resort, 2000. Courtesy of Suzanne Adan.

Although Adan didn't know it at the time, her black birds would soon take center stage in another Sacramento Metropolitan Arts Commission project, an 18-by-24-foot glass mosaic she called *Flying Colors*. It was one of three floor murals destined for the Sacramento International Airport's new Terminal B, the other two by artists Lynn Criswell and Joan Moment. Adan applied for the competitive project by submitting a two-dimensional interpretation of a four-sided German puzzle toy, in which the head, torso, and legs could rotate to create different configurations of animals. Adan's preliminary drawing/painting, which survives, was regarded highly enough for her to be asked to make an in-person presentation of her idea, which did not go well. [pp. 90–91] One of the government panelists—the one who controlled the budget—felt the animal parts might be interpreted as dismembered bodies and cause distress to those with a fear of flying. Though the other airport commission panelists disagreed, the naysayer won out, meaning Adan was asked to revise her design.

Adan was not happy but nevertheless complied, all the while remaining calcitrant that this version, too, should be equally emblematic of her work. After several attempts and back-and-forths with the project manager, she came up with an acceptable proposal. It included birds, along with birdhouses and perches, striped cattails, and other plant forms set within a pale gold background that obliquely referenced Sacramento's mineral history. [pp. 92–93] The work's central activity was framed within a black-and-white striped circle, which in turn was surrounded by darker gold ornamented with colorful abstract shapes. Unlike her other public projects, Adan did not have to fabricate these tiles nor help install them. Installation work was done by Franz Mayer of Munich, a firm that knew how to make the floor mosaic both beautiful and durable, as it would need to withstand thousands of passengers—along with their roller bags—traversing it each day.

In 2013, Adan and Stevens held another joint show at JAYJAY. Because it had been seven years since their last exhibition at the gallery, they titled it *Seven Year Itch*. Adan's pieces included paintings and detailed pencil-on-paper collages with an abundance of provocative writing, the latter new for her. Also new were her highly finished drawings on ceramic plates.

Adan's largest and most ambitious contribution to the exhibition was *Cabin Number Seven*, a 56-by-60-inch oil that dazzles the eye with confetti-like brushwork and detail. In it, amid an abundance of shapes, letters, and polka dots, are two large and rather menacing figures. One is Pinocchio-like, with dark sunken eyes, a tree branch growing from his nose, and a snake-like arm with a skull at the end. Mitigating these more sinister elements are his playful beanie, cat balloon, hobby horse, and sandwich board body. The other character is more skeletal and smoking a pipe, its body coiled like a spring, its head balancing a tiny hat connected to a set of floating stairs. There are also birds—one nesting in a boat atop a tree held by a disembodied arm—as well as a small dog resembling Pluto. Double helixes and ladders hang from tree limbs, as do a fish skeleton, bird house with anthropomorphic arms and legs, and a black cottage representing Cabin Number Seven.

It is a surreal and enigmatic image that is at once ominous and delightful, but it is also a real-life parody of the long-running, early July vacation that Adan and Stevens would take to Sardine Lake in the Lakes Basin area of Tahoe National Forest in California. While there, Adan and Stevens encountered all number of creatures, including birds, snakes, coyotes, and bears, as well as abundant trees and wildflowers. The boat in the tree represents the couple's love of trout fishing, the fish skeleton what was left of the day's catch. The title stems from the fact that Adan and Stevens stayed in the same cabin for twenty-seven years in a row, their last visit taking place in 2024, when they decided that they had too many pets to take along, and that there were too many campsite stairs to climb while carrying gear.

No Spring Chicken

Adan and Stevens exhibited at JAYJAY again in early 2019. The impetus for the show was *Kit n' Kaboodle,* an interactive installation for children and their parents that the artists had made the previous fall for the Crocker Art Museum's education galleries. The installation at the museum consisted of large, saccharinely adorable cutouts of 1950s-looking children that

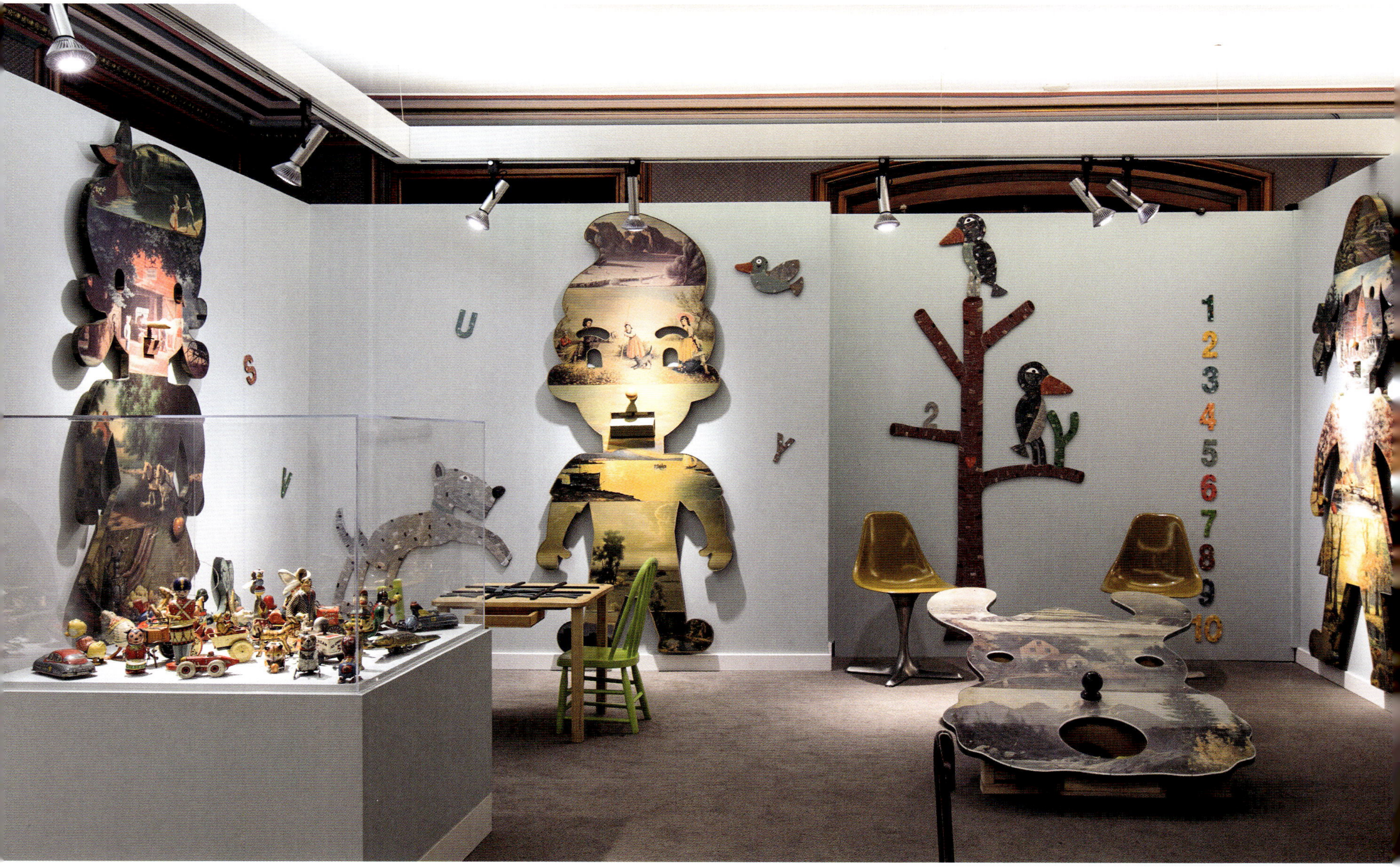

hung on the wall, each layered with Stevens's found, thrift-store reproductions of paintings. There were also playful, plywood images of dogs, cats, birds, trees, and numbers painted by Adan, as well as treasures from their collection of vintage toys. At JAYJAY, the large cutouts anchored other of the artists' works dating back to 1979, the show a mini retrospective of sorts.

That same spring, Adan curated her own version of the *Gun* show that she had participated in twenty-four years earlier at the Michael Himovitz Gallery. For this, she convinced the venturesome couple Mima and Numan Begovic—respectively director and curator of artspace1616 on Del Paso Boulevard—to host it. The updated version, called *The Gun Show,* was more overtly anti-gun than the first, the Columbine High School massacre and numerous subsequent mass shootings having occurred in the interim. Though Adan "had some reservations" about organizing the show given how volatile issues around guns and gun violence had become, she felt that the issue was so consequential that she could not remain complacent. Guns were also significant to her own history:

> There definitely has been a history in my life attached to guns. Growing up in the post-war baby boom generation, all of the boys that I knew in the 1950s (including my brother) had an arsenal of guns: cap guns, ray guns, BB guns, homemade rubber band guns, etc. . . . In the late 1960s and early 1970s, every male artist/friend created art using the gun as subject matter. Maybe it was due to the turmoil and chaos of our times, since we were fascinated with assassinations, civil rights issues, riots, the draft, the Vietnam War, etc.[43]

Adan asked 35 artists she knew and respected to contribute artwork, including herself and Stevens.[44] One of the most controversial submissions was by her old friend Ron Peetz, who submitted an AR-15 rifle atop a child's school desk with bibles strewn underneath. The work's title, derived from platitudes given in the wake of gun tragedies, was *Thoughts & Prayers.*

Artspace1616 closed in early 2021, in large part due to the COVID-19 pandemic. JAYJAY closed that May for much the same reason. The virus also forced Adan and Stevens into seclusion, as both were fearful of contracting it because of their age, 75 and 76 respectively, and because they had friends who had become very ill or died. Adan's brother, Jim, also died in October 2021, though not from COVID, his passing affecting Adan deeply. She had always relied on her older brother as a friend and source of emotional support.

For more than two years, Adan and Stevens did not socialize nor see people. They even questioned whether making art was a legitimate pursuit in the face of such tragedy, though they did not stop. Stevens created a series of pop-out portraits of people with found object backgrounds and carved board (bored!) pieces in relief. Adan worked on pencil drawings with collage elements cut from magazine photos and additional found objects. She made one of these in honor of her brother: *The Magic Chef (In Memory of James Adan).* It includes a "portrait" of Jim attached to a Magic Chef stove surrounded by Spanish recipes from her grandmother's cookbook, a remembrance of their cooking days in 4-H. **[p. 101]**

← Kit n' Kaboodle installation, Crocker Art Museum, 2018.

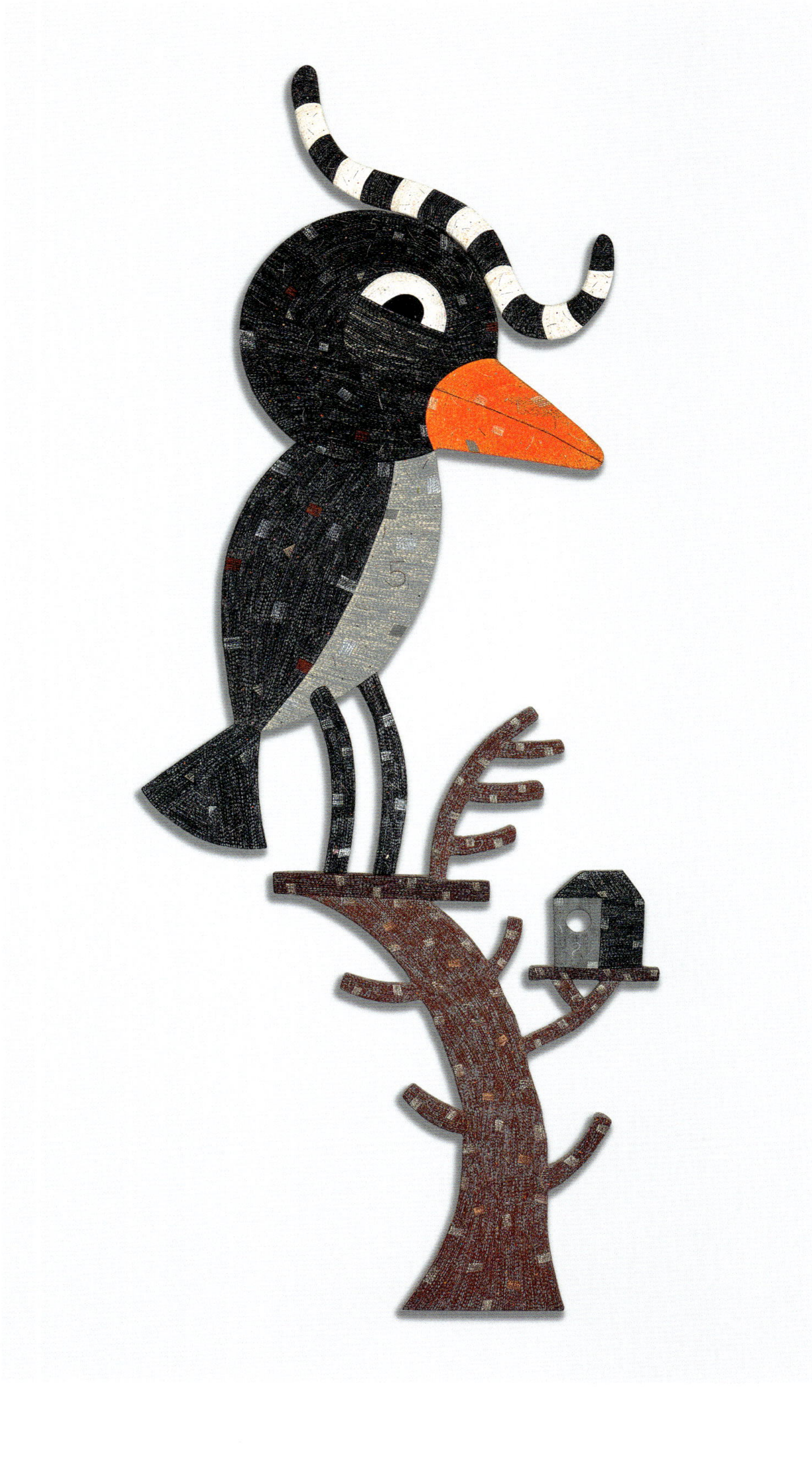

Crow's Feet, 2019.
Acrylic on plywood, 52 ½ × 22 ½ in. Collection of Susan, Pamela, and Catherine Hopper.

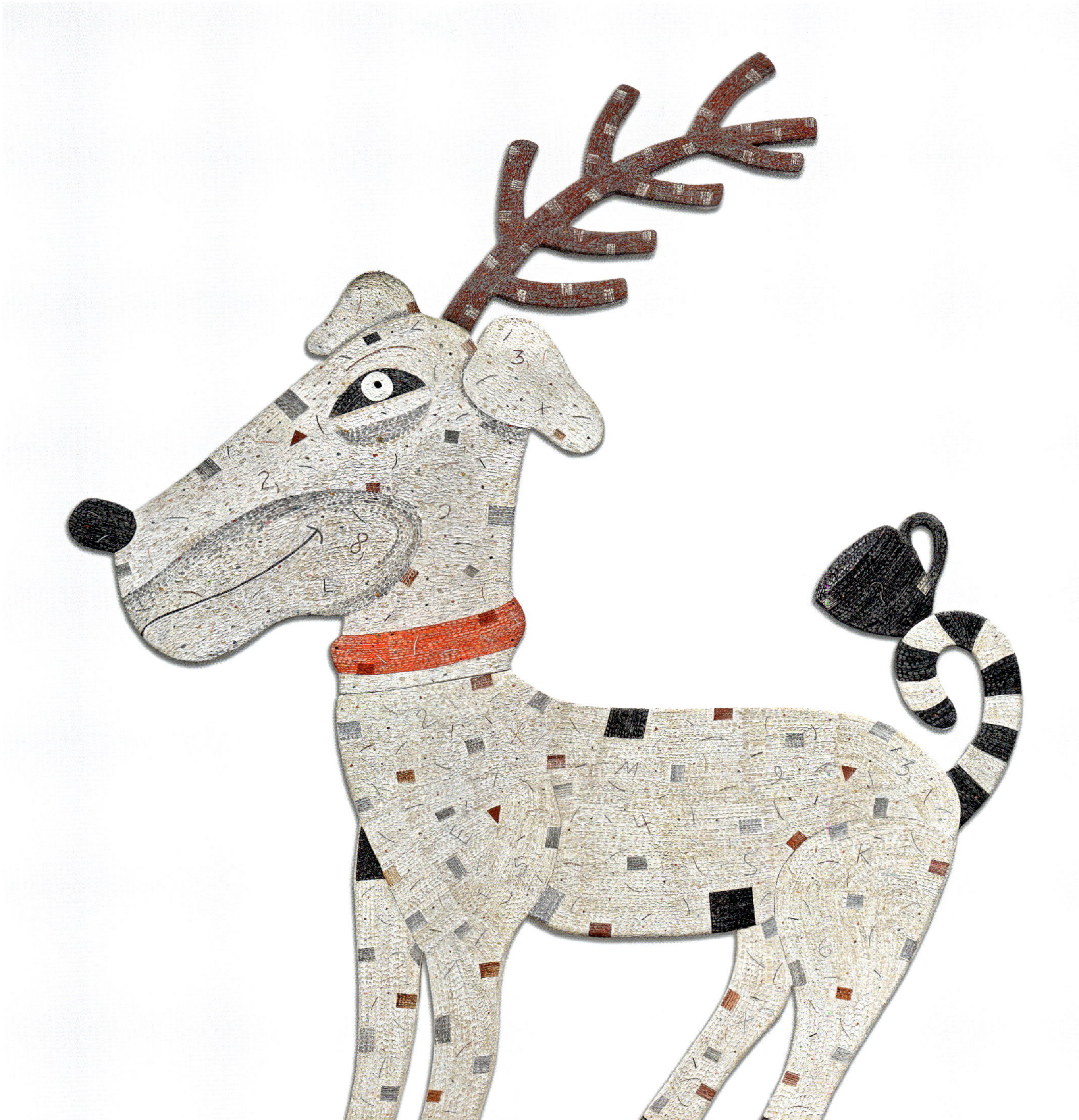

Murphy (In Memory of John Stevens), 2019.
Acrylic on plywood, 34 × 29 × ½ in. Collection of Keri Stevens and Beau Stevens.

Adan and Stevens gradually re-emerged back into society starting in the second half of 2023, wearing masks as they returned to restaurants, galleries, and an occasional dinner party. In late 2023, Adan accepted an invitation to hold an exhibition of her work at the Crocker Art Museum, a retrospective to take place in her eightieth year. She came up with the exhibition's title herself, *Suzanne Adan: I'm No Spring Chicken,* which was not only honest but conveyed her typical, self-deprecating humor with a hint of Aunt Bee nostalgia, making it clear that her talent, humor, and idiosyncratic views of the world remained still very much intact.

1 Renny Pritikin, *Flatlanders 3: A Regional Roundup* (Richard L. Nelson Gallery and The Fine Arts Collection, University of California, Davis), 6.

2 Adan remembers one Sunday school teacher, Almira Borach, with special fondness. Borach was married to Leon Borach, who co-owned the local Borach's Store with his brother.

3 "Cacheville School Plans Fun Festival," *Daily Democrat* (Yolo County), circa 1950–1951. Suzanne Adan Archive, clipping, n.p.

4 Suzanne Adan, interview with author, March 26, 2025.

5 Suzanne Adan, interview with author, May 1, 2025.

6 Suzanne Adan, "A 4-H'er Reports," Suzanne Adan Archive, clipping, 1963.

7 Suzanne Adan, "4-H Club Member's Record," 1965, 6.

8 Adan interview with author, May 1, 2025.

9 Adan interview with author, March 26, 2025.

10 Jacqueline Kennedy letter of June 4, 1965. Copy in Suzanne Adan, "4-H Club Member's Record," 1965, letters and correspondence.

11 Adan interview with author, March 26, 2025.

12 Paul Mapes, "Yolo and Willow Oak Youths 4-H All Stars," *The Daily Democrat* (Yolo County), July 13, 1965, 1.

13 Suzanne Adan, "4-H Club Member's Record," 1965, 4–5.

14 Suzanne Adan, interview with author, May 7, 2025.

15 *The Daily Democrat* (Yolo County), July 13, 1965, 1.

16 Suzanne Adan, "Artist Statement," Suzanne Adan Archive, November 6, 2017.

17 Adan, "Artist Statement."

18 Adan, "Artist Statement."

19 Adan, "Artist Statement."

20 Suzanne Adan, "Artist Autobiography," 2023, in Elaine O'Brien's exhibition *She Laughs Back: Feminist Wit in 1970s Bay Area Art,* 2024. Suzanne Adan Archive.

21 Adan interview with author, May 1, 2025.

22 Adan interview with author, May 7, 2025.

23 Adan, "Artist Autobiography," n.d., 1.

24 The nicknames came from Adan's name and penchant for painting rainbows, Stevens's unruly bushy hair, and Peetz's frequent sunburned skin from being a swimmer.

25 Adan, "Artist Autobiography," n.d., 1.

26 See Scott A. Shields, *Knock on Wood: Sculpture by Michael Stevens* (Crocker Art Museum, 2003), n.p.

27 Adan, "Artist Autobiography," n.d., 2.

28 The Candy Store Gallery was celebrated in two exhibitions at the Crocker Art Museum, first in 1981 and then again in 2022.

29 Adan, "Artist Autobiography," n.d., 2.

30 Robert Doty, *Extraordinary Realities* (Whitney Museum of American Art, 1973), 9–12.

31 Doty, *Extraordinary Realities,* 9.

32 Roberta Smith, "Extraordinary Realities," *Artforum* 12 (January 1974): 74.

33 Womanspace gallery records, 1970–1974. Box 2, Folder 9: Exhibition of Works by Suzanne Adan (1974 May 25–June 15), 1974. Smithsonian Archives of American Art.

34 Suzanne Adan, "Artist's Statement," Suzanne Adan Archive, October 1998.

35 Suzanne Adan, "Artist Statement," Suzanne Adan Archive, n.d.

36 "All's well in love and art at CSUS exhibition," California State University Public Affairs Department, published online October 22, 2001, http://www.csus.edu/news/102201mrmrs.htm.

37 Shields, *Knock on Wood,* n.p.

38 "Encina Art Gallery Celebrates Its Fifth Anniversary," *The Connection* [San Juan Teachers Association] 2 (September 1998): 9.

39 Suzanne Adan and Michael Stevens, "Finalist Statement for Art Educators of the Year Award," Suzanne Adan Archive, January 9, 2018.

40 Tom Gemma, quoted in Bob Sylva, "A Brush with the Past," republished online June 11, 2004; http://www.encinahighschool.com/teachers/bios.htm

41 Michael Stevens, quoted in Bob Sylva, "A Brush with the Past."

42 "Encina Art Gallery Celebrates Its Fifth Anniversary," 9.

43 Suzanne Adan, "The Gun Show Statement," Suzanne Adan Archive, 2019.

44 Adan, "The Gun Show Statement," 2019.

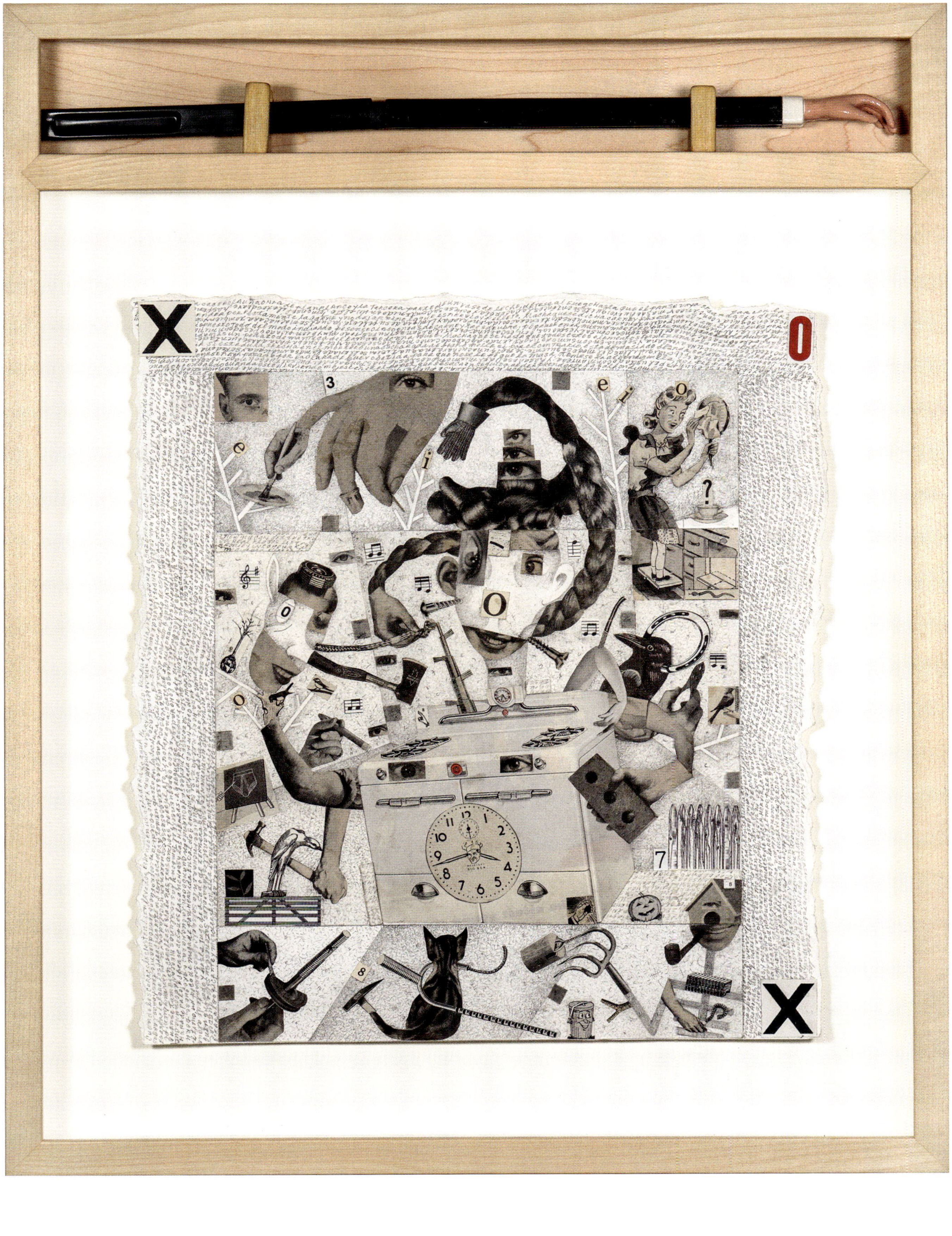

The Magic Chef (In Memory of James Adan), 2021–2023.
Paper, graphite, plastic, and wood, 24 × 19 in. Collection of the Artist.

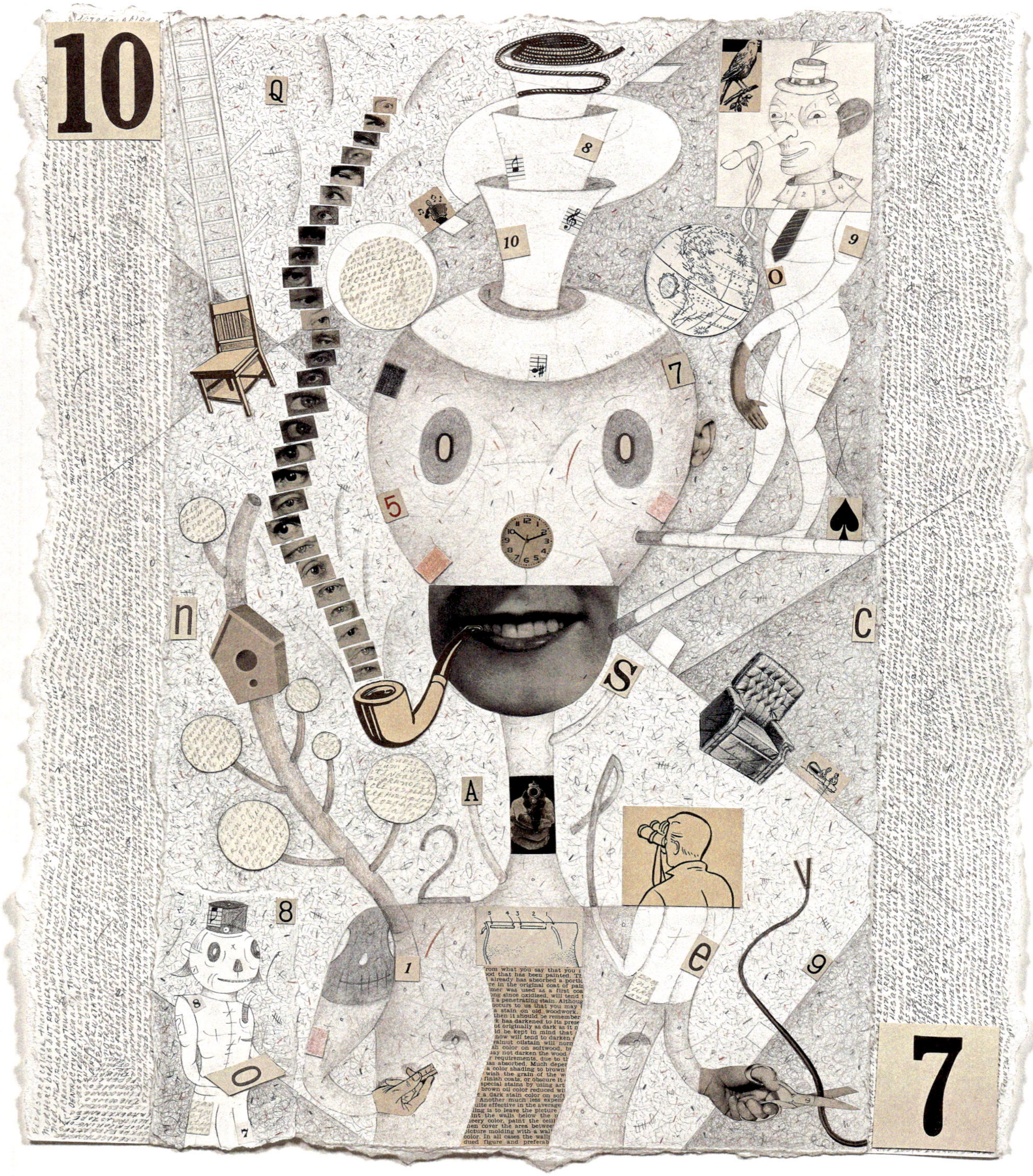

Gazoontite, 2016.
Graphite, magazine, and wood on paper, 18 × 15 ¼ in.
Collection of Patrick Whitnell.

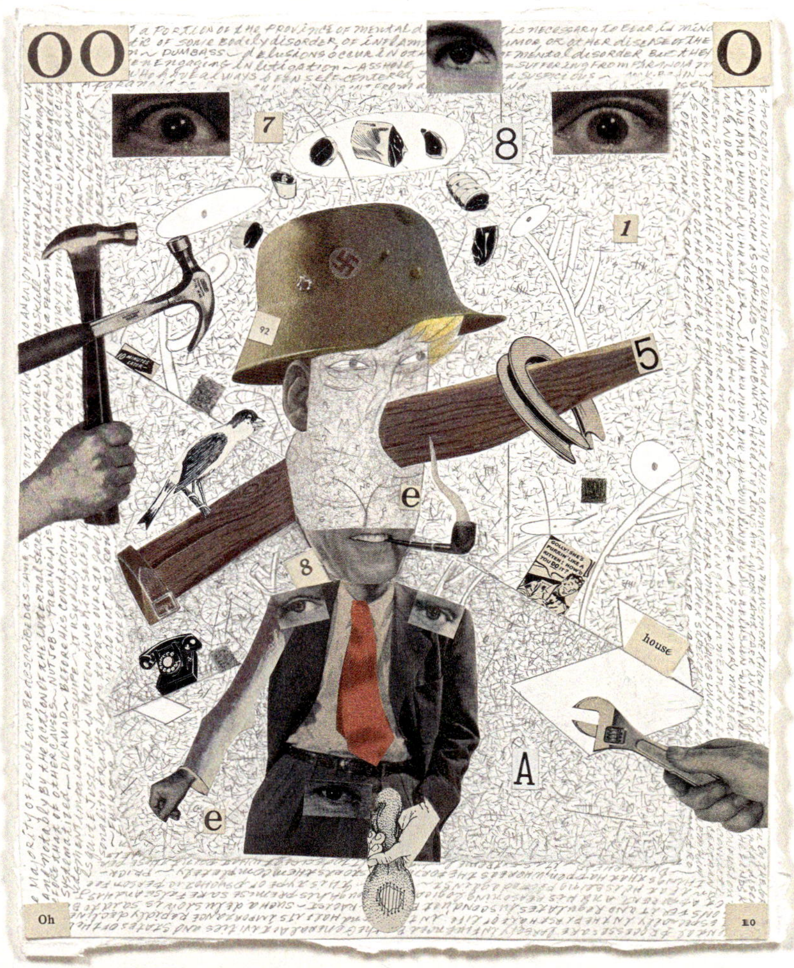

Tweet!, 2017.
Mixed media, graphite, and collage on paper, 10 × 8 in.
Crocker Art Museum, gift from the estate of Nancy Lawrence, 2024.77.2.

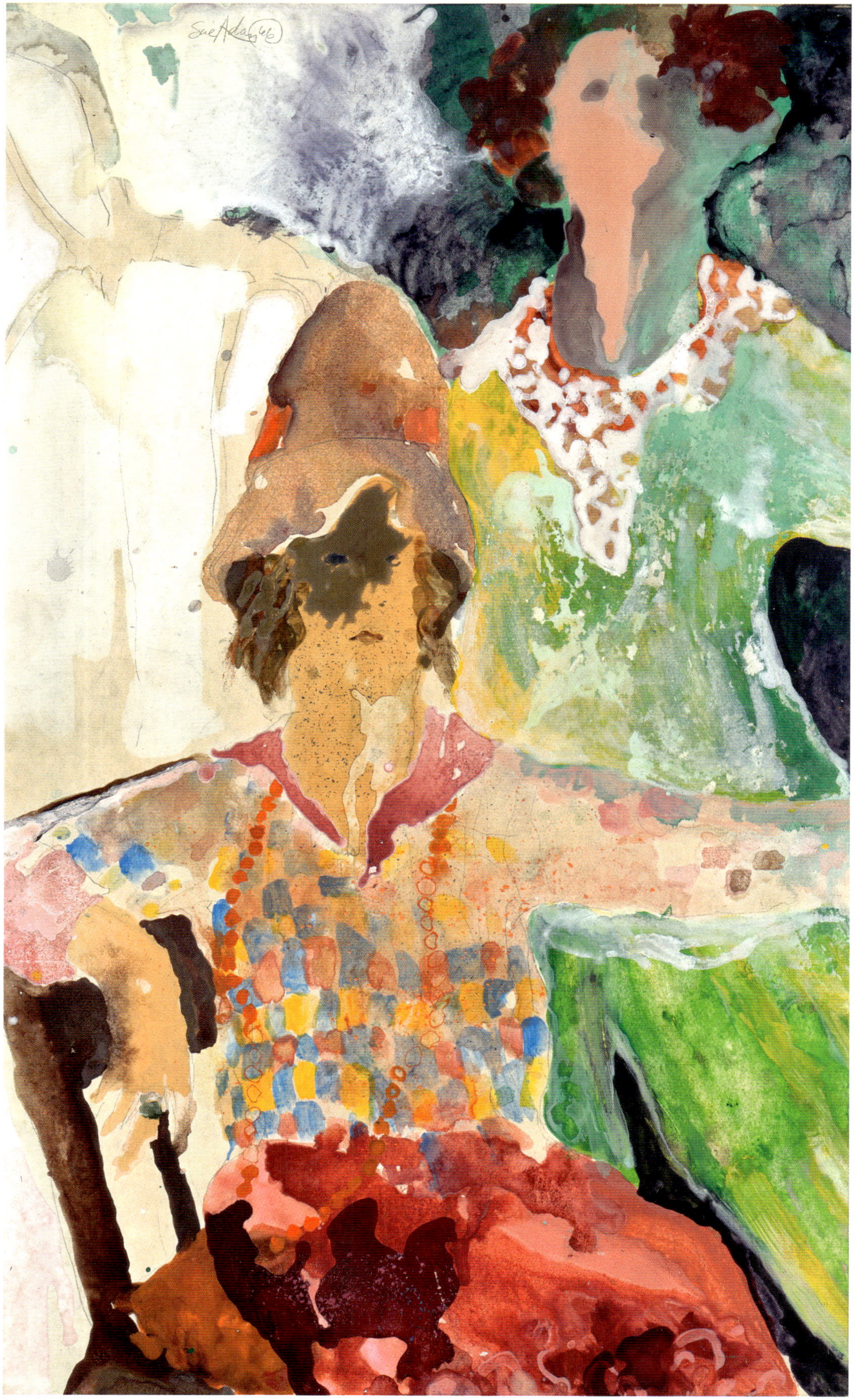

Self Portrait in a 1920s Setting, 1966.
Watercolor, 33 ½ × 21 ¼ in. Collection of the Artist.

Making Art Out of Rainbows: The Education of Suzanne Adan at Sacramento State

Elaine O'Brien

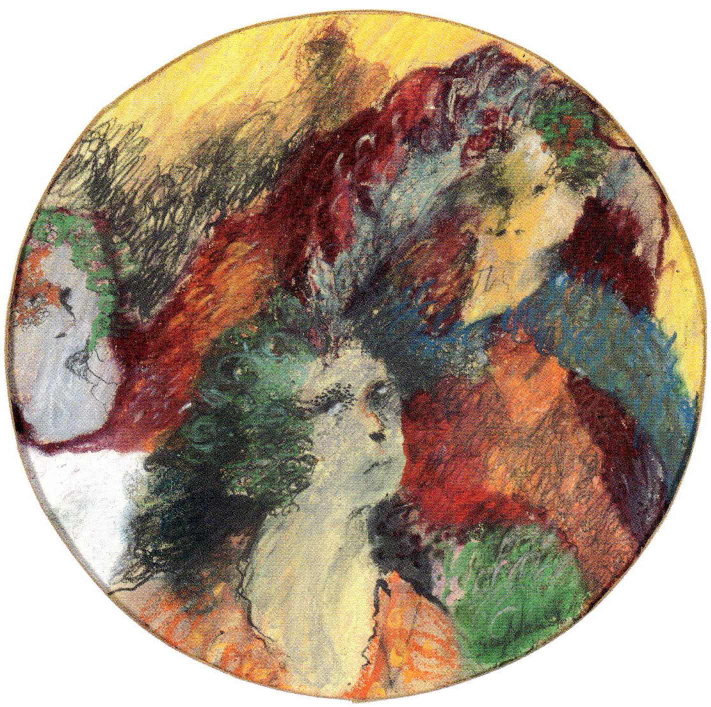

Untitled, 1965.
Oil pastel on paper, 8 in. (diam.).
Collection of the Artist.

Rainbow Sue
we called her
15 years ago.
She made art
out of rainbows.

Phil Weidman, 1983

Sacramento State and Suzanne grew up together.
When she arrived, things were just sort of blooming.

Jack Ogden, 2025

Suzanne Adan: I'm No Spring Chicken includes a selection of the artist's early work created at Sacramento State between 1966, when she declared art as her major, and 1971, when she completed her master's degree in painting. During that time of discovery, "she kind of bounced off all of us," remembers Jack Ogden, one of Adan's most influential teachers.[1] In her student work, we are struck by Adan's experimental confidence as she discovers what she will appropriate and refashion for her own art, beginning with the paintings of her professors. Her 1966 *Self Portrait in a 1920s Setting,* for example, painted in Jerald Silva's watercolor class, draws inspiration for its subject and style from the abstract figurative paintings that Irving Marcus, her oil painting professor, showed at the Candy Store Gallery the previous year: "It was like, well, I'd never seen anything like it before. It just had a huge impact on my brain and my eyes. I came back to the class and started being Irv junior."[2]

Adan's student work is true to the spirit and visual intelligence that characterizes this six-decade survey. Its explorative range and variety in style and content evidence a brilliant, ambitious student and what was available to her at Sacramento State.

The artist's student years ended in 1971 with the completion and exhibition of her master's project, a series of Neo-Dada conceptual paintings on butcher paper, including *Panty Hose, Fragment of a Formal Idea, Debutante Ball Slippers,* and *The Restless Balls.* **[pp. 107–109, p. 121]** Begun in 1969 as a graduate study in visual wordplay under Jim Nutt, it was pursued in notebooks that Adan filled with verbal puns and sketches of their visual equivalents. The completed project surpasses student work, achieving the originality, authenticity, and relevance of advanced contemporary art. Adan's graduate series of pun paintings destabilizes the names and purposes of ordinary things by absurdly doubling their meaning and poking fun at the fixity of conventional thinking. Selections from the portfolio, first exhibited in Adan's 1971 master's show at the Kaleidoscope Gallery in Sacramento, garnered exceptional attention from the national art world for the new graduate.[3]

The first day I stepped on campus, I thought, "This is great!" And then when I started doing art, I was obsessed with it. Nobody had to tell me to get into the studio.[4]
Suzanne Adan

In September 1963, Adan began her first semester at Sacramento State. The new public college was as young as she was; both grew and matured astonishingly fast during the artist's years of matriculation. Sacramento State drew students like Adan from working- and middle-class families who commuted from Sacramento and nearby towns. Like her, most were first-generation college students. By 1971, when Adan completed her MA in painting, full-time enrollment had tripled, and 75% of the faculty had arrived after 1964.[5] Importantly for Adan's education, the 1960 California Master Plan for Higher Education, which decentered the traditional focus on teacher education and supported fundamental changes in curriculum and faculty expertise, was coming into effect.[6]

When Adan arrived in the fall semester of 1963, a new and larger art building was ready to welcome students. The modernist building, with its professional art gallery and studio classrooms, suggested that teaching and learning contemporary studio art were prioritized. When they moved into the new building, nine of the twelve full-time professors held degrees in art education and taught studio as well as art education classes. The remaining three professors included one art historian, Dr. Riis Bohr, and two artists: Irving Marcus and Ruth Rippon. The 1965 hire of a third artist professor, Jack Ogden, and the appointment of Marcus as Department Chair in 1966, were definitive steps toward building the department as a studio program.[7]

Adan's years as an art major at Sacramento State coincided with the chairmanships of Irving Marcus (1966–1969) and John Fitz Gibbon (1970–1971). In those five years, Marcus's radical hiring agenda (carried forward by Fitz Gibbon) created an Art Studio program on par with any

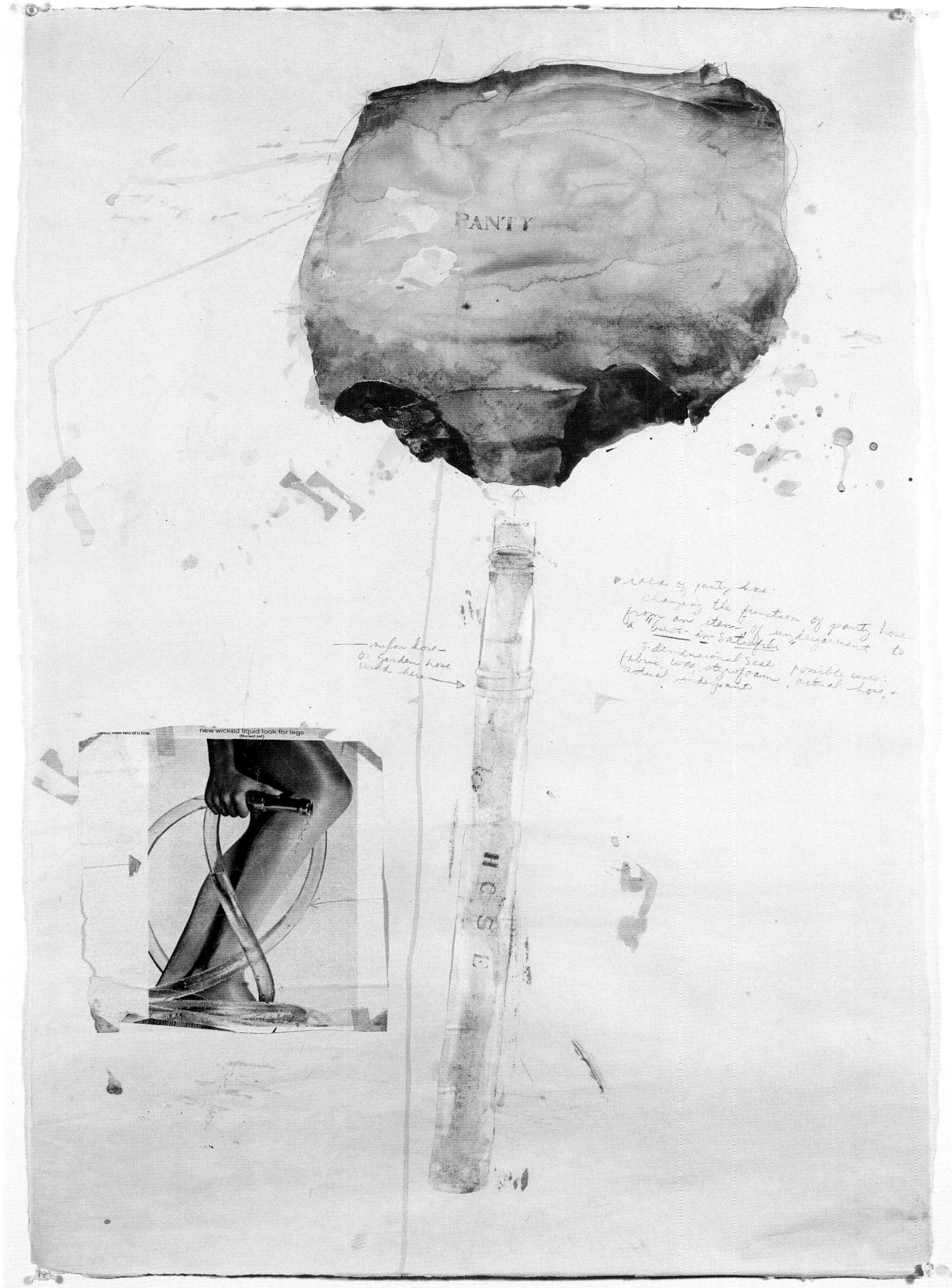

Panty Hose, 1969.
Watercolor, pencil, Elmer's glue, and magazine on butcher paper, 38 ¼ × 26 ¼ in. Collection of the Artist.

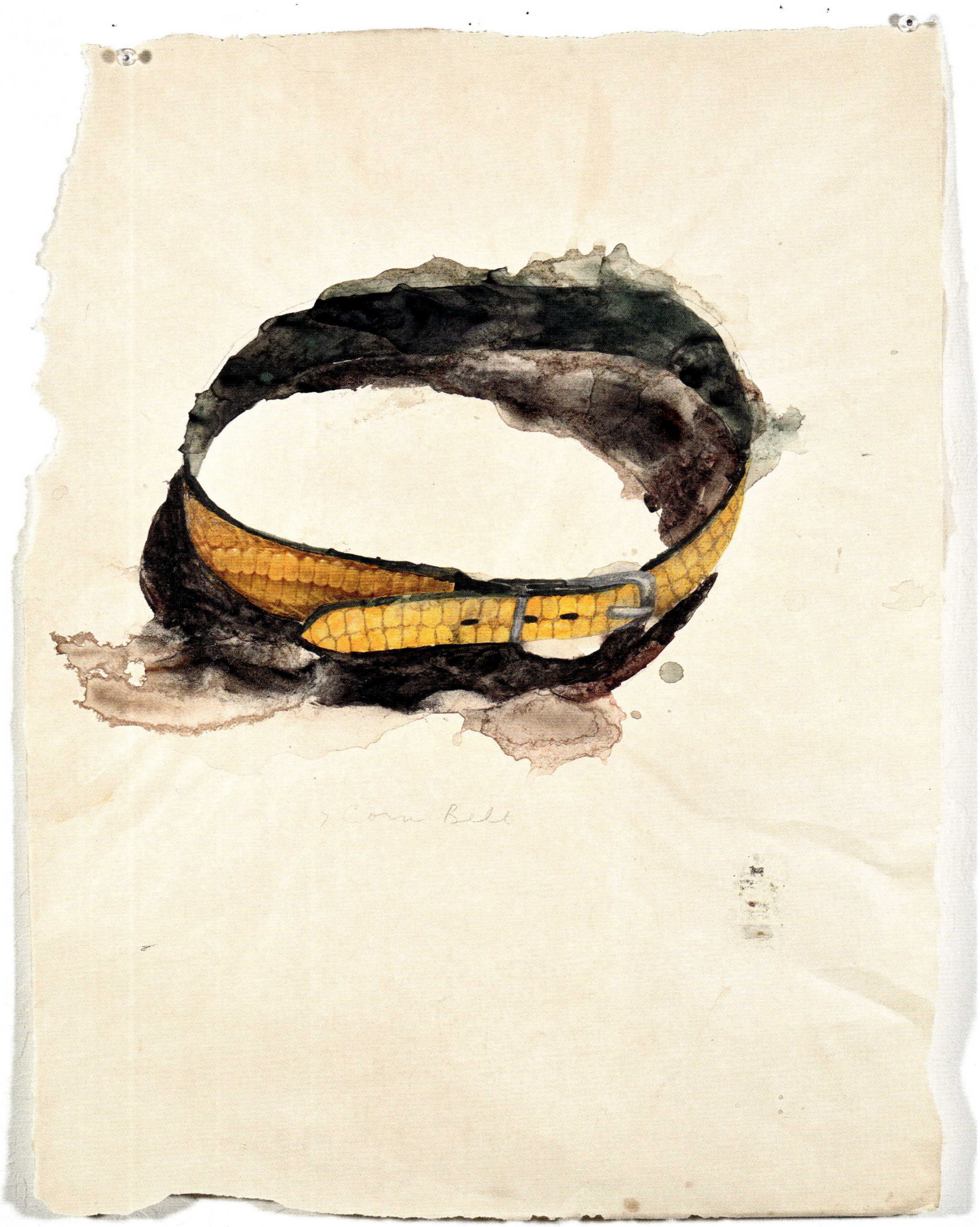

Corn Belt, 1973.
Watercolor, pencil, Elmer's glue, and magazine on butcher paper, 24 ½ × 18 ¼ in. Collection of the Artist.

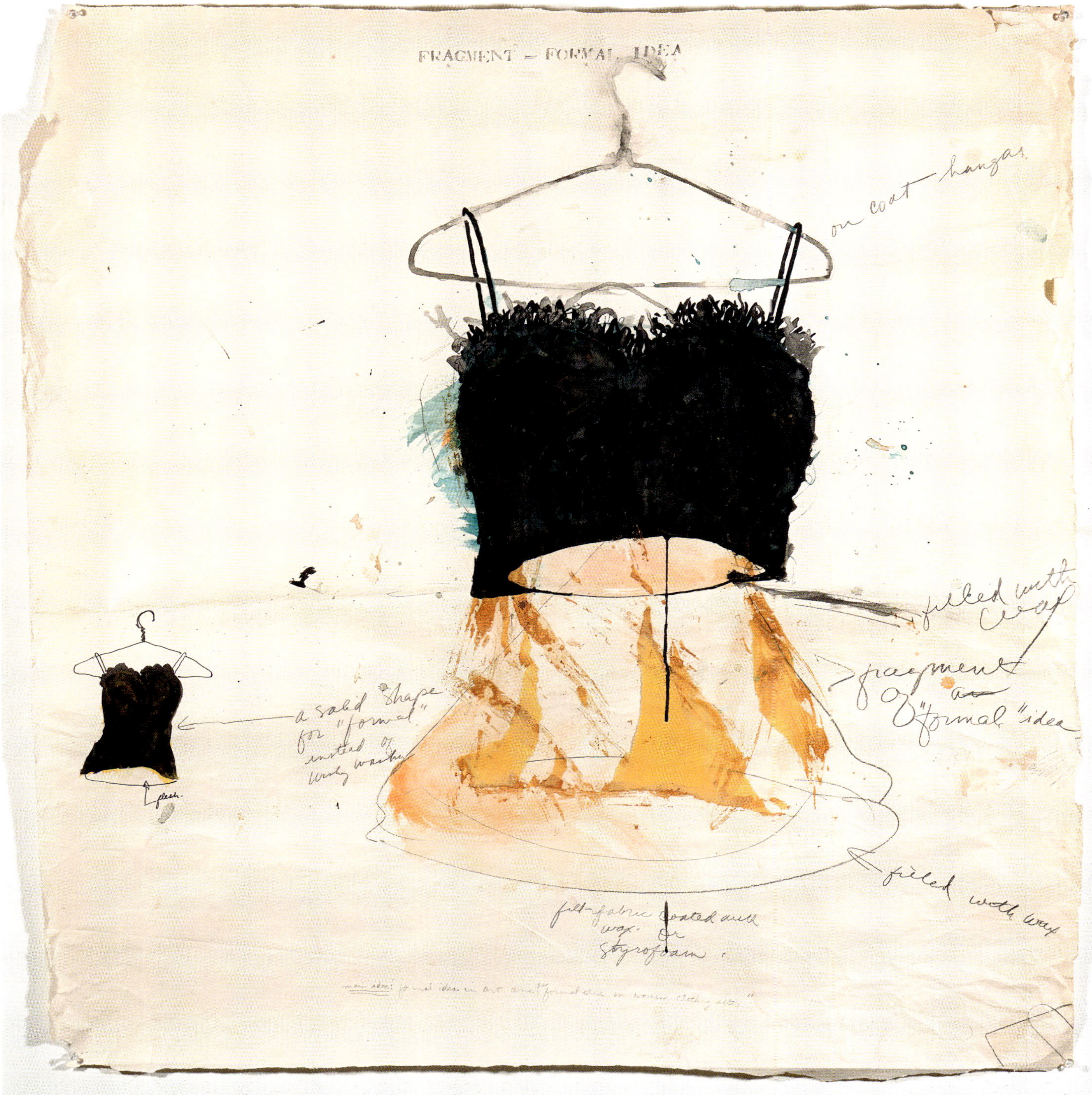

Fragment of a Formal Idea, 1969.
Watercolor, pencil, and Elmer's glue on butcher paper, 42 × 40 ¼ in. Collectior of the Artist.

in the California State University system.[8] Marcus had been educated by progressive practicing artists at the University of Minnesota and the University of Iowa. He knew the value of that education for students and wanted the same in Sacramento. Inspired by Richard L. Nelson's recent success in assembling a faculty of outstanding artists at the University of California, Davis, Marcus seized the opportunity he had as department chair to achieve that same kind of result at Sacramento State.

During every year of his chairmanship, Marcus recruited more young artists with impressive résumés to teach studio courses. The 1960 California Master Plan for Higher Education supported his hiring agenda. The sympathetic Dean of Arts and Sciences, Harvey Reddick, waived degree requirements for artist professors with equivalent real-world credentials. In 1968, Marcus recruited Hairy Who artist Jim Nutt from Chicago, a stroke of good fortune for Adan, who would learn much from Nutt.[9] Sculptors Gerald Walburg, a recent graduate of UC Davis, Richard Randell from Oberlin College, and William Geis from San Francisco, as well as the experimental San Francisco filmmaker Robert Nelson, also arrived in 1968. New hires in 1969 were art critic John Fitz Gibbon from Berkeley, art historian Kurt von Meier from Los Angeles, and painters William Allan from San Francisco and Joseph Raffael from New York. In 1970, Allan Gordon, a new PhD in Art History from The Ohio State University; Steve Kaltenbach, a UC Davis graduate based in New York; Carlos Villa from San Francisco; Eduardo Carrillo from San Francisco; and Oliver Jackson from Iowa all joined the faculty.[10]

From 1965 to 1968, Adan worked in the art office as a work-study assistant. She helped Marcus's secretary, Eleanor Van Valkenburg, and art historian Riis Bohr, who required slide assistance for his lectures. Beginning in 1966, she also assisted Richard Jackson in the department's art gallery. Adan admired Marcus as an artist and teacher. Watching him operate as chair, negotiating what Nutt remembers as "ceaseless faculty wars," she saw that Marcus "had a vision to shape the department in a whole different direction."[11] Although his chairmanship was only one three-year term, "He made the most of it. He brought Jim Nutt into the mix."[12]

By the time Adan graduated in 1971, the number of full-time artists on the faculty had increased ninefold from when she started, growing from two to eighteen. Professional artists dominated the department and set about making the changes needed to teach art practice. In 1970, the department's footprint grew to include the large Art Sculpture Lab, a converted storage facility situated on the edge of campus that provided space for unrestricted artmaking and graduate studios.[13]

Looking back on his ambitious and successful chairmanship years later, Marcus shared his sense of accomplishment: "The word had gotten out, and I was all pumped up! Wow, I can really do wonders! We had between sixty and seventy people apply to graduate school each semester!"[14]

The young studio faculty, most of them only about ten years older than their students, was actively engaged in the contemporary art world. They exhibited in major national and international venues, such as the Whitney Museum of American Art in New York and the Venice Biennale. They were a resource beyond the studio classroom for local Sacramento area students, who learned to follow current directions in advanced art at the national and international level and use that knowledge to inform

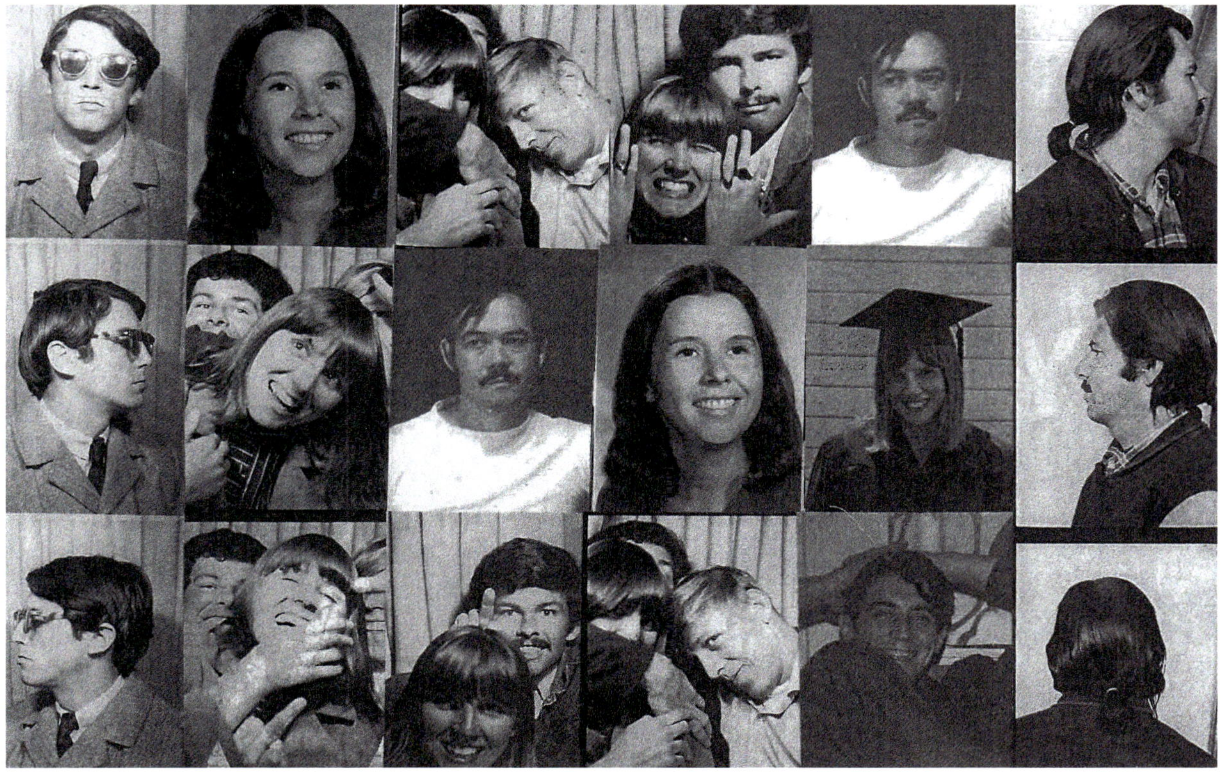

their own practice. The new professors linked students to artist professors and graduate students at art schools in the greater San Francisco region, primarily UC Davis, the San Francisco Art Institute, UC Berkeley, and the California College of Arts and Crafts in Oakland. Connections also included regional art museums, such as the E. B. Crocker Art Gallery (now the Crocker Art Museum) and the San Francisco Museum of Art (now the San Francisco Museum of Modern Art), as well as galleries that showcased advanced contemporary art. In Sacramento, the Artists Contemporary Gallery and the Belmonte Gallery showed the kind of art produced by Sacramento State and UC Davis professors and students.[15] The most culture-defining gallery for the Northern California region when Adan was studying at Sacramento State was the Candy Store Gallery in Folsom, which promoted Funk and Nut art, figurative painting and ceramic sculpture made by UC Davis and Sacramento State faculty and graduate students, and Chicago Hairy Who artists Jim Nutt, Gladys Nilsson, and Karl Wirsum, who were then teaching at Sacramento State. The Candy Store was crucial to Adan's education. It was there that she saw canvases that inspired her signature painting style, and where she first exhibited that work.

> *Those college days were all for fun and made going to class enjoyable.*[16]
> **Ron Peetz**

Adan's group of art student friends at Sacramento State enriched her education. Collaborative, competitive, supportive, and playful, they took the same classes, discussed ideas, shared information, and created art events and installations. When asked about her fascination with puns and wordplay, the basis of her graduate work, Adan replied, "Well, when we were all at Sac State, we were all looking for puns to outdo each other."[17] Ron Peetz, Adan's close friend and part of her group, confirms, noting that

1969*: A Fifty-Year Anniversary of Sacramento State College Art Students/Friends,* exhibition postcard, 2019. Courtesy of the Artist.

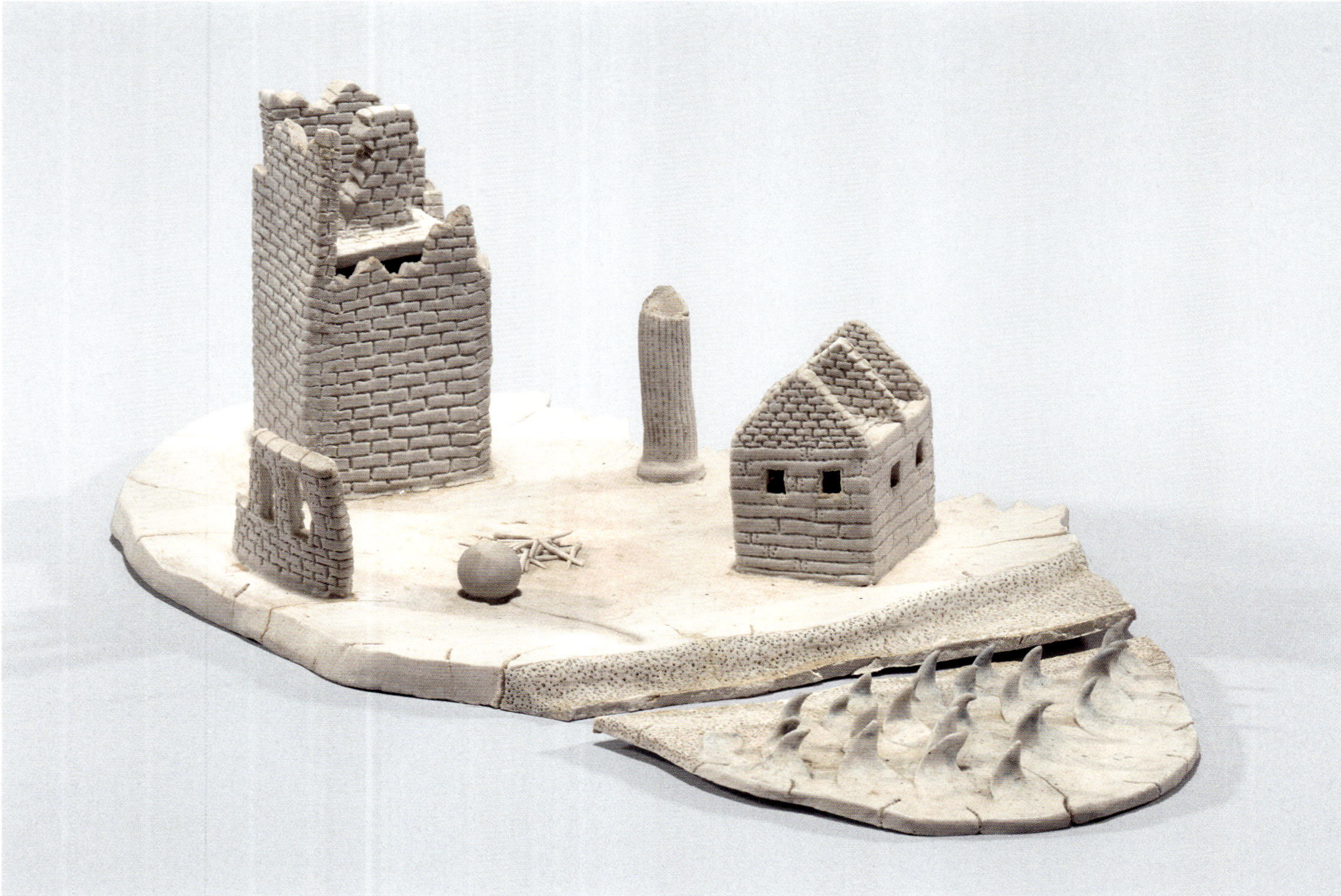

they got into punning because William T. Wiley and Bruce Nauman made punning a part of their conceptual practice. "Suzanne's brother Jim was very good at it," recalls Peetz, "as were Mike [Stevens] and Suzanne. Working with puns and wordplay also solved the whole problem of titles. We would ask a silly question to get a silly answer."[18]

Adan celebrated the vibrancy of her artist group five decades later, curating an exhibition titled *1969: A Fifty-Year Anniversary of Sacramento State College Art Students/Friends* for the Kondos Gallery at Sacramento City College, which she managed with Michael Stevens, her husband and best friend since college. The exhibition postcard featured a grid of photos of group members Phil Weidman and Vicky Wallace from the late 1960s, as well as period photobooth mug shots of Stevens and Adan; her brother, Jim Adan; Ron Peetz; and Nick Steinmetz.[19] **[p. 111]** Rodney Atha and Jim Stewart were included in the show but are not pictured. The exhibition presented the late 1960s production of the artists' group during a "crazy time" when "stuff got real" for college students who were at the forefront of Vietnam War protests, racial justice and liberation movements, rock music, and youth counterculture.[20]

Adan put a lot of thought and effort into the *1969* show:

> I even included books, books that were important for all of us in the 1960s and early '70s. I included correspondence. I included things that were actually done in 1969, like my brother's vacuum-formed hats. . . . It really gives you a sense of that time, that place, and all the different kinds of things we were doing.[21]

↑ *Towerscape*, 1976.
Porcelain, 13 × 14 × 8 in; 1 ½ × 3 ¾ × 5 ¼ in.
Collection of Vicky Wallace and Ron Peetz.

→ *Cupscape*, 1976.
Porcelain, 3 × 5 ½ × 6 in. Collection of Susan Howe and Rebecca Goodchild.

Adan's *1969* show featured nine artists, only two of whom were women, which points to the fact that the art world was dominated by men, at Sacramento State and everywhere else. The 1969 Whitney Annual, intended and assumed to be a selection of the best new American art that year, featured 143 artists, only eight of whom were women, a ratio of 1 in 18.[22] Sacramento State's full-time art faculty was entirely male, except for ceramicist Ruth Rippon.[23] Adan's artist statement for a 2017 exhibit of work by Rippon's students expresses admiration and gratitude for her example and mentorship, "when it was truly a 'man's world' . . . she paved the way and inspired many of us who took her classes to continue our dreams."[24]

Adan took two semesters of ceramics with Rippon in 1966. Frustrated by wheel-throwing, she taught herself to make hand-built sculptures inspired by the beautiful ceramic boxes she saw in a show of Rippon's work at the Artists Contemporary Gallery. "A light bulb went off," Adan recalled, "I came back to class and started doing hand-built pieces."[25] One of them was *Spacey Fur-Lined Airplane Box,* a small stoneware box decorated with a tiny finger-shaped airplane and forms that suggest a "spacey" travel narrative. [p. 34] The incongruous fur lining recalls Meret Oppenheim's Surrealist sculpture *Object (Breakfast in Fur)* (1936).

Adan's *The Face of Fear* drawing and large oil painting *The Face of Fear Showing Sunshine Superman, M & D, or Have You Lost Your Zoo Keys?* were made in Jack Ogden's spring 1967 oil-painting class. [p. 114] Adan had spent that summer experimenting with collage and drawing, hoping to have fresh ideas for the new semester and do some experimental work in Ogden's class.

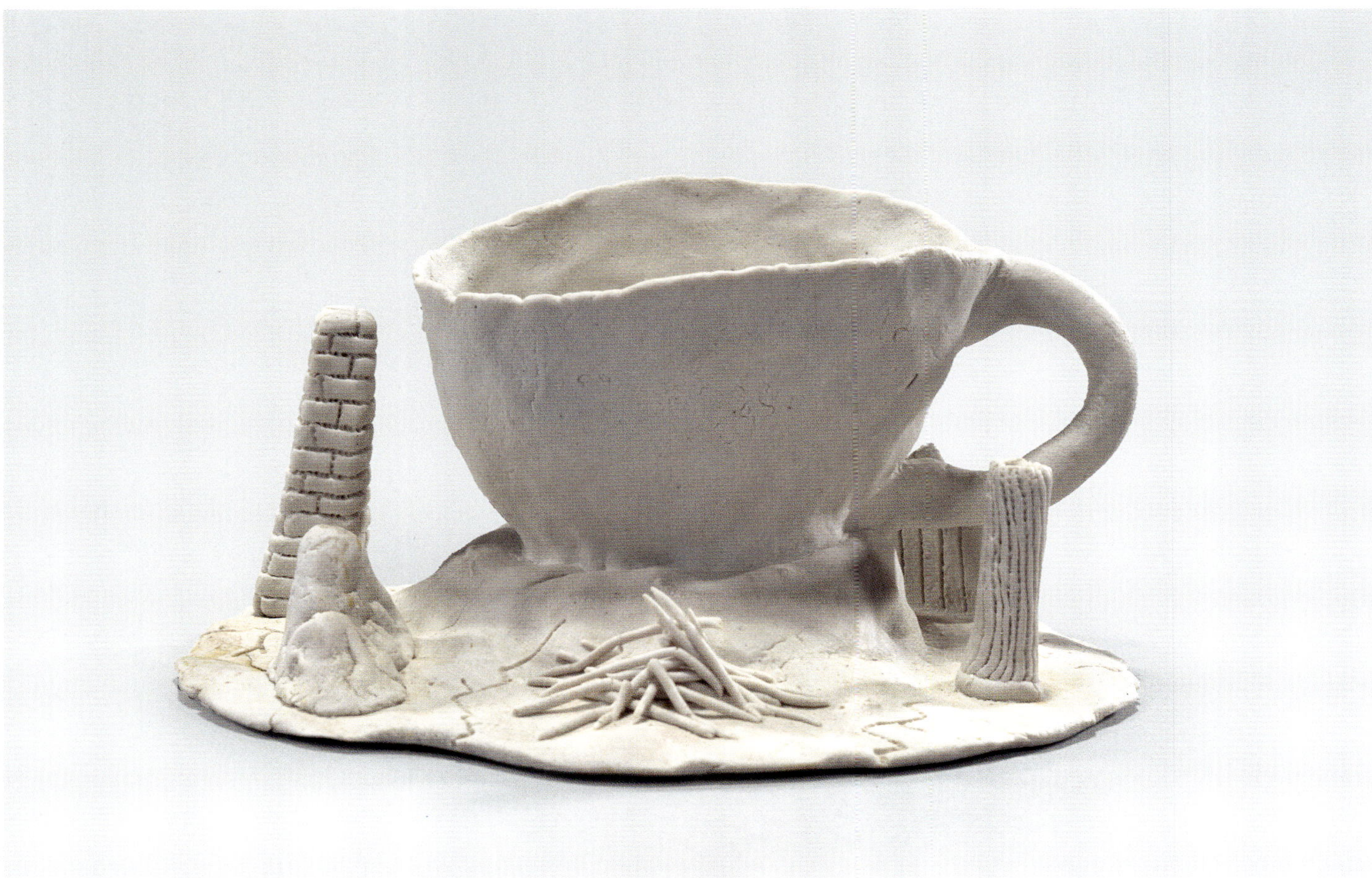

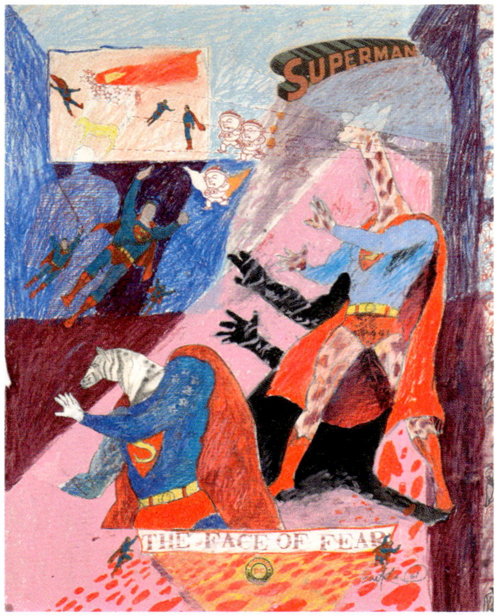

A fruitful experiment in *The Face of Fear* drawing was to imprint it with the rubber stamps she was using on ceramic sculptures in Rippon's class. Ogden loved the effect, asked to buy Adan's stamps, and was soon using stamps in his own work. As other artist friends started using them, it became "the great rubber stamp competition."[26]

The Face of Fear Showing Sunshine Superman, M & D, or Have You Lost Your Zoo Keys? was in part inspired by the artist's frequent sketching trips to the Sacramento Zoo with Stevens and Dean Steiner ("M & D" in the painting's title), who appear as silhouettes, Michael with a green, worm-like body, Dean with the long neck and spots of the horse-headed giraffe. Two female nudes, one cut off by the left edge, the other floating near the top, were taken from life-drawing studies. The large scale, unusual for Adan, emphasizes the work's theatricality.[27]

The art department gallery at Sacramento State exposed students to new work they would otherwise have seen only in reproduction. Opening in 1963 with the art building, the gallery presented a full schedule of

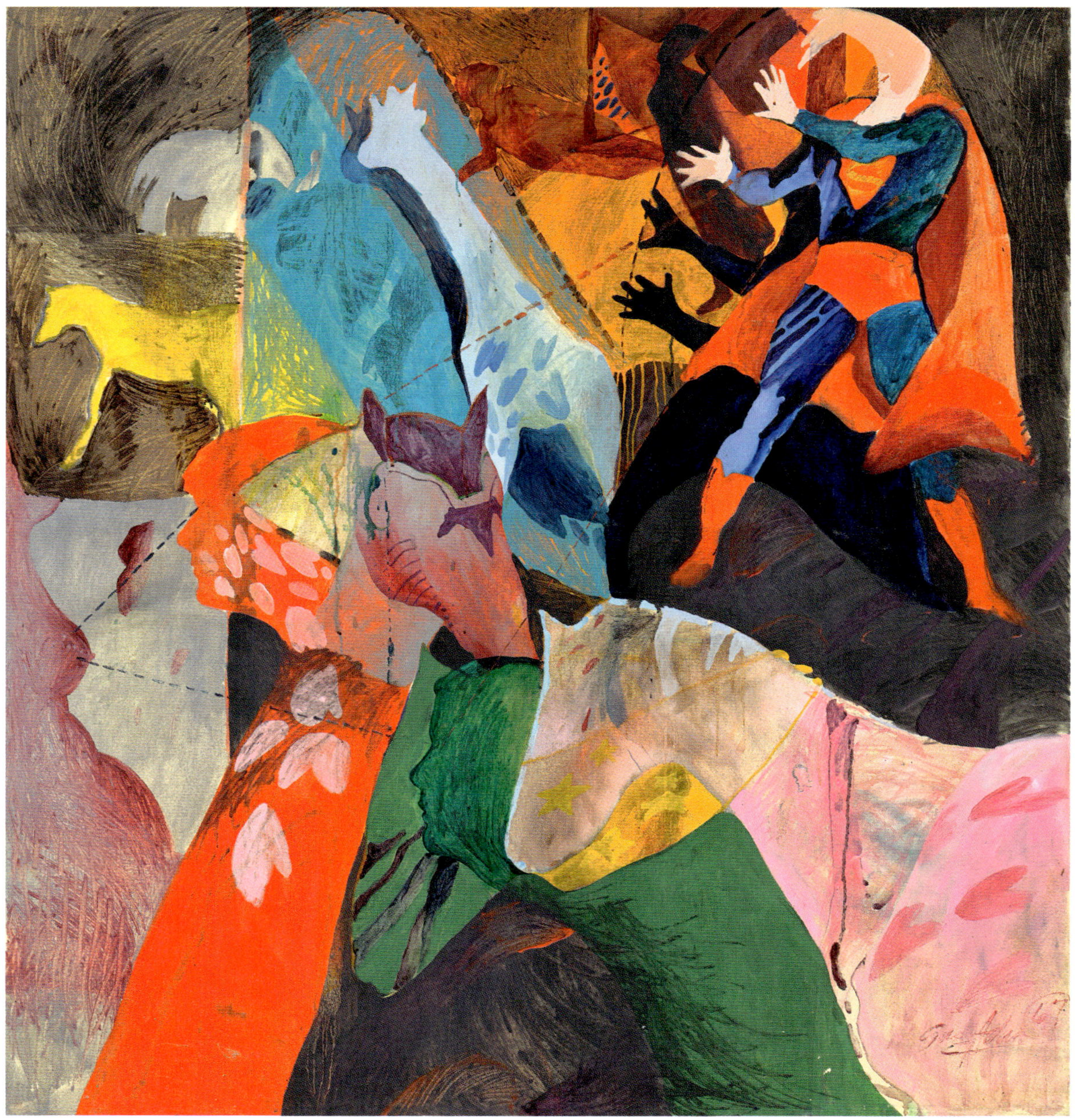

↑ *The Face of Fear*, 1967.
Oil pastel, pencil, comics, and rubber stamps, 18 ½ × 14 ¾ in. Collection of the Artist.

→ *The Face of Fear Showing Sunshine Superman, M & D, or Have You Lost Your Zoo Keys?*, 1967.
Oil on canvas, 59 ½ × 55 in. Collection of the Artist.

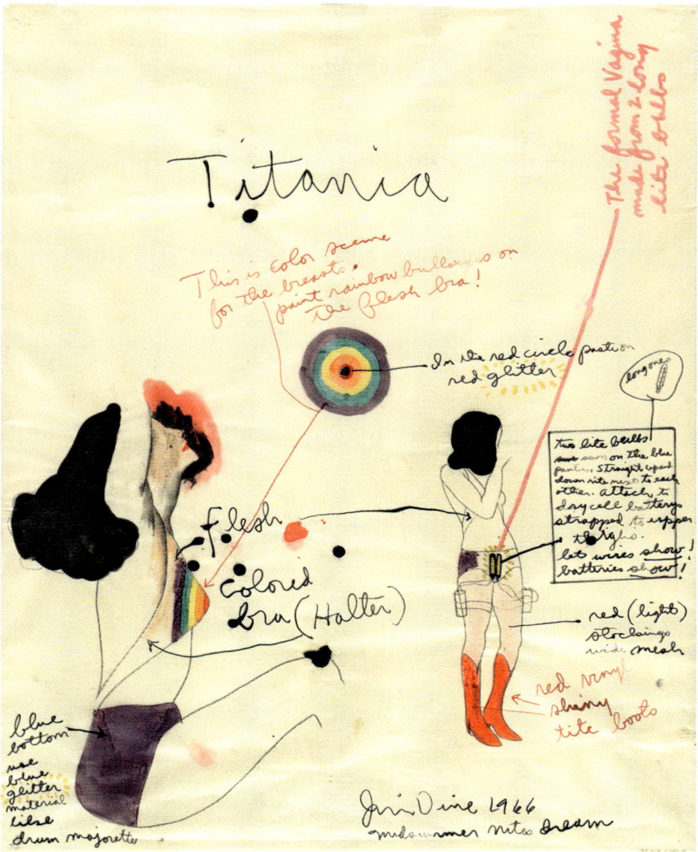

Jim Dine (American, born 1935), *Titania:* Costume design for *A Midsummer Night's Dream,* 1966. Glitter on cut-and-pasted paper, watercolor, pencil, pen and ink, and felt-tipped pen on tracing paper, 23 ⅞ × 19 in. MOMA, Gift of Mrs. Donald B. Straus, 410.1966. Digital Image © The Museum of Modern Art/Licensed by SCALA / Art Resource, NY. © 2026 Jim Dine / Artists Rights Society (ARS), New York.

contemporary art exhibitions, artist talks, performances, and installations. Graduate student Ken Waterstreet ran the gallery between 1963 and 1965 and remembers its rough start: "I kept asking [the art faculty], 'What do we want to do for the gallery?' I kept getting, 'I don't care, do what you want.' Along with Bill Yates and some other people I knew at Davis, we scheduled some shows. [In 1965] Bruce Nauman and Ed Higgins, who were studio mates at Davis, did a show there. I just asked them, and they did it."[28]

In 1966, Marcus became department chair and hired his former student Richard Jackson to run the gallery.[29] Adan assisted Jackson as part of her art department job, as he brought in an outstanding sequence of exhibitions, events, and artist talks. The 1967 show of Peter Saul's Vietnam paintings was the first time Adan had seen Saul's work. She explains:

> Jackson knew everybody. . . . And because Ed [Kienholz] and Richard were very tight, Ed came to Sac State in 1968 and gave a talk. So we had access to listening to people like that, people you could read about in art magazines and relate to. . . . And there was just this in the sixties: a constant stream of people coming to campus.[30]

Department art exhibitions that directly influenced Adan's work included the June 1968 show of Blalla W. Hallmann, a German self-taught artist who was then temporarily working in San Francisco. Hallmann's obsessive technique and flat, figurative, and musical-narrative compositions would later characterize Adan's signature painting style. Adan also studied the work of other outsider artists, such as Adolf Wölfli, who had inspired Jean Dubuffet's Art Brut.[31]

The exhibition *Jim Dine Designs for A Midsummer Night's Dream* (1968) directly influenced Adan's advanced student work, most notably the paintings she would make for her graduate project. Jackson borrowed the Jim Dine show from the Museum of Modern Art in New York shortly after it was exhibited there in 1967. The exhibition catalogue illustrates Dine's dominant rainbow motif for the theatrical production, as well as his mixed-media instructional drawings for the "Black Comedy " on view in the gallery.[32] The influence of Dine's composition, handwritten notes, arrows, identification labels, collaged elements, and pencil drawings was first evident in Adan's 1968 *Rainbow Popsicle Melted,* a singular mixed-media work on tracing paper. [p. 117] Handwritten notes slanted across the top describe Adan's playful and improvisational process of creating *Rainbow Popsicle Melted* according to the laws of chance. Sugary, melting popsicle ice in red, blue, and yellow colors that remained vivid for years was allowed to pool on tracing paper, with the two popsicle sticks apparently left in place.[33] Adan's first mixed-media pun paintings, such as *Fragment of a Formal Idea,* [p. 109] were created just months after the Dine exhibition. "I was really influenced by the show," Adan remembers. "I loved everything about what he did. Fluid kind of pencil drawing and drippy, and this and that. I just loved that work."[34]

In February 1969, when D R. Wagner ran the gallery, art students inflated a World War II Army vehicle decoy on the gallery patio during an exhibition of collaborative ink drawings by William Geis, Robert Nelson, Robert Hudson, and William T. Wiley. Once the drawing exhibition was down,

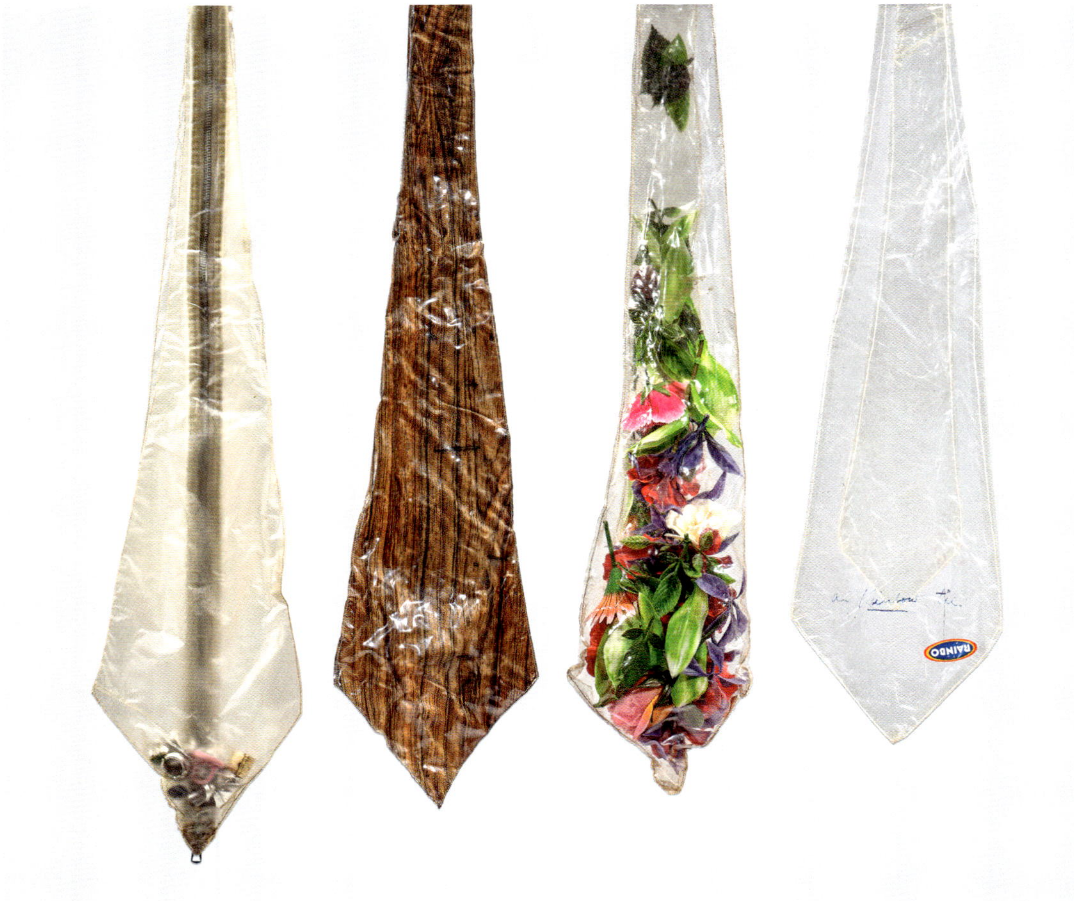

the students reinstalled the inflatable truck in the gallery until it nearly filled the space.[35] Professors Ogden and Walburg bought the inflatable at a federal surplus warehouse, and Ogden dragged it to the gallery for students to inflate. "[It was] like a Claes Oldenburg," Ogden explained.[36] Adan, who had been studying Oldenburg, recalls it vividly, remembering, "We all thought it was pretty damned cool, and we were thoroughly involved in watching it inflate." Four months later, Adan would submit a research paper on Oldenburg for Contemporary Art History 112, taught by Lynn Louden, and another for an independent study with Jim Nutt. She notes as well that, "We kept up with reading art magazines such as *Artforum, Art in America,* and *Art News.* We would go to the library to check them out, so we were quite aware of what was going on in Los Angeles, Chicago, and the East Coast."[37] Like Jim Dine's designs for *A Midsummer Night's Dream,* Oldenburg's drawings for his soft sculptures were primary sources for the paintings in Adan's master's series. [p. 118]

> I was thoroughly entranced by Oldenburg's drawings that he did for his soft sculptures. I liked everything about them—the scribbling, the writing, the cut-out pictures, the sloppiness of the material used. He just had a special touch in creating these fluid, elegant drawings that were very influential in my early watercolor pun paintings.[38]

Neckties, 1968–1969.
Plastic, mixed media, and found objects, varied dimensions. Collection of the Artist.

Suzanne Adan graduated in June 1971 with a Master of Arts in painting. From the first exhibition, her graduate series of concept-based paintings was well-received in regional and national venues, notably the 1974 solo

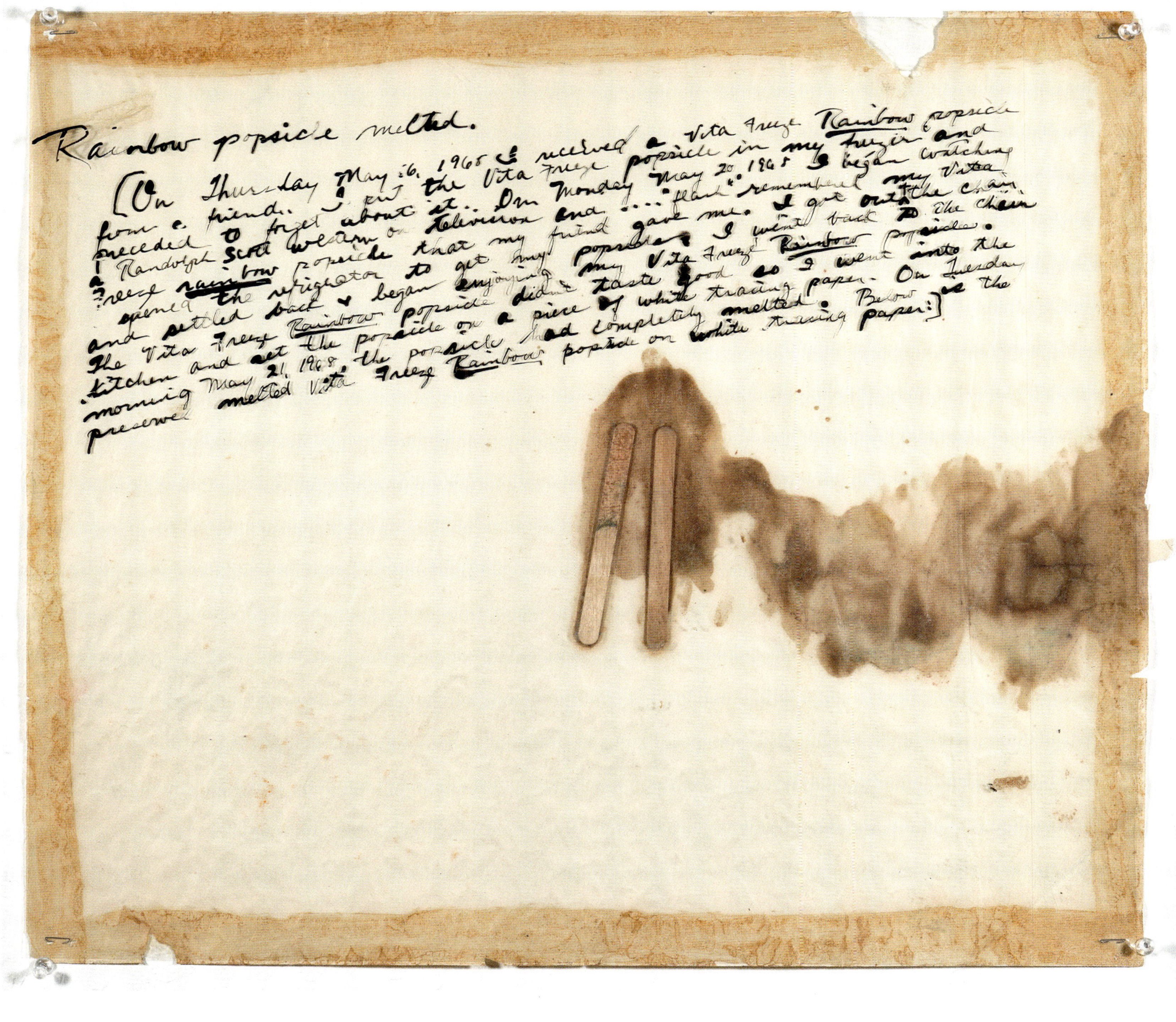

Rainbow Popsicle Melted, 1968.
Plastic, ink, melted popsicle, and popsicle sticks on paper, 19 × 21 ¼ in. Collecticn of the Artist.

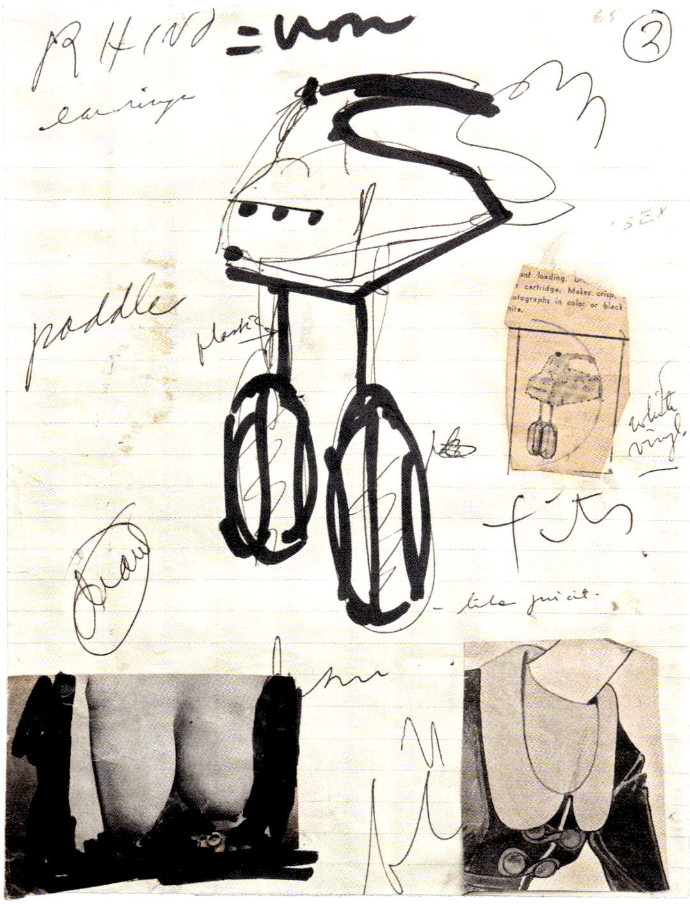

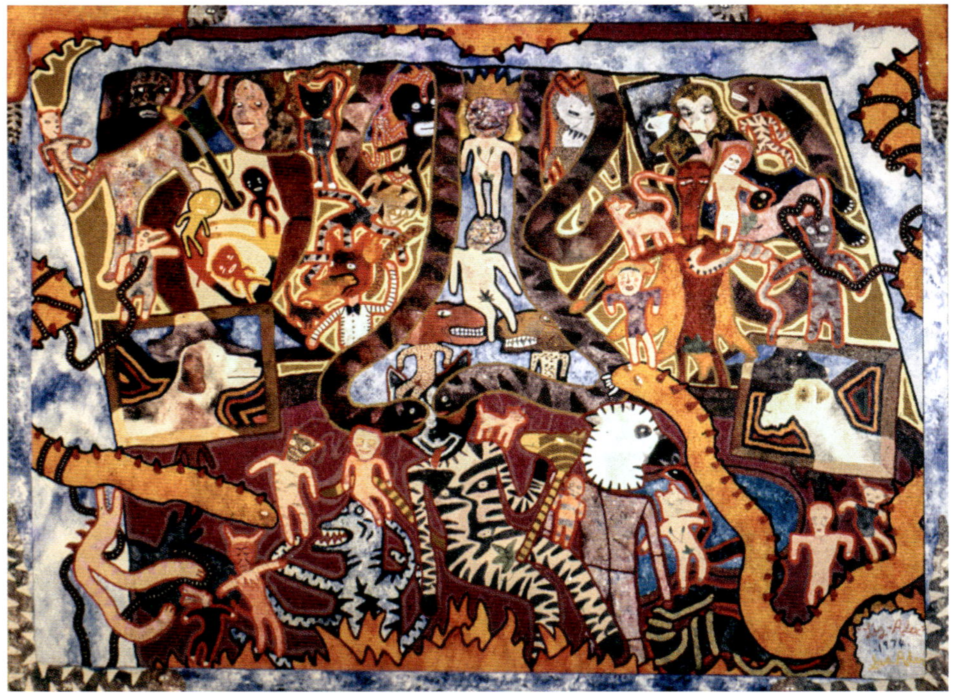

show at the legendary Womanspace gallery in Los Angeles, and three shows at the Candy Store Gallery in 1971, 1973, and 1975.[39] By 1976, when she created her last pun piece, Adan had returned to oil painting.

Asked why she turned away from a direction admired by pathbreaking artists and curators, Adan replied, "I just think I was interested in getting back to painting with oils again, especially after visiting the Chicago Art Institute in the summer of 1977. Seeing Seurat's paintings, Hopper's *Nighthawks,* Georgia O'Keeffe's large-scale cloud painting, and, of course, the Van Gogh self-portrait . . . I was ready to move on."[40] Adan specifically credits commissions from her brother, Jim Adan, for two *Adan Family Portraits* in 1972 and 1974 for making her want to paint on canvas again. The 1974 *Adan Family Portrait* is the first to employ the stippling technique, which solved the problem of energizing negative space and would later develop into Adan's distinctive embroidered marks.[41]

By 1979, with *Crosses to Bear,* Adan had achieved her signature style, described by Phil Weidman in the last stanza of his poem *Rainbow Sue:* [pp. 128–129]

Now her paintings
are filled with
strange dream-like
images stitched across
canvas in thousands
of tiny brush strokes.

↑ Claes Oldenburg (American, born Sweden, 1929–2022), *Notebook Page: Dormeyer Mixer,* 1965. Felt pen, ballpoint pen, clippings, collage. Photo courtesy of the Oldenburg van Bruggen Studio.

↗ *Adan Family Portrait #2,* 1974. Courtesy of the Artist.

1 Jack Ogden, interview with author, July 15, 2025.

2 Adan learned watercolor techniques in Jerald Silva's class, such as taping unsized paper to Masonite and adding Elmer's glue to the paint, which she used in her graduate series of pun paintings on butcher paper. (Suzanne Adan, interview with author, July 22, 2025).

3 The admiration of prominent artists and curators began immediately, with Adan's 1971 MA show at the Kaleidoscope Gallery in Sacramento, when ceramic sculptor Robert Arneson offered to exchange one of his sculptures for *Panty Hose.* (Suzanne Adan, interview with author, August 19, 2025).

That same year, Walter Hopps, Director of the Corcoran Gallery in Washington, D.C., and guest juror of painting for the San Francisco Art Institute's 1971 Centennial Exhibition, selected four paintings from Adan's graduate portfolio, including *Panty Hose,* to exhibit at the San Francisco Museum of Art (now SFMOMA). Jim Nutt remembers that the installation "absolutely stopped me in my tracks," and that "Walter [Hopps] was really struck by [Adan's work], and told me that, 'Jasper Johns would trade one of his drawings for that one [*Panty Hose*], you know, flat out. He would really like that.'" (Jim Nutt, interview with author, August 8, 2025).

In 1973, Adan's 1970 watercolor on butcher paper *Happy Trails to You . . . Until We Meet Again* was included in Robert Doty's Whitney exhibition, *Extraordinary Realities,* alongside work by advanced artists such as William Allan, Roy De Forest, H. C. Westermann, and Roger Brown.

Finally, underlining the historical significance of Adan's graduate series is her 1974 solo exhibition in the groundbreaking Womanspace gallery in Los Angeles, one of the first galleries to show and promote work by women artists. Adan's feminist humor is evident in the pun paintings on display in the exhibition. (See the Archives of American Art "Womanspace gallery records, 1970–1974": https://www.aaa.si.edu/collections/womanspace-gallery-records-8766).

4 Suzanne Adan, interview with author, July 22, 2025.

5 George S. Craft, Jr., *California State University, Sacramento: The First Forty Years: 1947–1987* (Hornet Foundation Publication, 1987), 108, 114, 127, 130.

6 Craft, *California State University,* 43–106; and Sacramento State College, *The Statesman* 1963 (yearbook): https://archive.org/details/css_003715/page/n11/mode/2up?view=theater&ui=embed&wrapper=false.

7 It is notable that Robert Else, an art educator recruited in 1950 and a department founder, supported hiring more artist professors. Else hired Irving Marcus in 1959 when Else was Department Chair (1958–1961); later, he advocated for Jack Ogden and supported Marcus's chairmanship and recruiting agenda. (Irving Marcus, interview, July 13, 2016).

See also Robert Else's autobiographical essay in *Robert Else: A Retrospective Exhibition* (Crocker Art Gallery Association and E. B. Crocker Art Gallery, 1977, 7). Recalling his education at Columbia Teachers College, Else writes, "It never occurred to me that any of my college teachers . . . had serious ambitions as artists. They were primarily teachers. Important painting went on outside the learning institutions. Things have certainly changed. . . . Three of my younger painting colleagues at the university have had recent one-person shows at the Whitney Museum, a splendid record for any art department."

8 Marcus agreed to step down as chair after one term if the art faculty would appoint John Fitz Gibbon, who Marcus knew would pursue his hiring agenda. (Irving Marcus, interview, July 13, 2016). The 1970 start date for Fitz Gibbon's term as chair is from the *Sacramento State College General Catalog*; however, he did not complete the standard three-year term. Allan Gordon recalls that Marcus hired him in 1969, but when Gordon arrived on campus in 1970, Fitz Gibbon was the chair. In 1971, Gordon replaced Fitz Gibbon as chair (Allan Gordon, interview with author, June 27, 2015, telephone confirmation and clarification, September 15, 2025).

9 Hairy Who artist Gladys Nilsson, married to Jim Nutt, moved with him and their son, Claude, to Sacramento and taught part-time at Sacramento State. A third Hairy Who artist, Karl Wirsum, moved to Sacramento in 1971 and taught part-time for a few years.

10 Chicano activist artists Esteban Villa and José Montoya, founders of the Royal Chicano Air Force at Sacramento State, were hired as art educators by Marcus and Fitz Gibbon in 1969 and 1970. They taught silk screen classes, collaboratively produced many RCAF event posters, and established the ongoing Barrio Art Program. Hiring Montoya and Villa began the next significant chapter in the history of the Sacramento State Art Department.

11 Jim Nutt, interview with author, August 25, 2025.

12 Suzanne Adan and Michael Stevens, interview with author, January 14, 2014. Adan and Stevens had read about Jim Nutt before Nutt arrived on campus. They saw the Hairy Who show at the San Francisco Art Institute in May 1968.

13 See Rachel Clarke, "Interview with Jack Ogden, Jerry Walburg, and Steve Kaltenbach," in Rachel Clarke, Mya Dosch, and Eliza Gregory, *Art Sculpture Lab, 1970–2024* (California State University, Sacramento, 2024), 20–35.

14 Irving Marcus, interview with author, July 13, 2016. According to Sacramento State's "Graduate Statistics on Master's Degrees for the School of Arts & Sciences," the Art Department awarded eight master's degrees in 1963 and thirty-nine in 1973 (Craft, 265).

15 For the Belmonte Gallery, see Tim Foster, "Memoirs of Belmonte," *Midtown Magazine,* February 1, 2018, http://www.midtownmonthly.net/art/memories-of-belmonte/. It was at the Belmonte Gallery that Adan first saw Robert Arneson's groundbreaking ceramic Funk sculptures, including his *Funk Johns* (toilets) soon after they were shown in Peter Selz's historic 1967 *FUNK* exhibition at UC Berkeley. Adan was impressed by Arneson's iconoclastic humor and use of ceramics as an individually expressive, contemporary art medium. (Suzanne Adan and Michael Stevens interview with author, January 14, 2014).

16 Ron Peetz, text message to author, August 22, 2025.

17 Suzanne Adan, interview with author, September 22, 2025.

18 Ron Peetz, interview with author, March 28, 2025.

19 Phil Weidman was ten years older than the others and considered the leader of the group. Artist and writer, he authored the 1969 *Slant Step Book* and published thirteen collections of his poems, some of which are about his artist friends. "Rainbow Sue," the first lines of which inspired the title and serve as an epigraph for this essay, reflects on Adan's art, beginning with the art she made of rainbows at Sacramento State.

20 Sam Whiting, "1969: Stuff Got Real," *San Francisco Chronicle,* undated photocopy, Suzanne Adan Archive, 1969 exhibition folder.

21 Suzanne Adan, interview with author, August 19, 2025.

22 For the ratio of men to women artists in the 1969 Whitney Annual and how quickly it changed in subsequent years due to pressure from the new feminist movement in art see Lawrence Alloway, "Institution: Whitney Annual," *Artforum* 2, no. 1 (1973): 32–35. For women activists' perspective on the 1969 Whitney annual, see Lynn Hershman Leeson, *! W.A.R. ! Women Art Revolution,* A Hotwire Production, 2010, distributed by Zeitgeist Films, 2010.

23 Joan Moment's arrival in 1971 would begin to correct the imbalance. Moment was hired as a tenure-track professor in 1972.

24 Suzanne Adan, "Statement," November 6, 2017, Suzanne Adan Archive.

25 Adan, "Statement."

26 Adan didn't sell Ogden her stamps because they were a gift, very old, and irreplaceable. Ogden went out and bought his own stamps. Suzanne Adan, interview with author, July 22, 2025.

27 Adan, interview with author, July 22, 2025.

28 Ken Waterstreet, interview with author, September 4, 2025. Waterstreet was hired as the gallery "technician," a position that soon included curating the exhibitions and events.

29 Irving Marcus, interview with author, July 13, 2016. The talented, well-connected young Richard Jackson left for Los Angeles in 1969 at the end of Marcus's chairmanship. He became a significant figure in post-Abstract Expressionist theatrical painting. See John Welchman, *Richard Jackson* (Hauser & Wirth Publishers, 2020), 21.

30 Suzanne Adan, interview with author, August 26, 2025.

31 See Charles Johnson's review of the Sacramento State Blalle W. Hallmann show, "Art Views," *Sacramento Bee,* June 9, 1968.

32 David Zack, "James Dine Designs Sets for 'A Midsummer Night's Dream'," *Artforum* 4, no. 9 (1966): 32–34. Zack discusses the avant-garde theatrical experience of Jim Dine's designs as part of a total work of art. Dine donated the designs and documents for *A Midsummer Night's Dream* to the Museum of Modern Art, which has made them available online, including a PDF of the exhibition catalog: https://www.moma.org/calendar/exhibitions/2605

33 Suzanne Adan telephone interview with author, October 29, 2025. Adan's text for *Rainbow Popsicle Melted* reads in part: "On Thursday, May 16, 1968, I received a Vita Freeze Rainbow popsicle from a friend. On Monday, May 20, 1968, I began watching a Randolph Scott western on television, and . . . flash . . . I remembered my Vita Freeze Rainbow popsicle. . . . The Vita Freeze Rainbow popsicle didn't taste good, so I went into the kitchen and set the popsicle on a piece of white tracing paper. On Tuesday morning, May 21, 1968, the popsicle had completely melted. Below is the preserved melted Vita Freeze Rainbow popsicle on white tracing paper."

34 Suzanne Adan and Michael Stevens interview with author, August 26, 2025.

35 Ron Peetz, text to author, September 1, 2025.

36 Jack Ogden alludes to Claes Oldenburg's inflatable sculptures, especially *Lipstick (Ascending) on Caterpillar Tracks,* the 1969 anti-Vietnam War sculpture by Oldenburg and Coosje van Bruggen; see Jack Ogden, Jerry Walburg, and Steve Kaltenbach interview with Rachel Clarke in Clarke, et al., *Art Sculpture Lab,* 32. Charles Johnson comments on the inflated army truck in his *Sacramento Bee* review: "Its gross ugliness, a mockery of function and, in this context, a mockery of man's war machines, make the truck a curious reflection on the artist's awareness of our time." *Art Views,* February 12, 1969.

37 Suzanne Adan, email to author, August 21, 2025.

38 Ibid.

39 See note 4 for more on the critical reception of Adan's graduate painting series.

40 Suzanne Adan, email to author, August 28, 2025.

41 Suzanne Adan, text message to author, October 28, 2025.

The Style and Subjects of a Pretty Artist from Yolo

Diana L. Daniels

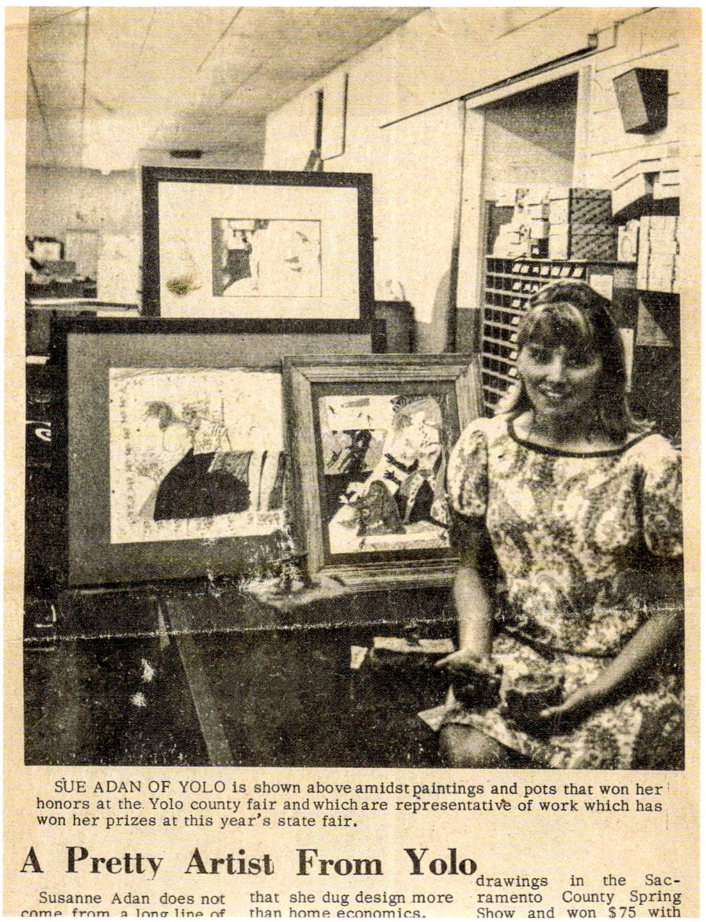

SUE ADAN OF YOLO is shown above amidst paintings and pots that won her honors at the Yolo county fair and which are representative of work which has won her prizes at this year's state fair.

A Pretty Artist From Yolo

Susanne Adan does not come from a long line of

that she dug design more than home economics.

drawings in the Sacramento County Spring Show and won $75 with

"A Pretty Artist From Yolo", *Woodland Record*, August, 31, 1967. Courtesy of the Suzanne Adan.

Painting for Suzanne Adan does not come easily. She describes working in oil as torture, albeit an exquisite one. The pleasure of artmaking and its dopamine reward comes to her through rapidly drafted pencil drawings or the confident marks of her scratchboard compositions. The quickly rendered lighthearted characters captured in her sketchbooks are near opposite that of the controlled brushwork and textured fields of her works in oil. Her paintings—for all their wit, charm, and enigma—are for Adan each a long-deliberated confrontation with the canvas.

Before her "confinement in the studio," as she jocularly calls it, lies an extensive period of pre-visualization. She considers and reconsiders every possible complement and juxtaposition of the elements with which she tells stories. This engaged problem-solving is critical to building a laser-sharp focus for handling oil paint with ultra-fine brushes, unguided by preliminary drawings. At times her contemplation lasts months, at times years. Building a narrative in this manner is for her a construction zone of the visual problems of form and composition. Aptly, she describes her compositions as puzzles pieced together physically and figuratively.

The controlled manner with which Adan paints has produced the distinct, consistent style that she has worked in for more than forty years. It is also the result of additional, self-imposed constraints, such as limiting her palette and always proceeding from one corner of the canvas to the other. With the latter, the fluidity of slow-to-dry oil paint creates risk as well as reward. A slip of the wrist easily mars what has already been laid down.[1] Hers is a painstaking precision that speaks of obsessive habit. It is thus surprising to see her loose execution and use of abundant color in works from the late 1960s and 1970s.

A series of small watercolors she produced in this period illustrate the point. In these, feminine objects are her subjects: a hanging corset bra or a single, flirty kitten heel are executed in color washes and rapid, brushy strokes. Each subject is brightly lit in an ambiguous, shallow space that makes for a cheeky presentation hinting at the future humor and wit so closely associated with Adan's production. The treatment of subject is spare, but bold, and the artist clearly delights in showcasing these

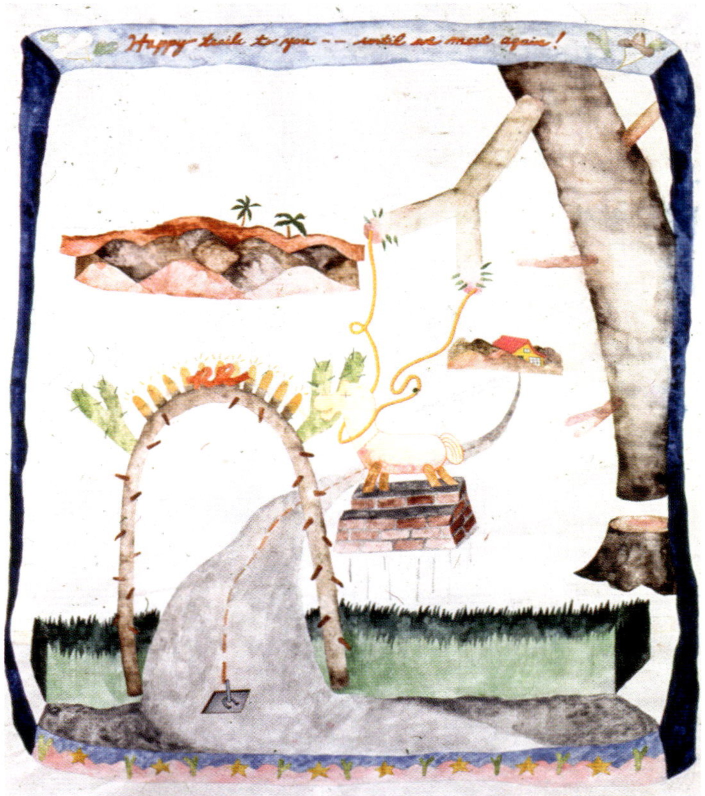

← *Happy Trails to You . . . Until We Meet Again,* 1970.
Watercolor. Courtesy of the Artist.

↓ *The Restless Balls,* 1972.
Watercolor, pencil, and Elmer's glue on butcher paper, 26 ½ × 38 ½ in. Collection of the Artist.

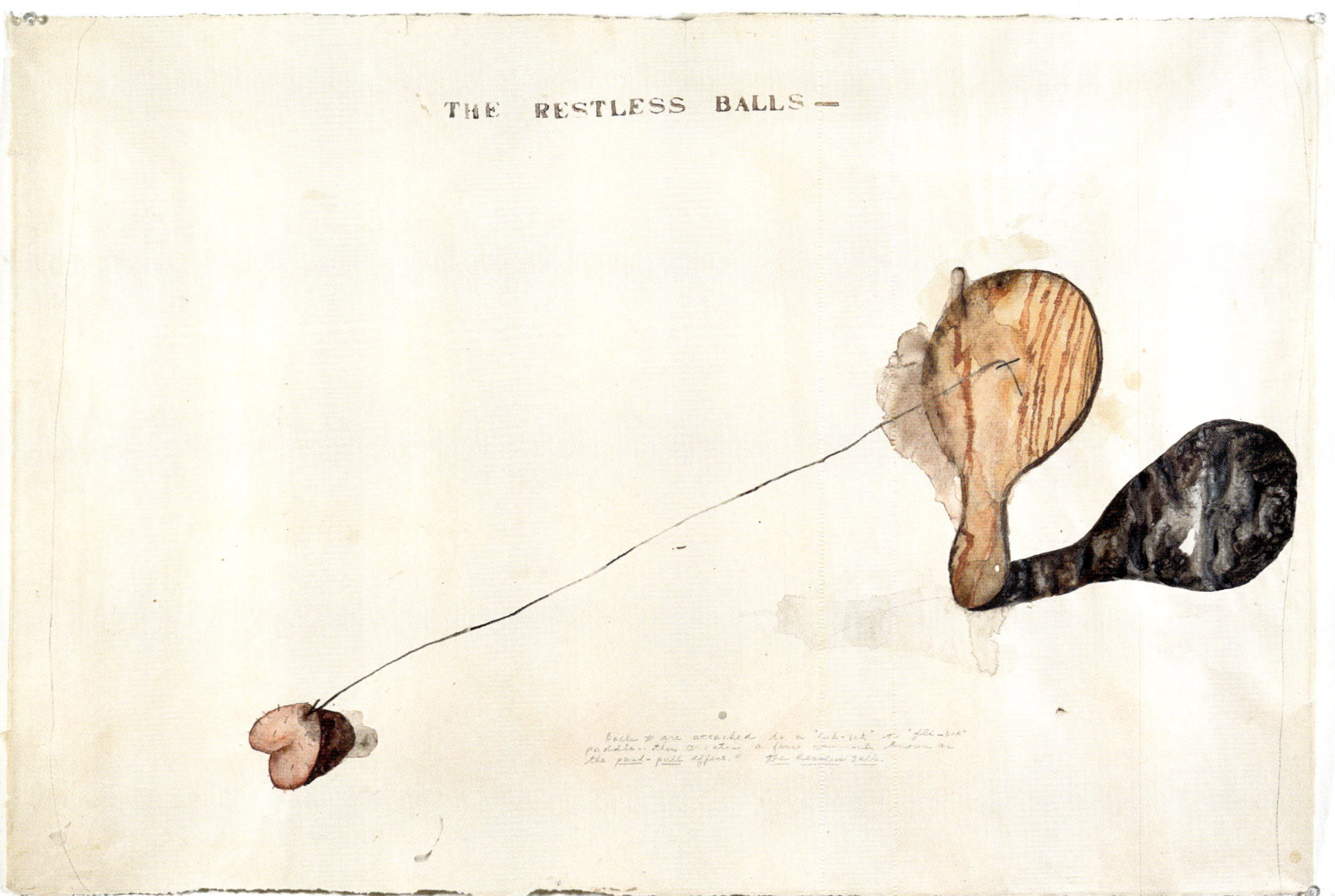

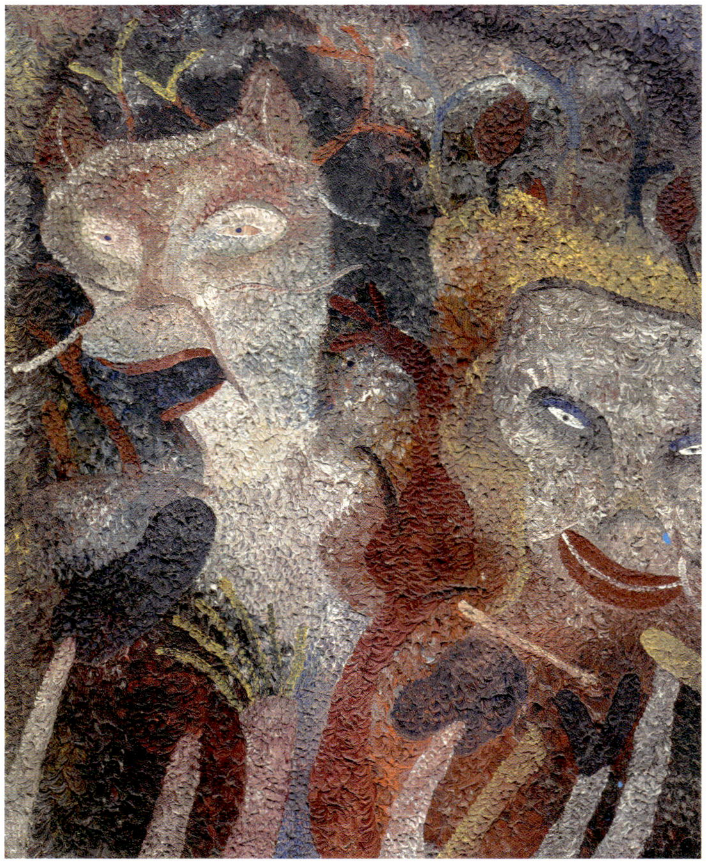

Masked Faces/Landscape, 1975.
Oil on canvas, 22 ½ × 18 ½ in.
Collection of the Artist.

everyday femininities. But there is a droller sassiness in the suggestion of sex in *The Restless Balls,* which is decidedly more masculine and features a classic child's paddleboard game. [p. 121] Spotlit in the same manner as the watercolor *Fragment of a Formal Idea,* [p. 109] the paddle appears isolated on a shallow stage, standing upright so that it casts a dramatic shadow. This paddle, however, has tethered to it male genitalia rather than the expected toy ball attached by rubberized string. It is an unexpected, suggestive, and conflicted visual. Sexual desire is her true subject. But it is an open question if this is male desire thwarted from a feminine point of view, in which the paddle is the victor, or if it depicts the momentary exhaustion of a man who fully enjoys the game.

This suggestive humor is her own, although it was arguably the dominant artistic sensibility of Sacramento and Davis in a period that favored Pop art sensibilities and the bawdy and irreverent delights of its Funk artists. But beyond following their example, Adan also shrugged off her more personal burdens with humor. Her own upbringing was one in which well-behaved children were seen, not heard. Layered atop this was a generalized normative estimation of gender that did not know what to make of accomplished women. One article showering her with early attention leads with the headline "A Pretty Artist from Yolo," followed by a brief write-up in which the author was clearly unprepared to explain the 1967 pastel drawing of a fanciful animal costumed as Superman with which Adan is pictured.[2] [p. 114] Indeed, the article's author is more comfortable implying that Adan's destiny is to be attractive, and a housewife, albeit with talent. The provocation of "pretty artist" is mild, but not without its rub. Certainly, the conflict of achieving any acclaim amid the confused reaction to doing so was not atypical for women in the visual arts in this era. Continuing to seek her artistic voice involved shedding the many confining values of acceptable feminine manners and conduct with which she had grown up.

While a general broadening of gender roles and loosening of mores was already underway in American society, Adan as a student found the associative strategies of early twentieth-century Surrealism and the fantastical, suggestive worlds created by Surrealist painters especially liberating. Indeed, clever wordplay in tandem with visual puns stoked her own sensibilities. While she may have been an upstanding Yolo County citizen and dedicated 4-H'er, she also grew up surrounded by raucous laughter and at times biting wit. In her mother's banter with her sisters, Suzanne's aunts, Adan came to relish how they entertained one another, lobbing aphorisms and pulling inside jokes. She also observed and absorbed how amid select company women could be free not only to enjoy a good laugh, but to exercise the liberty of satire and racy humor. During graduate school, Adan likewise began to develop the "feeling that I can say what I want and that I can enjoy the freedom to be funny."[3] Her cohorts at Sacramento State served as her select company, especially her future husband Michael Stevens, and she increasingly seized the opportunity to step up, speak out, and be counted among the opinionated, outspoken, and witty males with whom she "had to keep up."[4]

During the 1960s the role of humor in art received divided reception among art critics. Intellectual rigor was still the domain of realism,

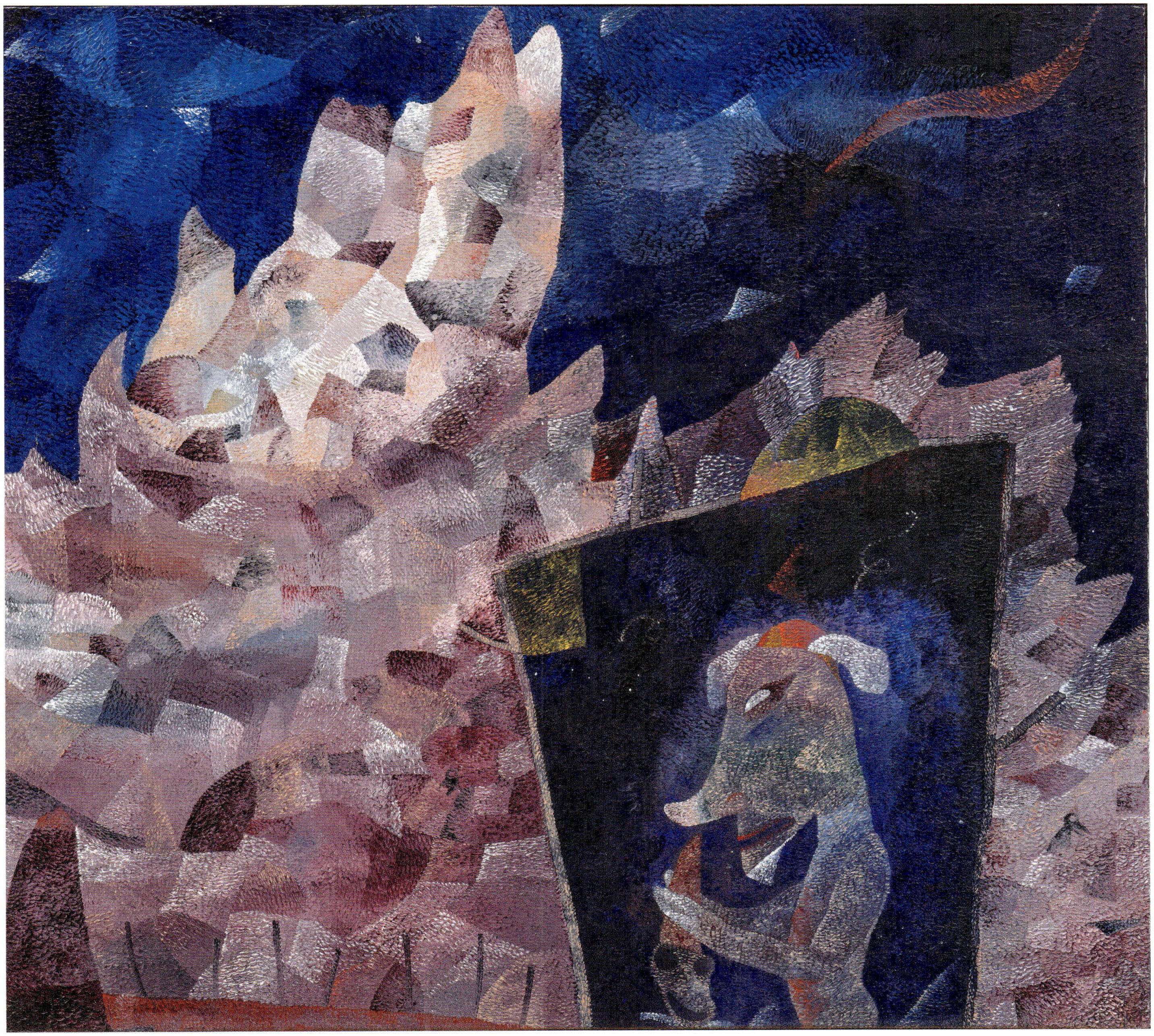

The Fantom Faith Healer, 1977.
Oil on canvas, 21 ¼ × 23 ½ in. Collection of Donna and Tony Natsoulas.

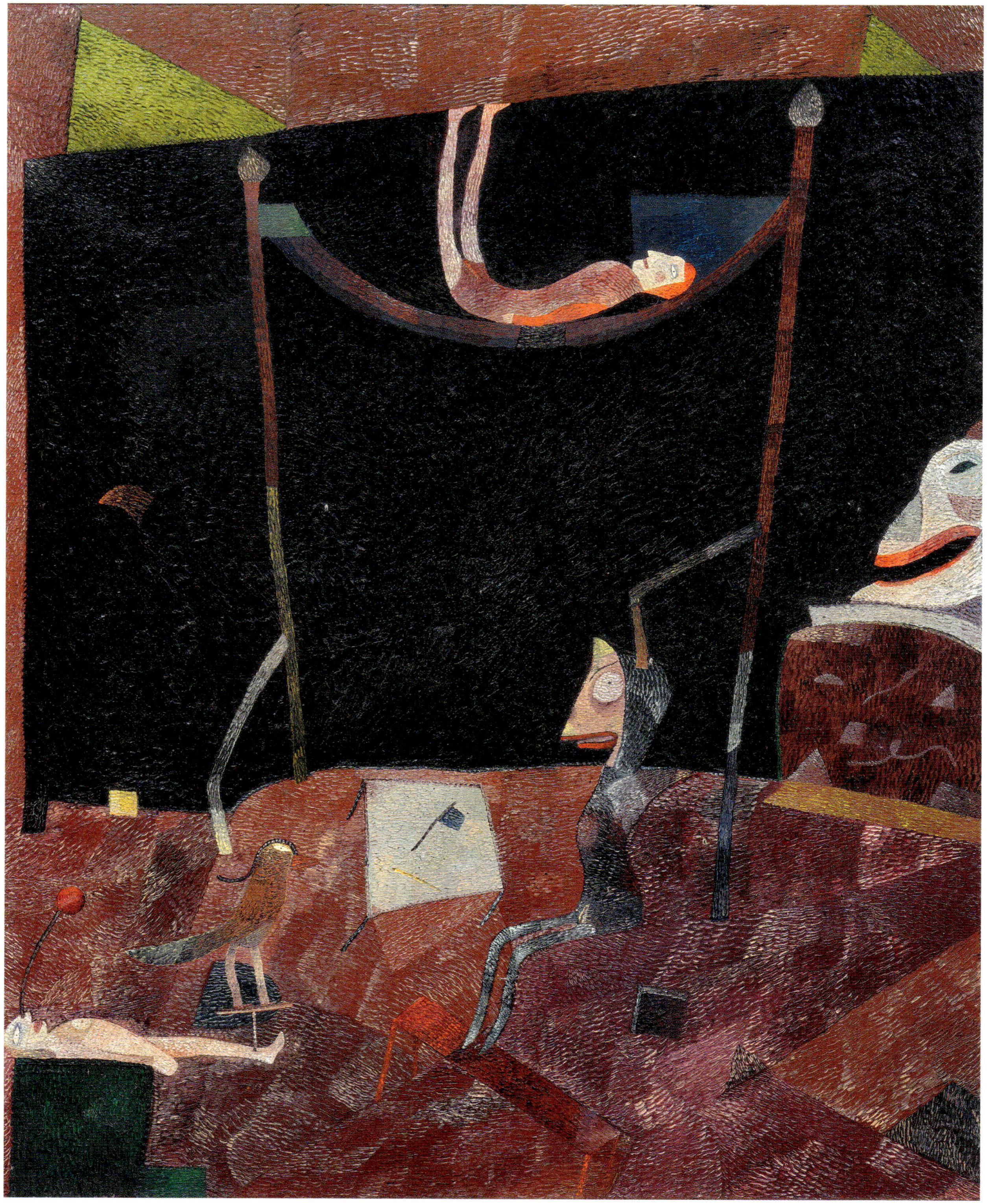

Sideshow: Balance Act, 1979.
Oil on canvas, 20 ½ × 16 ½ × 2 ¼ in. Collection of the Artist.

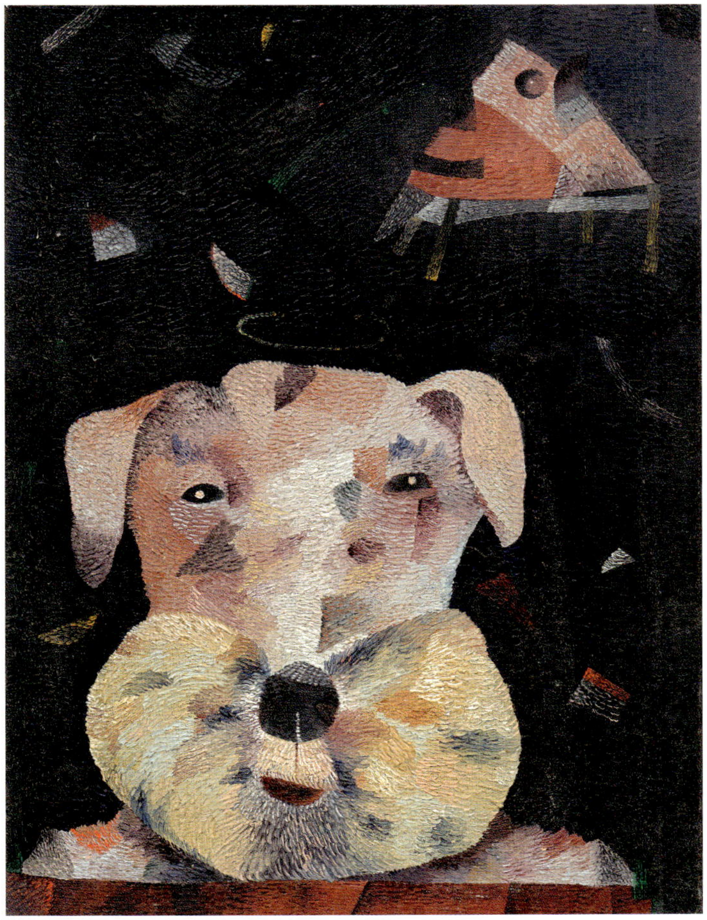

Felix, aka Devil Dog Adan Stevens (For Mike), December 25, 1978.
Oil on canvas, 9 ½ × 12 in. Collection of Michael Stevens.

formalism, and offshoots of Abstract Expressionism. Beyond Sacramento, in Chicago and New York, the bravery of "tongue-in-cheek" subject matter and garish or exuberant color were received as more fitting for the time, as old-fashioned manners increasingly felt quaint amid the realities of political assassinations, the expansion of foreign wars, and gross, political misconduct. Adan aimed neither to copy nor emulate the work of artists such as Gladys Nilsson and Jim Nutt, but the friendship she and Stevens developed with the two Chicagoans was important both in terms of artistic exchange and exposure, introducing the couple to artists and art figures outside of northern California. Like Nilsson, Adan gravitated to exaggerated depictions and the everyday psychological dramas of interpersonal relationships, but her style was never gestural in the manner of Nilsson. Instead, she took from Nilsson and other artists who exhibited at Folsom's Candy Store Gallery the ways the universal could be conveyed through imagery that was personal and imaginative, comedic or mysterious, seemingly naively executed or precisely detailed.

Adan's work in the 1970s, however, did not become more brilliantly colored due to the influence of Nilsson, Nutt, Robert Arneson, Clayton Bailey, and others featured at the Candy Store, but quite the opposite; they became expressionist with a new, darker palette. The figures she created were increasingly imaginative, often wearing outlandish masks and appearing with or as animals possessed of exaggerated visages and bodies. Paintings such as *Masked Faces/Landscape* clearly show her admiration for twentieth-century European Expressionists such as Paul Klee, George Grosz, and Jean Dubuffet, but more importantly reveal a period of experimentation in which she explored portraying psychological tension via exaggerated brushwork, abstracted form, and moody, dark tones. [p. 122]

In 1974, her watercolor *Happy Trails to You . . . Until We Meet Again* was included in the Whitney Museum of American Art's exhibition *Extraordinary Realities*, which art critic Roberta Smith, writing for *Artforum*, noted featured works with "cartoonlike figuration or writing; verbal and visual punning; tight, meticulous painting often extended to patterns of repeating details; flat, often hot color and small scale."[5] [p. 121] While Smith gives no positive endorsement of the exhibition, it featured not only William T. Wiley, but Lucas Samaras, Richard Artschwager, Lynda Benglis, and Chris Burden, all recognized today for their masterful psychological tensions in painting and sculpture. Alongside them were works by "33 of 55" total artists who were "under thirty-five years of age," for whom, per Smith, it was too early to evaluate their staunch individualism.[6] What Smith does conclude from the show is that "perversity is a complicated idea" and that "in order to be strong and interesting, it must manifest itself formally, regardless of content."[7]

The importance of formal strength resonated with Adan, and a refinement in her technique became evident in 1979. In the oil painting *Felix aka Devil Dog Adan Stevens (For Mike)*, she is already using tighter, more layered handling, which by the next year became a major shift to a new obsessive manner. This shift was in part the result of Adan's and Stevens's 1977 visit to the Art Institute of Chicago, where she engaged deeply with one of Vincent van Gogh's self-portraits. Each stroke she

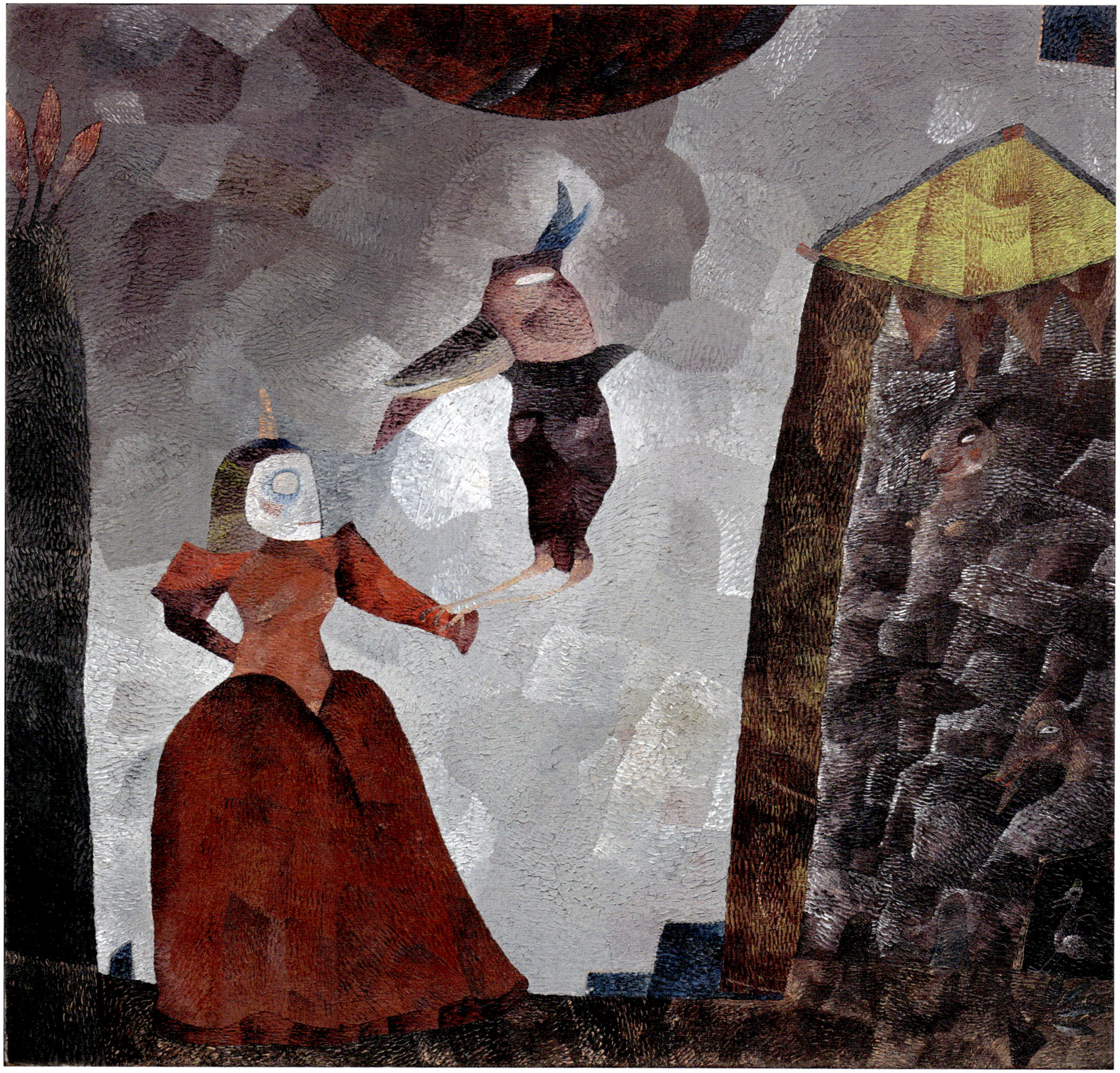

Curtain Call, 1978.
Oil on canvas, 18 × 18 in. Adan Family Collection.

noted was not one color, but many from a loaded brush. And the directional way in which van Gogh applied the brush to canvas produced a rich impasto that, in combination with his color, produced a scintillating effect. It was van Gogh's luminosity that she wished to capture in her own oil painting. Adan muses, "I'm not sure how I got to be so rigid, but I became obsessed with the technique. The torture of it. When you start painting it's a hill to climb."[8] Behind each stroke is the guiding principle that every color, no matter how unorthodox in blend, should work together—a requirement often entailing much reworking of either paint or figurative elements until she is satisfied with the result. Both the mixing and layering of color, even when applied with the tiniest brushes, achieves atmospheric backgrounds filled with light-reflecting impasto made by loading her brush with pigment.

Adan's palette represents a personal color theory dominated by muted reds, pinks, grayish blues, creams, and flesh tones, and she increasingly leaned into the drama of black and white. As learned through her observation of van Gogh, every color, even her blacks and whites, is thus comprised of multiple hues, sometimes in shade, sometimes in tint. "I don't like working with red, blue, and green," says Adan, "so I use weird mixes of colors. My blue is not a regular blue, and my green is not a regular green. In my work a pure color may well be mixed with purple, cream, and even one more toning shade."[9] By problematizing her use of color in this manner she set up an ongoing theorem that she proves to this day.

What came next was a leap in scale. With her 1979 oil painting *Crosses to Bear*, this jump is seen in a canvas nearly 70 inches wide upon which thousands of minute strokes create a shifting color field. Fantastical figures are set against this shimmery backdrop. At far left appears a clown, a figure that for Adan represents states of being other than who we are, a being that is disguised in masquerade physically and psychologically. It also represents her own personal distaste for clowns, so that when she incorporates them into her art, they serve as an expression of emotional concealment, as well as the sublimation of what makes her personally uncomfortable. [pp. 128–129]

Seen in profile view and suspended in space, one leg planted, the other lifted, the clown in *Crosses to Bear* appears to be running. The flare of a collar and a belly deployed as ballast suggest he is leaning into a strong headwind. At the clown's crown is a gray-blue, triangular tuft of hair, a side section, low beneath his ear, and just behind a similar gray-blue shape suggests his coiffure being whipped away. Immaculately detailed, this figure is a combination of simplified geometric forms modeled in light and dark, shimmering with color and texture.

The precise technique and overall sheen of her paintings result from her choice of the very finest paint brushes, sometimes consisting of only a few hairs, a fineness requiring that she compose the painting methodically and meditatively. She begins working at the upper left and progresses to the upper right, then down and across again, until reaching the lower right corner. The characters and signs in her paintings tend to emerge intuitively as she works, and she likens their emergence to the piecing of different thoughts together. Previously she had begun to develop scratchboard drawings by combining different fragments of paper, sometimes adding, sometimes subtracting sections. It was a method

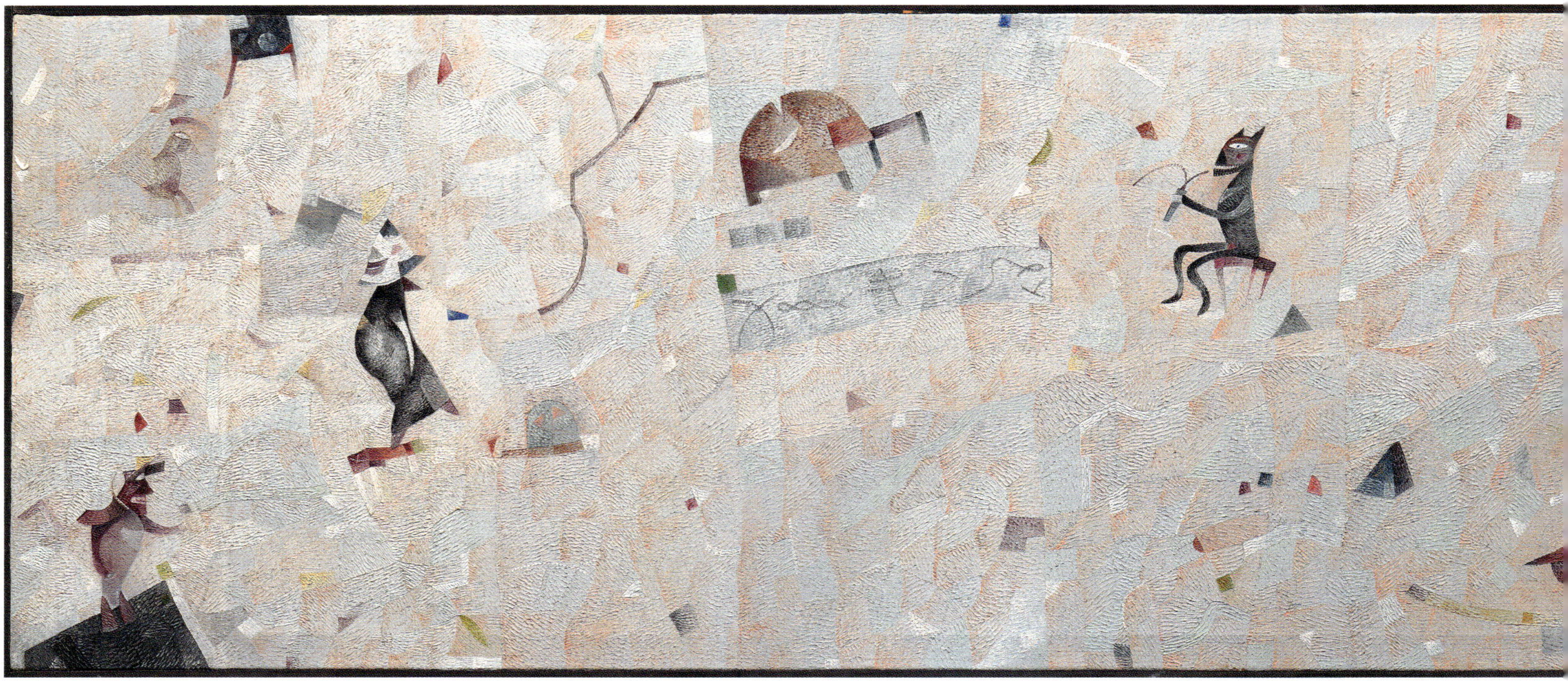

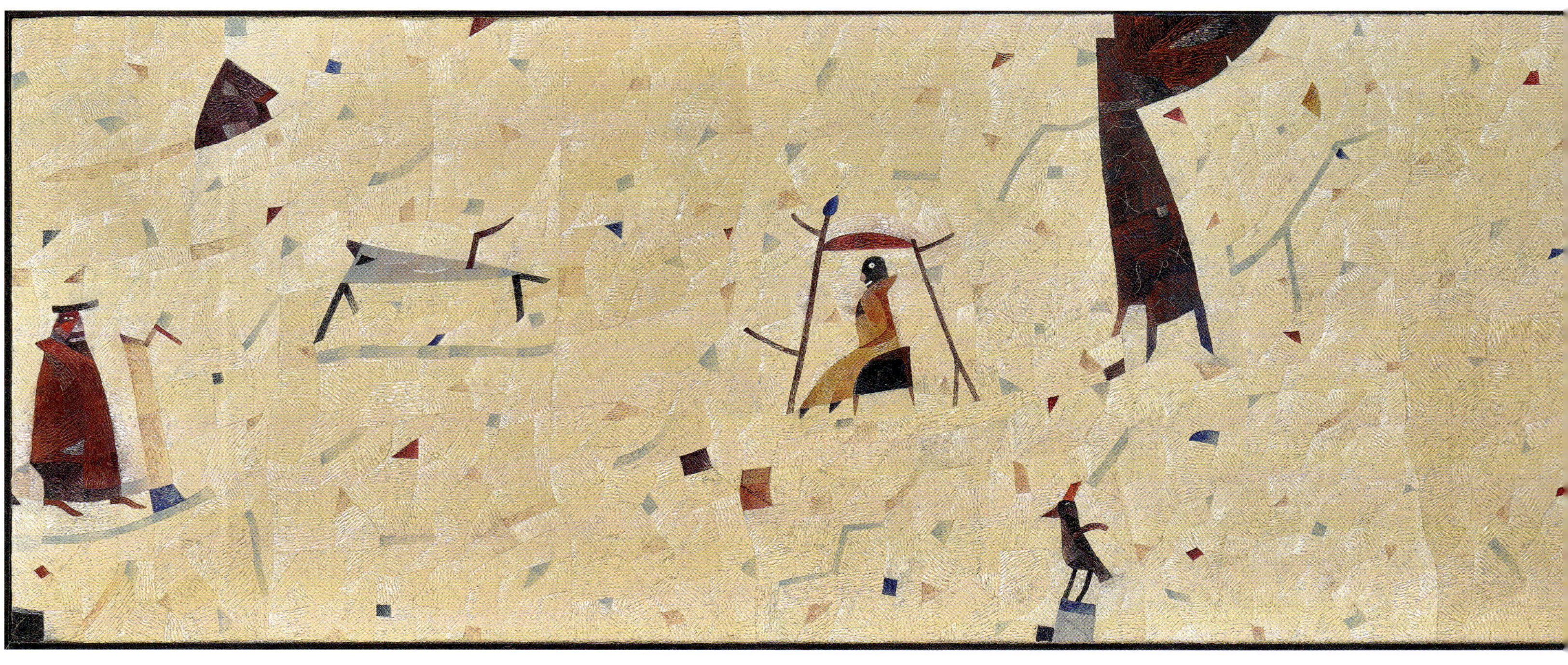

↑ *Crosses to Bear*, 1979.
Oil on canvas, 15 × 68 ½ in. Collection of Steve and Beth Jones.

↓ *Curtain Call (For Michael)*, 1979.
Oil on canvas, 14 × 69 in. Collection of Lucas and Julia Himovitz.

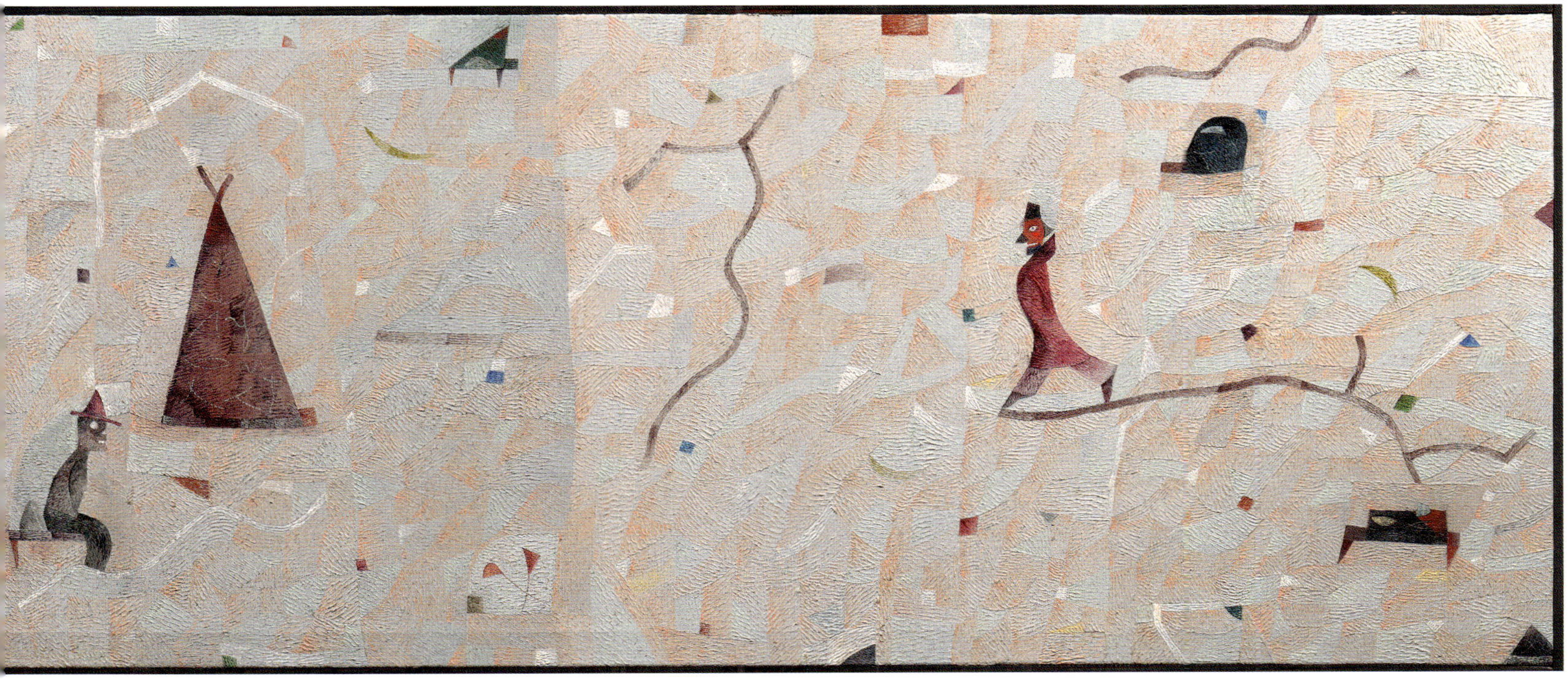

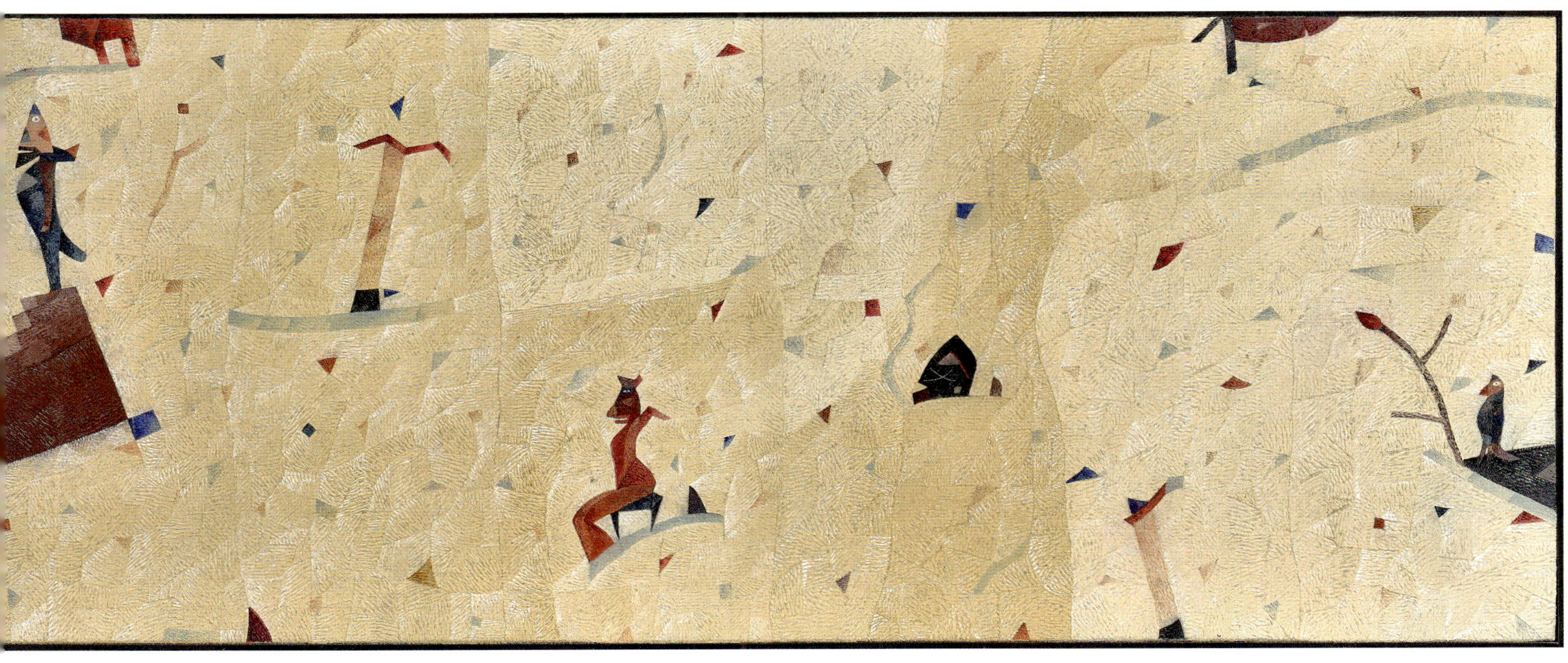

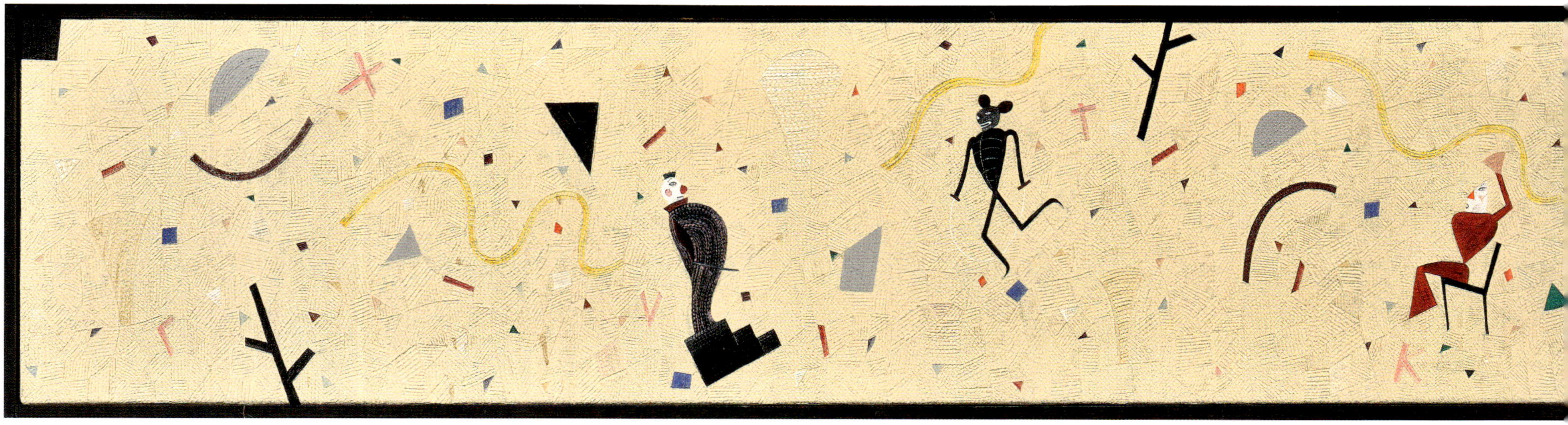

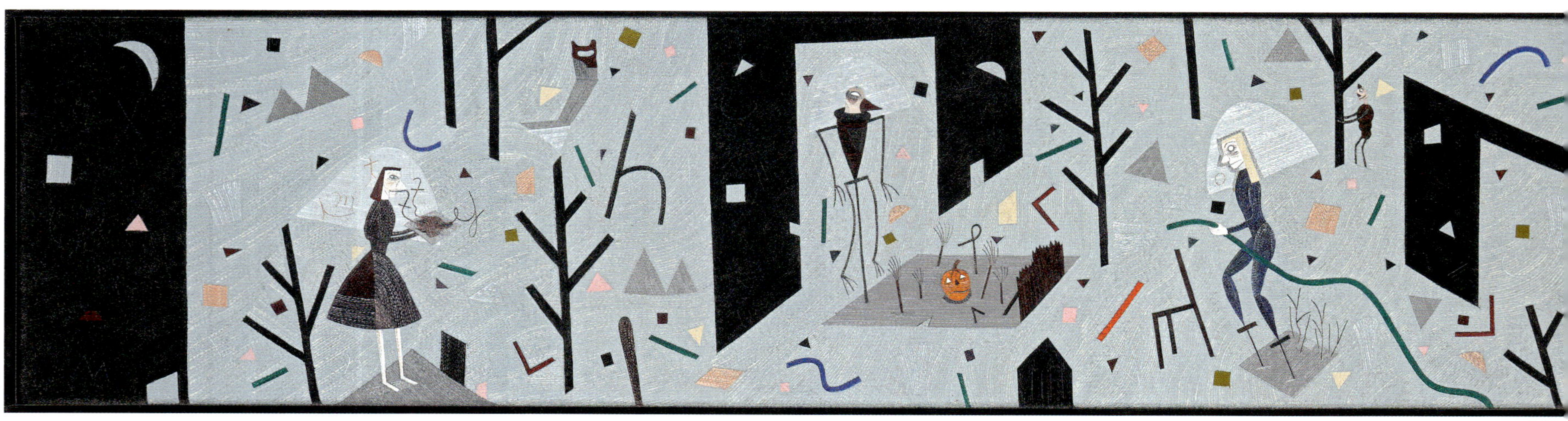

↑ *Blonde and Blueeyed,* 1982.
Oil on canvas, 7 × 90 ⅜ in. Collection of Marny and Rick Wasserman.

↓ *Cross-Examine,* 1986.
Oil on canvas, 7 × 90 in. Collection of Jeffrey Goodrich and Mary Jameson.

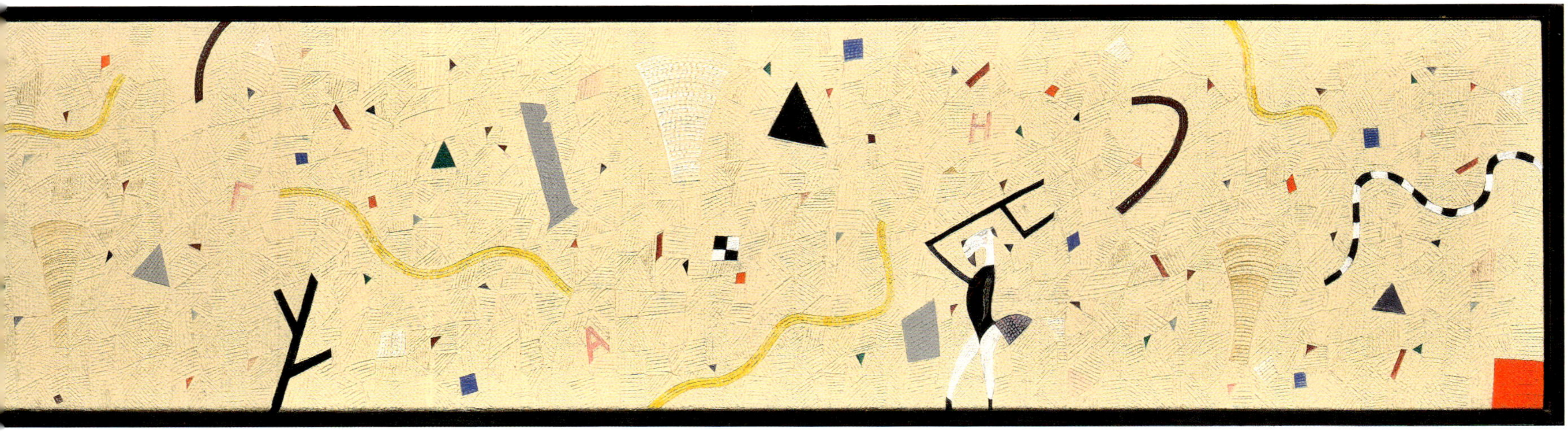

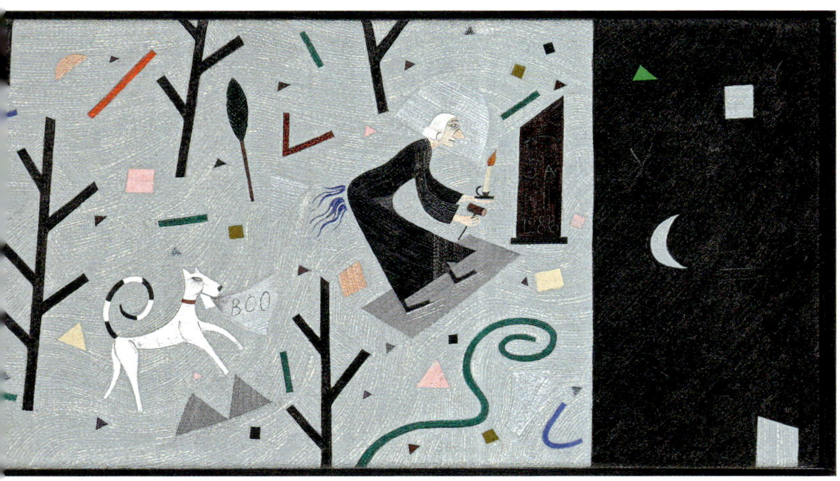
BOO

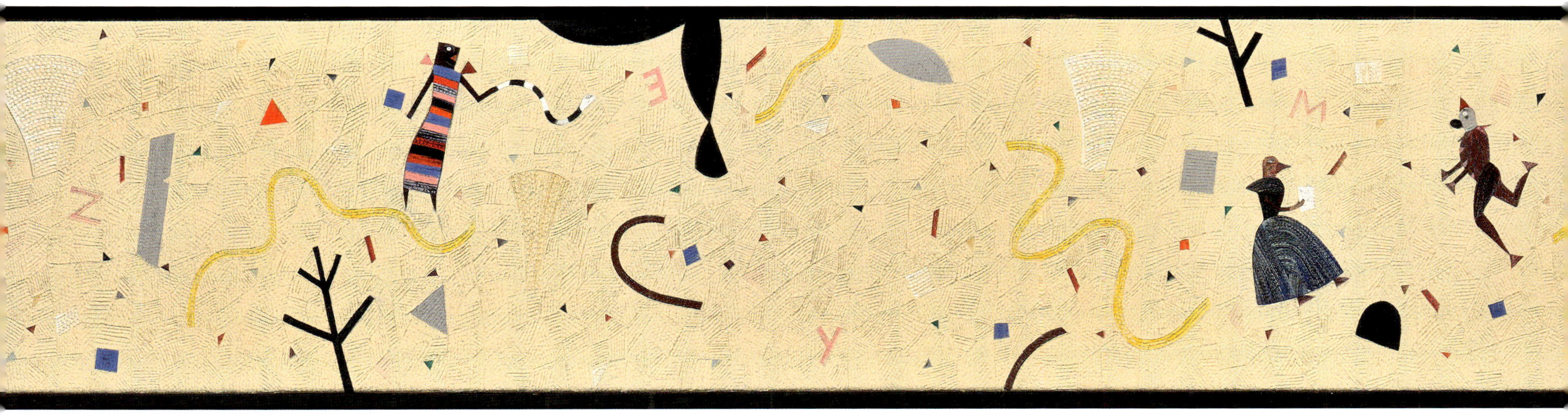

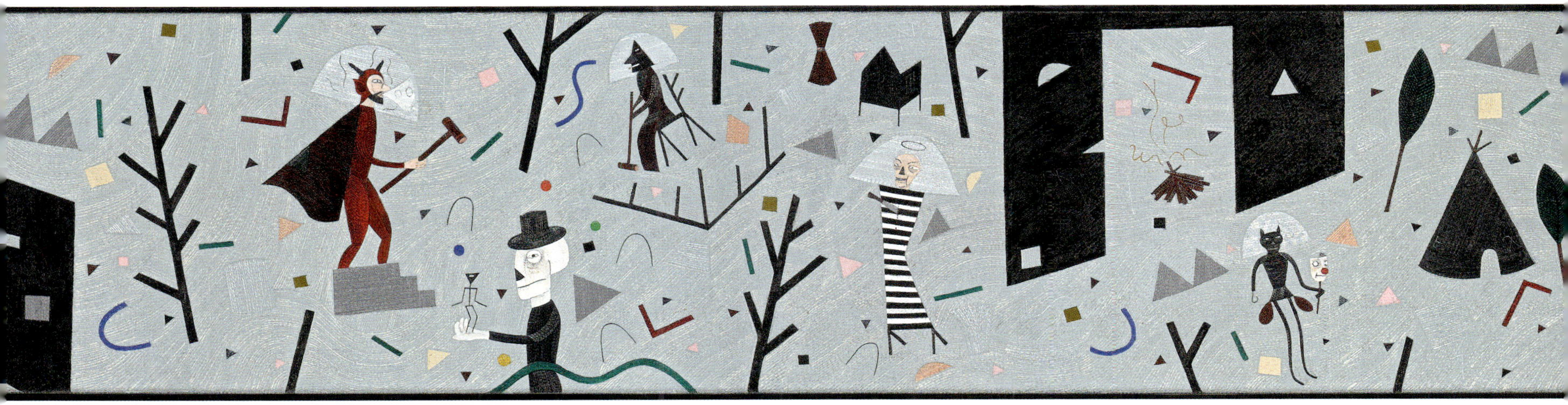

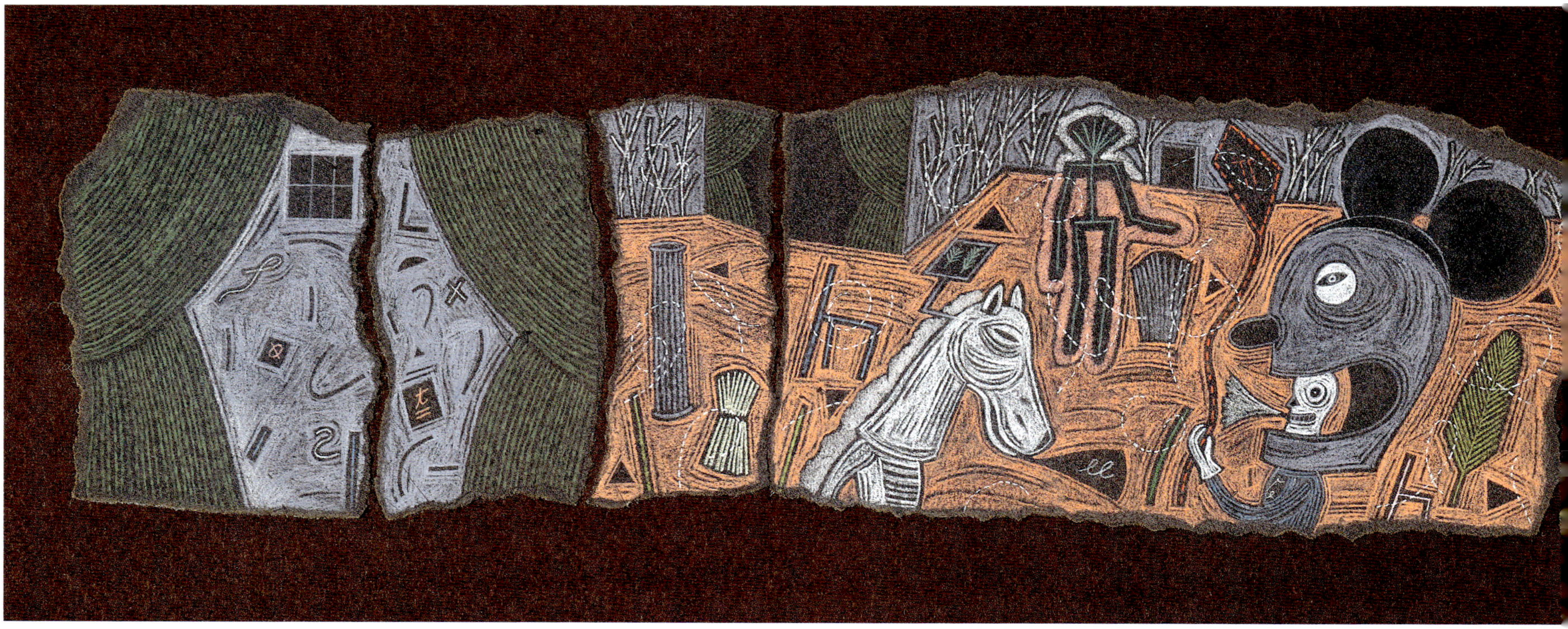

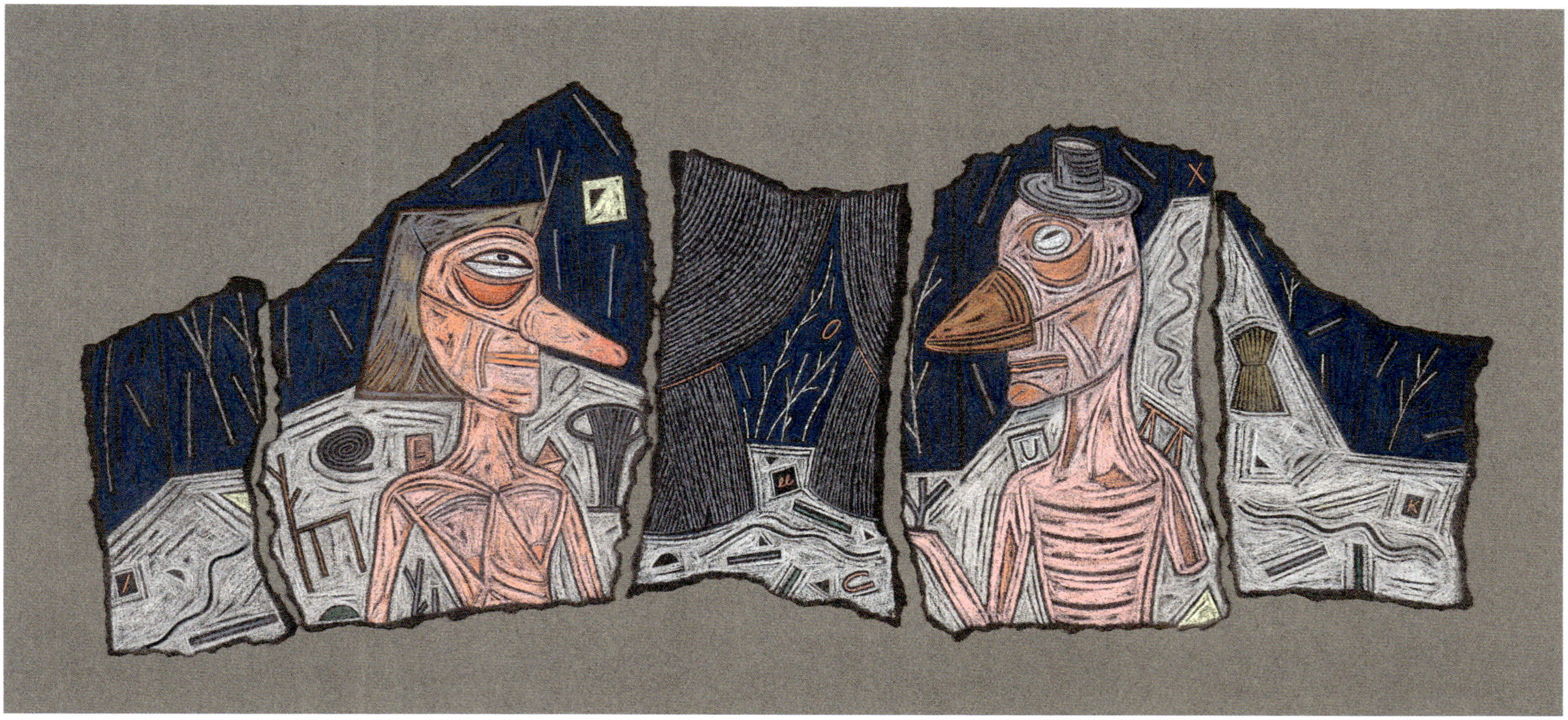

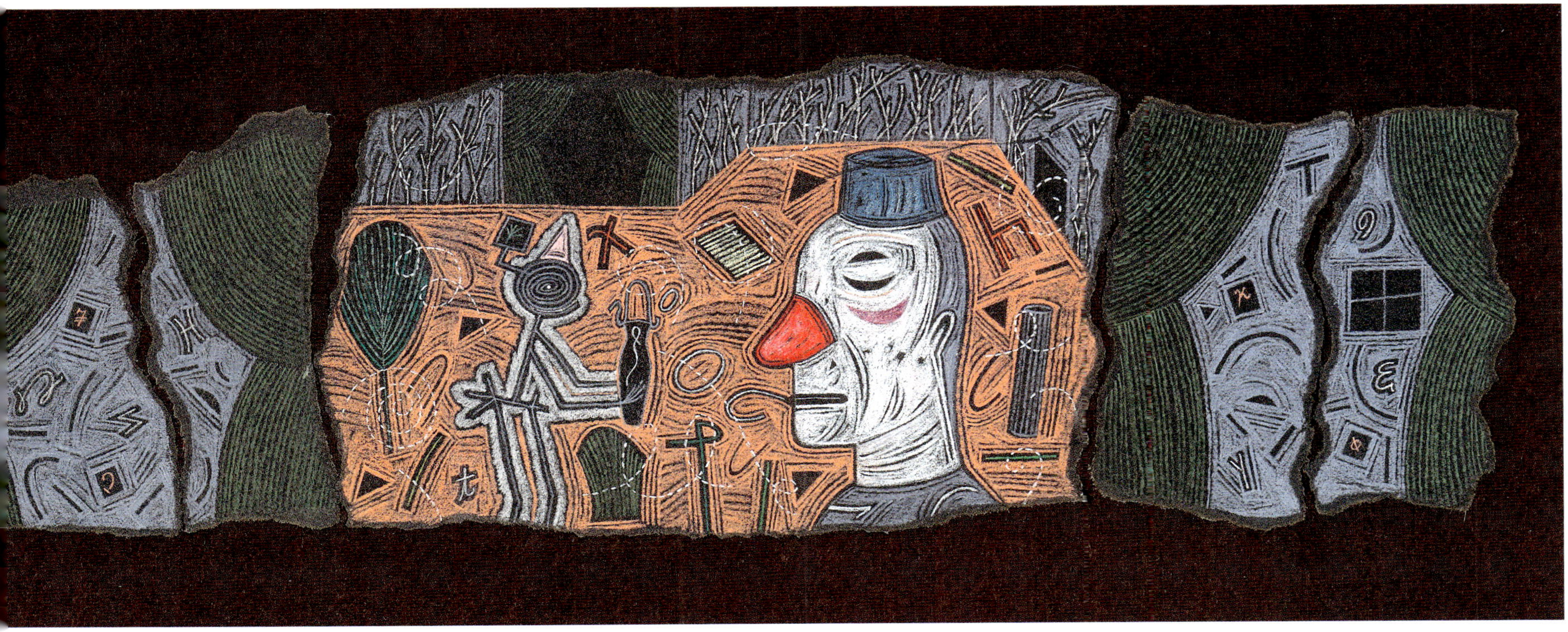

that suited working in her small, at-home studio, and resulted in new effects in oil.[10] Between each section of *Crosses to Bear*, slight ridges of impasto arise, giving its multi-hued surface a complex texture that plays with the light. [pp. 128–129]

In this instance, the dream continues to reveal itself inch by inch. At the center of this wide canvas appears a man sitting on a low seat. He leans forward, hands tucked between his legs with neck craned in a position of engagement, as if in conversation. His facial features are cartoonish, formed of basic circles, triangles, and rectangles for the eyes, nose, and mouth, akin to a jack-o-lantern. Such deliberate abstraction of features and posture effaces specific identification; in Adan's work hybrid, imaginative figures become vessels for the viewer's associations, whether the figure is fantastical, clownish, or playfully toy-like. Additional hints also appear of popular characters from television and decades of children's lunchboxes, which the artist collects, but never directly quotes. Only the occasional appearance of Mickey Mouse ears on a character offers critique. In Adan's career-long celebration of absurdist narratives, her figures escape stock types and are used to trigger curiosity rather than pure recognition of caricature.

As her career progressed, Adan's subject matter included a revolving cast of birds, clowns, skeletons, and other characters that tease or directly reference her husband, herself, and the dynamics of their special universe, including their many beloved dogs and cats.[11] While Adan continued this exceedingly wide format in several more paintings, including *Pen Pal, Trick or Treat,* and *Horse Sense,* she also turned to the intimate, using square canvases that varied in exact dimensions but typically measure approximately 10 × 10 inches. [p. 140, p. 2, p. 145] In each of these new scenes, she created shallow stage-like settings. Figures are sparely modeled and forms appear flattened, painted with exceedingly tight brushwork. Both scale and technique evoke the preciousness of medieval miniatures.

↑ *Smoke Signals,* 1986.
Torn paper and colored pencils on black paper, 10 ¼ × 31 in. Collection of Scott and Ruixia Howe.

← *Nose 2 Nose,* 1986.
Torn paper and colored pencils on black paper, 11 × 20 in. Collection of Vicky Wallace and Ron Peetz.

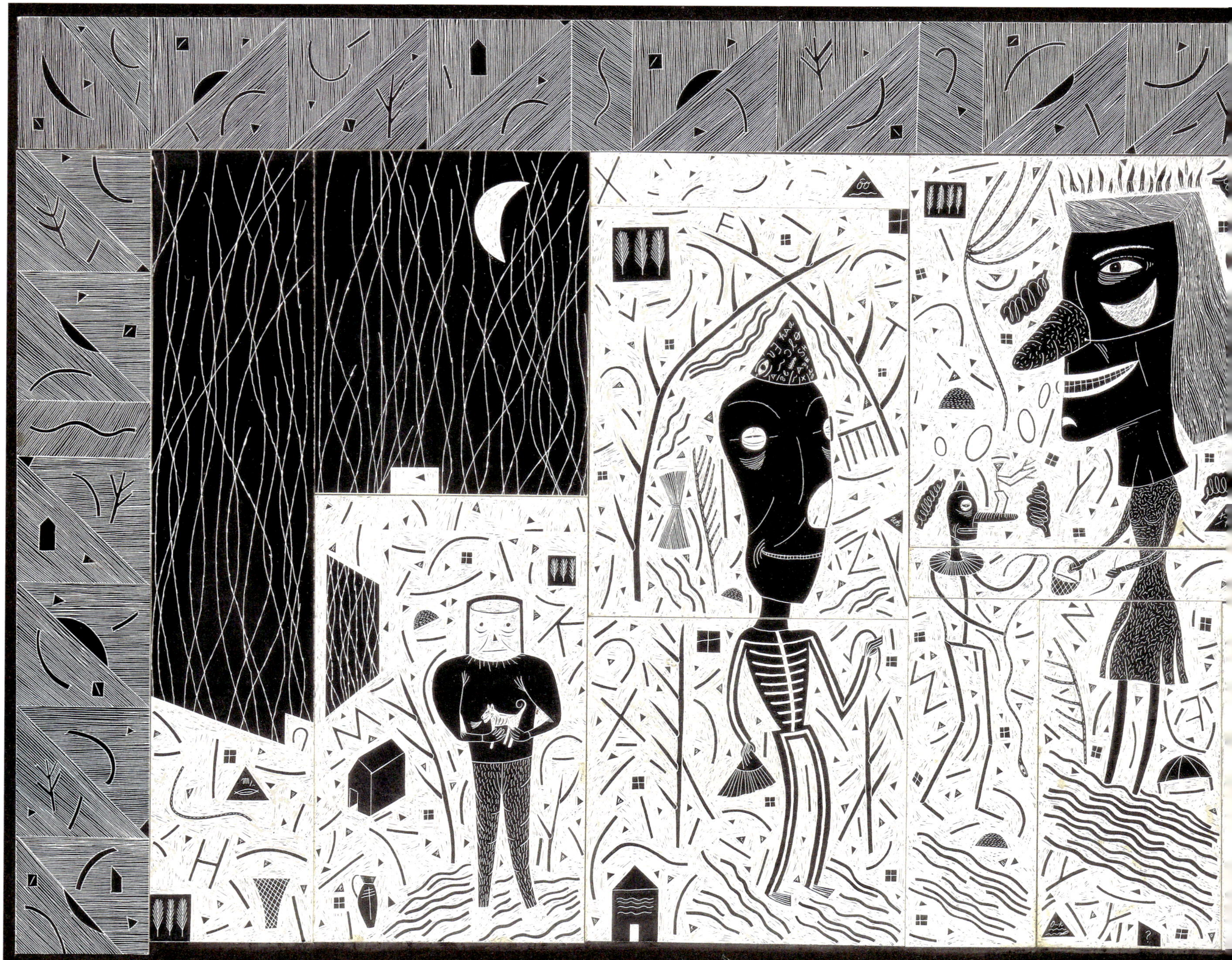

Wise Cracks, 1987.
Scratchboard and wood, 16 × 33 in. Collection of the Artist.

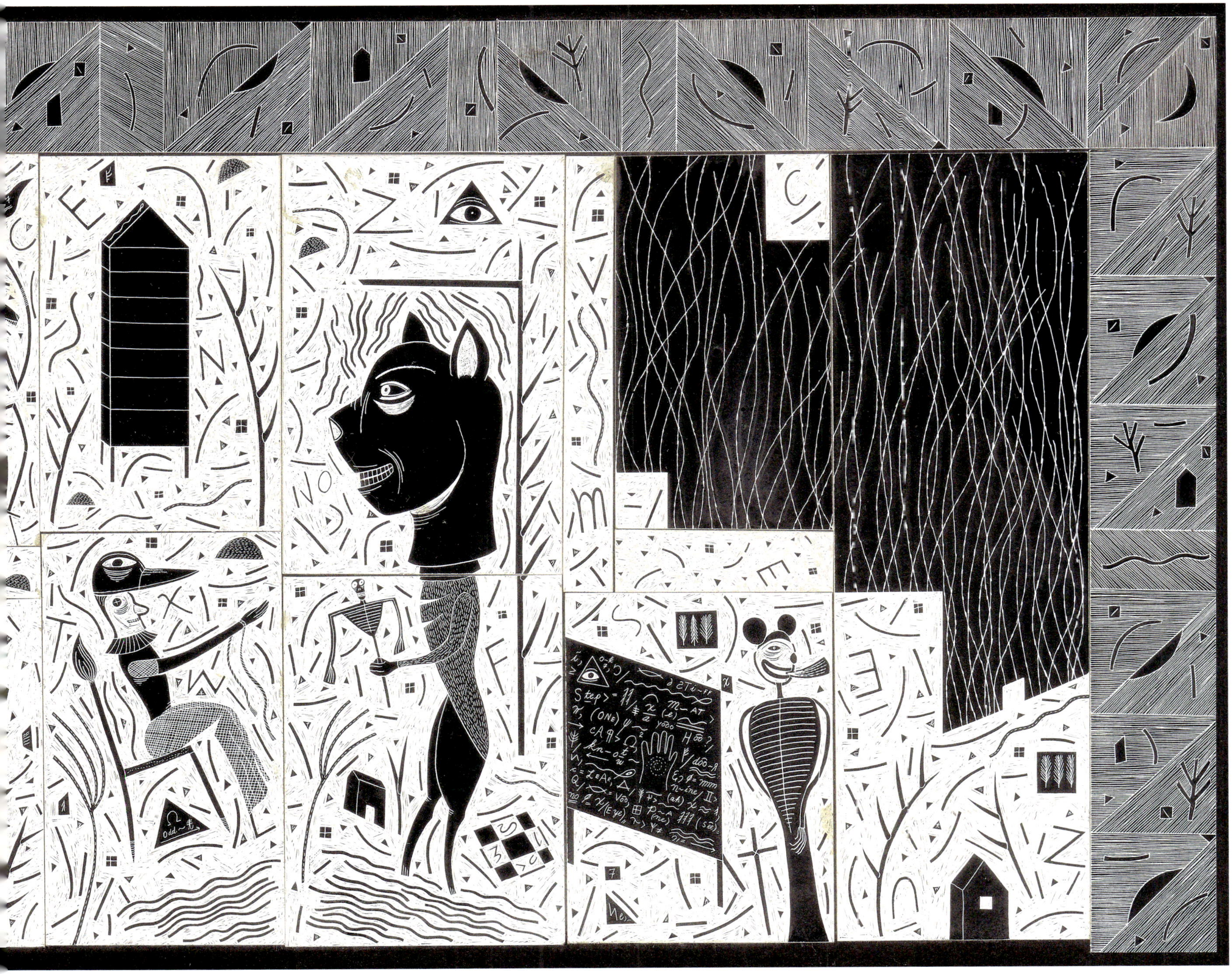

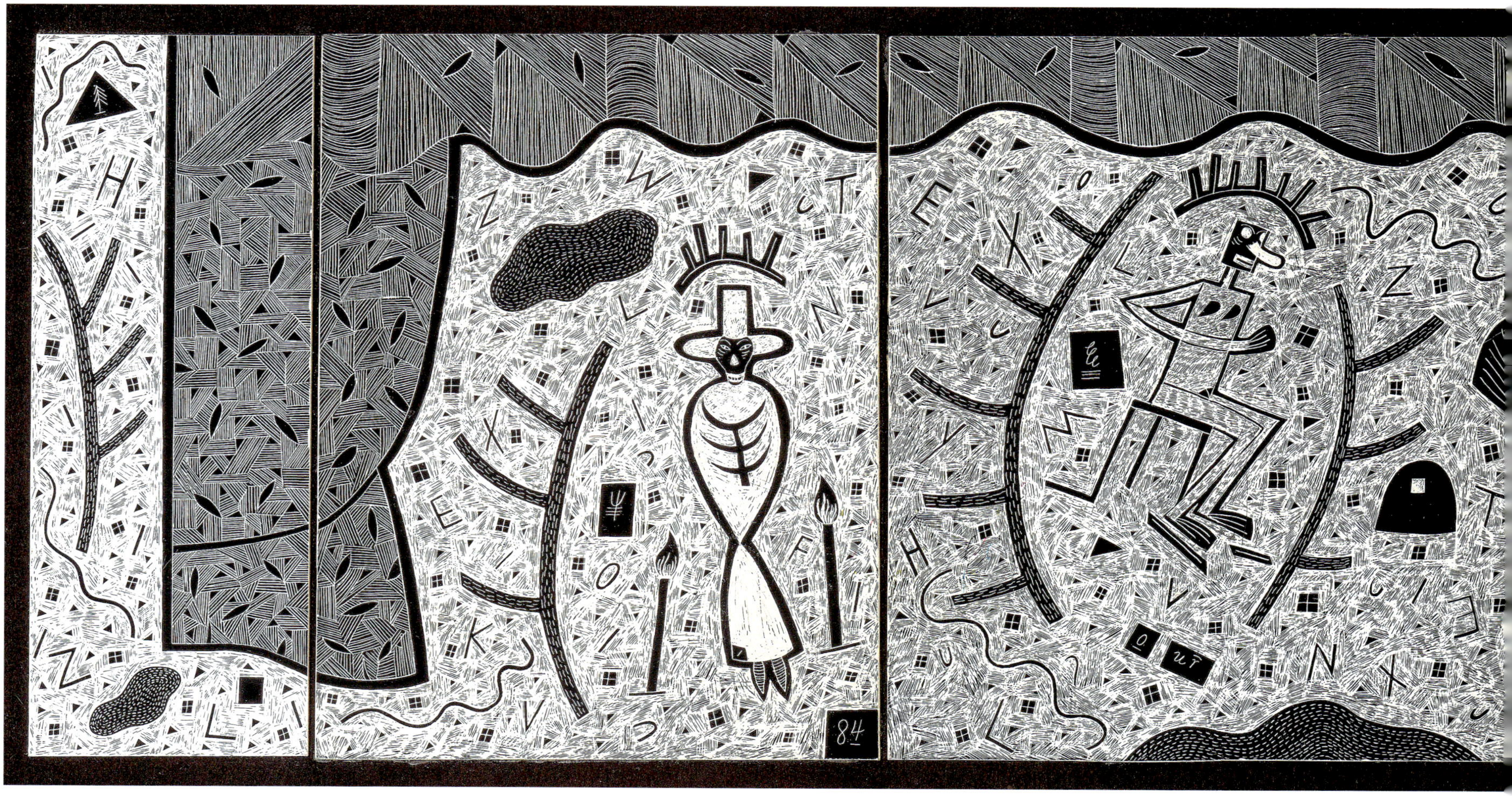

Holey Smokes!, 1984.
Scratchboard, 10 × 31 in. Collection of Pat Mahony and Randy Getz.

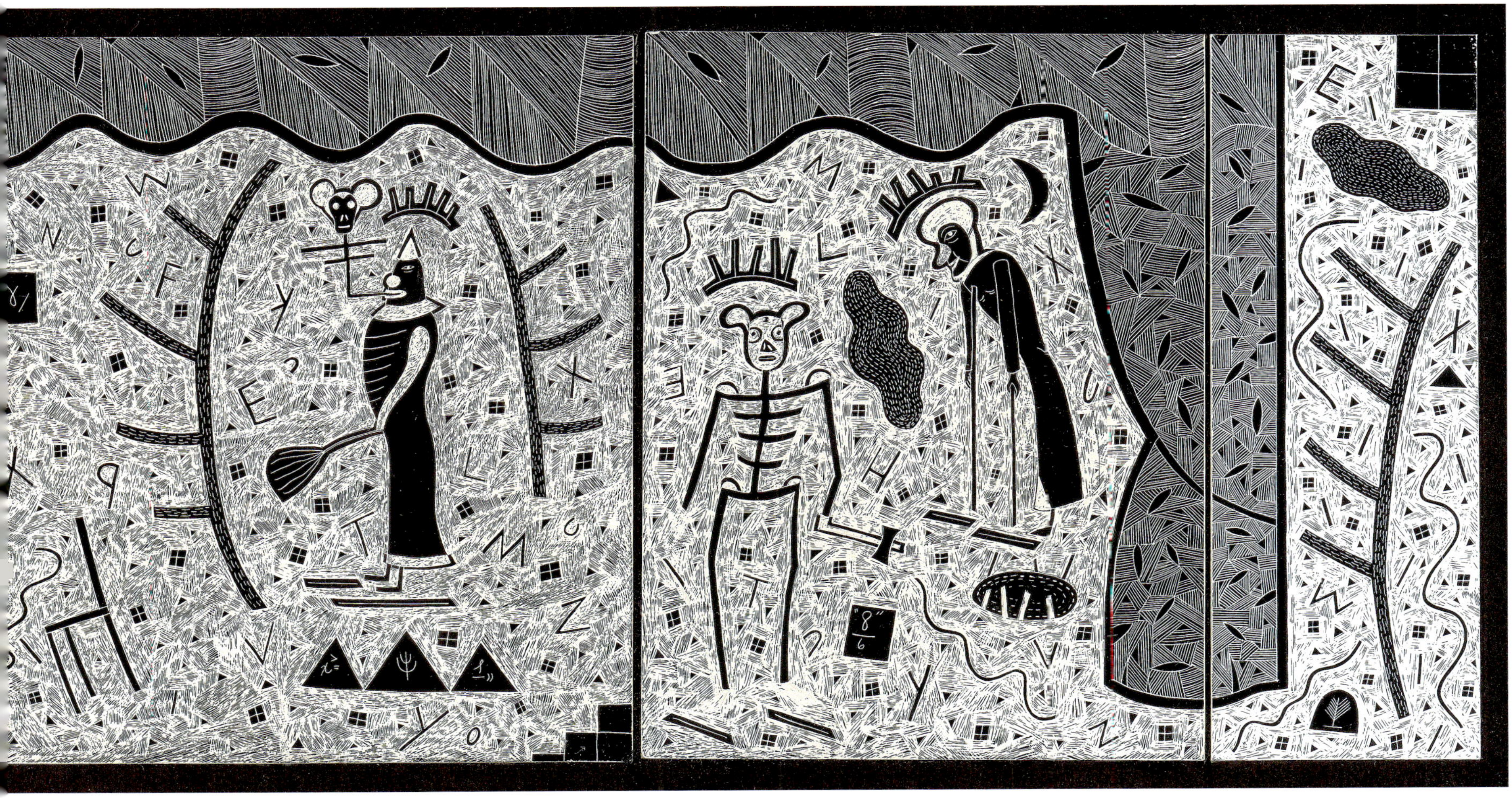

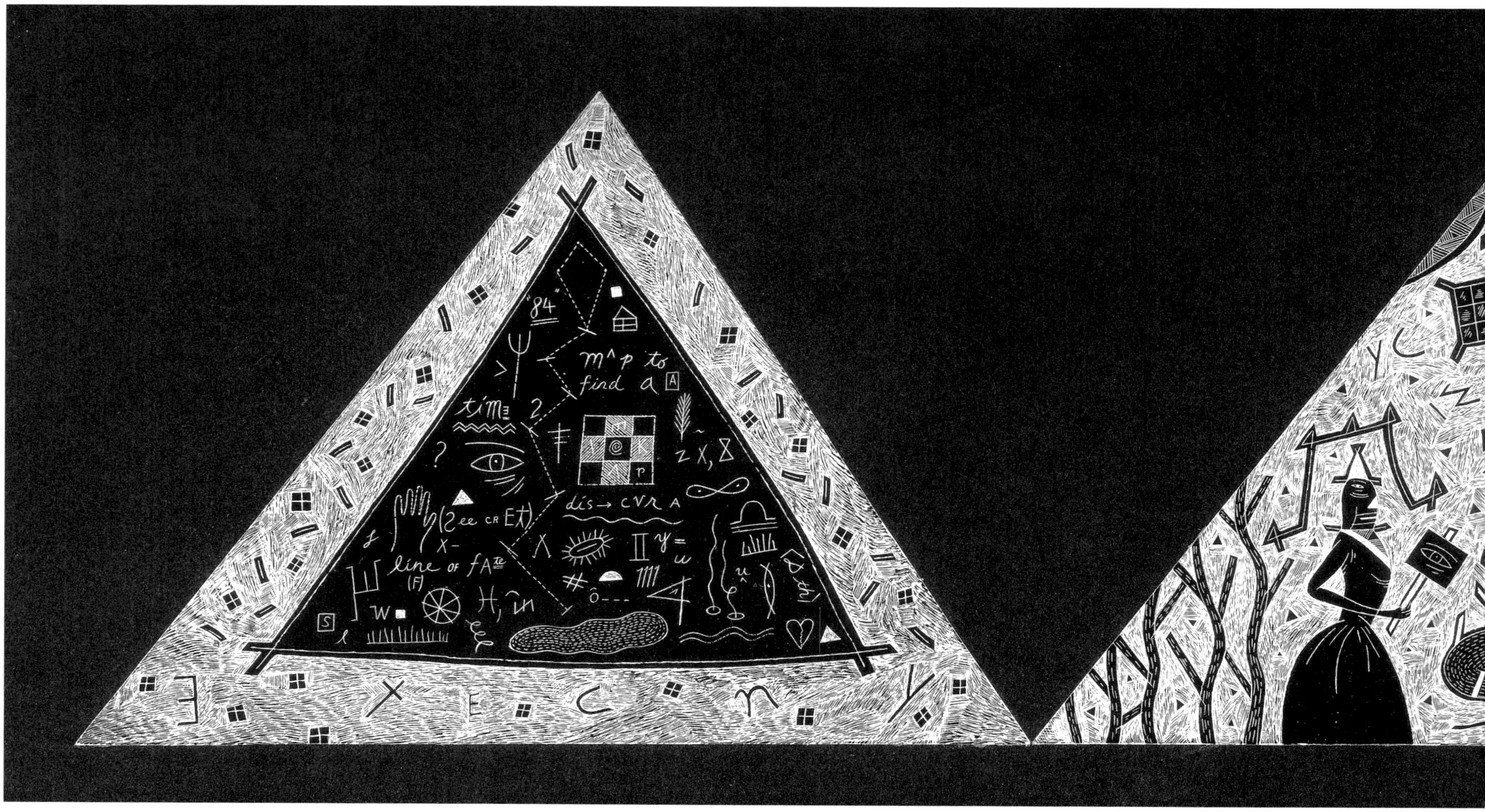

Eternal Triangle, 1984.
Scratchboard, 6 ¼ × 26 ¾ in. Collection of Marny and Rick Wasserman.

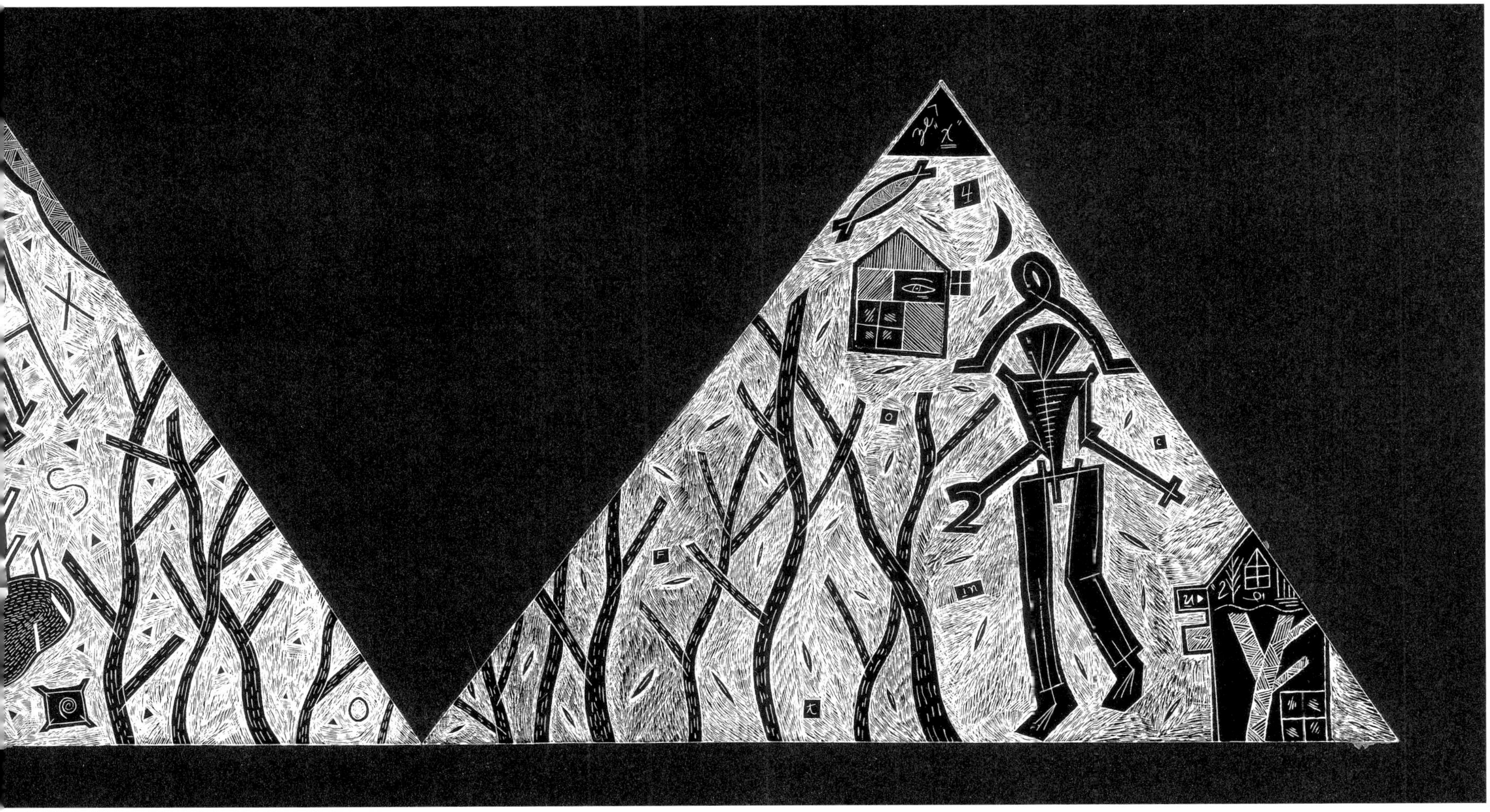

Her imagery remains enigmatic but more densely populated. New forms and figures emerge, including stick trees, clown figures with Mickey Mouse ears, the black-and-white checkerboard, a stepstool seat, and female antagonists. Such works, which have been described as "introverted, the stuff of dreams, symbols, and finely detailed innerscapes"[12] —as evidenced in *Even Steven*—act as discourses on Adan's everyday dramas, especially the interpersonal dynamics and tensions of relationships. [p. 143]

With *Even Steven*, Adan offers a morality play, or perhaps *commedia dell'arte*, in which a man costumed as the devil confronts a bare-chested woman, incongruently wearing a colossal cat's head mask. Their conflict takes place on a shallow stage, upon which the main curtain has been raised to reveal the architecture of a living room. Curtains surround a pane window that hovers supernaturally, while upright beams suggest timber framing, domestic furnishings, and trees in the Garden of Eden. Only the devil and the woman are solidly planted in a funhouse that both tilts toward and recedes from the viewer. Amid vase shapes, triangles, and squares are two family dogs and a representation of the wood sculpture *The Conjuror* (1983) by Stevens. Without shadows and arranged eccentrically, each element suggests energy and motion. Adan's directional brushstrokes further activate the canvas and the countless ridges of impasto result in busy,

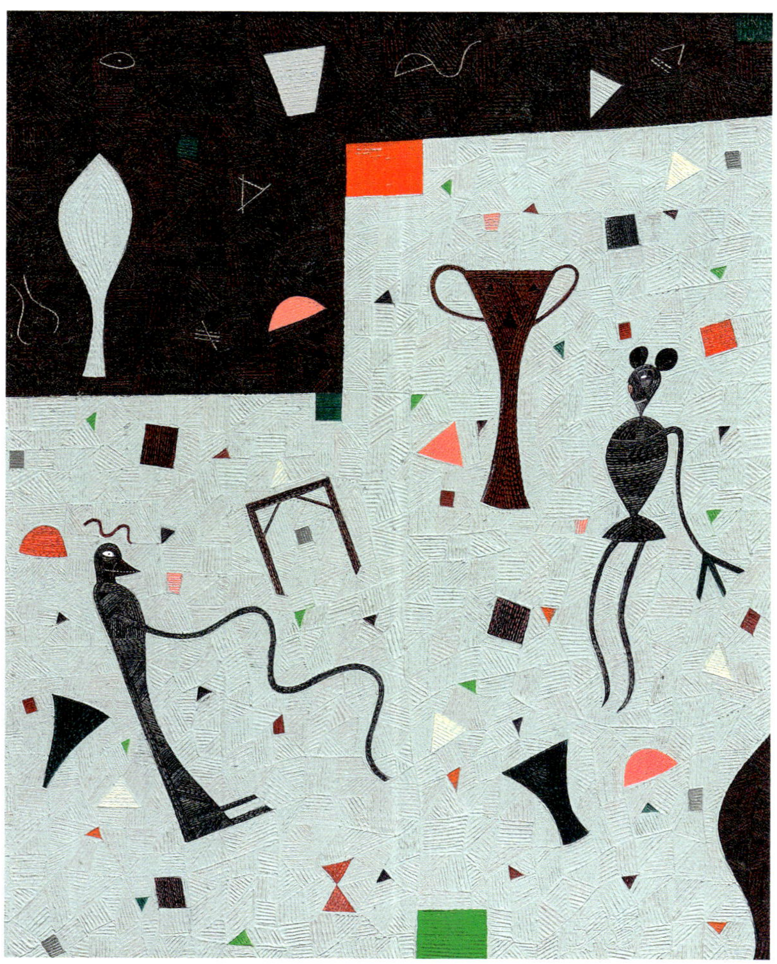

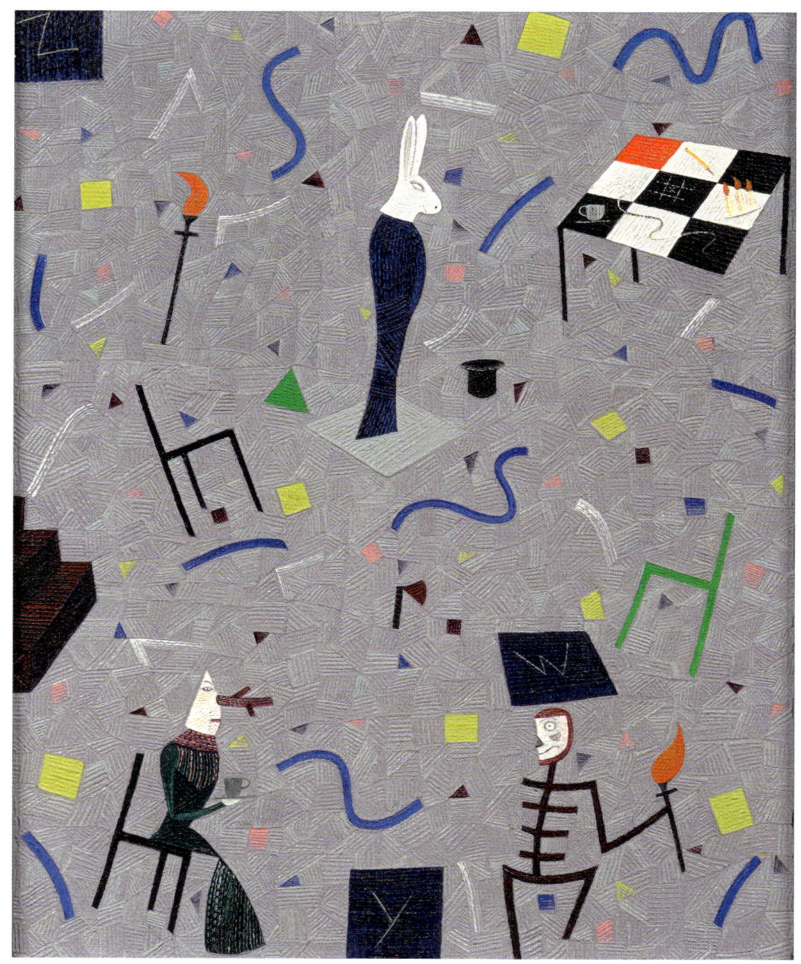

repeating patterns that increase the scene's visual tension—a tension like vibrations along a taut piano wire.

This living room is a domestic, suburban Eden that has suffered a terrible disruption. Neither the woman nor the man is cast out, but the devil holds before him a black-and-white serpent, while another sinuous serpent slithers below. A mysterious small slab stands to his left, which unlike anything else in this composition does cast a slight wedge of shadow that grounds it to the stage. Perhaps Adan has painted a household door to complement the window almost directly across from it? Or, maybe, with its pediment and short stature, the artist intends the viewer to read this as a tombstone, suggesting that this devil has dug his own grave. Original sin, however, is clearly not Adan's subject, though the mundane, daily trespasses of married life are. The melodramatic play sees Adan and Stevens cast as the bare-chested woman in an A-line skirt and as the devil respectively. They face each other, but the distance separating them emphasizes their discord. Suzanne laughs, "Mike is always the devil. I'm lucky he is good-humored about this."[13]

By 1989, Adan realized that the art world favored large works and grand statements, so that for her to reach a new audience a shift in scale was necessary. Her canvases leapt in measurement to 56 ¼ × 71 ¼ and 66 × 60 inches, for example. The larger scale obliged her to use broader,

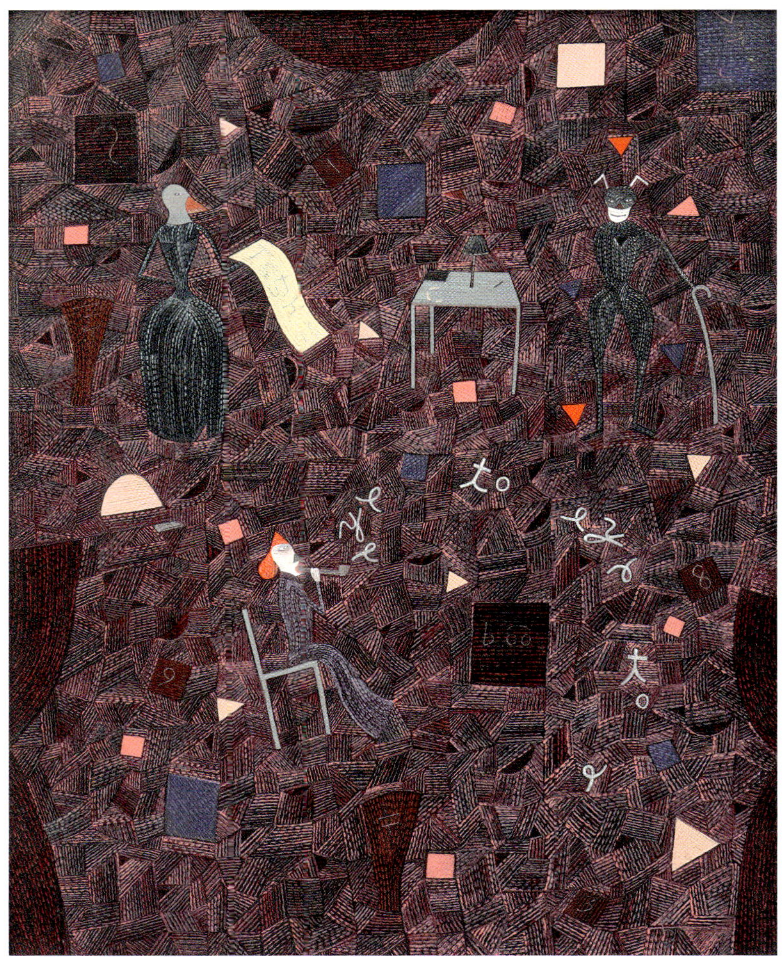

←← *Pen Pal,* 1983.
Oil on canvas, 10 ¼ × 8 in. Crocker Art Museum, gift of Dr. Samuel and Mrs. Sharon Goby, 1984.25.

← *Sleight of Hand,* 1983.
Oil on canvas, 9 ¾ × 7 ½ in. Collection of Elaine O'Brien.

→ *Words of Wisdom,* 1983.
Oil on canvas, 10 × 7 ½ in. Collection of Lucas and Julia Himovitz.

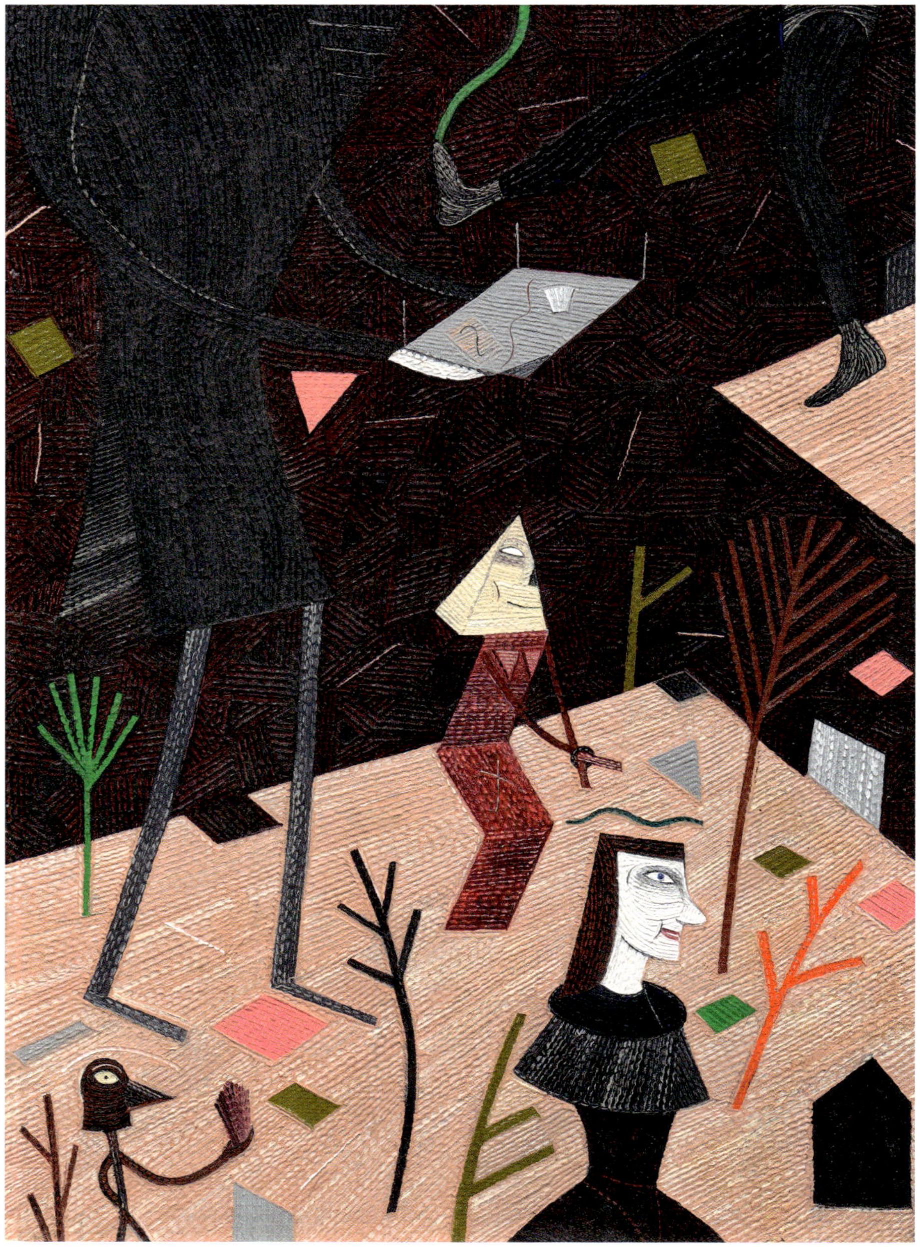

Fit to be Tied, 1986.
Oil on canvas, 13 × 11 in. Collection of Jerald Silva.

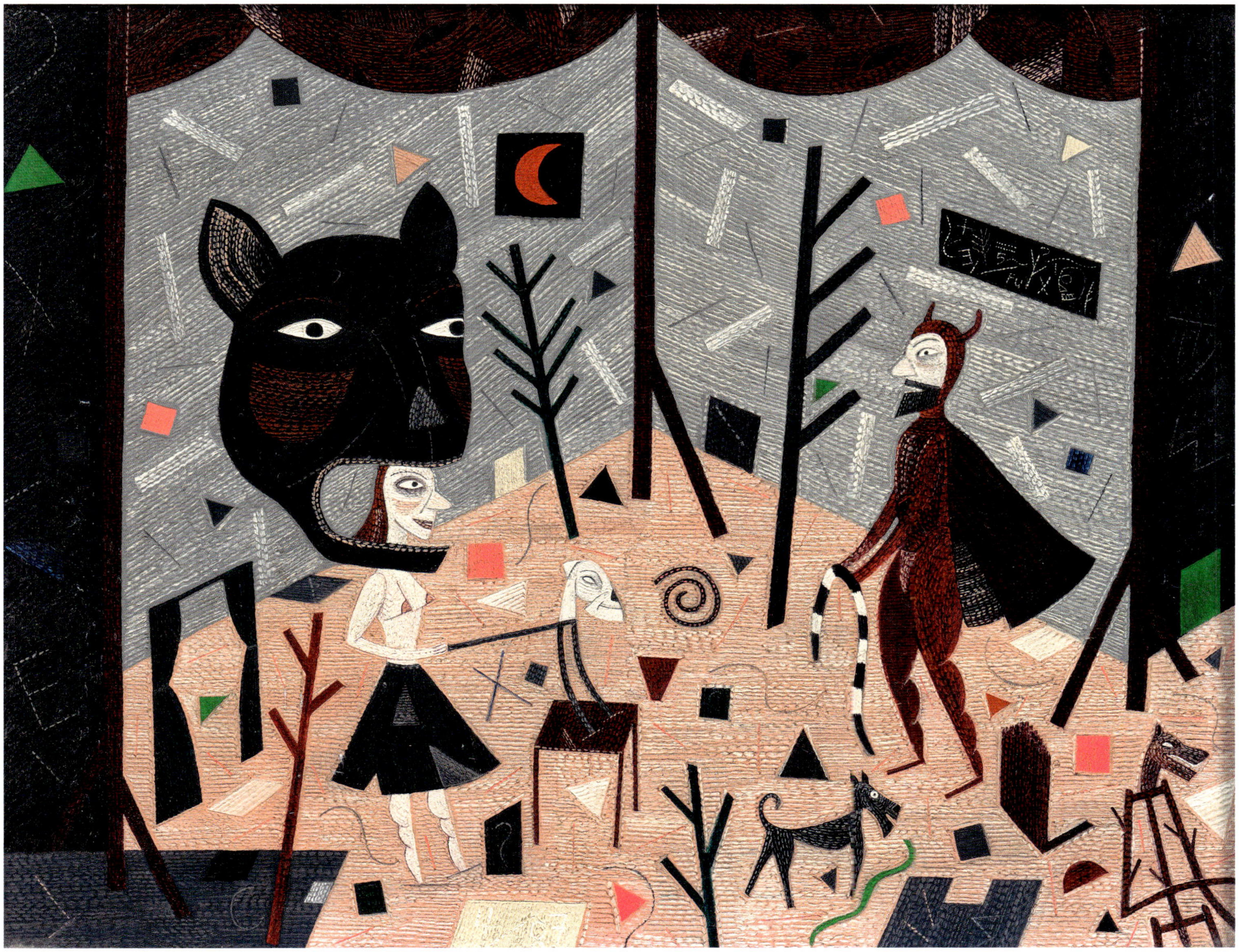

Even Steven, 1987.
Oil on canvas, 11 ¾ × 13 ¾ in. Collection of Michael Stevens.

bolder brushstrokes, but even in those changes she kept the lessons of van Gogh in mind. In applying thick paint, she layered her preferred muted colors and activated the canvas with ridges of impasto. These hallmarks of her mature style appear in her 1989 painting *Cattails*. [p. 146] It depicts houses and doors, twig trees, and black-and-white striped cattails. A dog and a horse walk this dormant forest, which is a careful, complex abstraction of space, tilting both away from and toward the viewer. The vase she includes may signify the long arc of art's history; it is among her favorite symbols, and here evokes a Greek form. The main figure references art and whimsy, suggesting the sculptural figures of Michael Stevens, its tin-can head made friendly, not threatening, by smiling eyes and the brief description of a raised cheekbone. Appearing along the right edge is the border device that she frequently included in paintings from the late 1980s onward. This new strip of black-and-white squares gives the viewer a full stop to scenes dancing with characters, multi-directional strokes, and the rhythmic kaleidoscope of space were no single focal point dominates. Much of her production from this point on assumes a more cheerful and bemused continence than even a work made a year prior, such as *Life of Reilly*, in which the artist revisits a depiction of herself, seated amid the swirl of daily chaos surrounding her. [p. 147]

The formal strength of Adan's art and the ongoing appeal of her eccentric, whimsical, open-ended narratives remain undeniable. Over the decades she has achieved a consistent, technically demanding, highly recognizable style. Viewers may be challenged to decipher meanings, but the artist profoundly believes that making associations and speculations is not only intellectually stimulating but a pleasure unto itself. She has made her work one of rich examination, especially of outsized emotions and how richly humorous their effect can be upon our motives and actions. She is an astute observer of human nature, and throughout her body of work she echoes the banter of life with Michael Stevens and of her mother and aunts, who found comfort and joy in jesting over the miseries and victories of ordinary life. Her art is a complex detailing of psychological states, interpersonal tensions, character strengths, and character faults, which are universal to us all.

1 Michael Stevens once created for Adan a canvas attachment intended to support her wrist and prevent her from smearing her work. She laughs that her attempts to use it failed.

2 "A Pretty Artist from Yolo," *Yolo County Record,* August 31, 1967.

3 Suzanne Adan, conversation with the author, July 20, 2025.

4 Ibid.

5 Roberta Smith, "Extraordinary Realities," *Artforum,* January 1974, www.artforum.com/events/extraordinary-realities-232932/.

6 Ibid.

7 Ibid.

8 Suzanne Adan, conversation with the author, June 14, 2025.

9 Ibid.

10 Ibid.

11 Among them dogs Felix, Reilly, and Murphy, and cats Deenie, Olive, Dashiell, Prancer, and Squeak.

12 Dianne Heimer, "Going Places," *Sacramento Magazine* (April 1993): 13.

13 Suzanne Adan, conversation with the author, July 20, 2025.

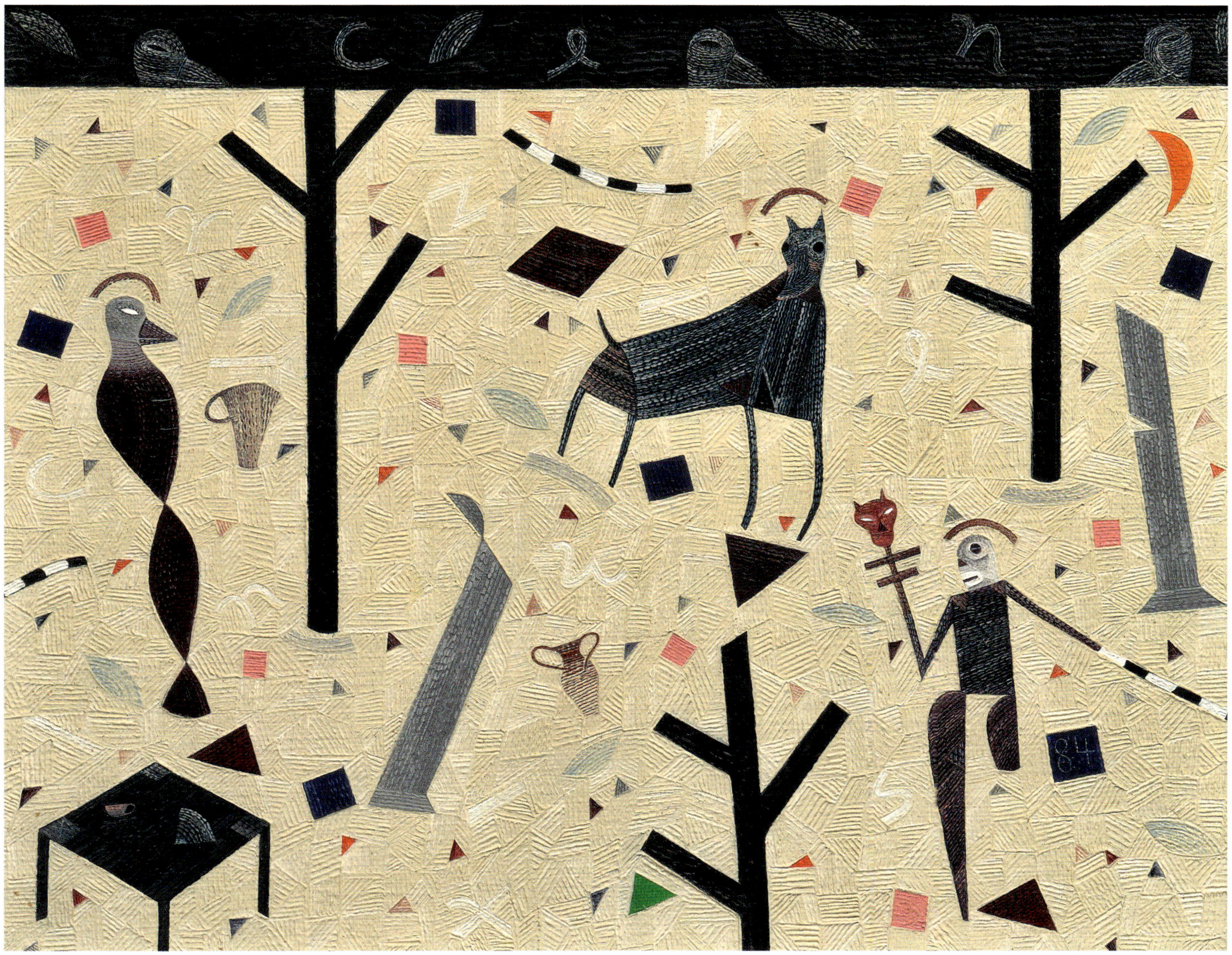

Horse Sense, 1984.
Oil on canvas, 7 ¾ × 9 ¾ in. Collection of Julia Couzens and Jay-Allen Eisen.

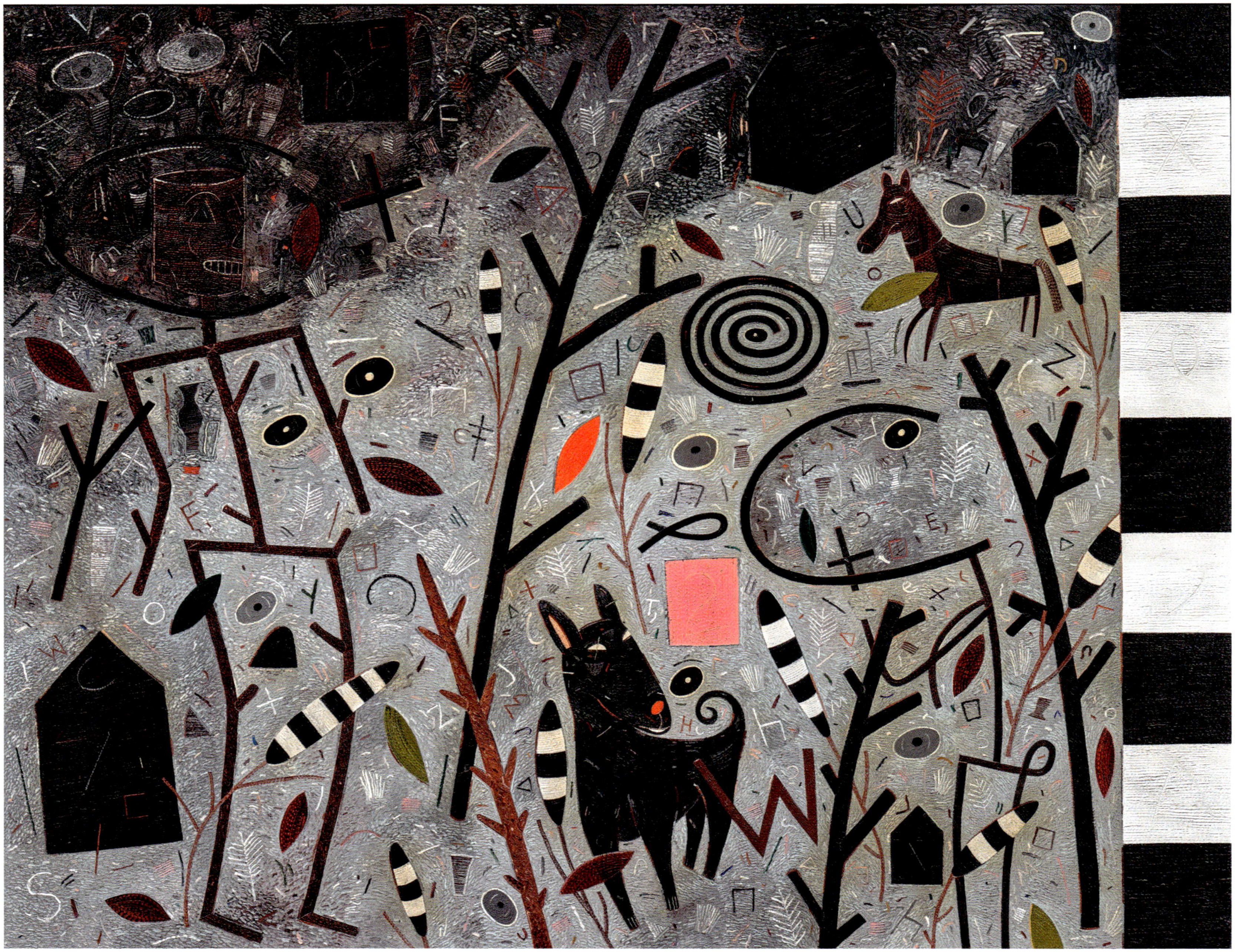

Cattails, 1989.
Oil on canvas, 57 × 73 in. Collection of Gene and Carol Livingston.

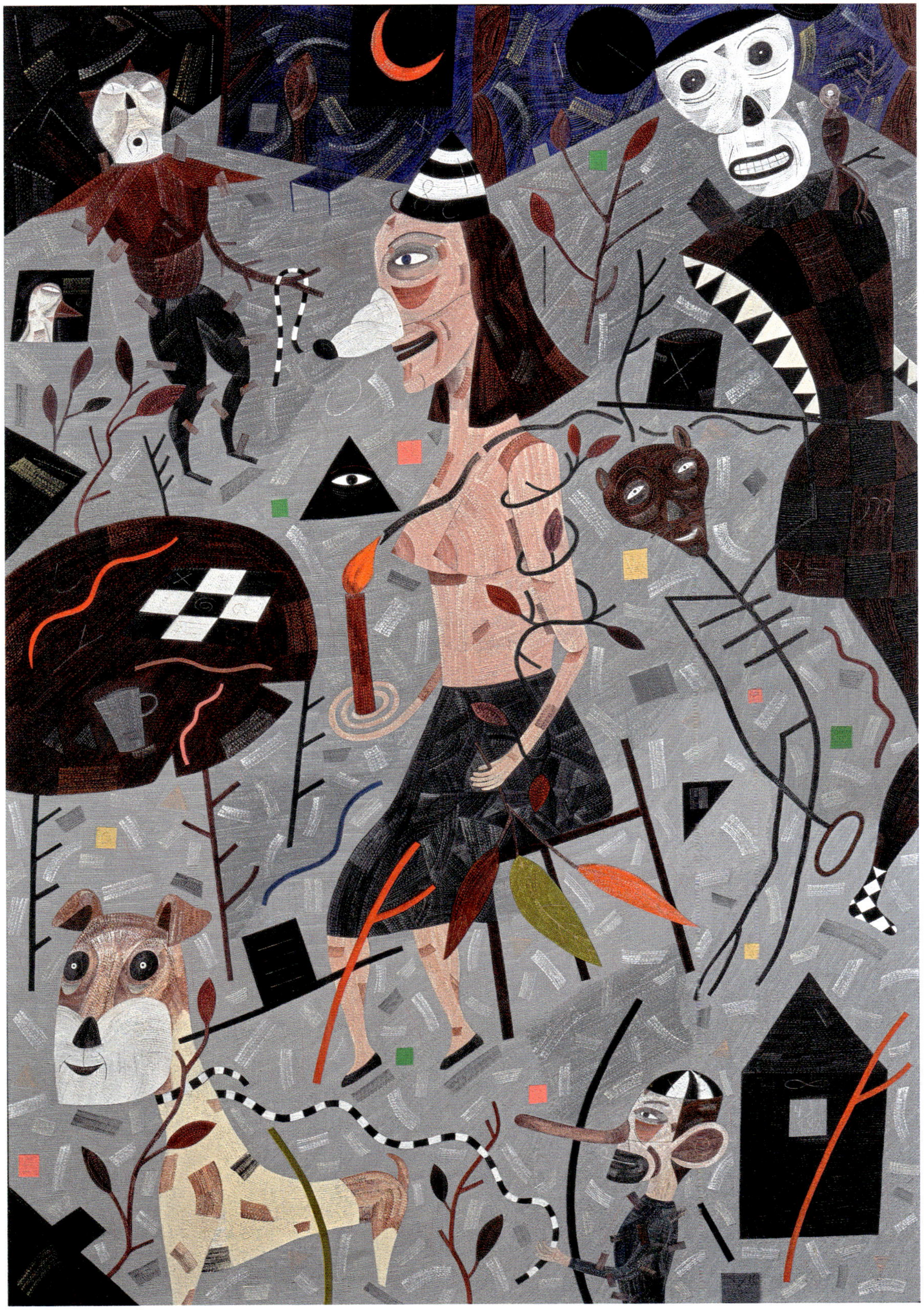

Life of Reilly, 1988.
Oil on canvas, 56 × 37 ½ in. Collection of the Artist.

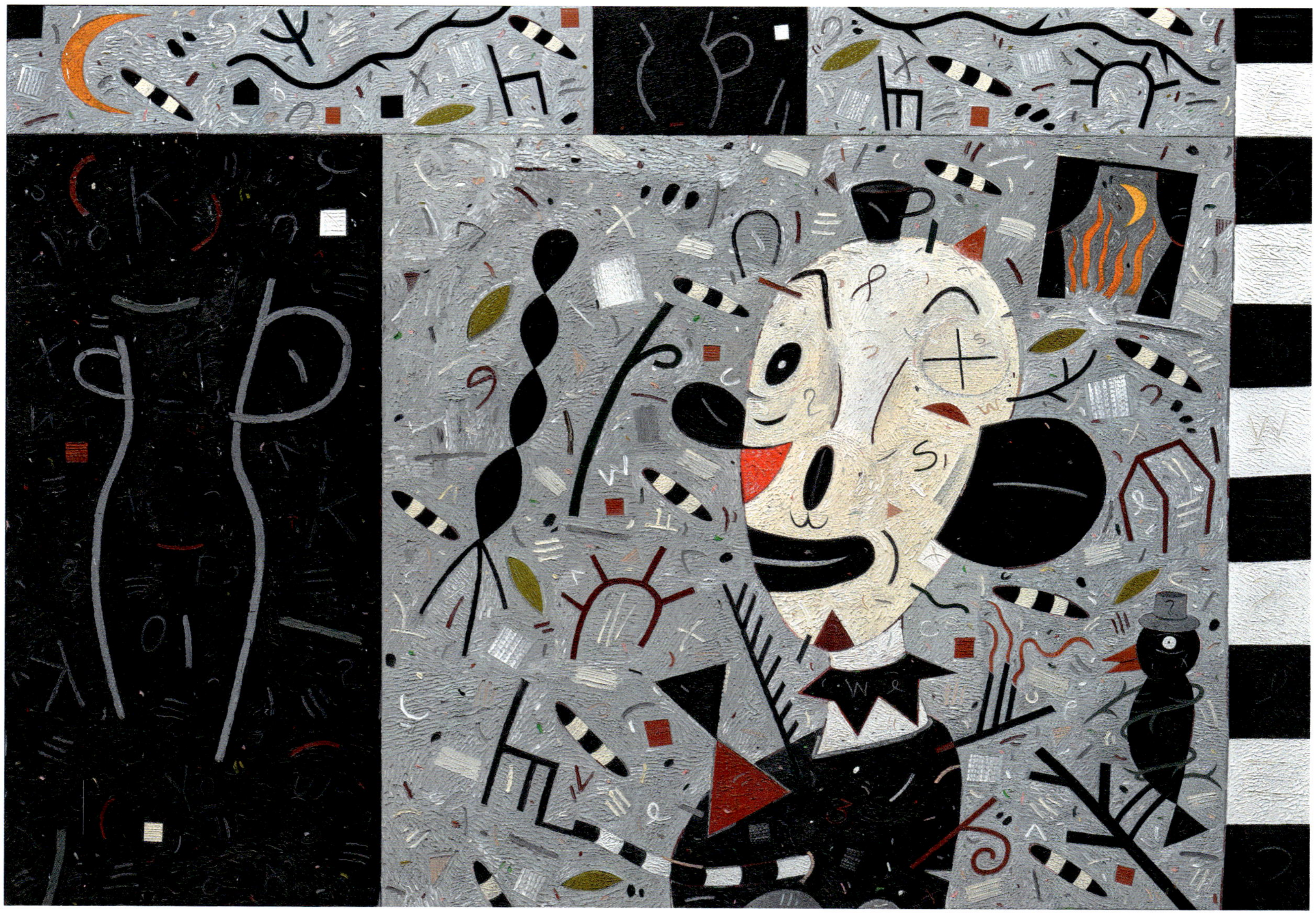

Kloun, 1992.
Oil on canvas, 49 ¼ × 68 in. Collection of Kay Lehr.

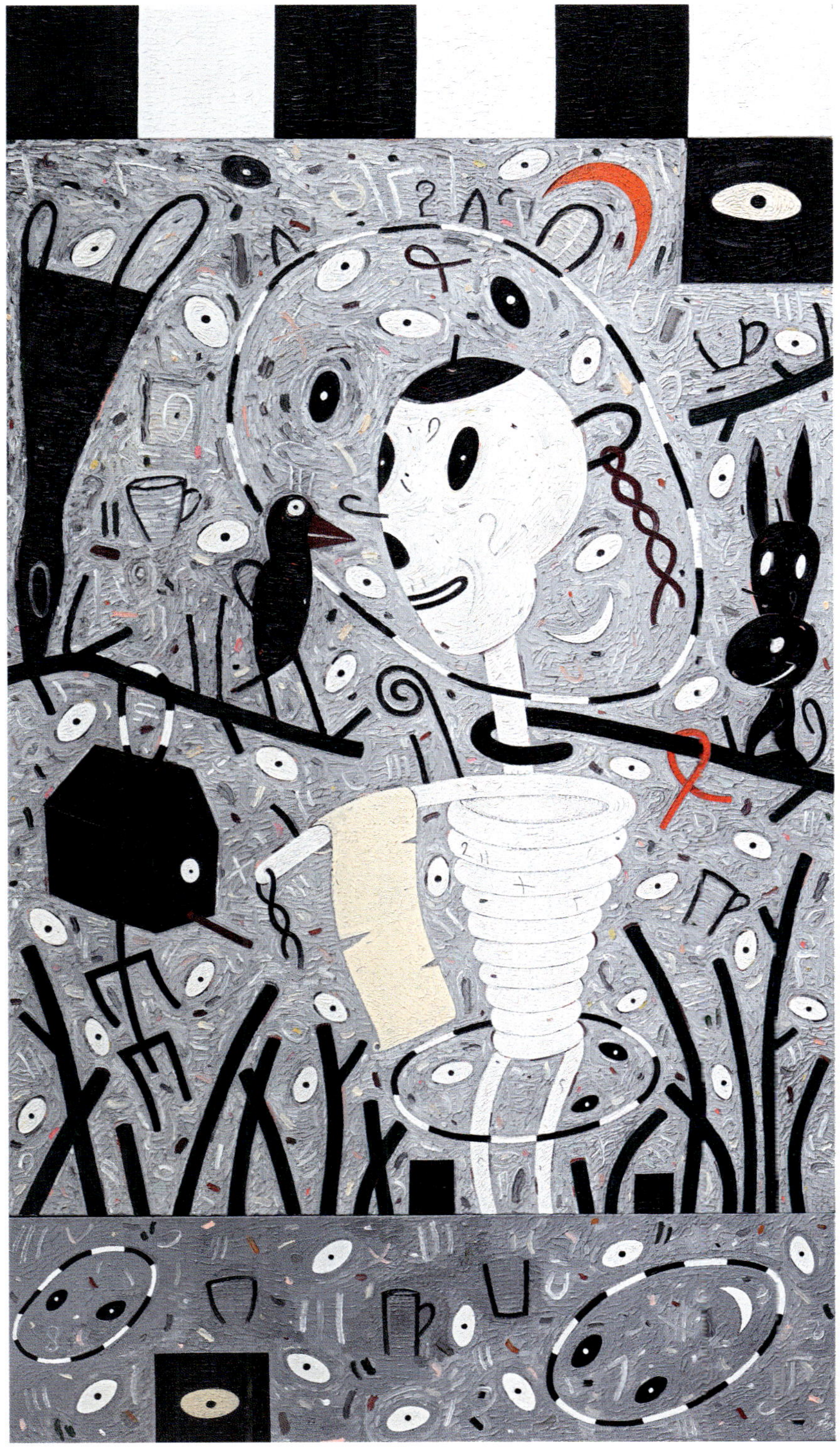

Divinity (The M.H.H. Series), 1996.
Oil and acrylic on canvas, 66 ½ × 38 in. Collection of Andrea and Rob Stone. Photo by Rob Stone.

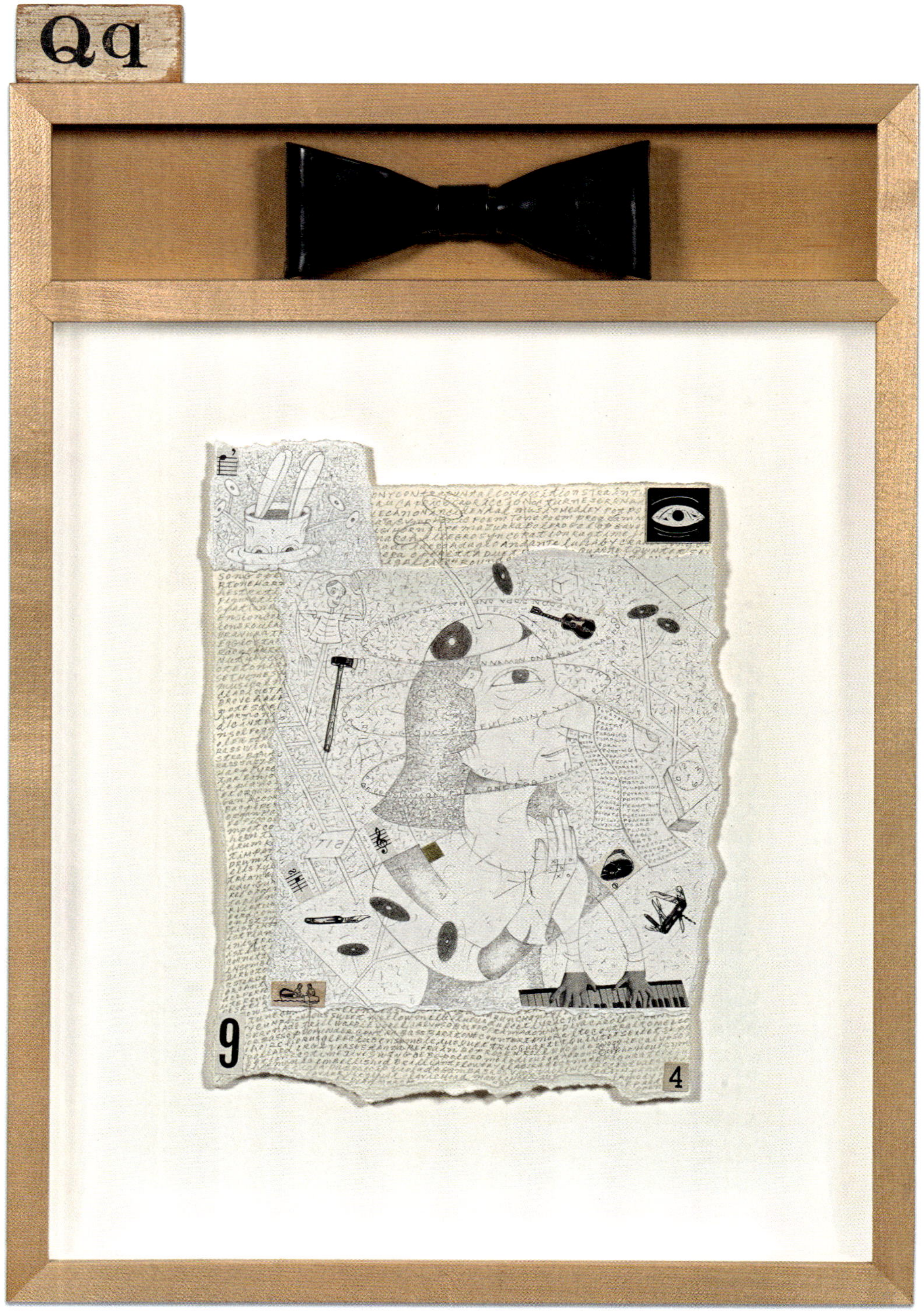

Mind Your P's and Q's, 2013.
Graphite, Prismacolor, paper, wood, and plastic, 20 × 14 in. Collection of D. Oldham Neath.

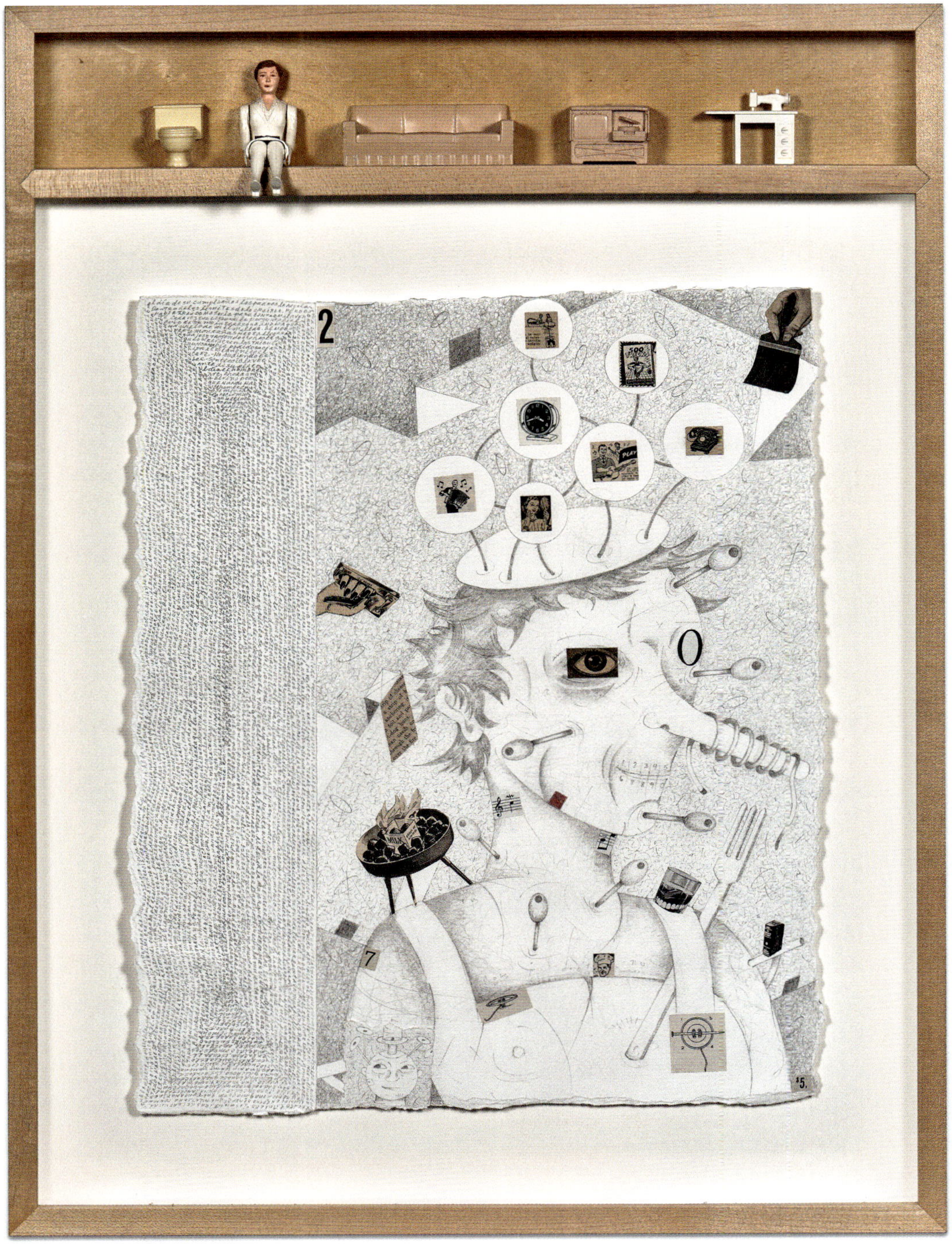

Spanish Olive, 2013.
Graphite, Prismacolor, paper, and plastic. Collection of Libby and Kevin Sanchez.

Chronology

1946 February 12: Born in Woodland Memorial Hospital in Woodland, California, to Myrtle Adan, a homemaker (later a postal worker), and Raymond Adan, a truck driver. Her brother, James (Jim), is two years older.

1951–1959 Attends Cacheville Elementary School from first through eighth grade
June 3, 1959: Graduates from eighth grade

1956 Baptized at the Yolo Methodist Church (at age 10)

1959–1963 Attends Woodland High School

1963 Spring: Enrolls in first formal art class, an entry-level course called Arts and Crafts
Summer: Graduates from Woodland High School

1963–1969 Attends Sacramento State College, Sacramento as an undergraduate.

1965 Visits the Candy Store Gallery in Folsom, CA, for the first time
Spring: Enrolls in Introduction to Oil Painting course with Irving Marcus
July 13: Appears on the front page of the *Daily Democrat* in an article highlighting her being honored as a Yolo County 4-H All-Star **[p. 25]**
Fall: Enrolls in Beginning Ceramics with Ruth Rippon

Exhibitions
Northern California Arts, Inc.'s 12th Annual Open Art Exhibition, E. B. Crocker Art Gallery (later Crocker Art Museum), Sacramento

1966 Spring: Enrolls in watercolor class with Jerald Silva
Meets Michael Stevens
Fall: Declares Art as her major and Anthropology as her minor

Exhibitions
Kaleidoscope Gallery, Sacramento
13th Annual Sacramento County Fair: Art exhibition; wins first and second place in the drawings and collage category
Yolo County Fair Arts and Crafts Exhibition; wins four prizes: second place in the abstract or non-objective graphics category; first place in representational graphics, painting, and pottery categories; wins best-of-show in painting and in pottery categories
California State Fair Art exhibition; wins third place in the college junior and senior oil painting category
SOLO SHOW at Sierra College in Rocklin, CA

1966–1967 **Exhibitions**
Northern California Arts, Inc.'s 13th Annual Open Exhibition, E. B. Crocker Art Gallery; wins third place in the watercolor category

1967 Spring: Begins dating Michael Stevens
Enrolls in painting class with Jack Ogden
Receives the Kingsley Art Scholarship

Exhibitions
14th Annual Sacramento County Fair: Art exhibition; wins first place in drawing
Yolo County Fair Arts and Crafts Exhibition; wins first and second place
California State Fair Art exhibition; wins two prizes for her ceramics
Student Show, Sacramento State College Art Gallery
Sacramento Valley Artists Association Show, Carmichael, CA
California Crafts V, E. B. Crocker Art Gallery

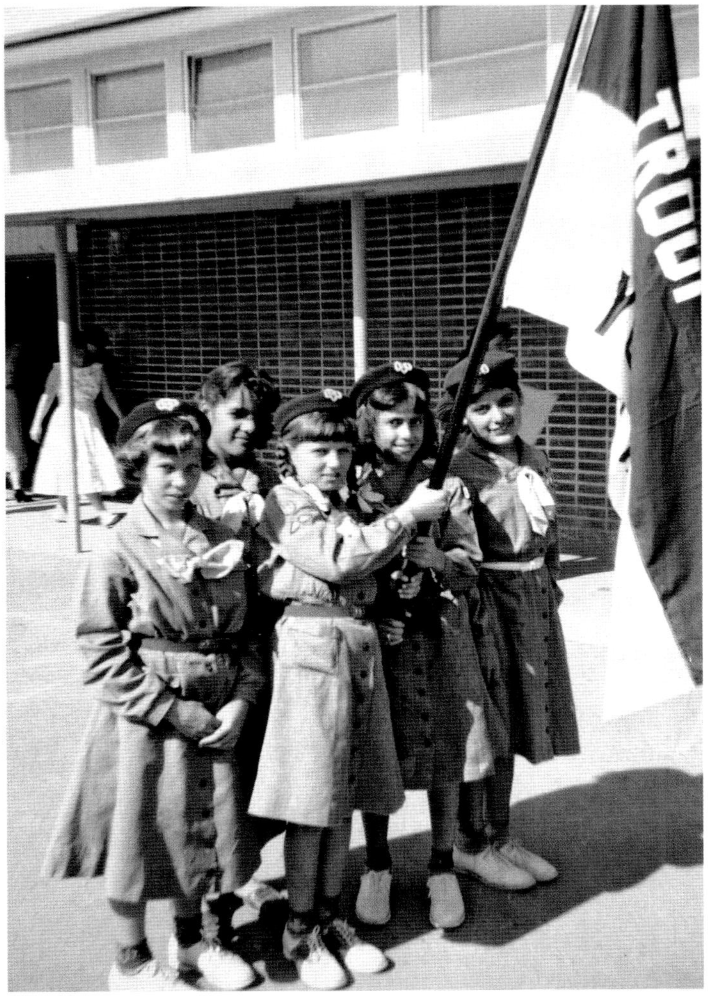

← Suzanne Adan and her Girl Scout troop, Cacheville Elementary School, 1954. Courtesy of Suzanne Adan.

↓ Cacheville Elementary School Band (Suzanne front row, third from left), 1956–1957. Courtesy of Suzanne Adan.

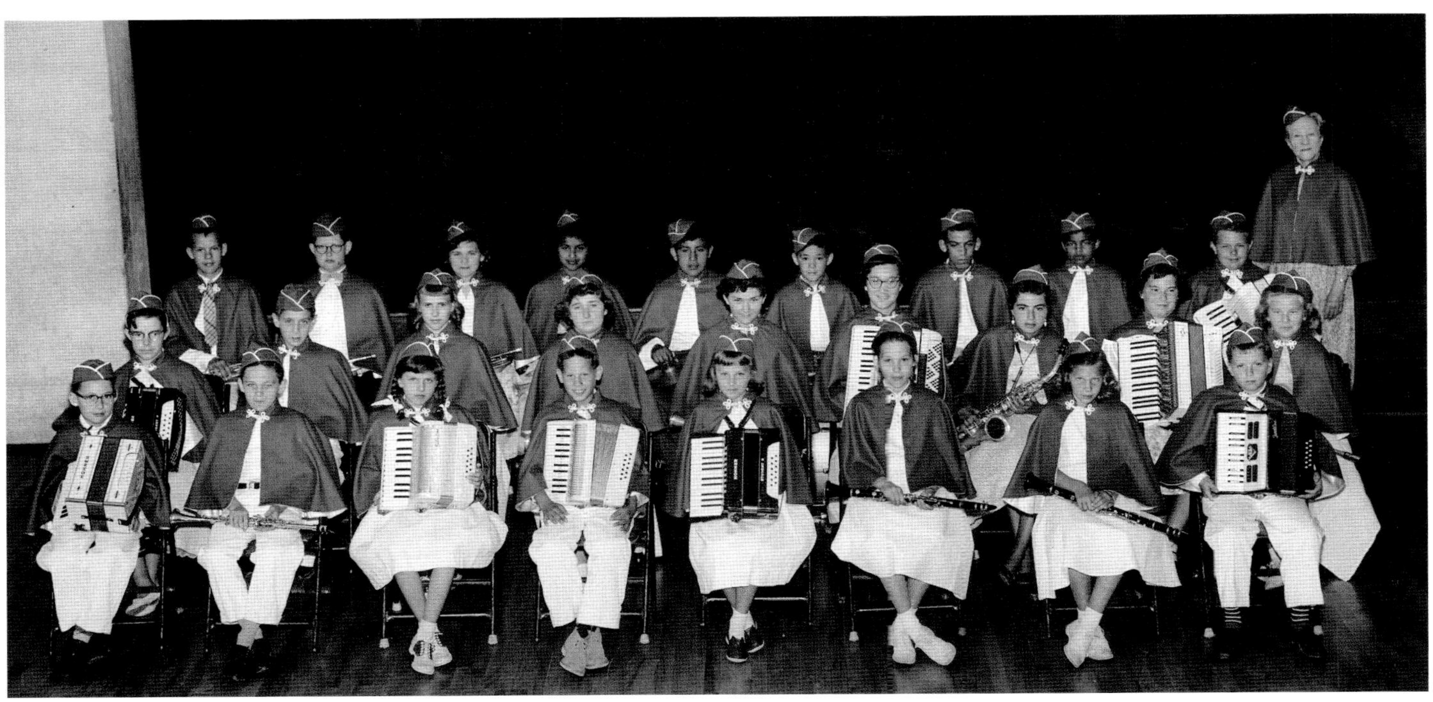

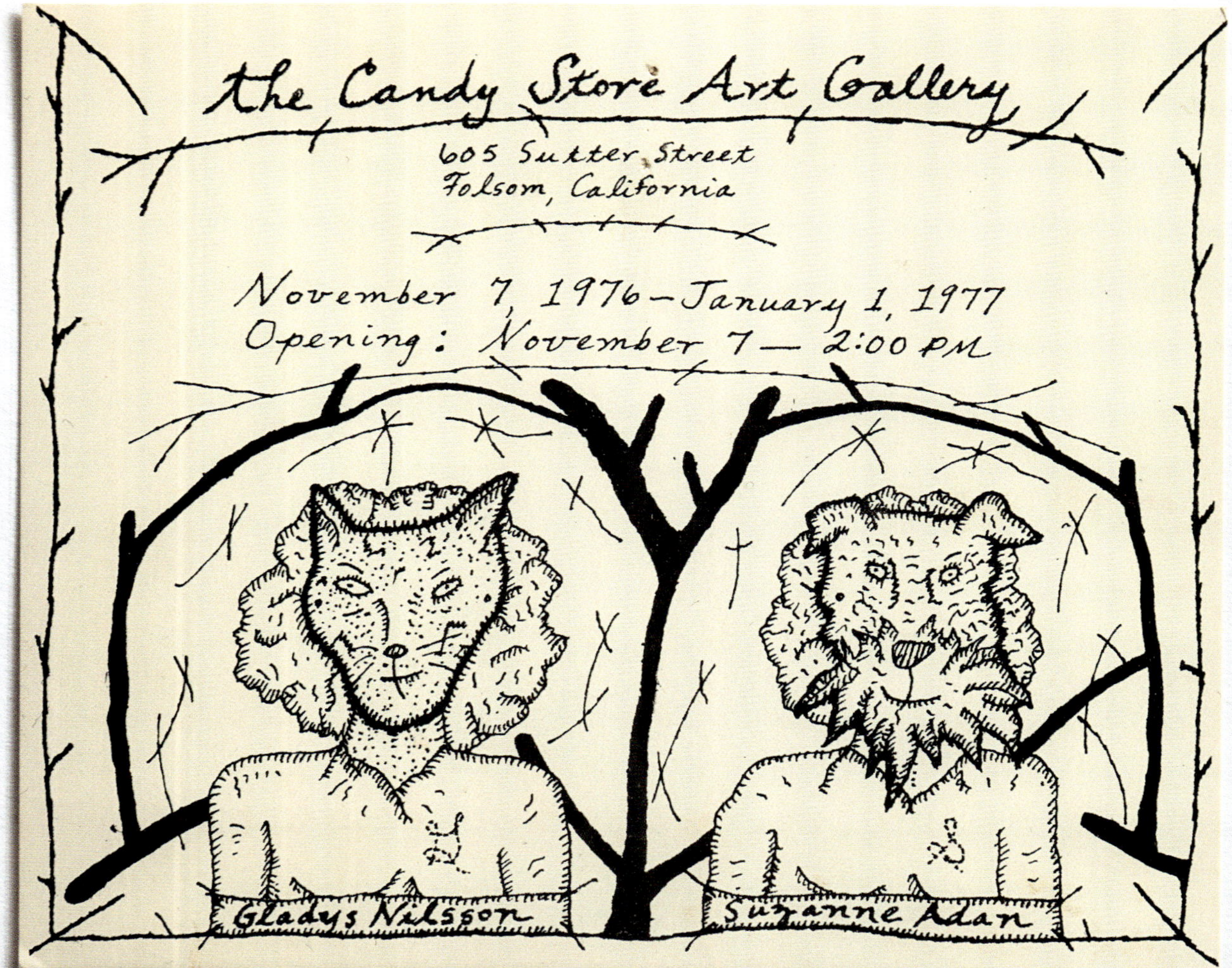

Postcard for Gladys Nilsson and Suzanne Adan Show at the Candy Store Gallery, 1976.
Courtesy of Parker Gallery, Los Angeles.

1968 Jim Nutt and Gladys Nilsson of Chicago's Hairy Who move to Sacramento and later become Adan's friends/mentors.

Exhibitions
43rd Annual Crocker-Kingsley Exhibition, E. B. Crocker Art Gallery, wins the Ayling Water Color Award
California State Fair Art exhibition; wins a Purchase Award

1969 January: Graduates from Sacramento State College with a BA in art. She immediately enters the MA program.
Begins her thesis project, a new series of works rooted in feminism, the first of which is *Panty Hose* **[p. 107]**

1969–1971 Attends Sacramento State College for graduate school
Is elected to the Phi Kappa Phi honor society

1970 September 5: Marries Michael Stevens
Fall: Is granted a two-semester graduate teaching assistantship in Irving Marcus's oil painting class

Exhibitions
Drawing Invitational Exhibition, E. Walters Gallery, San Francisco Art Institute

1971 May: Sends Stevens to defend her thesis before the faculty review committee
June: Graduates from Sacramento State College with an MA in art
Fall: Stevens has federal hearing regarding the draft

Exhibitions
San Francisco Art Institute Centennial Exhibition, San Francisco Museum of Art, San Francisco
Group Show, Candy Store Gallery, Folsom, CA, her first time showing at the Candy Store
Shazam: Monumental Arte, Kaleidoscope Gallery, Sacramento

1972 **Exhibitions**
Sacramento Valley Show, E. Walters Gallery, San Francisco Art Institute
47th Annual Crocker-Kingsley Exhibition, E. B. Crocker Art Gallery

1973 Kingsley Art Club purchases *Gumshoe* for the Crocker's collection, Adan's first museum acquisition **[p. 42]**

Exhibitions
Auburn Arts Festival
Lodi Art Annual; wins honorable mention
San Mateo County Fair Fine Arts, Crafts, and Photography Exhibition; wins second place
48th Annual Crocker-Kingsley Exhibition, E. B. Crocker Art Gallery; wins a Patrons' Purchase Award
7th National Drawing and Small Sculpture Show, Art Gallery, Del Mar College, Corpus Christi, TX

1973–1974 **Exhibitions**
Extraordinary Realities, Whitney Museum of American Art, New York (also shown at Everson Museum of Art, Syracuse, NY, and Contemporary Arts Center, Cincinnati, OH)

1974 Fall: Appointed adjunct professor of art at American River College in Sacramento

Exhibitions
20th Annual Open Art Exhibition held by Northern California Arts, Inc., Sacramento Public Market, Sacramento
SOLO SHOW *Suzanne Adan: Drawings—Watercolors,* Womanspace gallery, Los Angeles

1975 **Exhibitions**
Fifty Years of Crocker Kingsley, E. B. Crocker Art Gallery
Jim Nutt, Gladys Nilsson, Suzanne Adan & Michael Stevens, Candy Store Gallery, Folsom, CA

1976 **Exhibitions**
Gladys Nilsson & Suzanne Adan, Candy Store Gallery, Folsom, CA
Candy Store Gallery Artists, American River

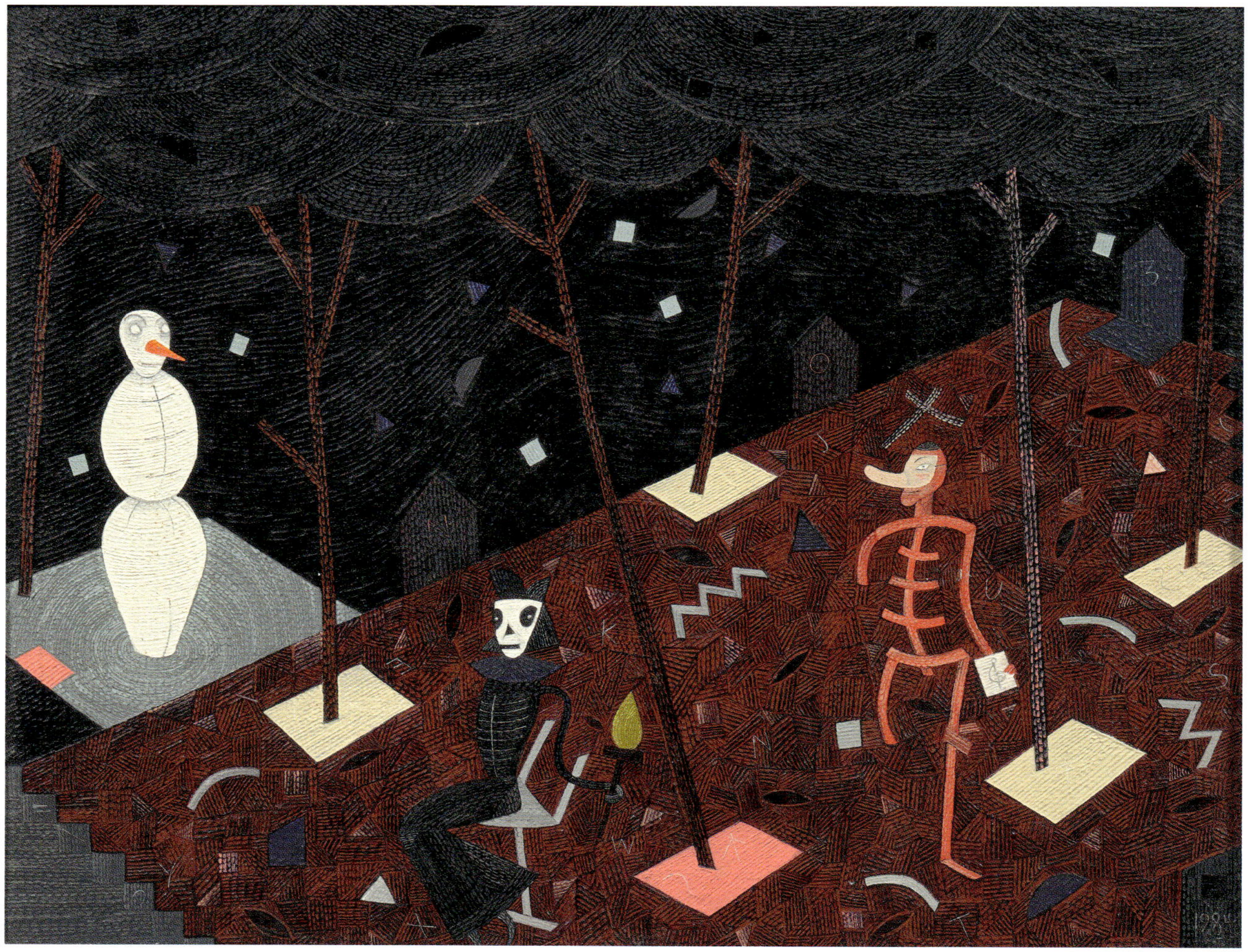

Snow Job, 1984.
Oil on canvas, 7 ¾ × 9 ½ in. Collection of Lucas and Julia Himovitz.

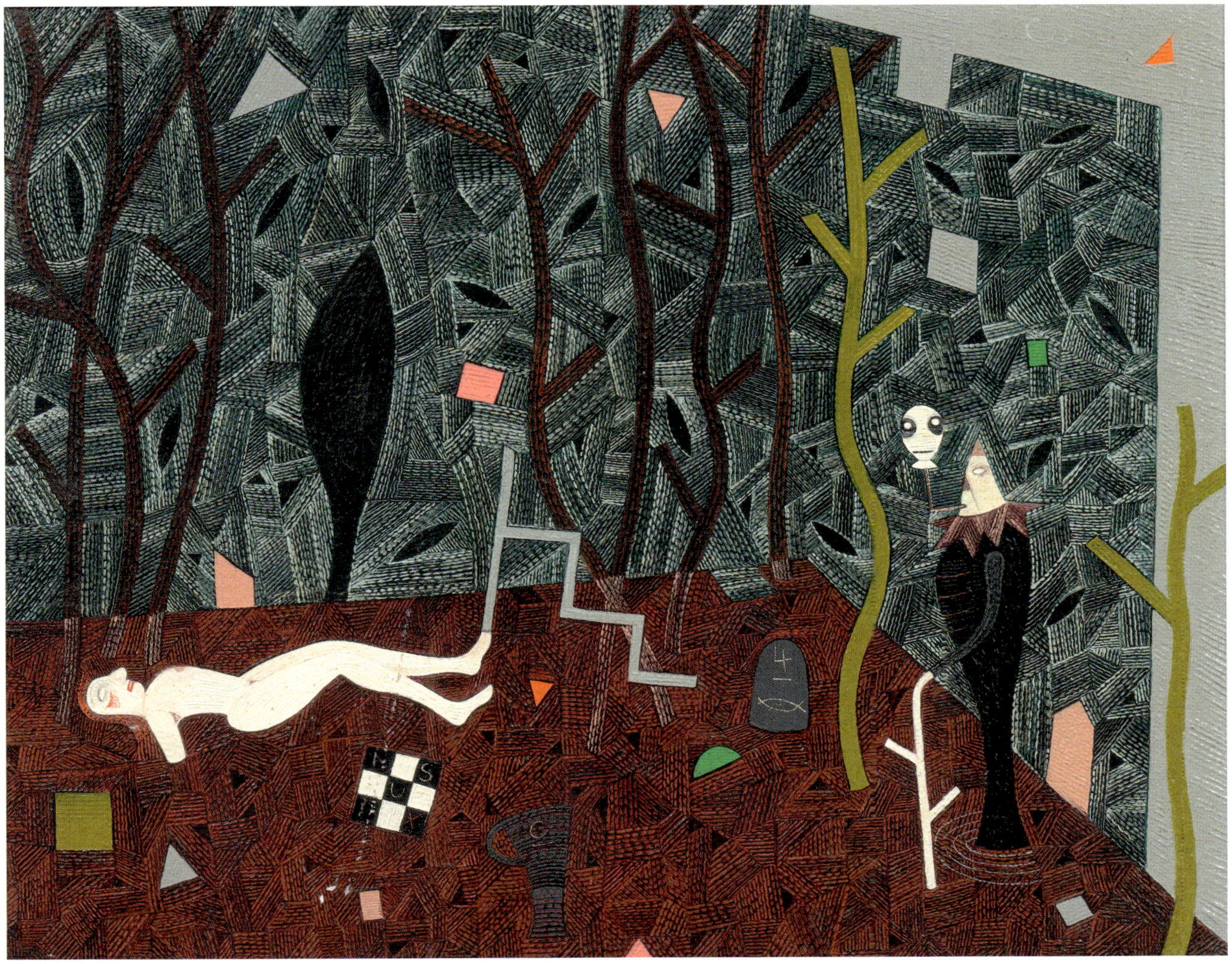

Naked Edge, 1984.
Oil on canvas, 7 ¾ × 9 ¾ in. Collection of Lucas and Julia Himovitz.

College Art Gallery, Sacramento
Invitational Show at The Clock Tower, Benicia Art Center, Benicia, CA

1976–1977 Works as a community services art instructor for the San Juan Unified School District in Carmichael, CA

1977 June: Visits the Art Institute of Chicago and sees Vincent van Gogh's 1887 *Self-Portrait,* sparking a change in her style.

Exhibitions
Group Show, Candy Store Gallery, Folsom, CA
Jim Nutt, Gladys Nilsson, Suzanne Adan & Michael Stevens, Candy Store Gallery, Folsom, CA

1978 April: Meets Andy Warhol at The Factory in New York

Exhibitions
California State Fair Fine Arts exhibition; wins third place for a painting
Private Vision, Ohlone College, Fremont, CA
Group Show, Candy Store Gallery, Folsom, CA
Your Show, Cal Expo, Sacramento

1979 **Exhibitions**
Suzanne Adan, Judith Linhares & Don Meyer, Richard L. Nelson Gallery, University of California, Davis

1980 **Exhibitions**
Suzanne Adan & Michael Stevens, Crocker Art Museum, Sacramento
27th Annual Painting Exhibition, Richmond Art Center, Richmond, CA; wins the Hardison, Komatsu, Ivelich & Tucker Award
Peaceable Kingdom, Fuller Goldeen Gallery, San Francisco

1981 **Exhibitions**
Welcome to the Candy Store, Crocker Art Museum, Sacramento

1982 Secures representation at the prestigious Betsy Rosenfield Gallery in Chicago, her first committed gallery outside California
August 26: Adan's father, Raymond Adan, dies.

Exhibitions
California Connections: Sacramento State College, The Early 70's, Joseph Chowning Gallery, San Francisco, and Laguna Beach Museum of Art, Laguna Beach, CA
SOLO SHOW at Betsy Rosenfield Gallery, Chicago

1983 **Exhibitions**
Interface: The Artists of the Himovitz/Salomon Gallery, Richard H. Reynolds Gallery, University of the Pacific, Stockton, CA
SOLO SHOW at Betsy Rosenfield Gallery, Chicago

1984 **Exhibitions**
A Dozen Women, Himovitz/Salomon Gallery, Sacramento
Small Wonder, Jan Baum Gallery, Los Angeles
The Finals in Painting and Sculpture, Jan Baum Gallery, Los Angeles
SOLO SHOW at Himovitz/Salomon Gallery, Sacramento

1985 Receives Best and Brightest Award, *Sacramento Magazine*
Begins making yearly contributions to the Fred Uhl Ball Memorial Fund for Artists in Crisis

Exhibitions
Suzanne Adan & Michael Stevens, New Mexico State University, Las Cruces
Recent Acquisitions, John Berggruen Gallery, San Francisco
Sacramento/Davis Interface, Richmond Art Center, Richmond, CA
Sacramento Valley Painting and Sculpture, Creative Growth Gallery, Oakland, CA
SOLO SHOW *Suzanne Adan* at Betsy Rosenfield Gallery, Chicago

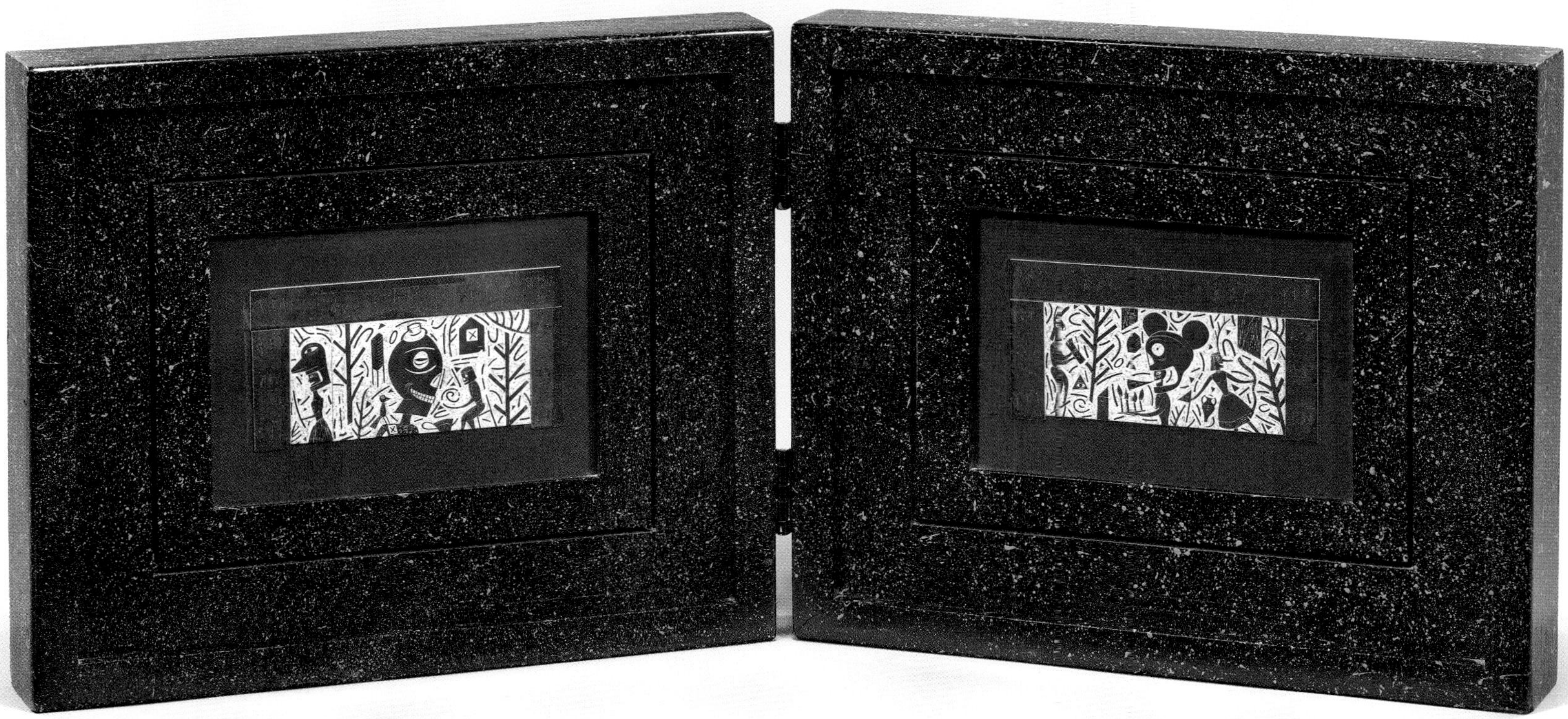

Two Face, 1988.
Scratchboard and wood frame, 10 ¾ × 11 ¾ in. (each). Collection of Lynda Jolley.

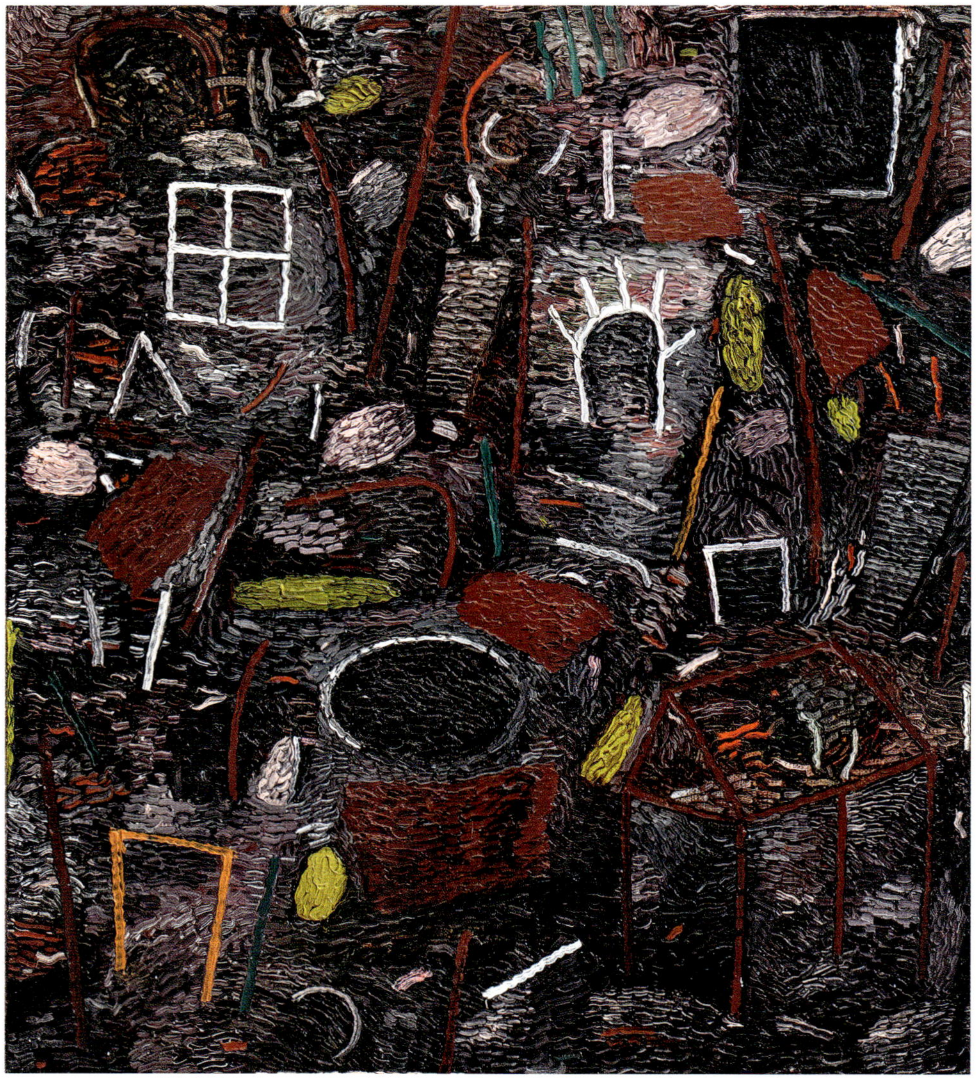

Wooly Bully (What the Music Looks Like), 1989.
Oil on Masonite, enamel on wood, 23 × 36 × 4 in. Collection of Phillip and Marilyn Araki Isenberg.

1986 Exhibitions

Art Bridge, Kobe International Community Center, Kobe, Japan
Drawings from Northern California, Memorial Union Art Gallery, University of California, Davis
SOLO SHOW at Himovitz/Salomon Gallery, Sacramento

1987 Exhibitions

Suzanne Adan & Michael Stevens, Richard H. Reynolds Gallery, University of the Pacific, Stockton, CA
Contemporary Illumination, Himovitz/Jensen Gallery, Sacramento
SOLO SHOW at John Berggruen Gallery, San Francisco

1988 Exhibitions

Contra Costa Contemporary Collections, Hearst Art Gallery, Saint Mary's College of California, Moraga
Humorists: Artists from the Michael Himovitz Gallery, Merced College, Merced, CA
Animal Imagery, Susan Cummins Gallery, Mill Valley, CA
The Dog Show, Braunstein/Quay Gallery, San Francisco
Northern California Art Since 1945, Crocker Art Museum, Sacramento
Inaugural Exhibition: A Commitment to the Crocker Art Museum, Attia, Bartel, Eng & Torngren [law offices], Sacramento
CSUS Forty Years of Art, Robert Else Gallery, California State University, Sacramento

1989 Exhibitions

What the Music Looks Like, Michael Himovitz Gallery, Sacramento
Artscape '89, Sacramento Public Library

1990 Receives New Works Grant, Sacramento Metropolitan Arts Commission
Creates commission *Untitled,* hand-made ceramic tile mural, courtyard, University of California, Davis, Medical Center, Sacramento
Creates commission *Horse Sense* and *Catawampus* for River West Corporation, four black and white hand-made ceramic tile murals, Natoma Station, Folsom, CA

Exhibitions

Suzanne Adan & Michael Stevens: A Survey, Memorial Union Art Gallery, University of California, Davis
All Creatures Great and Small, John Natsoulas Gallery, Davis, CA
Women of The 90's, Michael Himovitz Gallery, Sacramento
California Eccentrics, Illini Union Art Gallery, University of Illinois Urbana-Champaign

1991 Serves as visiting artist, Figurative Sculpture Workshop, California State University Summer Arts Program, Humboldt State University, Arcata, CA

Exhibitions

A Tribute Exhibition: Works on Paper and Sculpture by Crocker Kingsley Artists, Crocker Art Museum, Sacramento
Group Exhibition: James D. Phelan Art Awards in Printmaking, Kala Art Institute Gallery, Berkeley, CA; wins the James D. Phelan Art Award in Printmaking from The San Francisco Foundation
Black and White in Color, Spectrum/Himovitz Gallery, San Francisco
All Creatures Great and Small, John Natsoulas Gallery, Davis, CA
SOLO SHOW *The Seven Deadly Sins . . . More or Less,* Brent Smith Design and Michael Himovitz Gallery, Sacramento

1992 Exhibitions

Ceramic Figures, Michael Himovitz Gallery, Sacramento
California Contemporaries, Michael Himovitz Gallery, Sacramento, and United States Information Services, American Center, Mumbai, India
Discovery/ Contemporary California Narrations, Himovitz/Miller Gallery, The Pavilions, Sacramento, and United States Embassy, Brussels, Belgium

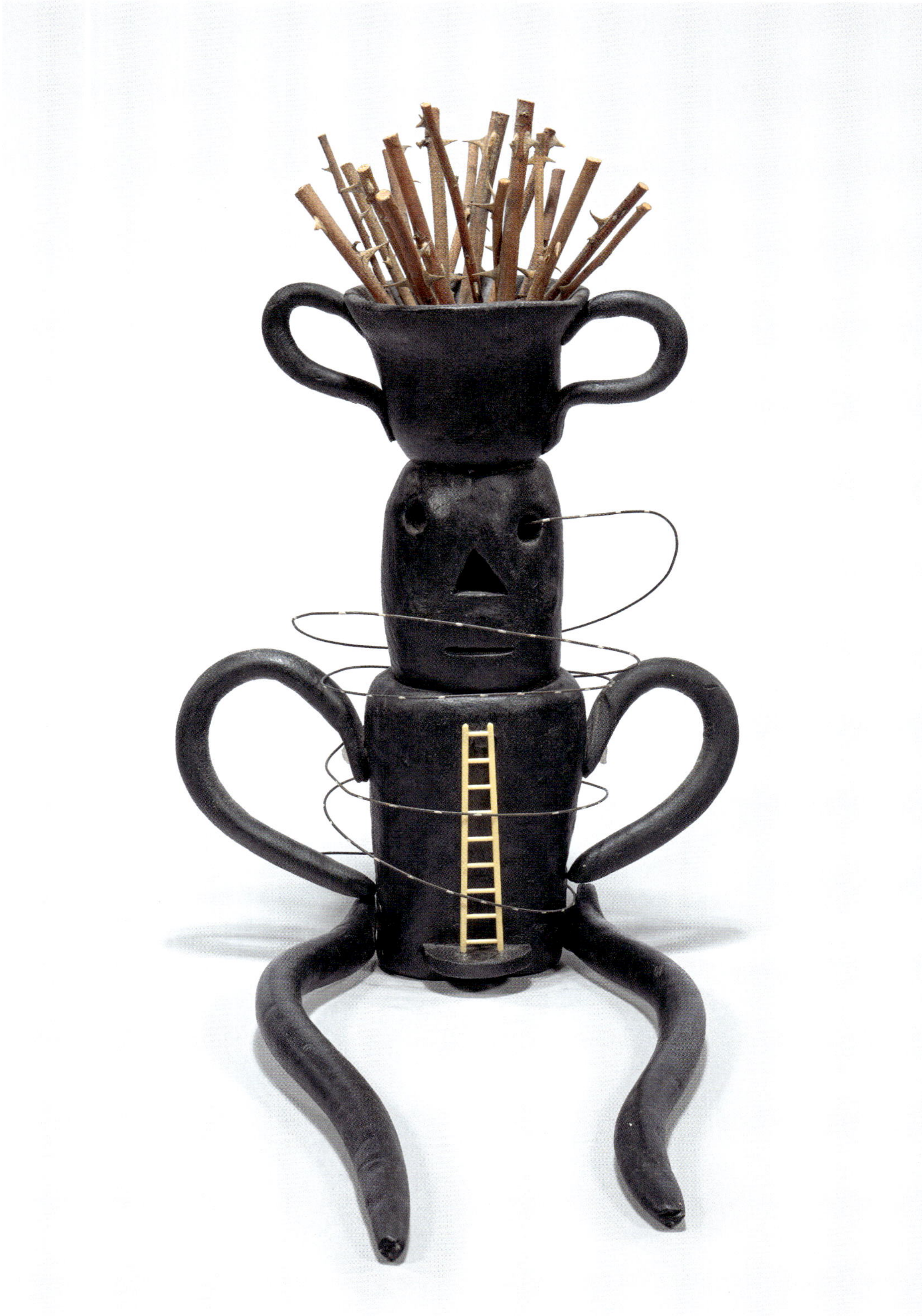

Twister, 1992.
Clay, acrylic paint, plastic, wire, and rosebud vines, 25 ½ × 8 ½ × 5 in.
Collection of Scott and Ruixia Howe.

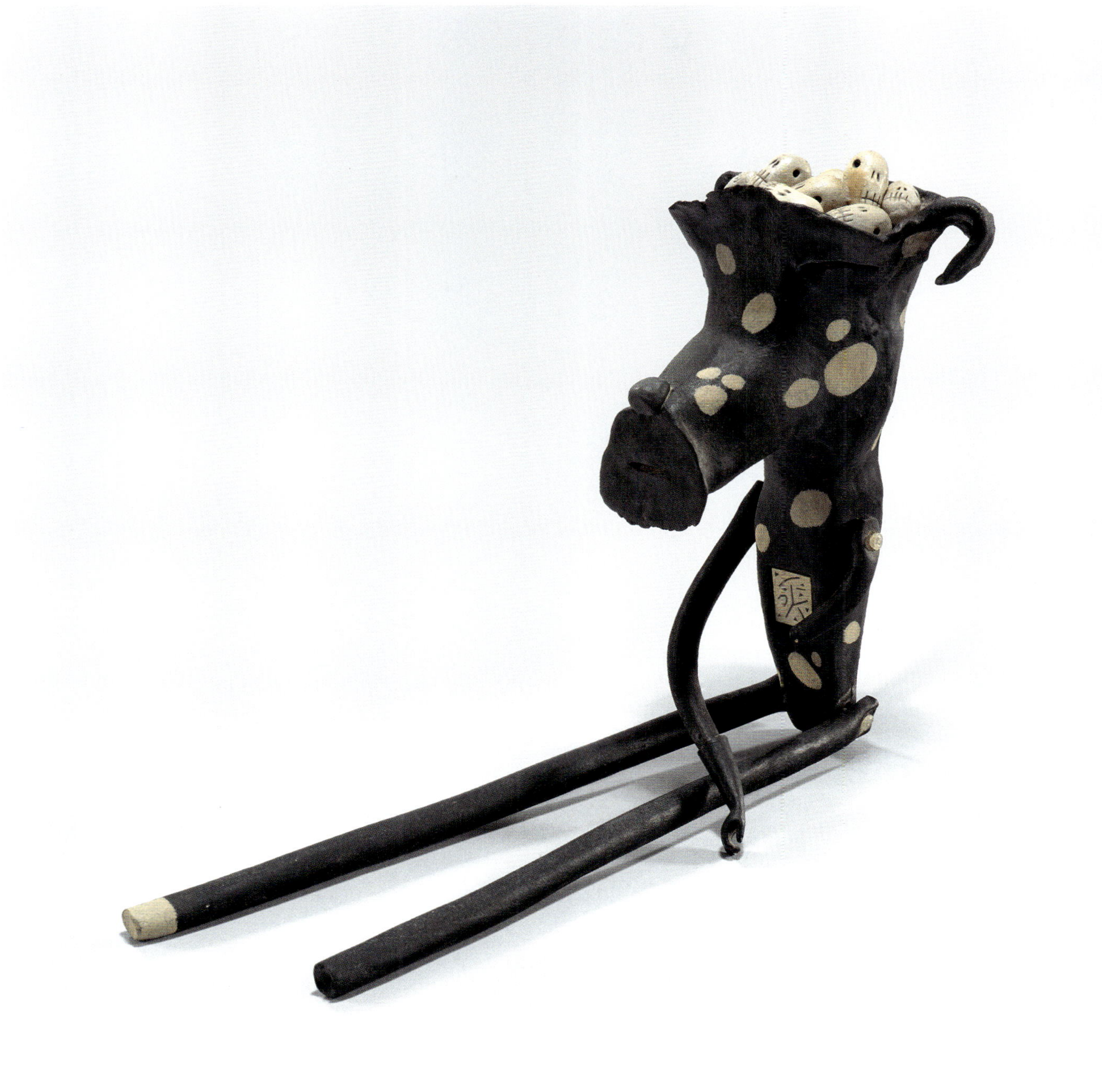

Bone Head (Good Dog), 1992.
Clay, acrylic paint, scratchboard, and plastic, 23 × 5 ¾ × 6 in.
Collection of the Artist.

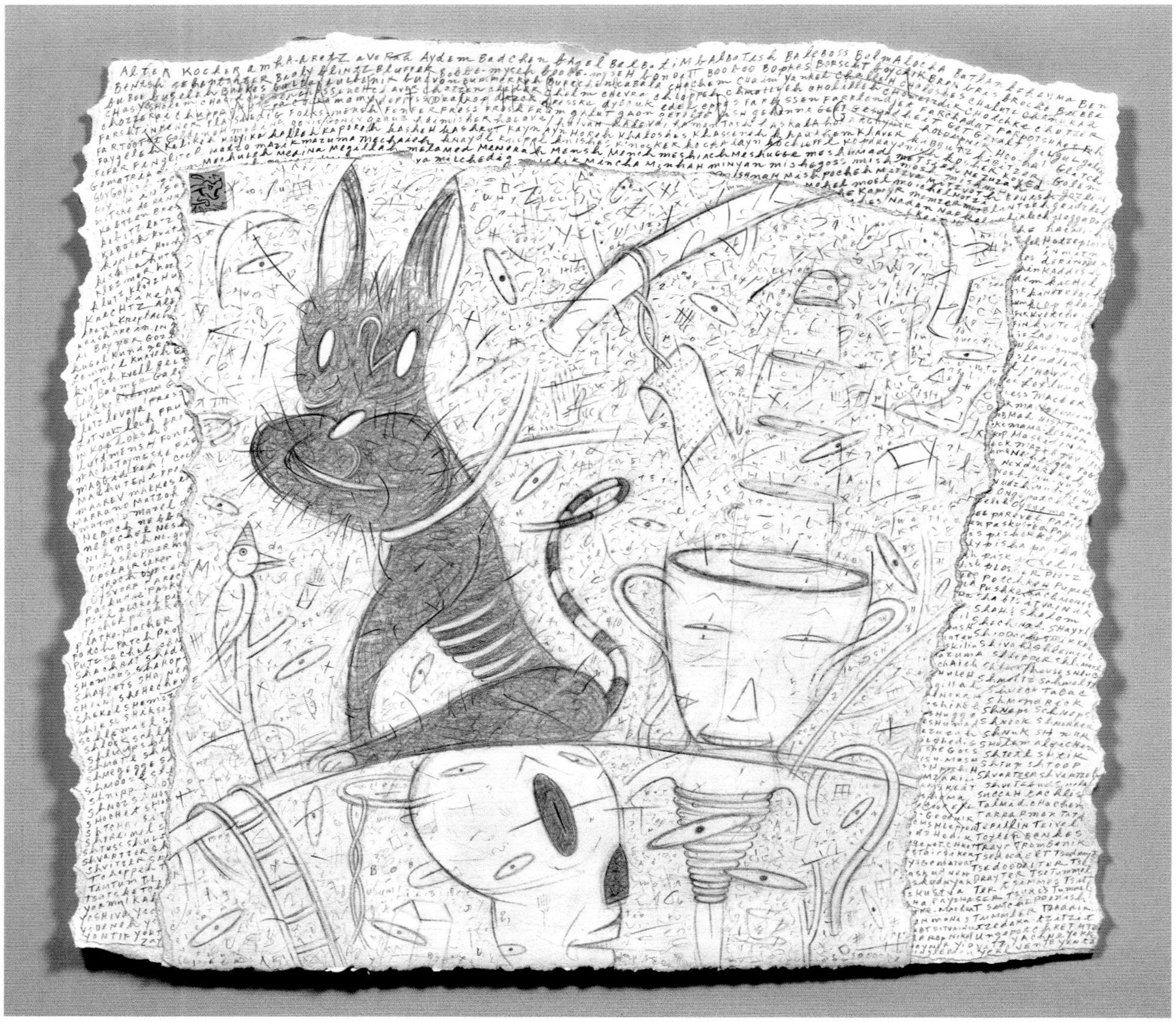

Death Watch Dog (In Memory of Michael Himovitz), 1996.
Paper and graphite, 24 ½ × 26 in. Collection of the Artist.

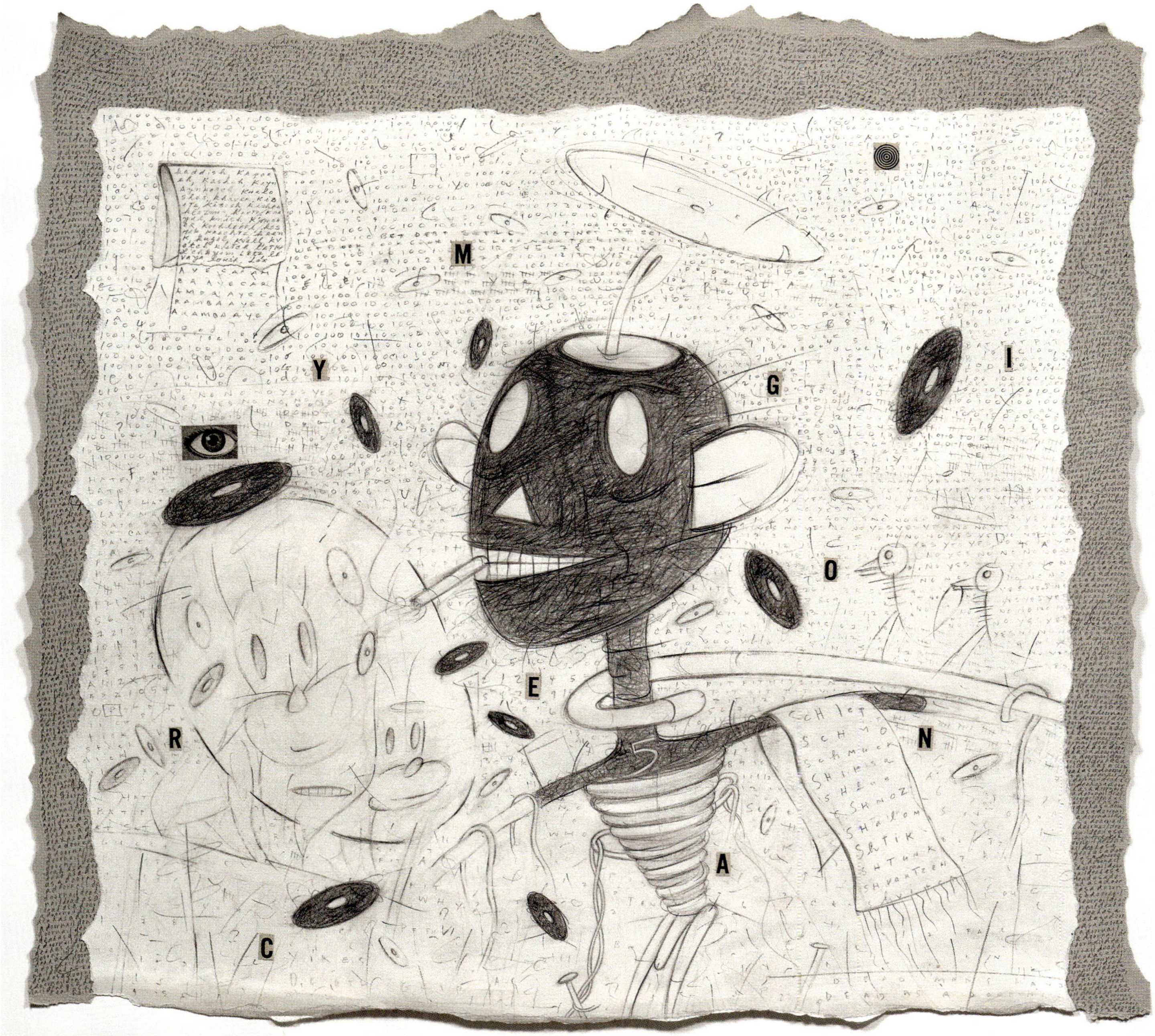

Swan Song (The M.H.H. Series), 1997.
Graphite and mixed media on paper, 27 × 28 ¾ in. Collection of Jon Stevenson.

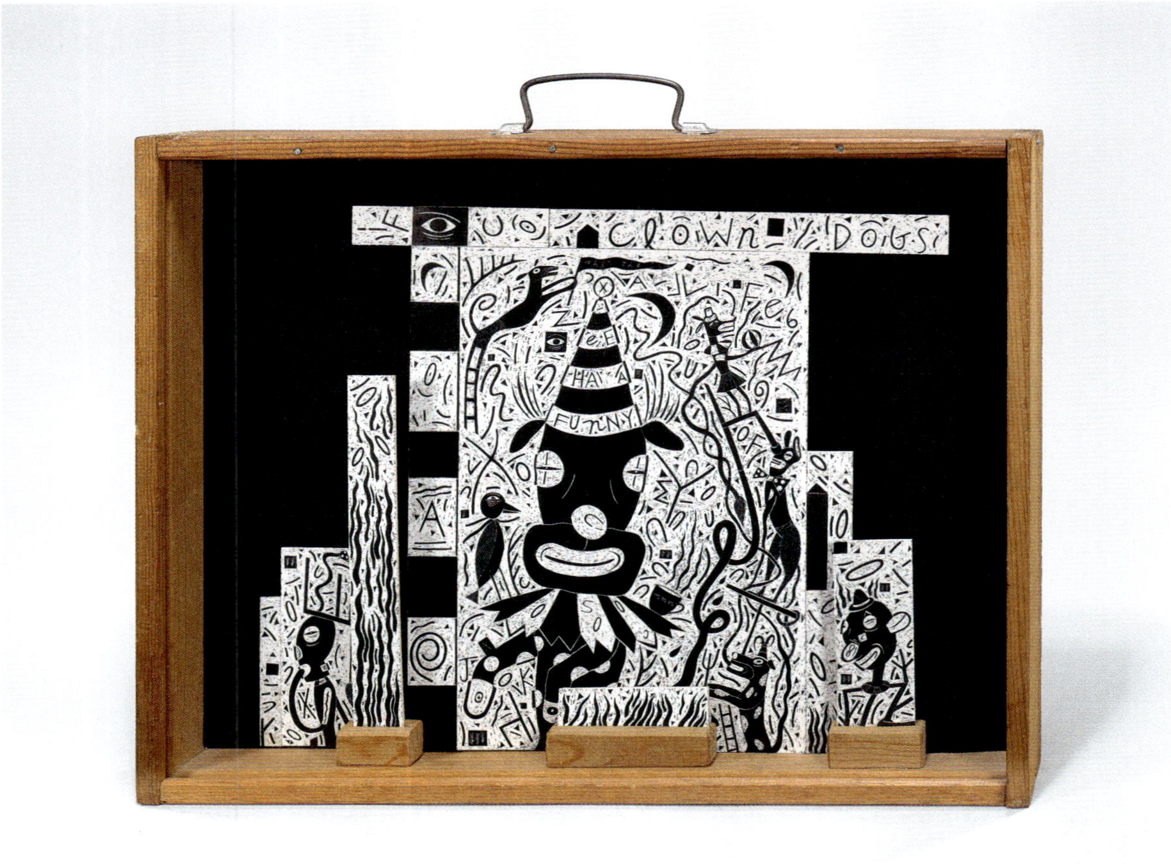

Clown Dogs in Hell, 1999.
Scratchboard, wood, and glass,
16 ⅛ × 12 ½ × 2 ¼ in. Collection of Julie Spezia.

1993 **Exhibitions**
Mr. & Mrs., Michael Himovitz Gallery, Sacramento
Ink and Clay, Holmes Fine Art Gallery, San Jose, CA

1994 **Exhibitions**
Building a Collection: Building a Decade of Gifts, Crocker Art Museum, Sacramento
Michael Himovitz Gallery, Crocker Art Museum, Sacramento
The Art of Collection: The Artist as a Collector, Memorial Union Art Gallery, University of California, Davis

1994–2004 Serves as curator for the Encina Art Gallery at Encina High School, Sacramento

1995 **Exhibitions**
Gun, Michael Himovitz Gallery, Sacramento

1996 Receives New Works Grant, Sacramento Metropolitan Arts Commission

Exhibitions
Mr. & Mrs., Suzanne Adan and Michael Stevens, American River College Art Gallery, Sacramento
Made in Sacramento, Crocker Art Museum, Sacramento
The Abstract Surface/The Illusion, Sierra College Library Gallery, Rocklin, CA
Painting Exhibition, John Natsoulas Gallery, Davis, CA
Tenth Annual 30 Ceramic Sculptors Exhibition, John Natsoulas Gallery, Davis, CA

1997 **Exhibitions**
Small Works, Susan Cummins Gallery, Mill Valley, CA
CSUS/50, Crocker Art Museum, Sacramento
For Funk's Sake, John Natsoulas Gallery, Davis, CA
SOLO SHOW at Susan Cummins Gallery, Mill Valley, CA

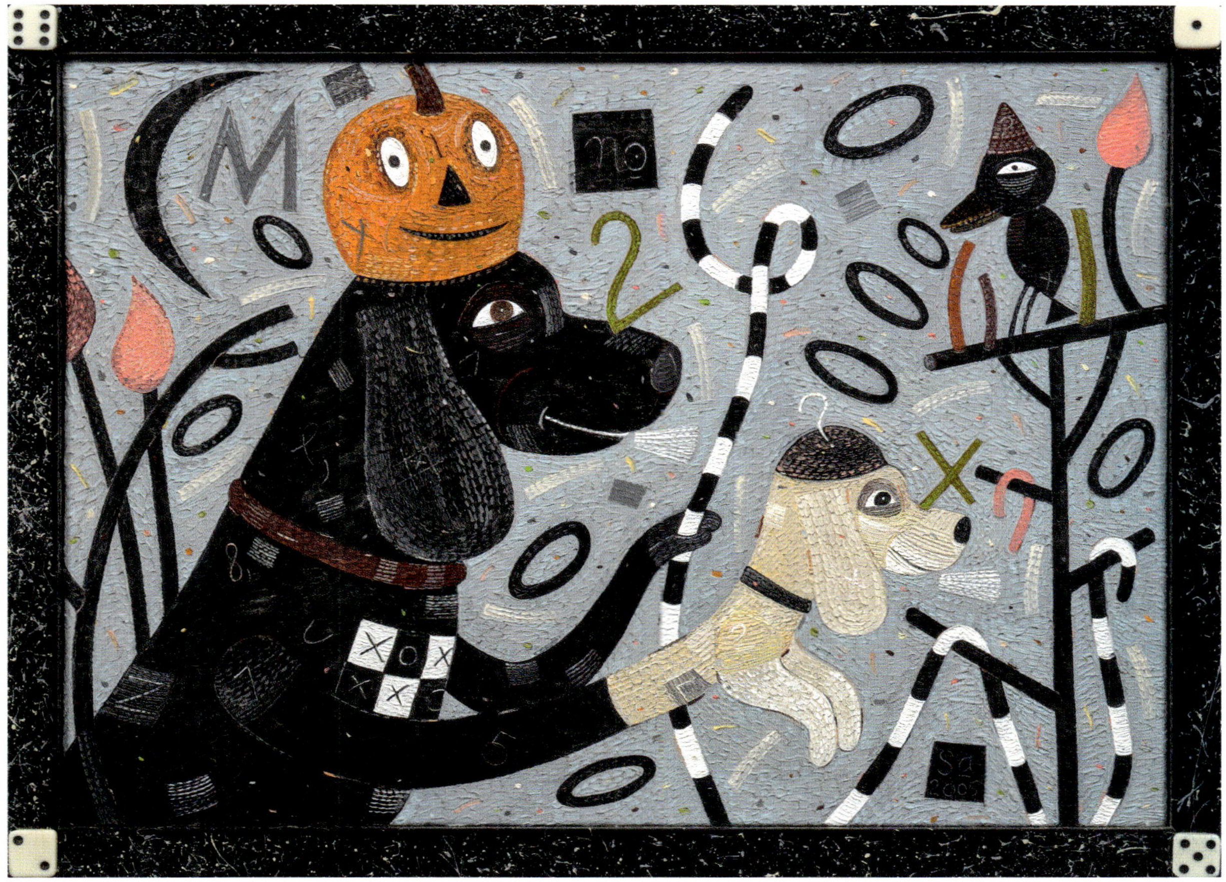

Zoe and Lulu, 2005.
Oil on canvas, enamel on wood with dice, 11 ⅜ × 15 ½ in. Collection of Michael and Lindy Dunlavey.

1998 **Exhibitions**
Mr. & Mrs. with Michael Stevens, San Joaquin Delta College, Stockton, CA
The Death & Desire Show, Center for Contemporary Art, Sacramento
Self Expressions 1998, Solomon Dubnick Gallery, Sacramento
Once Upon a Playground, Black Box Theater, Encina High School, Sacramento

1999 **Exhibitions**
Bob Arneson and Friends, John Natsoulas Gallery, Davis, CA
The Figure, The Fairfield Art Center, Fairfield, CA

2000 With Stevens, receives a Distinguished Service Award from California State University, Sacramento, sponsored by the CSUS Alumni Association

Exhibitions
Two Decades of Art at the John Natsoulas Gallery, John Natsoulas Gallery, Davis, CA
Cats and Dogs, Jean Albano Gallery, Chicago

2001 **Exhibitions**
Mr. & Mrs. with Michael Stevens, Robert Else Gallery, California State University, Sacramento
Altares Nuevos: Offerings by Contemporary Artists, Crocker Art Museum, Sacramento

2002 Creates commission *Knick, Knack, Paddywhack,* seven black and white hand-made tile murals, East End Child Care Center, California Department of Education, Capitol Area East End Complex, Sacramento

2004–2019 With Stevens, serves as an adjunct professor of art at Sacramento City College

2005 Exhibitions
New from the Stable show, JAYJAY, Sacramento

2006 Exhibitions
His & Hers, JAYJAY, Sacramento
Artful Jesters, Pence Gallery, Davis, CA
Art from Adeliza's Candy Store, Folsom History Museum, Folsom, CA

2008 Exhibitions
Eccentric Imagery, Blue Line Arts, Roseville, CA
Play Time, Terminal B, Sacramento International Airport, Sacramento
The Dark Side of The Mouse, Center for Contemporary Art, Sacramento

2009 Creates commission *Ruffled Feathers,* black and white hand-made ceramic tile mural, Jacinto Creek Park, Sacramento **[p. 89]**

2010 Exhibitions
Tomorrow's Legacies: Gifts Celebrating the Next 125 Years, Crocker Art Museum, Sacramento
In Public: Designing Art for the Sacramento International Airport, Center for Contemporary Art, Sacramento
Art of Painting in the 21st Century, John Natsoulas Gallery, Davis, CA
Flatlanders 3, A Regional Roundup, Richard L. Nelson Gallery, University of California, Davis

2010–2019 With Stevens, serves as a curator/director at the Kondos Gallery, Sacramento City College

2011 Creates commission *Flying Colors,* glass mosaic floor, Terminal B, Sacramento International Airport, Sacramento **[pp. 92–93]**

Exhibitions
Now and Then, JAYJAY, Sacramento
In the Studio, Public Artists in Their Private Spaces, Terminal B, Sacramento International Airport, Sacramento
Art of Painting in the 21st Century, John Natsoulas Gallery, Davis, CA
Totems and Plates, Blue Line Arts, Roseville, CA

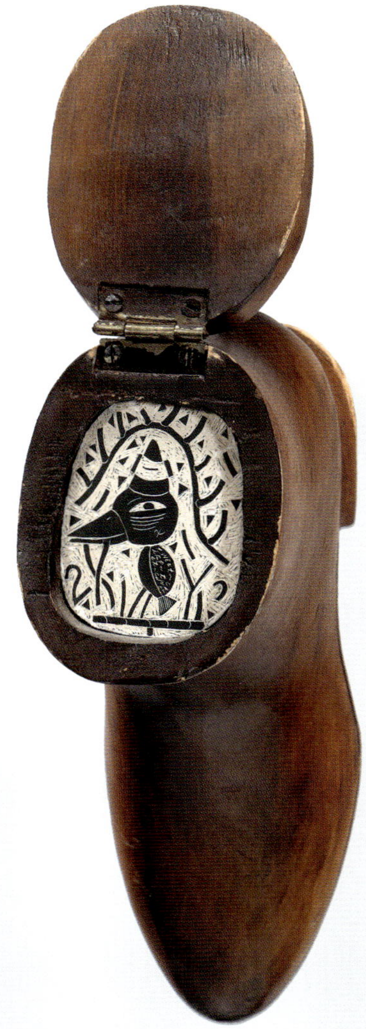

Birds of a Feather, 2011.
Wood and scratchboard, 9 ¾ × 4 ½ × 2 ½ in.
Collection of Steve and Beth Jones.

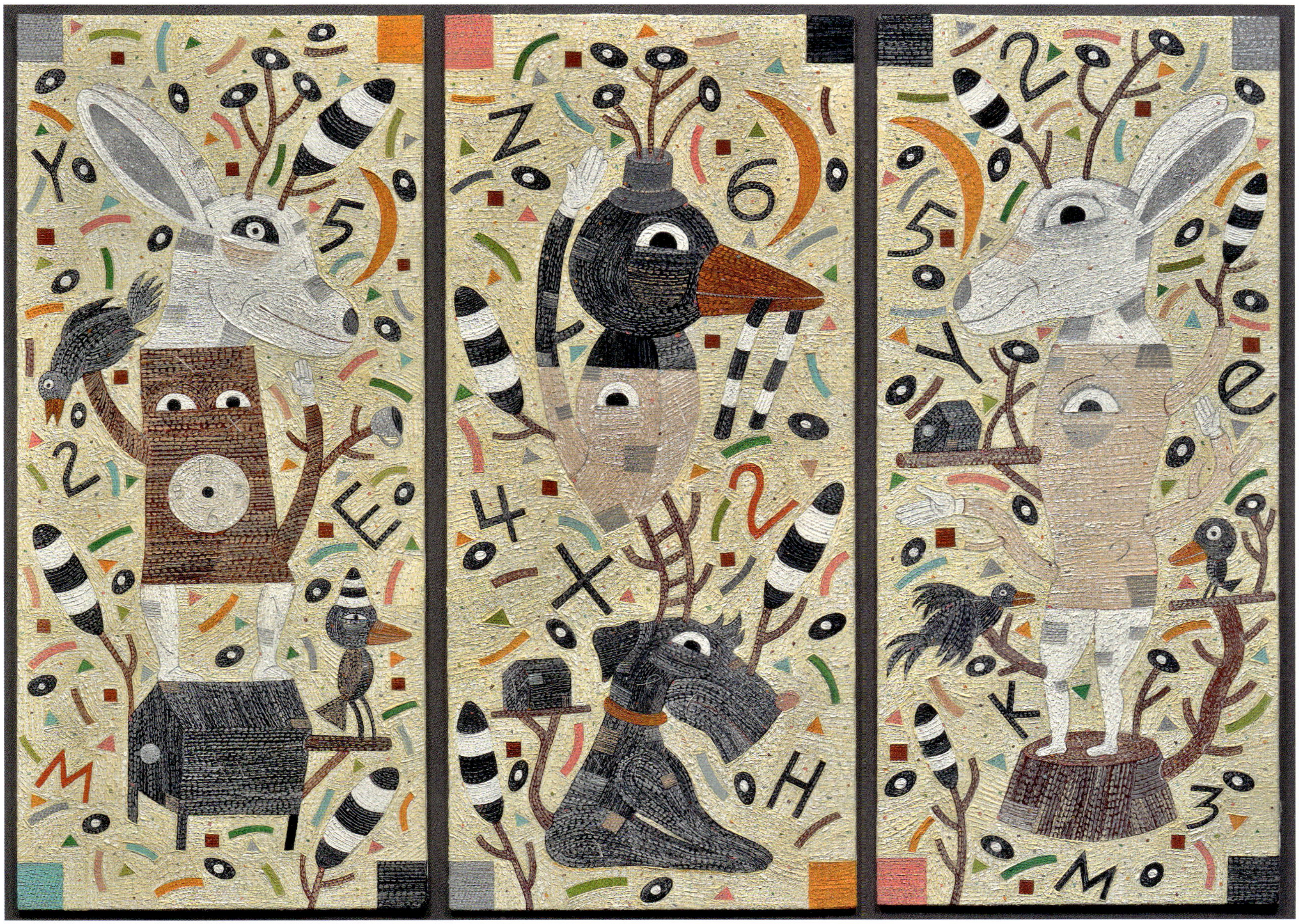

Maquette for "Play House," (McKinley Village), 2018.
Acrylic on canvas, 14 × 19 in. Collection of the Artist.

2012 **Exhibitions**
Flatlanders on the Slant: 50 Artists Celebrate the 50th Anniversary of the Slant Step, Richard L. Nelson Gallery, University of California, Davis
Toy Stories 2, William Havu Gallery, Denver

2013 **Exhibitions**
Seven Year Itch, JAYJAY, Sacramento

2014 February 8: Adan's mother, Myrtle Adan, dies.

2015 Creates commissioned outdoor sculpture for McKinley Village, LLC

Exhibitions
30 Painters to Collect, Blue Line Arts, Roseville, CA
It's All Relative, James Kaneko Gallery, American River College, Sacramento

2017–2018 With Stevens, creates interactive installation *Kit n' Kaboodle,* Crocker Art Museum, Sacramento **[p. 96]**

2018 **Exhibitions**
The Candy Store, Parker Gallery, Los Angeles

2019 **Exhibitions**
Return to Kit n' Kaboodle, JAYJAY, Sacramento
The Gun Show, artspace1616, Sacramento
Robots, JAYJAY, Sacramento
1969: A Fifty-Year Anniversary of Sacramento State College Art Students/Friends, Kondos Gallery, Sacramento City College, Sacramento
SOLO SHOW at Mayor Darrell Steinberg's Office, City Hall, Sacramento

2021 October 19: Adan's brother, James Adan, dies.

2022 **Exhibitions**
The Candy Store: Funk, Nut and Other Art with a Kick, Crocker Art Museum, Sacramento

2023–2024 **Exhibitions**
Nuts and Who's: A Candy Store Sampler, San José Museum of Art, San Jose, CA

2023 **Exhibitions**
AI: Authentic Intelligence, Twisted Track Gallery, Sacramento

2024 **Exhibitions**
She Laughs Back: Feminist Wit in 1970's Bay Area Art, University Library Gallery, California State University, Sacramento
15th Annual Art of Painting In the 21st Century Conference & Exhibition, John Natsoulas Gallery, Davis, CA

2025 **Exhibitions**
Working Through It (Women's History Month), John Natsoulas Gallery, Davis, CA

2026 **Exhibitions**
SOLO SHOW *Suzanne Adan: I'm No Spring Chicken,* Crocker Art Museum, Sacramento

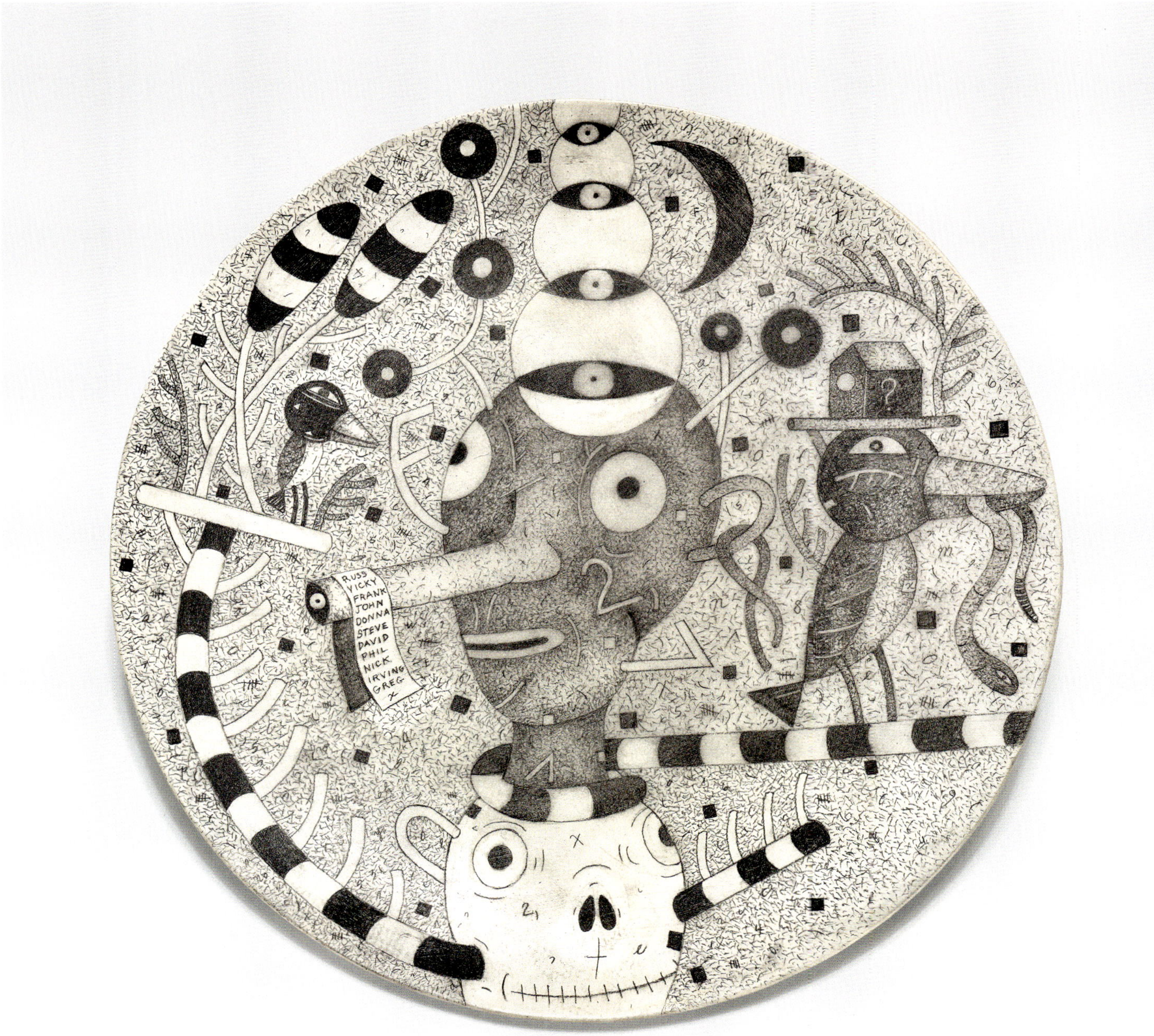

Toodle-Doo, 2021.
Graphite on ceramic, 13 in. (diam.). Collection of William Chambers.

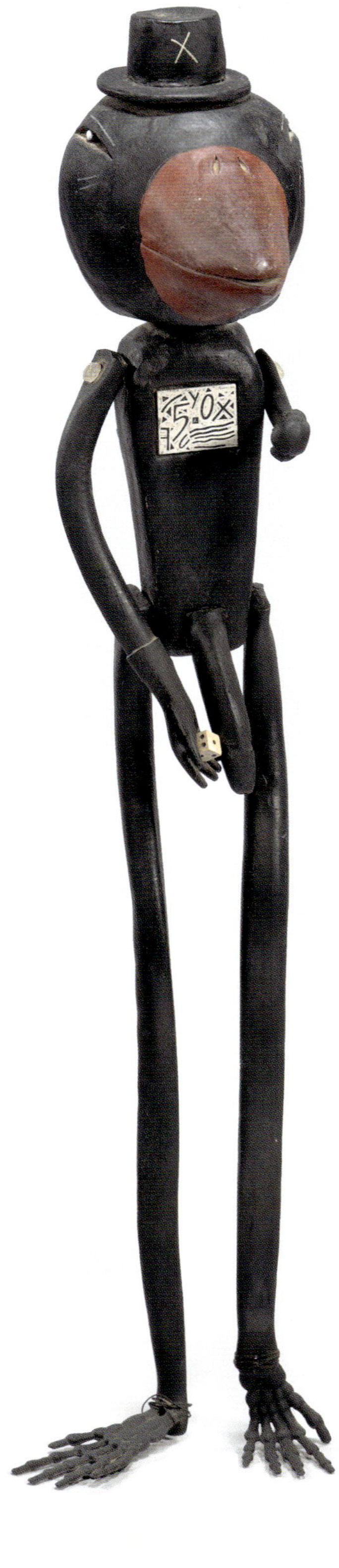

Birdy Num Num (For Jim on His 50th Birthday), 1993.
Clay, acrylic paint, scratchboard, wood, and rubber, 24 × 3 ½ × 6 ½ in. Collection of the Artist.

Index

A

B

C

D

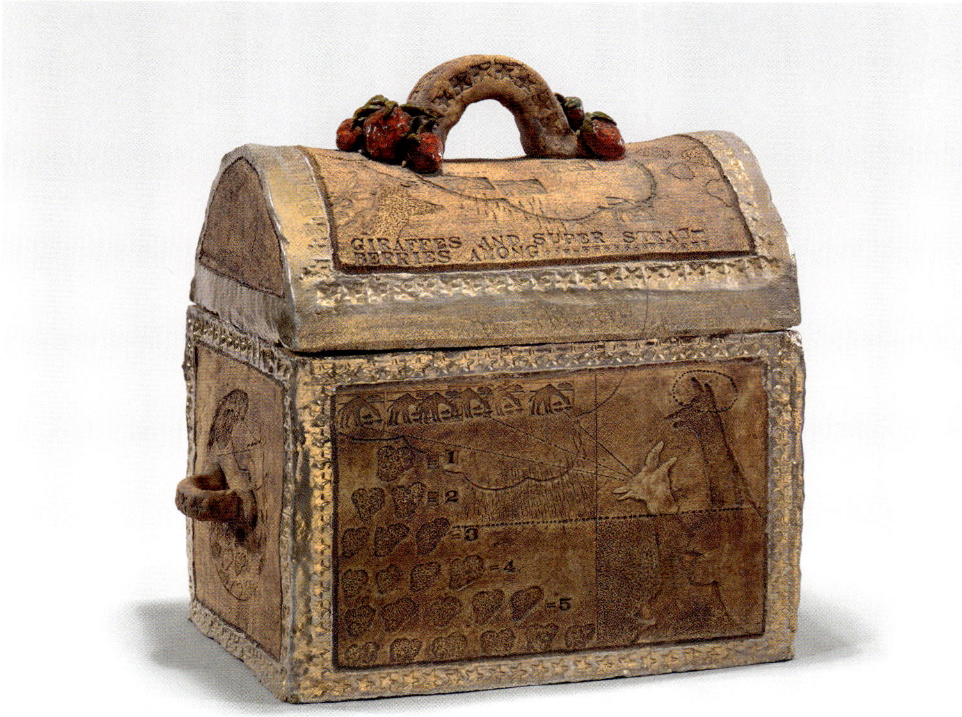

Giraffes and Super Strawberries Among Stars and Clouds, 1967.
Ceramic, 22 × 22 ½ × 13 ½ in. Collection of the Artist.

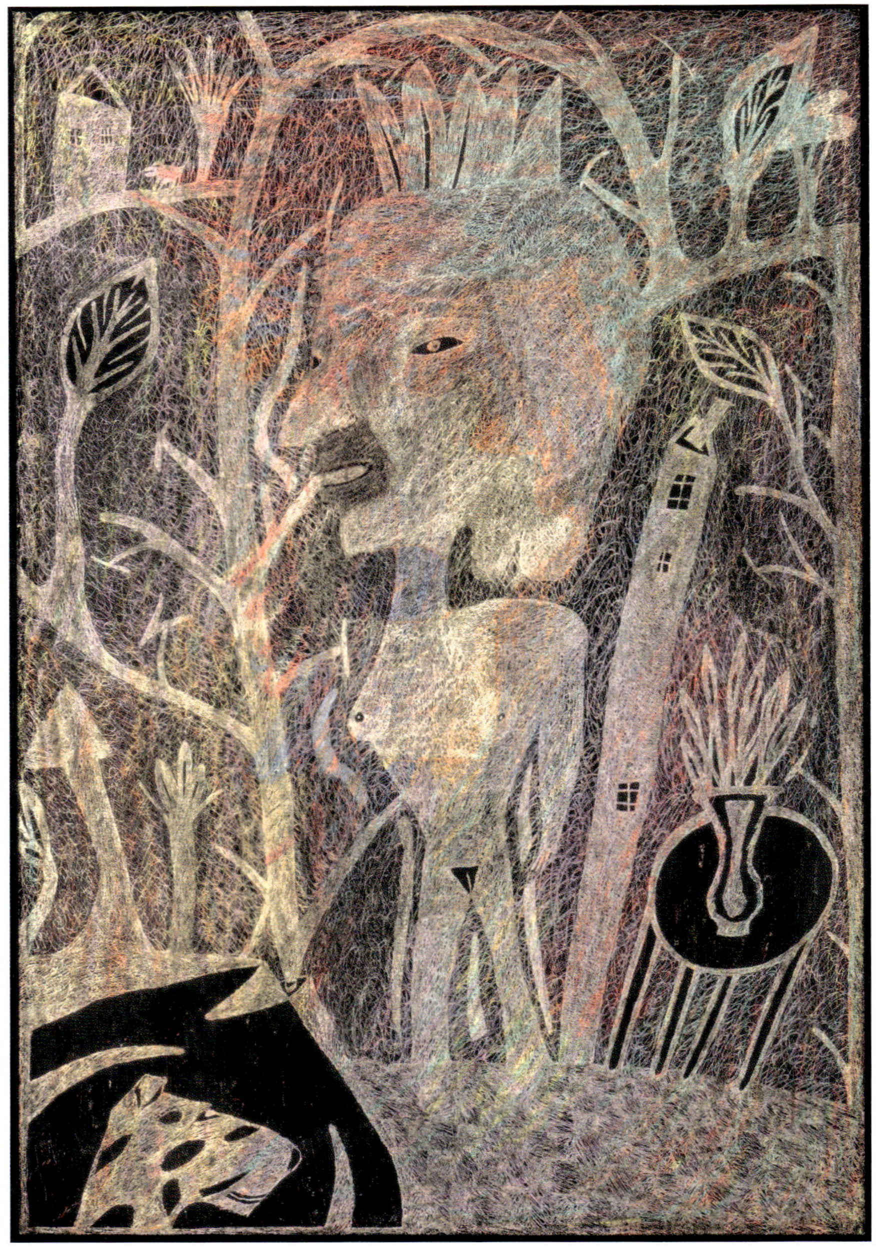

Landscape with Women and Felix, 1975.
Colored and black crayon on paper, 18 × 12 in. Adan Family Collection.

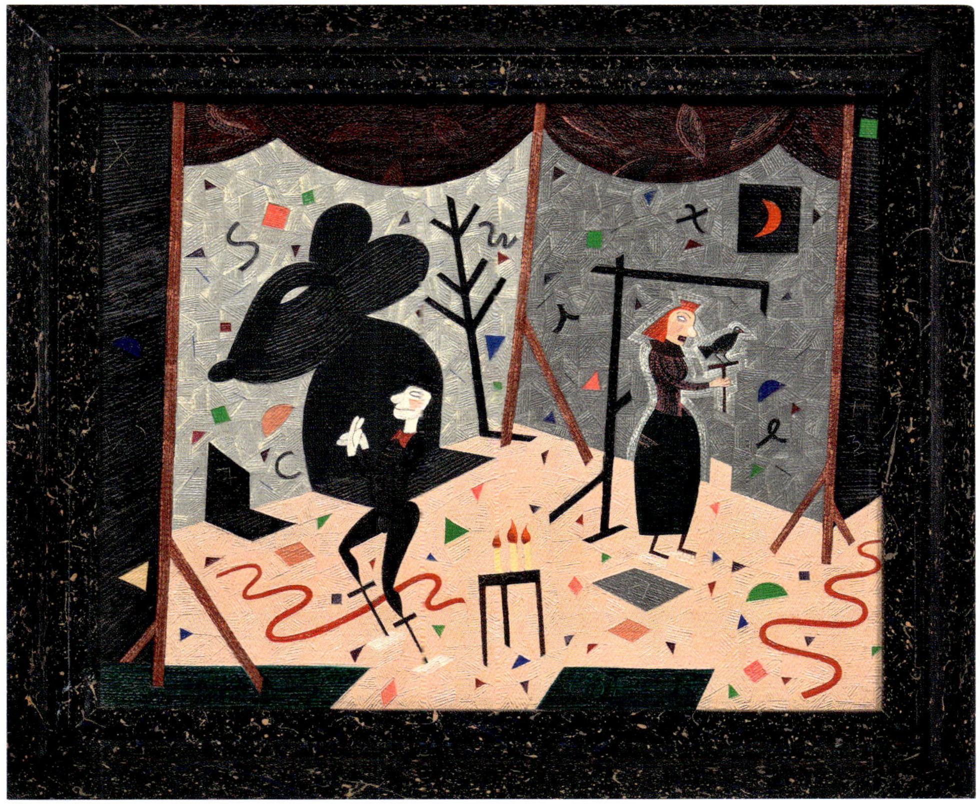

Shadow of a Doubt, 1984.
Oil on canvas, 8 × 10 ¹⁄₁₆ in. From the collection of Vince and Sage LaPena.

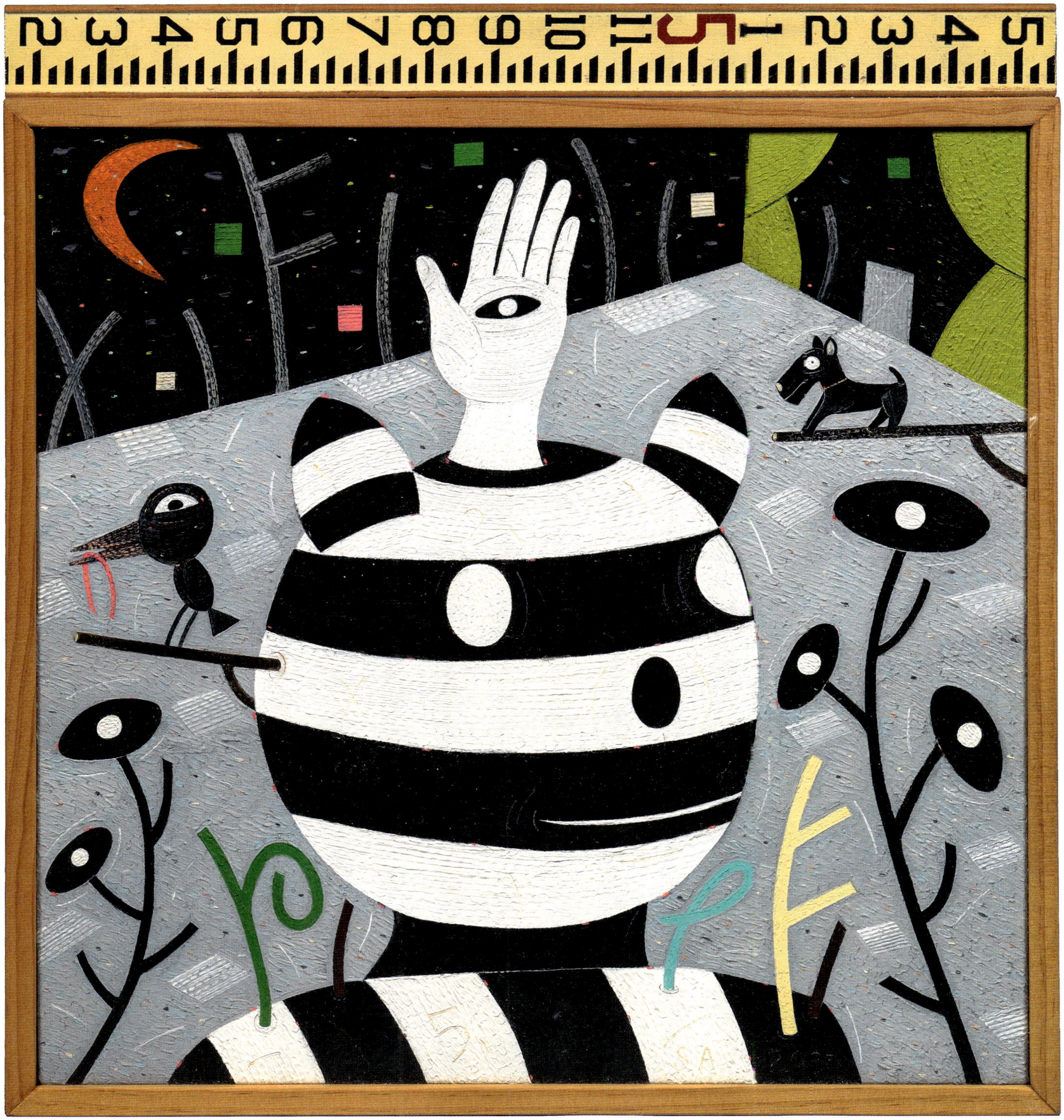

Whodeenie, 2007.
Oil on canvas and wood, 15 × 15 in. From the collection of Vince and Sage LaPena.

Colophon

This book has been published on the occasion of the exhibition

Suzanne Adan: I'm No Spring Chicken
Crocker Art Museum, Sacramento
June 28 – October 11, 2026

Editor
Scott A. Shields, PhD

Editorial team
Mariah Carmen Briel and Caitlin Schwarz

Picture editing
Gerard Vuilleumier

Senior Editor Hirmer Publishers
Elisabeth Rochau-Shalem

Project management Hirmer Publishers
Rainer Arnold

Copy-editing
David Sánchez Cano

Graphic design
Lukas Winkler

Prepress
Reproline mediateam GmbH&Co. KG, Unterföhring

Paper
Gardamatt Ultra 150 g/m²

Typefaces
Elza, GT Walsheim

Printing and binding
Printer Trento S.p.A.

Printed in Italy

MIX
Paper | Supporting responsible forestry
FSC® C015829

Bibliographic information published by the Deutsche Nationalbibliothek: The Deutsche Nationalbibliothek lists this publication in the Deutsche Nationalbibliografie; detailed bibliographic data is available on the Internet at https://www.dnb.de.

ISBN 978-3-7774-4689-9

Hirmer Publishers
(Hirmer Verlag GmbH)
Managing Director: Kerstin Ludolph
Bayerstraße 57–59
80335 Munich
Germany

www.hirmerpublishers.com
www.hirmerpublishers.co.uk

Cover
Skin and Bones (detail), 1987. Oil on canvas, 9 ¾ × 34 in.
Collection of Michael Stevens.

Endpapers
Cross-Examine (detail), 1986. Oil on canvas, 7 × 90 in.
Collection of Jeffrey Goodrich and Mary Jameson.

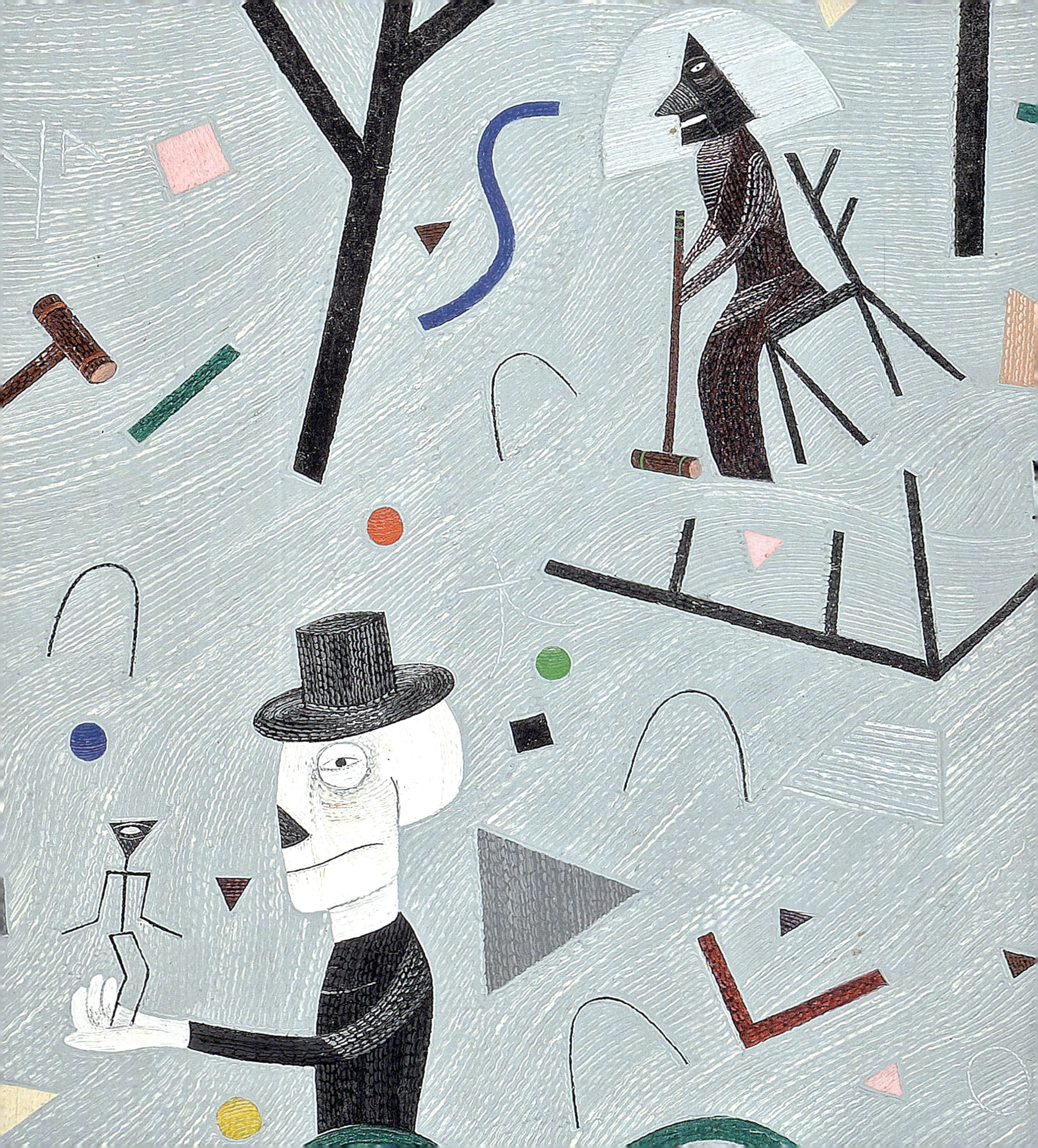